$19.95

641.5
Hal   Haller, Henry

           The White House
           family cookbook

THE
WHITE HOUSE FAMILY
COOKBOOK

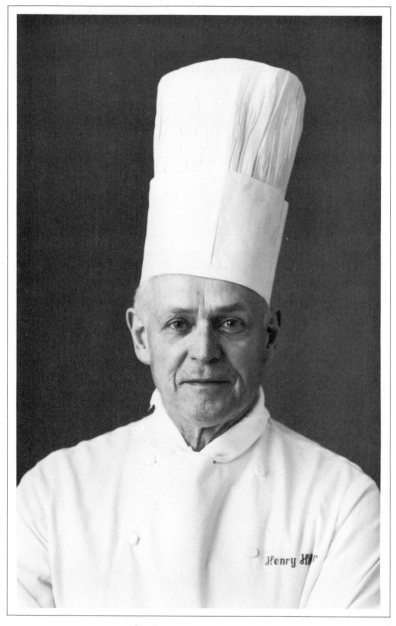

(© 1985 THE PORTRAIT PROJECT, INC. BY MICHAEL EVANS)

THE
WHITE HOUSE FAMILY
COOKBOOK

Henry Haller

with Virginia Aronson, R.D., M.S.

RANDOM HOUSE
NEW YORK

Library of Congress Cataloging-in-Publication Data

Haller, Henry.
The White House family cookbook.

Bibliography: p.
Includes index.
1. Cookery. I. Aronson, Virginia. II. Title.
TX715.H179 1987   641.5   87-9674
ISBN 0-394-55657-7

Manufactured in the United States of America

Typography and binding design by Jo Anne Metsch

23456789

First Edition

This book is dedicated to my wife, Carole,
whose years of support, patience, and love have nurtured
my career and warmed my homelife.

FOREWORD

The White House holds millions of memories that can recount for us the American story. The First Family's Washington home has always served as a mirror of the social customs of the times and as a pace-setter for social precedent. Thus the White House embodies the social history of America and presents us with a precise record of the changing life-styles of the last two centuries. There is only one White House, and it is indeed an honor to be able to serve the people who live and work here.

When I decided to pursue a career in cooking, I had no idea where I would find myself working or how I would get there. I was only a fourteen-year-old growing up in Altdorf, Switzerland, when my father first planted the idea of becoming a chef in my mind. Although he appreciated the world's fine food, he had never left Switzerland, but he encouraged me to travel. "Henry," he would say, "why don't you be a chef? You can travel all over the world. And you will never have to worry about a job. People everywhere have to eat." Yet even my father never expected my career path to lead me to the White House.

At the age of sixteen, I began a culinary apprenticeship at the famed Park Hotel in Davos, Switzerland. In my native country, an apprenticeship is mandatory for all trades and professions. I continued my training for nearly ten years in various Swiss hotels, including the Hotel Belle-Vue-Palace in Berne, and the Hotel des Balances in Lucerne, where I attended the Hotel Training School. This program was considered one of the world's best for professional chefs and offered me the additional opportunity of learning the English language.

When I was twenty-five, I left my position as the "chef tournant" at the beautiful Grand Hotel in Buergenstock to be the "chef entremetier" at the Ritz-Carlton Hotel in Montreal. In most restaurant and institutional kitchens, there are five stations, each with its "chef de partie": The "chef entremetier" is responsible for hot vegetables, soups, pasta, potatoes, and egg dishes; the "chef saucier" prepares the sauces and the entrées served with sauces; the "chef rotissier" roasts the meats and poultry; the "garde manger" makes the cold plates; the pastry chef position may be subdivided into specialties such as frozen desserts, cakes and batter recipes, chocolates and confectioneries. Larger kitchens may include a butcher, a fish chef, and a pantry station for preparing salads, sandwiches, and coffee. The "chef de cuisine" is the Executive Chef who must coordinate the activities of each of the kitchen stations and chefs de partie, plus serve as the "chef tournant," or substitute chef, whenever necessary.

In 1953, I finally arrived in the United States to work as the chef saucier at the Royal Palms Inn in Phoenix. About a year later, I moved to New York City, where I worked for four years as the Executive Chef of the exclusive Dellwood Country Club. I spent the following three years as the Executive Chef for the Hotel Hampshire House with its magnificent view of Central Park. And with a staff of twenty, I had time to fine-tune my art by developing my skills in creating ice sculptures and designing artistic food displays. At the Sheraton-East Hotel (formerly The Ambassador), I had a staff of fifty. Here, I was able to further enhance my supervisory skills as well as enrich my culinary expertise with input from a large and experienced kitchen crew.

When the White House publicly announced their search for an Executive Chef in January 1966, my wife suggested that I apply. "If they want me, they can call me," I told her with bland equanimity. My attitude abruptly changed, however, when the White House *did* call me in for a personal interview with First Lady Mrs. Lyndon B. Johnson, who had heard about me from a number of her friends. I was given an impressive tour of the White House, including the kitchen I would call home for the next twenty-plus years. I was thrilled when, on January 20, 1966, I was named Executive Chef for the White House.

On February 1, 1966, I arrived without fanfare at the North Gate of the White House to begin an exciting new life. A friendly kitchenman helped me carry my suitcases up the stairs of the White House and down the third floor hallway to my new temporary housing. For the first six months, I lived "over the store," which is like living above a historical museum and within earshot of where history is being made. I still remember being awakened each morning by the clanging of a metal ladder right outside my window, as the American flag was hoisted to its place of honor. So I was usually up at sunrise ready to execute my important new role, and available twenty-four hours a day to spot-check the operation. President Johnson liked that.

Although I had not met President Johnson until I arrived at the White House to serve as his Executive Chef, the President had tasted my cooking on a number of occasions. As Vice-President, he had frequented the Sheraton-East Hotel when in New York City and had tasted some of my specialties there, including one of his favorites, Lobster Thermidor. The White House hired me not only because I could prepare such elaborate dishes to the President's satisfaction, but also because I could cook a wide range of food-stuffs, from pâté to pastrami. I am still a very flexible cook, which is an absolute must in any productive kitchen, and especially at the White House.

The White House has served for almost 200 years as one of America's great emblems. Envisioned by city planner Pierre L'Enfant as having "the sumptuousness of a palace . . . and the agreeableness of a county seat," the Executive Mansion (as the White House used to be called) has long represented beauty and dignity, power and glory, heritage and tradition, pomp and circumstance. It provides a clear reflection of social trends and sets in motion social innova-tions, representing both tradition and foresight. Above all, the White House symbolizes the homes of the nation, and the family installed there, by democratic extension, represents all American families. Each of the First Families has colored the White House with its individual personalities and tastes, and with its diverse reactions to life in the First Home. Each First Family has left an imprint of its own on the home, the nation, and the world.

During my twenty-plus years at the White House, I have pre-pared much of the food served to five different families with five very different dietary patterns. Geographical, cultural, and familial influences have all helped to inspire the menus for each of the First Family's dining tables. After all, the United States has been quite accurately labeled as a "melting pot" of peoples, and Ameri-can cuisine serves as a revealing representation of the vast variety in individual tastes and backgrounds of the past and present pop-ulace. Nowhere has this rich heritage been more clearly in evi-dence than at the White House—at America's First Dining Table.

The White House invariably evokes patriotism and pride in

Americans. My own role as the Executive Chef at the White House has certainly been the most rewarding position I have ever held. Now, more than twenty years since the day I walked up the long drive with my humble suitcases and an overwhelming sense of honor, I am pleased to be able to share my experiences in the American First Family's home. It is my sincere hope that *The White House Family Cookbook* will inspire and inform, amuse and arouse, edify and educate cooks, would-be cooks, and noncooks everywhere.

—Henry Haller, Executive Chef
The White House
September 1987

ACKNOWLEDGMENTS

No book is composed solely by its authors. We are grateful to all who helped us, and we give special thanks to: Maurice Bonté and Roland Mesnier for their expert advice on desserts; Becky Saletan for her creative and proficient editorial guidance; Jason Epstein, our esteemed editor; Connie Clausen, our top-notch agent; Helene Marks, our skilled typist; and our families and friends for their understanding and support throughout the lengthy and demanding process of turning two decades of White House dining into an informative, attractive, and eminently useful cookbook.

CONTENTS

INTRODUCTION

Cooking well takes time and research, patience and practice. Artistic skill helps, too, in achieving a proper presentation. But the most important requirement is a true interest in cooking. It is my hope that the recipes in this cookbook can be used with pleasure and success by anyone who is interested in cooking and willing to experiment in the kitchen, even those who do not know how to cook. The recipes have been kept as simple as possible without sacrificing flavor or appearance, even those that sound "fancy" to the novice cook, or appear a bit lengthy to the convenience food user. Equipped with an open mind and a sense of adventure, even an inexperienced cook can turn out results fit for a king.

A good cookbook should enable the user to feel at home in the kitchen and to gain confidence in culinary abilities. It is important to understand that a cookbook is really only a guide; cooks must learn to trust their tastebuds to teach them how to create truly delicious dishes. Flexibility is an essential tool. Sometimes the available ingredients will vary, as will cooking equipment. Personal taste and culinary style are equally important in determining eventual outcome. Thus, to "follow" any recipe is really to re-create it as your own.

It is important to measure ingredients as accurately as possible, and to concentrate on each recipe, paying close attention to detail. Reading through each recipe in advance is unquestionably the best way to start. Since this book is much more than a cookbook, there is much more to read than just the recipes; there are fascinating stories about behind-the-scenes life at the White House, and bits of White House history and lore. The "Special Event" recipes at the end of each section were prepared in the White House during that administration to be served at State Dinners and other official functions and historic events, including three weddings. Since many of these recipes would be perfect for serving to your own guests, I have scaled down the recipes for the most popular dishes so that home cooks can re-create the White House menus for their own special dinners, parties, even wedding receptions. The yields tend to be greater than those of the "Family Recipes," so that you can use these recipes to feed a practical number of guests at your own "Special Events."

Since this book does not follow a conventional soups-to-nuts sequence, you should make use of the index, which includes listings by category and major ingredients.

In preparing any dish, from the simplest fruit platter to the most intricate pastry, there are some standard rules to keep in mind. The following "Baker's Dozen" are my own basic guidelines for working in the kitchen, whether in the White House or your own house. The Appendix at the end of this book includes additional suggestions for improving the nutritional value of your family's menus and for ease in using this book.

CHEF HALLER'S BAKER'S DOZEN

1. Plan your menus in advance. In order to achieve an appealing balance of meal components and ease daily food preparation, it is essential to learn how to menu plan, shop by a list, and then prepare food step by step, with all ingredients ready in advance. The French call it *mise en place.* I call it kitchen common sense.

2. Keep your menus seasonal. Nothing will make food taste fresher nor prove to be more economical. Food at the peak of perfection is your best buy; it is usually more nutritious and always more delicious. No cook can produce a dish of a quality higher than that of the raw ingredients, and foods at their seasonal peak provide the best base from which to begin. In fact, "good cooking" is often no more than selecting the freshest ingredients and altering them as little as possible.

3. Follow each recipe carefully and pay close attention to details. Remember that there are variables that can contribute to variations in the final outcome (i.e., ingredients differ in composition; temperature gauges may vary from oven to oven; weather, altitude, and humidity can have an effect; and cooking equipment and personal cooking styles are unique). It is also important to test in advance any recipes you wish to scale down or multiply, as I have done with many of the recipes included in this book. If you reduce a recipe to serve 4 instead of 40, or 5 rather than 10, the formula is changed and unexpected outcomes can occur. It is safer to prepare the recipe as given and enjoy leftovers later.

4. *Use standard ingredients unless the recipe indicates otherwise.* Eggs should be Grade A large, butter is salted unless unsalted is called for, flour is all-purpose unless another kind is specified, sugar is granulated, and bread crumbs are dry and unseasoned. Wash and dry fresh produce before use, and select medium-size fruits and vegetables unless the recipe indicates otherwise.

5. *Use standard procedures in preparing and cooking foods.* I dice foods carefully into even little squares that the French call *brunoise,* and I chop or mince in a more random manner into the desired size, either finely or coarsely. To butter a pan, use real butter; if burning is a possibility, I suggest greasing the pan with vegetable shortening or oil instead. *Sauté* means to cook quickly in a hot pan over medium-high heat while stirring contantly. *Simmer* means to cook slowly over low heat, just below a boil, as indicated by tiny surface bubbles. Food is *blanched* by parboiling in boiling water for a few minutes. To *make a roux,* butter is melted but must not be allowed to brown; flour is added at once, mixed in with a wire whisk, then cooked for a minute to remove the starchy taste and develop a sweet, nutlike flavor.

6. *Use standard cooking equipment when available.* The recipes in this book assume that any beating is conducted with an electric mixer unless otherwise indicated; using a hand beater will lengthen the time required to achieve the desired outcome. Sometimes a food processor or blender is unavailable; if it is possible to do without, I have suggested an alternate method. A commercial ice cream freezer is called for in some recipes. Deep-fat frying is best conducted in a French fryer, but a Dutch oven can be substituted; with most shallower pans, one runs the risk that hot grease may boil over or splatter. In cooking starchy foods such as potatoes, nonstick pans are preferable; seasoned pans are best for egg dishes. Line pans with buttered brown paper when baking or roasting vegetables, but substitute silicon (parchment) paper at high temperatures as it will not burn; both types can be purchased in large rolls. Wax paper is easily burned, so it should be generously greased before use in baking. In working with pastries, a marble slab is preferable to a wooden board as it is smoother, making the dough easier to clean off, and its even coolness facilitates handling. To avoid kitchen accidents, keep knives sharp; a damp kitchen

towel under a cutting board or mixing bowl helps avoid slippage. My own favorite tool for stirring is a cook's spatula—a hard, thin, plastic spatula with a wooden handle that is more efficient than the customary wooden spoon.

All in all, delicious dishes can usually be created using the simplest equipment. But the proper piece of equipment is often required to accomplish the task efficiently and proficiently. In equipping a home kitchen, begin by buying standard size equipment that is sturdy and easy to clean. Expensive but essential kitchen tools—such as a professional mixer, blender, food processor, and commercial ice cream freezer—should be regarded as a long-term investment.

7. Use standard measurements and standard measuring tools. Be sure to measure ingredients carefully and evenly. Do not "pack" ingredients unless called for, and use items that are of average size unless indicated otherwise. For a pinch, a dash, or a drop, add ingredients "to taste." It is essential for cooks to learn to employ their own tastebuds as precise and personal measuring tools.

8. Food substitutions should be made with care. Olive slices may be used in place of the costly black truffle in garnishing, for example, but the final results cannot be expected to be of equal quality. Fresh herbs are best when available; the more pungent dried form can often be substituted in reduced amounts, as indicated throughout this book. Although bouillon, broth, and stock can be used interchangeably, the salt contents will differ, so taste-testing is essential in seasoning the dish. Bottled chili sauce is acceptable; tomato sauce and mayonnaise may be either commercially prepared or homemade. In the end, there is sometimes no substitute for the "real thing."

9. Note the few suggested name brand products. Lea & Perrins Worcestershire Sauce and genuine Cointreau, for example, each offer consistent high quality and fine flavor. In most recipes, however, various commercial brands can be used interchangeably, depending on personal preference and availability.

10. Note the few suggested imported specialty products. Usually, readily available substitutions are also listed. For the adventuresome cook, a trip to local specialty shops, ethnic markets, and health food stores can yield a surprising cache of unusual ingredients. For a complete brochure on Swiss imported specialty items, write to: Albert Uster Imports, 9211 Gaither Road, Gaithersburg, Maryland 20877.

11. Use proper temperatures in pastry making to ease preparation and improve final results. For example, add 1 tablespoon of *hot* water when beating egg yolks with sugar for a lighter, fluffier yield. In beating cream, use a *cold* bowl; I pour the cold cream into a mixing bowl and chill for 30 minutes before whipping. Egg whites should be at *room temperature* before beating in a clean, dry bowl to ensure the best yield. Dough is better chilled before handling, and can be kept *cool* by rolling out on a marble slab instead of a wooden board.

12. Use proper temperatures in making sauces, soups, and stocks. Avoid overcooking sauces. When working with whole eggs or yolks, stir constantly over medium-low heat and remove from heat at once if any curdling is observed. In order to avoid separation, warm sauces should be of equal temperature (around 95°F) when combined. If there is time, soups and stocks can be chilled to allow fat to rise to the top for easy removal, before reheating.

13. Individuality is an essential ingredient in every recipe. Personal taste and individual style can be incorporated at each step when preparing a recipe, from testing for flavor to eyeing for doneness and garnishing for visual appeal. Character is as important as talent in attempting a new recipe or repeating one that is "tried and true." Each time you cook, you can become the master of your latest composition, and your dinner guests can serve as an appreciative audience for your unique culinary creations.

Over the past twenty-plus years, the White House has received hundreds of letters from America's home cooks requesting our recipes for the dishes served to the Presidents and their families and guests. All of these recipes can now be reproduced with equal success in the average home kitchen. Home cooks can plan menus and prepare foods for their own families that adhere to the axiom outlined in the *Executive Residence Procedures Manual* in the section on "Menu Planning for the First Family": "Purpose—To ensure that the First Family's menus are prepared to the highest standards and in accordance with the Family's tastes and preferences." So, to all cooks and would-be cooks as well as their fortunate dining companions, I wish you much fun and success in the home kitchen, and I bid you bon appétit!

THE
JOHNSON FAMILY

*Morning Favorites from
the LBJ Ranch*

Johnson Family Favorite Entrées

*Side Dishes and Salads
Johnson~Style*

Johnson Family Favorite Desserts

Special Event Recipes

MORNING FAVORITES
FROM THE LBJ RANCH

President Johnson liked to accomplish some of the day's work before he even got out of bed in the morning. As early as 6:00 A.M., he would watch the news on three television sets while scanning the day's papers. Mrs. Johnson used her own bedroom suite as an office, spending much of her day there working on projects and answering the some 1,500 letters she received each week. She would join the President each morning to have breakfast in his four-poster bed. Once in a while, Mrs. Johnson would also join him in indulging in a thickly cut, well-cooked bacon, which they called "ranch-style."

Ranch-Style Bacon was prepared every morning in the White House in case the President called for a slice or two. Any extra bacon would be used later on for making sandwiches or in dishes such as Mrs. Johnson's Quiche Lorraine.

Makes 8 slices

1 pound whole bacon

1. Preheat oven to 375°F.
2. Slice bacon into 8 very thick (⅛- to ¼-inch) slices.
3. In a cast-iron skillet, arrange bacon slices in a single layer. Set skillet on middle shelf of hot oven.
4. Cook for 10 minutes; drain off excess fat and turn bacon over, using a metal spatula. Cook for 10 minutes more, or until bacon is very crisp.
5. Drain on paper towels and keep warm. Just before serving, crisp bacon by reheating it in oven for several minutes.

THICK RANCH-STYLE BACON

Martha Jefferson Randolph, the daughter of our third President, provided some advice on breakfast eating to the readers of her cookbook, The Virginia Housewife, *published in 1824:*

Early rising is also essential to the good government of a family. A late breakfast deranges the whole business of the day and throws a portion of it on the next, which opens the door for confusion to enter.

CHIPPED BEEF ON TOAST

After President Eisenhower suffered a heart attack (also in 1955), he modified his hectic habits and advised the American public of his plans to lead a term "of ordered work activity, interspaced with regular amounts of exercise, recreation, and rest." The American public soon followed suit, emphasizing the importance of leisure time, regular physical activity, and attention to life-style in the prevention of heart disease and maintenance of good health.

The typical morning meal prepared in the White House for President Johnson consisted of his favorite chipped beef covered with cream, and a cup of hot tea. Even when the President was trying to shed a few extra pounds, he insisted on having chipped beef. So, we developed a low-calorie bouillon-based sauce to replace the rich cream.

Before his first heart attack in 1955, Lyndon B. Johnson led a stereotypical "stressed executive" life-style. Working from 7:30 A.M. to 11:30 P.M., LBJ was constantly on the go, eating his meals on the run. After his heart attack, LBJ organized his recovery like he managed his campaigns. Restructuring his typical caloric intake into a sensible diet plan, LBJ lost weight and altered his eating habits to emphasize low-fat, reduced-calorie eating. President Johnson also discovered that his physician's prescription for daily naps worked to his own professional advantage. His post-luncheon nap made two days out of every one. On arising at 6:00 P.M. after a two-hour rest, the President explained in delight, "It's like starting a new day."

Serves 1

¼ *pound chipped beef, cut into*   ½ *to* ¾ *cup beef bouillon*
    1-inch squares   *1 thick slice bread, toasted*
1 tablespoon butter   *3 twists freshly ground black*
1 tablespoon flour   *pepper*

1. In a small saucepan, cover beef with water and bring to a boil; drain.
2. In a small sauté pan, heat butter over medium heat; add flour, stirring well, and continue to cook until the mixture browns lightly. Stir in enough bouillon to make a smooth, thick sauce.
3. Add chipped beef to the sauce, and simmer gently for 5 minutes, stirring often.
4. Spoon the chipped beef over hot toast (HOMEMADE BREAD LOAF [page 6] is delicious). Sprinkle with pepper, and serve at once.

MRS. JOHNSON'S TINY BREAKFAST PANCAKES

Mrs. Johnson loved breakfast foods, including eggs and omelets, pancakes and waffles, even grits. A warm, feminine woman, Mrs. Johnson was also independent and intelligent. She was a sharp businesswoman, and handled the family money and household

matters with amazing skill. State dinners at the White House are paid for by the government, but the First Families are responsible for their own meals. Thus, Mrs. Johnson utilized her accounting skills in reviewing my weekly menus carefully, with an eye to economy as well as appeal. She frequently inserted her economical, tasty little pancakes into the weekend breakfast menu.

Makes 24

¾ cup flour
1 teaspoon baking powder
¼ teaspoon salt
1 egg yolk

½ cup milk
¼ cup shortening, melted
2 egg whites, at room
    temperature

1. Mix together dry ingredients and sift.
2. In a large mixing bowl, beat egg yolk with milk until well blended. Mix in melted shortening.
3. Blend dry ingredients with egg mixture until batter is smooth.
4. In a clean, dry bowl, beat egg whites until stiff; fold into batter.
5. Heat nonstick skillet until very hot, drop batter by tablespoonfuls onto hot surface, and brown on both sides. Serve hot with melted butter and Vermont maple syrup, or top with warmed MRS. JOHNSON'S PEACH PRESERVES (page 8).

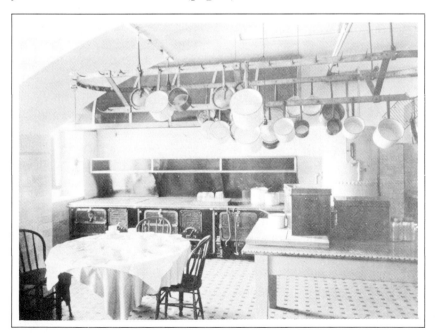

Pancakes have long served as a popular breakfast item on White House menus. Thomas Jefferson so valued his pancakes that he brought his governess up from Monticello to be sure that he had his favorite "batter cakes, fried apples, and hot breads served with bacon and eggs" for breakfast while living in the White House. President Andrew Jackson reportedly favored buckwheat-cornmeal flapjacks with hot molasses or buttered maple syrup. Franklin D. Roosevelt also liked hot buttered maple syrup on his pancakes, while President Eisenhower preferred cornmeal pancakes smothered with light molasses. And America's most thrifty President, Calvin Coolidge, usually served buckwheat cakes with Vermont maple syrup at the low-cost breakfast meetings he held regularly in the White House dining rooms.

The White House kitchen circa 1890. (COURTESY: LIBRARY OF CONGRESS)

HOMEMADE BREAD LOAF

Freshly baked bread was endorsed in the 1887 edition of The White House Cook Book *("A Comprehensive Cyclopedia of Information for the Home, Containing Cooking, Toilet and Household Recipes, Menus, Dinner-Giving, Table Etiquette, Care of the Sick, Health Suggestions, Facts Worth Knowing, Etc." written by White House steward Hugo Ziemann and Mrs. F. L. Gillette) at a time when the act of baking bread was considered to be a household necessity rather than a culinary art:*

Among all civilized people bread has become an article of food of the first necessity; and properly so, for it constitutes of itself a complete life sustainer. . . . As there is no one article of food that enters so largely into our daily fare as bread, so no degree of skill in preparing other articles can compensate for lack of knowledge in the act of making good, palatable and nutritious bread.

Mrs. Johnson can be credited with bringing back old-fashioned home-style cooking to the White House. She was a strong advocate of serving home-baked bread, so fresh loaves were made, two at a time, using Mrs. Johnson's own recipe. Mrs. Johnson often gave away her delicious bread as gifts, with or without a jar of her homemade preserves.

In Switzerland, the bakeries offer a wide selection of fresh breads made with different flours and shaped into all kinds of loaves. The breads vary from canton (Swiss state) to canton, but are always delicious. In America, the typical white bread that is sold commercially is not nearly as tasty as freshly baked loaves of what the Swiss call "gentleman's bread"—the same home-style white bread that Mrs. Johnson introduced to the White House.

Makes 2 loaves

3 tablespoons shortening	*1 egg*
½ cup sugar	*1 teaspoon salt*
1 cup milk, scalded	*4½ to 5 cups flour*
2 packages active dry yeast	
¼ cup warm water (105°F–115°F)	

1. In a large mixing bowl, cream shortening and sugar. Pour in scalded milk and let cool to lukewarm.
2. Dissolve yeast in warm water; add to milk mixture.
3. Beat egg until light, add egg and salt to milk mixture, and beat well.
4. Add flour, one cup at a time. Mix with dough hook or turn out and knead by hand until dough is smooth and elastic. (This will take about 5 minutes.)
5. Place dough in a large greased bowl, cover with a hot damp cloth, and place in a warm spot to let rise until doubled in bulk, approximately 2 hours.
6. On a lightly floured board, knead dough. Work outside edges in, adding flour and kneading for about 3 minutes, or until dough no longer sticks to the board. Dough should be bubbly and puff back up on pressing.
7. Use a sharp knife to divide dough into 2 equal loaves, and place in greased bread pans. Cover with a hot damp cloth, and let rise again for 30 minutes, or until doubled in bulk.
8. Bake at 350°F on lower oven shelf for 35 to 40 minutes, or until

browned and shrinking from the sides of the pans. Loaves should sound hollow when tapped on the bottom with a knife.

9. Turn bread out onto wire racks to cool. Cut into thick slices as needed.

The Johnsons all adored hot biscuits fresh from the White House ovens. The family's affinity for plain biscuits led Mrs. Johnson to include Hot Biscuits often on breakfast, lunch, and dinner menus. Hot Biscuits were also served at many of the parties that the Johnsons hosted at the White House, including the wedding receptions for both Luci and Lynda.

President Johnson enjoyed snacking on Hot Biscuits stuffed with ham or his favored deer sausage (page 11). Mrs Johnson and the girls liked the rolls plain, served in place of the Homemade Bread Loaf they liked for breakfast. The First Families that have followed the Johnsons have also proven partial to fresh biscuits and breads, so the White House has never lacked the enticing aroma of home-baked breadstuffs.

Makes 12

2 cups flour
1 tablespoon baking powder
1 teaspoon salt

3 tablespoons butter
¾ cup milk

1. Mix together dry ingredients and sift.
2. Add butter in pieces, and work into dry ingredients by hand until mixture is lump-free.
3. Stir in milk quickly, mixing by hand to form a soft dough.
4. Transfer dough onto lightly floured board and press down by hand to around ¾ inch thickness; even dough out by hand.
5. Cut dough into 2-inch biscuit rounds and arrange on a lightly greased baking sheet.
6. Bake at 425°F for about 10 to 15 minutes, or until lightly browned.
7. Serve stuffed with country ham (HAM-STUFFED BISCUITS [page 43]) as a snack or appetizer, on top of LAMB HASH WITH BISCUITS (page 13) for a filling supper, or dotted with butter and MRS. JOHNSON'S PEACH PRESERVES (page 8) for Sunday breakfast Johnson-style.

HOT BISCUITS

Bess Truman brought her own cook to the White House during her husband's administration so that they could continue to enjoy the "homey" foods—such as hot biscuits—that were popular in Independence, Missouri. Well before that time, the 1887 edition of The White House Cook Book *provided a recipe for the Baking Powder Biscuits popular in many small towns:*

Two pints of flour, butter the size of an egg, three heaping teaspoonfuls of baking powder and one teaspoonful of salt; make a soft dough of sweet milk or water, knead as little as possible, cut out with the usual biscuit cutter, and bake in rather a quick oven.

MRS. JOHNSON'S PEACH PRESERVES

Thomas Jefferson has been called the greatest gourmet to occupy the White House. Yet he actually favored simple fare and relied heavily on fresh produce. He reportedly spent a good deal of time in planning near-vegetarian menus, shopping in local markets, raising unusual crops, and charting the growth of his gardens. Jefferson was partial to fruit, and brought several varieties from Europe to America—and even introduced such delicacies as dried peaches. Thomas Jefferson added over 1,100 peach trees to his abundant orchards at Monticello.

Mrs. Johnson, who referred to her home-canned jellies and preserves as "fruit of the land," stocked the White House kitchen with a variety of preserved produce from the LBJ Ranch. Mrs. Johnson often gave away jars of her preserves as gifts, noting, "nothing tastes as good as when it comes from your own garden." The Johnsons requested that only Texas-grown peaches be included in their popular peach preserves.

The LBJ Ranch was the Johnsons' most cherished relaxation spot. During the Johnson administration, the family retired to the ranch for long holidays and vacations. The rambling stone and frame ranch house, located on some three hundred acres of land on the banks of Texas's Pedernales River, captivated casual friends, VIPs, and almost anyone who crossed over the doormat that promised: ALL THE WORLD IS WELCOME HERE.

Makes 3 quarts

4 cups sugar
1 cup water
1 tablespoon vanilla extract

1 tablespoon lemon extract
6 pounds (around 24) ripe peaches, peeled and sliced

1. In a large saucepan, dissolve sugar in water over medium-high heat and bring to a boil; cook for about 5 minutes, or until syrup is clear. Skim off any froth.

2. Add vanilla and lemon extract, stir in peaches, and return to a boil. Watch carefully to prevent from boiling over.

3. Boil for 5 minutes. Remove from heat and skim off any froth.

4. Fill hot, sterilized jars (quart-size screw-top Mason jars) and adjust caps; a suction seal will form with cooling. Store in a cool, dark place. Serve with HOT BISCUITS (page 7), or warm over vanilla or TEXAS PEACH ICE CREAM (page 32).

JOHNSON FAMILY FAVORITE ENTRÉES

After I had been at the White House only a short while, Walter Cronkite reported the following prediction on the *CBS Evening News:*

> We have been unable to determine if the new chef has passed the test on chili con carne. If he has used ground round steak, as Mrs. Eisenhower used to do, that news would be automatically suppressed in the interests of public order in Texas. If he learns to use chuck meat, on the lean side and from an old critter, he can expect a long and happy life in the White House kitchen.

Actually, Texas cooking was not overemphasized during the Johnson administration. President Johnson liked his Texas-style dishes, but we generally served these foods as hors d'oeuvres for parties and receptions. My basic cuisine is French, but I am very flexible, so when the President wanted me to cook other types of food, I did so to the best of my ability—it was his kitchen, after all. But I stayed away from his spicy favorites myself, because the first time I bit into a hot pepper I almost went through the ceiling!

CHILI CON CARNE

Serves 8 to 10

2 pounds lean ground chuck or round steak
1 large onion, diced
2 garlic cloves, crushed
Tabasco sauce
1 teaspoon ground oregano
1 teaspoon cumin seed
2 tablespoons chili powder
Two 14½-ounce cans whole tomatoes
Two 14½-ounce cans kidney beans
2 cups hot water

1. In a large heavy skillet, sear meat with onion and garlic until lightly browned.

2. Add 5 or more shakes of Tabasco sauce (amount depends on individual taste) and rest of ingredients; bring to a boil.

3. Reduce heat, cover, and simmer for about 1½ hours; stir occasionally and skim off fat as it cooks out.

4. Serve hot with warm, crisp tortilla chips and, if desired, a side dish of jalapeño peppers. Chili tastes best after refrigerating overnight and reheating in a double boiler.

BEEF STROGANOFF

President Johnson liked this dish, along with other soft-textured meat dishes such as chipped beef, lamb hash, chicken chow mein, and chop suey. Mrs. Johnson hired me to serve as Executive Chef because of my experience in preparing simple American fare, as well as more elaborate Continental foods. So although I favor French cooking, I am equally at home with Swiss, German, Austrian, Italian, and American cuisine. This is fortunate because the White House—like America itself—is a melting pot of nationalities and cuisines. And there is no such thing as a routine meal in the White House.

Serves 6

3 tablespoons butter
3 tablespoons minced shallots
2 tablespoons flour
1 cup dry white wine
1 cup beef bouillon, heated
1 pint sour cream
½ teaspoon freshly ground black pepper
1 bay leaf
1 teaspoon Worcestershire sauce
1 tablespoon vegetable oil
2 pounds lean tenderloin of beef, cut into 1½ × ¼-inch strips

1. In a 3-quart saucepan, melt butter over high heat, and sauté shallots until golden brown.

2. Using a wire whisk, mix in flour. Cook for a minute over medium heat to remove the raw taste of the flour. Whisk in wine and hot bouillon. Bring slowly to a boil, stirring occasionally.

3. Stir in sour cream, pepper, and bay leaf. Simmer slowly for 10 minutes.

4. Add Worcestershire sauce and remove bay leaf. Keep warm.

5. In an iron skillet, heat oil until very hot; brown beef strips evenly on all sides, turning often. Drain well.

6. Stir beef strips into sauce; bring to a boil, and serve at once with plain rice or noodles or wild rice.

Fortunately, it was not my duty to prepare President Johnson's own recipe for deer sausage, which he liked to send to members of his staff and a few favored journalists at Christmastime, accompanied by little packages of the sausage and the following note:

> *GREETINGS FROM THE DEER COUNTRY OF TEXAS.* We hope your holiday season will be more delectable because of our hunting season. In Texas, from November 15 on, the hills are alive with the sound of hunters. Here is the result, killed this year by our trusty rifles on the LBJ Ranch.

President Johnson liked to eat deer sausage himself, either as a snack on hot biscuits or as part of his favorite Sunday breakfast menu: chilled melon, scrambled eggs and deer sausage, hominy grits, homemade biscuits, and hot (real hot!) coffee.

DEER SAUSAGE

About 200 pounds sausage

One-half deer	*8 ounces ground red pepper*
One-half hog	*2 ounces ground sage*
25 ounces salt	*Sausage casings*
20 ounces black pepper	

1. Remove the meat from the deer and hog carcasses and put through a grinder.
2. Combine the meats and mix in the seasonings. Pack into sausage casings.
3. Place the uncut sausages in open pans with a small amount of water. Bake at 400°F for 10 minutes, then turn and bake for 10 minutes more.
4. Slice into inch-long pieces and serve.

President Johnson liked saucy beef dishes and casseroles, but Mrs. Johnson preferred a plain steak. In fact, the Johnson family failed to agree on many of their meal choices, and often dined separately on different menus. This made for a busy kitchen and required flexibility on the part of the staff.

When I arrived at the White House in 1966, former chef René Verdon had already departed and had not left any guidelines. Since I had never seen a White House menu, I had no idea how the

STUFFED PEPPERS

"Hope you don't mind fillin' in until the new chef arrives on Tuesday."

meals should look or how the food should be presented. Fortunately, there were helpful staff members who gave me the necessary support. And Mrs. Johnson often popped into the kitchen to provide additional input. Preparing the First Family's meals was—and still is—a matter of following the sensible axiom given in the *Executive Residence's Procedures Manual:* "To ensure that the First Family menus are prepared to the highest standards and in accordance with the Family's tastes and preferences."

Serves 6 to 8

6 large green bell peppers
2 pounds lean ground beef
1 teaspoon oregano
1½ teaspoons paprika
2 teaspoons salt
1 teaspoon freshly ground
  black pepper
2 tablespoons vegetable oil
1½ cups diced onions

3 garlic cloves, finely minced
2 eggs, beaten
1½ cups chili sauce
2 cups cooked rice
2 tablespoons chopped fresh
  parsley
¼ cup bread crumbs
¼ cup grated Parmesan cheese
1 cup beef or chicken bouillon

1. Preheat oven to 350°F.
2. Cut peppers in half lengthwise and remove seeds and membrane.
3. Bring a large pot of water to a boil, add peppers and blanch for 3 minutes. Remove and drain well on paper towels.
4. In a large mixing bowl, mix ground beef with oregano, paprika, salt, and pepper.
5. In a small skillet, heat oil; add onions and garlic and sauté until golden brown. Add to meat mixture.
6. Add beaten eggs, half of the chili sauce, the cooked rice, and parsley; mix well.
7. Arrange peppers cavity up in a shallow baking pan. Divide meat mixture evenly among the peppers.
8. Spoon remaining chili sauce over peppers. Mix together the bread crumbs and Parmesan cheese and sprinkle over the peppers.
9. Pour bouillon between peppers to cover the bottom of the baking pan, and bake on lower shelf of preheated oven for 45 to 50 minutes. Add additional bouillon if it reduces too much. Serve hot.

When a large roast was served for a Johnson family dinner, there would occasionally be leftovers. The Johnsons were always glad when leftover lamb could be put to good use later in the form of this unusual hash served over their favored biscuits. The Johnson administration attempted to influence Americans to be more economical, and the White House was certainly the best place to start setting a good example.

Of course, the Johnsons had to endure a lot of good-natured teasing on the subject of White House economizing. Art Buchwald wrote a humorous column exaggerating the President's use of less costly menu substitutions: "... The chef almost quit the other night when you made him prepare Vienna sausages for the House and Senate Democratic Leaders' dinner. Please don't ask him to cook neckbones." And Bob Hope evoked national laughter with his comment after an elaborate White House dinner, "It's amazing what you can do with leftovers!"

LAMB HASH WITH BISCUITS

President Calvin Coolidge is remembered for his thrifty management of the White House. He reportedly pored over the menus and household accounts in search of unnecessary extravagances. He cut down on the amount of meat served in the White House, taught the cook how to make an inexpensive breakfast cereal, and conducted breakfast meetings in place of the more expensive luncheons. After President Coolidge left office, he claimed that his greatest disappointment in the White House had been his inability to find out what happened to the leftovers!

Serves 6

3 tablespoons butter
½ cup diced onion
2 garlic cloves, finely minced
½ cup diced celery
2 tablespoons flour
1 cup hot milk
½ cup lamb gravy
2 cups diced cooked lamb
1 tablespoon Worcestershire sauce

½ teaspoon freshly ground black pepper
½ teaspoon chopped fresh rosemary, or ¼ teaspoon dried
1 tablespoon chopped fresh parsley
HOT BISCUITS (page 7)

1. Melt butter in a medium-size saucepan, and sauté onion, garlic, and celery for 2 to 3 minutes.

2. Whisk in flour and mix well. Cook for a minute to remove raw taste from the flour. Stir in hot milk.

3. Add lamb gravy and bring to a boil; simmer until sauce is smooth and thick, about 5 minutes, stirring occasionally.

4. Stir in diced lamb; add Worcestershire sauce, pepper, and rosemary.

5. Cover, and simmer over low heat for 15 minutes, stirring often with a plastic spatula. Hash should have a creamy consistency.

6. Add parsley. Spoon hash over biscuits, and serve at once.

CHICKEN CHOW MEIN

The Johnsons liked chow mein and chop suey, so these Chinese-style dishes were included regularly in the First Family's dinner menus. President Johnson liked to spice up these dishes with the hot mustard commonly served in Chinese restaurants. Warning: This hot sauce has a real bite to it!

Serves 6

3 tablespoons vegetable oil
1 cup julienned onions
1 cup julienned celery
1 cup julienned carrots
1 cup julienned fresh
   mushrooms
1 cup snow peas
2 cups bean sprouts
Six 4-ounce boneless chicken
   breasts, skinned and
   julienned
1½ cups chicken stock

2 tablespoons soy sauce
1 tablespoon cornstarch
4 eggs, beaten
1 tablespoon diced red bell
   pepper
1 tablespoon chopped fresh
   parsley
½ teaspoon salt
¼ teaspoon freshly ground
   white pepper

1. In a large skillet, heat oil until very hot. Add vegetables a few cups at a time and sauté until crisp. Remove with a slotted spoon, drain well on paper towels and transfer to a large, high-rimmed sauté pan.

2. Add the chicken to the skillet and sauté until lightly browned.

3. Add chicken to vegetables and stir in 1 cup of the chicken stock.

4. Bring to a simmer and cook over low heat, stirring gently, for 1 to 2 minutes.

5. Mix soy sauce with the remaining ½ cup of stock, add to the cornstarch, and blend well. Pour into chicken-vegetable mixture and continue cooking, stirring gently, until thickened; keep warm.

6. In a mixing bowl, blend beaten eggs with the remaining ingredients. Use this batter to make 4 to 6 very thin pancakes, cooking them in a 6-inch nonstick pan until lightly browned on both sides. Let cool, and cut into julienne strips.

7. Garnish chicken chow mein with julienned eggs, and serve hot, with steamed rice and HOT MUSTARD, if desired.

HOT MUSTARD

Makes 2 tablespoons

1 tablespoon dry mustard
2 teaspoons white wine vinegar
1 tablespoon water
A pinch of salt

1. Combine all ingredients in a small bowl.
2. Mix until smooth.

CHICKEN LIVERS CASINO

Although liver was not one of Mrs. Johnson's favorite foods, this particular dish was popular with the entire Johnson family. Zephyr Wright, the Johnsons' family cook, would have included this low-calorie recipe on President Johnson's menu more often had he not been restricting his cholesterol intake as well. Organ meats are high in cholesterol, so are best eaten only on occasion by those monitoring their dietary cholesterol. Eating liver once a month is a sensible way to include this high-nutrient foodstuff in the diet. Bermuda onions are suggested for use in liver dishes as this variety is sweeter than other types.

Serves 6

2 tablespoons olive oil
1 cup thinly sliced Bermuda
  onions
1 garlic clove, finely minced
1½ pounds fresh chicken livers
1 teaspoon salt
6 twists freshly ground black
  pepper
1 teaspoon chopped fresh
  oregano, or ½ teaspoon dried
1 teaspoon chopped parsley

1. Heat oil in a large cast-iron skillet, add onions and garlic and sauté until golden brown. Remove with slotted spoon and let drain on paper towels.
2. Cut each chicken liver in half, and add to hot skillet.
3. Add salt, pepper, and oregano; cook over high heat for 3 minutes, stirring constantly, until livers are browned and heated through.
4. Mix in sautéed onions and garlic, sprinkle with parsley, spoon into a ring of RICE PILAF, and serve at once.

RICE PILAF

Makes 4½ cups

1 tablespoon butter
1½ cups long-grain rice
3 cups boiling chicken stock

1 bay leaf
A pinch of freshly ground
  white pepper

1. In a 2-quart saucepan, melt butter over medium-high heat. Add rice.
2. Add boiling stock to rice and stir in seasonings.
3. Bring to a boil, cover, and cook for 25 minutes over low heat, without uncovering. Remove bay leaf.
4. Press rice gently into a 1½-quart ring mold. Keep warm until serving time, then unmold to serve.

SEAFOOD CREOLE

This dish was one of President Johnson's favorites, as he really loved seafood. Whether prepared for a family meal, a private dinner, or a huge crowd, this recipe will yield attractive and tasty results. It was always a success with the Johnsons and their White House guests.

President Johnson always enjoyed hosting a party. Protocol mandates that the President must be the first to leave a party; other guests are not supposed to depart before he does. It was often difficult for President Johnson's guests to adhere to this rule, as he preferred to remain as long as possible, dancing into the wee hours. The Johnsons' social secretary once explained:

President Johnson loved people in small and large numbers. So much of a State Dinner is cast in concrete, so if he went up to the Family Quarters right after dinner, he felt as though he missed the fun. And he loved dancing. He would stay so late that we had to pass the word to people that it wouldn't be counted rude if they slipped away before the President.

Serves 8 to 10

2 pounds medium-size shrimp
   (22 to 25 per pound)
¾ cup vegetable oil
2 cups slivered onions
4 garlic cloves, finely minced
2 cups coarsely diced green bell
   pepper
1 cup diced celery
2 cups sliced fresh
   mushrooms
1 tablespoon curry powder
1 tablespoon salt

1 tablespoon mixed chopped
   fresh oregano, thyme, and
   marjoram, or 1½ teaspoons
   dried
6 tomatoes, seeded and diced
1 cup chili sauce
10 drops Tabasco sauce
1 bay leaf
½ cup dry sherry
1 tablespoon cornstarch
1 tablespoon chopped fresh
   parsley

1. Cook shrimp for 5 minutes in a large pot of boiling salted water; drain, peel and devein. Set aside.

2. In a large skillet, heat oil; sauté onions and garlic for 2 to 3 minutes, or until golden brown.

3. Add green pepper, celery, and mushrooms. Stir in curry powder, salt, and fresh herbs.

4. Add tomatoes, chili sauce, Tabasco sauce, and bay leaf. Bring to a boil.

5. Mix sherry with cornstarch until smooth, and add to boiling sauce.

6. Add shrimp, and simmer gently for 10 minutes. Remove bay leaf.

7. Pour into casserole dish, sprinkle with parsley, and keep warm until serving time. The creole is best served with steamed rice.

Quiche Lorraine is believed to have originated in the Lorraine region of France, although some claim that the dish was derived from the German *Kuchen*. Each area of Lorraine and Alsace has a specific kind of quiche that residents claim to be the sole "true" recipe. Typically served very hot as an hors d'oeuvre, quiche has become popular in America as an entrée as well. Quiche can be prepared using a wide variety of ingredients, including spinach or broccoli, cooked chicken or seafood, and spices and herbs.

MRS. JOHNSON'S QUICHE LORRAINE

Mrs. Johnson preferred to use Ranch-Style Bacon in her Quiche Lorraine. Mrs. Johnson liked her quiche recipe so much, in fact, that she included the dish on the menu for Lynda's wedding reception.

Makes two 9-inch pies

12 *thick slices bacon, cut in small pieces*
1 *cup diced onions*
6 *eggs*
2 *egg yolks*
1 *quart half-and-half*
1 *teaspoon salt*
¼ *teaspoon freshly ground white pepper*

¼ *teaspoon nutmeg*
¾ *pound Gruyère cheese, freshly grated*
¼ *pound Parmesan cheese, freshly grated*
Two 9-inch prebaked PIE CRUSTS
4 *tablespoons chopped fresh chives*

1. Preheat oven to 375°F.
2. In a cast-iron skillet, sauté bacon until very crisp. Remove with a metal spatula, and drain well on paper towels.
3. Add onions to the hot skillet and sauté in the bacon drippings until lightly browned. Drain well on paper towels.
4. In a mixing bowl, beat together eggs, yolks, and half-and-half. Add salt, pepper, and nutmeg.
5. Divide cheeses evenly between the prebaked pie shells. Top with equal portions of bacon, onions, and chives.
6. Pour egg mixture carefully into the pie shells. Do not overfill.
7. Bake on lower shelf of preheated oven for 45 minutes, or until golden brown and firm to the touch. Remove and let stand for 30 minutes before slicing in wedges. Serve as an entrée for a light lunch or dinner, or in thin slices as an hors d'oeuvre. Quiche can be reheated, wrapped in foil, in a 250°F oven for 20 minutes, or until warmed through.

PIE CRUST

Makes two 9-inch shells

3 *cups flour*
1 *teaspoon salt*

2 *sticks (1 cup) butter*
½ *cup cold water*

1. Preheat oven to 350°F.
2. In a medium-size bowl, stir together flour and salt.

3. Cut in butter with pastry cutter until it is thoroughly distributed and the mixture resembles coarse bread crumbs.

4. Add water a little at a time, mixing by hand until dough is smooth.

5. Divide dough in half. Place one part on a lightly floured surface and flatten by hand into a round. Roll out from center to ⅛-inch thickness.

6. Fit pastry loosely into a 9-inch pie plate or quiche pan. Trim edges leaving ¼-inch overhang; fold the excess up to form a rim, and flute.

7. Repeat with other portion of dough.

8. Line pie shells with greased wax or parchment paper; weigh down with uncooked dried beans or pie weights.

9. Bake on lower shelf of preheated oven for 15 to 20 minutes, or until lightly browned.

10. Remove beans and paper; let crust cool on wire rack. Save beans to use again in preparing pie crusts.

SIDE DISHES AND SALADS JOHNSON-STYLE

SPINACH SOUFFLÉ

In French, *soufflé* refers to a breath or a puff of wind. This light dish can be hot or cold, sweet or savory, of fruit or vegetable, a main dish, side dish, or dessert. A wide variety of vegetable soufflés can be prepared from purées of chestnut, lettuce, chicory, mushrooms, artichokes, asparagus, carrots, celery, cauliflower, turnips, potatoes, or sweet potatoes, thickened with egg yolks, lightened with stiffly beaten egg whites, and baked in soufflé dishes or individual "cassolettes." The baking time for a soufflé is important, as the puffy dish should be lightly browned but not dry.

Spinach was one of President Johnson's favorite vegetables. He especially enjoyed vegetable dishes prepared in unusual forms, such as light spinach soufflés. But President Johnson was somewhat of a vegetable perfectionist, even with the most basic presentations. He once told me in mock seriousness, "Henry, if you can't get all the strings out of the string beans, please don't serve them in the White House anymore." Needless to say, I always made sure that my spinach soufflés rose to perfection.

Serves 6 as a main course, 10 as a side dish

¾ cup butter
1 tablespoon minced shallots
1 garlic clove, minced
¾ cup flour
2 cups steamed fresh spinach,
   cooled to room temperature,
   or one 10-ounce package
   frozen spinach, defrosted
1 teaspoon salt

⅛ teaspoon freshly ground
   white pepper
A pinch of nutmeg
½ cup hot milk
4 egg yolks
8 egg whites, at room
   temperature
A pinch of cream of tartar

1. Preheat oven to 350°F.
2. In a large saucepan, melt butter. Use a pastry brush to lightly coat the inside of a 2-quart soufflé dish; then dust lightly with flour.
3. Sauté shallots in remaining melted butter. Add garlic and sauté until golden brown.
4. Add flour, and whisk well to make a roux. Cook for a minute or two over medium heat to remove raw taste from flour.
5. Squeeze as much liquid as possible out of cooked or defrosted spinach. Purée, and stir into the roux; season with salt, pepper, and nutmeg.
6. Add hot milk and stir; bring just to the boiling point. Remove from heat.
7. Add egg yolks one at a time, mixing well after each addition with a plastic or wooden spoon.
8. In a dry, clean bowl, beat egg whites with cream of tartar until stiff. Fold into spinach mixture just until combined.
9. Pour into prepared soufflé dish, leaving ½ inch at the top for the soufflé to rise. Lightly smooth the top with a spatula.
10. Bake in middle of preheated oven for 45 minutes, or until soufflé is lightly browned and puffed to at least 2 inches above the top of the dish.
11. Serve at once as a vegetarian entrée for six, or as an accompaniment to beef or lamb dishes for up to ten.

Sweet potatoes originated in the Americas and became an over-night success in Europe. Henry VIII of England imported the sweet tuber from Spain to be baked in heavily sweetened, spiced pies. Sweet potatoes should not be referred to as "yams," which are botanically different and rather rare in today's marketplace. Sweet potatoes can be baked, fried, boiled, tossed in a potato salad, or puréed into puddings and casseroles.

A seasonal dish that is typically served during the winter holi-days, sweet potato casserole was requested year-round during the Johnson administration. With only slight variations, it has been served in the White House to all of the families that followed the Johnsons. And this all-American casserole was a favorite of many of the presidential families who preceded the Johnsons as well.

Serves 6 to 8

6 medium-size sweet potatoes	⅓ cup brown sugar
1 cup orange juice	2 cups miniature
1 teaspoon grated orange peel	marshmallows
½ cup honey	

1. Boil sweet potatoes in lightly salted water for about 25 minutes, or until cooked through. Drain and let cool.

2. Preheat oven to 375°F. Lightly butter the inside of a large cas-serole dish.

3. Peel cold potatoes; cut diagonally into slices ⅓-inch thick, and arrange in prepared casserole dish.

4. Mix together juice, peel, honey, and brown sugar. Spoon over sweet potatoes.

5. Cover potatoes with a layer of marshmallows and bake on top shelf of preheated oven for 45 minutes, or until potatoes are bub-bling and marshmallow topping is golden brown.

SWEET POTATOES WITH TOASTED MARSHMALLOWS

President Hoover may be best remembered for his lavish entertaining, and for setting the most elaborate and most expensive table in the history of the First Fam-ilies. Yet, one of the Hoo-vers' favorite dishes was Marshmallow Sweet Pota-toes. A formal luncheon menu from President Frank-lin D. Roosevelt's admin-istration included Cubed Sweet Potatoes Topped with Toasted Marshmallow. And when the Eisenhowers entertained the Khrush-chevs at the White House, the formal dinner was an all-American meal with roast turkey, cranberry sauce, and those same sweet sweet potatoes. Use of marshmallow topping com-plies with one old rule for proper "Dinner Giving" from the 1887 edition of The White House Cook Book: *"Each dish should be gar-nished sufficiently to be in good taste without looking absurd."*

PRESIDENT JOHNSON'S YORKSHIRE PUDDING

The 1887 edition of The White House Cook Book *describes Yorkshire Pudding as "a very nice accompaniment to a roast of beef..." The old recipe is surprisingly similar to the one used during the Johnson administration and the subsequent presidencies, and one that the authors considered to be "much better than the old way of baking the pudding under the meat":*

...One pint of milk, four eggs, whites and yolks beaten separately, one teaspoonful of salt, and two teaspoonfuls of baking powder sifted through two cups of flour. It should be mixed very smooth, about the consistency of cream. Regulate your time when you put in your roast, so that it will be done half an hour or forty minutes before dishing up. Take it from the oven, set it where it will keep hot. In the

More like a thick pancake than a pudding per se, Yorkshire Pudding is the required accompaniment to roast beef at the English table, usually prepared with the drippings as the meat roasts. In America, this traditional dish is often reserved for special occasion meals.

Mrs. Johnson included Yorkshire Pudding on the menu for special events—such as the State Dinner given in honor of the President of Tunisia—as well as for the First Family's dinners, because she considered the dish to be a universal favorite. This is true, and it is a simple, dependable dish as long as the recipe is followed carefully. The art of fine cuisine and the success of basic cookery depend on the same premise: A good recipe will yield good results *as long as it is done right.*

Serves 6

1 cup flour
1 cup cold milk
½ cup cold water
⅛ teaspoon salt
A pinch of freshly ground
* white pepper*

A pinch of nutmeg
3 eggs
¼ cup meat drippings or
* rendered bacon fat*

1. Preheat oven to 350°F.
2. In a mixing bowl, blend flour with milk and water until smooth. Add salt, pepper, and nutmeg.
3. Add eggs and mix well with a wire whisk.
4. In a cast-iron skillet, heat drippings until very hot.
5. Carefully strain batter into the hot skillet and transfer to middle shelf of preheated oven.
6. Bake for 35 minutes, or until golden brown.
7. Use a metal spatula to remove from the skillet in a single piece. Cut into wedges and serve at once.

meantime, have this pudding prepared. Take two common biscuit tins, dip some of the drippings from the dripping-pan into these tins, pour half of the pudding into each, set them into the hot oven, and keep them in until the dinner is dished up; take these puddings out at the last moment and send to the table hot.

Jars of homemade Dilled Okra were stocked in the White House storeroom for the Johnson family.

DILLED OKRA

Okra is an interesting vegetable. People seem either to love it or hate it! Lightly fuzzy on the outside and sort of slippery on the inside, the texture of okra turns some people away. I was never wild about okra, but have found that pickled and served as a spicy relish for barbecued meats, it is really a terrific flavor enhancer. The Johnsons brought this recipe to the White House, along with some of the stock from the LBJ Ranch. President Johnson enjoyed the Texas flavor this relish added to his meals. And to stay in his good graces, I always served the President the foods he liked.

Makes 2 quarts

1 teaspoon dill seed
1 quart (about 1 pound) fresh
  okra
1 small hot green pepper
1 small hot red pepper

2 garlic cloves
1 quart cider vinegar
1 cup water
½ teaspoon salt

1. Place ½ teaspoon dill seed in the bottom of a sterilized 2-quart jar.

2. Pack whole okra into the jar. Pack in peppers and garlic, and sprinkle with the remaining dill seed.

3. In a saucepan, stir together vinegar, water, and salt; bring to a boil. Pour over okra.

4. Seal jar and allow to stand (unopened) for 2 weeks. Chill in refrigerator before serving.

ZEPHYR'S PICKLED BLACK-EYED PEAS

In 1942, Zephyr Wright arrived in Washington from Marshall, Texas, to serve as the family cook for the Lyndon B. Johnsons. Zephyr remained with the Johnsons until 1969, and helped to cook for the family during their stay in the White House.

President Johnson was quite fond of Zephyr, and she attempted to assist him in staying healthy and controlling his diet. In 1966, she sent the President a heartfelt memo:

> Mr. President, you have been my boss for a number of years and you always tell me you want to lose weight and yet you never do very much to help yourself. Now I'm going to be your boss for a change. Eat what I put in front of you and don't ask for any more and don't complain.

Zephyr cooperated with White House physician Vice Admiral George Burkley in planning the President's calorie-controlled diet, portioning out his food, and preparing low-calorie desserts. Unfortunately, Zephyr was not as successful with her own diet as she was with the President's. Upon leaving the White House in 1969, Zephyr complained that she had gained over 80 pounds during her stay there! With delicious Texas specialties always around and the stress involved in cooking for the First Family of America, dietary indiscretions were certainly understandable. Once Zephyr was able to relax, away from the White House kitchens, she quickly thinned down again. I, too, have had to be very careful, lest the temptations and stresses of my role as White House Chef induce undesirable weight gain.

Makes 1½ quarts

4 cups cooked, drained black-
    eyed peas (fresh, frozen,
    canned, or dried)
½ cup olive oil
5 tablespoons red wine vinegar
2 jalapeño peppers, diced
3 garlic cloves, minced

½ cup diced red onion
½ cup diced red bell pepper
½ cup diced green bell pepper
A pinch of salt
A pinch of freshly ground
    black pepper

1. In a large mixing bowl, combine black-eyed peas with the remaining ingredients.

2. Cover tightly with plastic wrap and chill overnight.

3. Serve cold as a side dish for picnic foods such as fried chicken and barbecued spareribs. Add more salt, pepper, and/or jalapeño peppers before serving, if desired.

It freshens without enfeebling and fortifies without irritating.
                                    —Brillat-Savarin, on salads

PRESIDENT JOHNSON'S CHOPPED GARDEN SALAD

Although there are dozens of varieties of lettuce, iceberg is most commonly found in America's salads because the heads are the easiest to pack and ship. The more fragile lettuces, which are less common but increasing in popularity, include Boston red or green, Bibb, field, oak leaf, lambs', and limestone. All lettuce should be used promptly and handled gently.

President Johnson preferred his salad chopped so fine that he could eat it with a spoon. He was a very rapid eater, basically because he led his whole day at breakneck speed. This hard-working President was grateful for dishes which he could eat quickly and still enjoy. He also liked bulky, filling foods that eased his hunger without adding to his waistline.

Serves 6

2 cups diced iceberg lettuce
2 ripe tomatoes, peeled, seeded, and diced
1 cup diced Bermuda onion
1 cup diced green bell pepper
1 cup diced celery
1 teaspoon salt

½ teaspoon freshly ground black pepper
Juice of 2 lemons
1 teaspoon cider vinegar
1 teaspoon vegetable oil
6 large lettuce leaves.

1. In a large mixing bowl, combine diced vegetables. Toss with salt, pepper, lemon juice, and vinegar.
2. Add oil and mix well. Chill.
3. Spoon salad onto lettuce leaves and serve at once.

LYNDA'S TUNA SALAD

George Washington was said to have preferred fish to meat, perhaps due to his bad teeth; he was toothless by the age of fifty-seven, and the ill-fitting dentures of the time necessitated a softer diet than usual. Franklin D. Roosevelt liked fish with his breakfast. President Kennedy loved fish in a chowder, prepared New England–style, with chunks of flaky fish in a thick cream soup.

Lynda was a pleasure to cook for because she liked simple food and would eat almost anything. Yet when it came to tuna salad, one of her favorite dishes, she made it clear just how she wanted the dish prepared: Lynda preferred her tuna chopped fine, not in chunks, and she liked it lightly sweetened with sweet pickles. A typical luncheon for this busy young woman would start with soup, end with peppermint ice cream, and include her tuna salad served with melba rounds.

Since the Johnsons did not always sit down together at set times for family meals, Lynda would often request that a tuna salad plate be sent to her room or brought out on the Truman Balcony where she could enjoy a majestic view of historic Washington. Despite the difficulties involved in growing up in the public eye, Lynda took advantage of the unique opportunities offered to White House residents. She matured into a successful adult, the wife of future governor Charles Robb, and the mother of tuna-loving children herself.

Serves 6

Two 6½-ounce cans solid white tuna, drained
1½ cups mayonnaise
¾ cup diced celery
1 small onion, diced
1 tablespoon diced sweet pickles

½ teaspoon salt
¼ teaspoon freshly ground black pepper
4 hard-boiled eggs, cooled and quartered
6 pimientos

1. Flake tuna finely with a fork.
2. In a large bowl, mix mayonnaise with celery, onion, and pickles. Season with salt and pepper.
3. Fold in tuna and blend well.
4. Mound tuna in a serving bowl and decorate top with quartered eggs and pimiento slices. Refrigerate until serving. Serve with whole-grain crackers or melba toast.

LUCI'S POTATO SALAD

Luci's potato salad was made to suit her request for "no onions, please." She often served this dish—along with hamburgers, soft drinks, and other popular teen fare—to her guests in the White House Solarium. The most private room in the Family Quarters of the White House, the third floor Solarium was redecorated by Luci and used as her own special niche. The tile floor was suitable for dancing to records, the comfortable chairs and sofas allowed for lengthy chats, and a "Coke bar" housed a soft drink machine for thirsty visitors. It was at a party in the Solarium that Luci first met Patrick Nugent, the young man she later married in the first White House wedding held in more than fifty years.

Like garlic, onions have long been the focus of concern for cooks, who recognize both the benefits and the drawbacks of the strong-smelling vegetable. The 1887 edition of The White House Cook Book *included as one of the "Hints in Regard to Health" the following suggestion for those who failed to opt for "no onions, please": "A cupful of strong coffee will remove the odor of onions from the breath."*

Serves 6 to 10

6 medium-size Maine boiling
   potatoes
2 cups diced celery
2 cups mayonnaise
½ teaspoon salt
¼ teaspoon freshly ground
   black pepper

Boston lettuce
6 hard-boiled eggs, peeled and
   halved lengthwise
1 tablespoon chopped fresh
   parsley

1. In a large saucepan, cover potatoes with water, salt lightly, and bring to a boil.
2. Cover and cook over medium heat for 25 minutes, or until a sharp knife pierces the potatoes easily. Do not overcook.
3. Drain potatoes and let cool for at least an hour.
4. Peel cooled potatoes, and dice coarsely.
5. In a large bowl, mix potatoes with celery and mayonnaise. Season with salt and pepper.
6. Arrange lettuce leaves on a serving platter. Top with a mound of potato salad, and decorate with egg halves.
7. Sprinkle with parsley and chill. Potato salad is best served on the day it is prepared.

JOHNSON FAMILY FAVORITE DESSERTS

TAPIOCA PUDDING

Tapioca pudding was a popular American dessert at the turn of the century, but without instant tapioca the preparation of this simple dish was time-consuming. An old-fashioned version of the recipe from the 1887 edition of The White House Cook Book *reads as follows:*

Five tablespoons of tapioca, one quart of milk, two ounces of butter, a cupful of sugar, four eggs, flavoring of vanilla or bitter almonds. Wash the tapioca and let it stew gently in the milk on the back part of the stove for a quarter of an hour, occasionally stirring it; then let it cool, mix with it the butter, sugar, and eggs, which should be well

Tapioca is the root of the cassava plant, which thrives in tropical climes. The root is roasted, dried, ground, and sifted to make the three different grades of tapioca—fine, medium, and pearl—used to thicken soups and broths. Tapioca is also the basis for a highly digestible milk pudding.

President Johnson was very fond of tapioca pudding, so we had it on hand at all times. After his first heart attack (in 1955) and subsequent life-style modifications, his lower-caloric diet precluded most desserts. But tapioca pudding endured as President Johnson's primary indulgence. He preferred the pudding cold, served without any topping. And occasionally the pudding was prepared using half sugar and half sugar substitute in order to reduce its caloric value.

Serves 6 to 8

3 cups milk
5 tablespoons instant tapioca
2 teaspoons vanilla extract
6 tablespoons sugar

¼ teaspoon salt
2 egg yolks
3 egg whites, at room
   temperature

1. Bring 2½ cups of the milk to a boil.
2. Using a wire whisk, stir tapioca into boiling milk. Reduce heat, and cook over very low heat, stirring constantly, until thick (about 3 to 4 minutes).
3. Remove from heat and add vanilla, sugar, and salt.
4. Mix egg yolks with the remaining ½ cup of milk, and stir into tapioca mixture.
5. In a clean, dry bowl, beat the egg whites until stiff; fold into the tapioca mixture.
6. Pour into a serving dish and refrigerate. Serve chilled, plain or topped with RASPBERRY SAUCE and whipped cream.

beaten, and flavor with either of the above ingredients. Butter a dish, put in the pudding and bake in a moderate oven for an hour. If the pudding is boiled, add a little more tapioca and boil it in a buttered basin one and a half hours.

A helping hand in beating egg whites is appreciated in the White House kitchen.
(FRANCIS MILLER, <u>LIFE</u> MAGAZINE, © TIME INC.)

RASPBERRY SAUCE

Makes 1½ cups

One 10-ounce package frozen raspberries, defrosted

1. Purée raspberries in blender; strain.
2. Pour over puddings, ice cream, or frozen fruit soufflés.

SPANISH CREAM

A number of America's presidents have led battles with their bulges. President Taft was the most overweight President in U.S. history, and his wife's attempts to assist him in reducing were futile. Theodore Roosevelt, a more athletic President with little empathy for his portly peer, publicly advised that Taft should forego horseback riding as it would be "dangerous for him and cruelty to the horse." And as Governor-General of the Philippines, Taft once cabled Secretary of War Elihu Root "Took long horseback ride today; feeling fine." Root cabled back, "How is the horse?"

This smooth banana pudding was a real favorite of President Johnson. In order to assist the President in his weight-watching endeavors, skim milk was substituted for the whole milk and sugar substitute for half of the sugar. On occasion, a dish of the lower-calorie pudding was served to the President while his guests indulged in richer fare. At the State Dinner given in honor of King Olav of Norway in the spring of 1968, for example, President Johnson's dish of "diet pudding" must have paled next to his guests' Baked Alaska with warm Cherries Jubilee. Dieting is certainly a difficult challenge, perhaps even more so if one happens to be the President of the United States.

Serves 6

3 egg yolks
⅓ cup sugar
1 cup warm milk
1 teaspoon vanilla extract
3 medium-size bananas, very ripe
1 package (¼ ounce) unflavored gelatin

¼ cup warm water
3 egg whites, at room temperature
A pinch of salt
A pinch of cream of tartar

1. In the top of a double boiler, combine egg yolks with sugar; add milk and stir well, using a wire whisk.
2. Cook mixture over medium heat for 6 to 7 minutes, stirring constantly, until thickened; do not boil. Let cool, and add vanilla.
3. Purée bananas and blend with egg mixture. Transfer to a mixing bowl.
4. In the top of a double boiler, dissolve gelatin in warm water; stir into banana mixture.
5. In a clean, dry bowl, beat egg whites with salt and cream of tartar until very stiff; fold into banana mixture.
6. Spoon into a 1½-quart mold; chill for at least 3 hours, or until firm.
7. To unmold, immerse mold in hot water for several seconds before reversing onto a serving platter. Decorate with banana slices and whipped cream rosettes. Serve with cold RASPBERRY SAUCE (page 29), if desired.

As long as a dessert tasted sweet, President Johnson would eat it. Even this light dessert was sometimes prepared in a lower-calorie version—made with a sugar substitute—to assist in the President's weight-watching endeavors. Yet this dessert is so light that whenever President Johnson was served Lemon Snow Pudding, he would call out, "Give me some more of that hot air!"

LEMON SNOW PUDDING

Serves 6

3 packages (¾ ounce)
  unflavored gelatin
1 cup water
½ cup lemon juice
Grated peel of 1 lemon

1 cup sugar
4 egg whites, at room
  temperature
A pinch of salt

1. In the top of a double boiler set over hot water, dissolve gelatin in ½ cup water. Add lemon juice and peel. Set aside.
2. In a saucepan, mix sugar with remaining ½ cup water and boil over high heat until the mixture reaches the medium ball stage (238°F on a candy thermometer).
3. In a clean, dry bowl, beat egg whites with salt until soft peaks form.
4. Gradually add sugar syrup to egg whites, beating constantly, until the mixture is frothy like meringue.
5. Add dissolved gelatin and beat in thoroughly.
6. Pour into a 1½-quart mold and chill for at least 2 hours, or until firm.
7. To unmold, set form in hot water for several seconds before turning out onto a deep serving platter. Serve with colorful fruits such as strawberries or black cherries, and CUSTARD SAUCE, if desired.

CUSTARD SAUCE

Makes 3 cups

5 egg yolks
½ cup sugar

2 cups warm milk
½ teaspoon vanilla extract

1. In the top of a double boiler, beat egg yolks with sugar, using a wire whisk.
2. Stir in warm milk.
3. Cook over medium heat, stirring constantly, until custard sauce coats the spoon. Do not boil.
4. Remove from heat and stir in vanilla.
5. Set pan in a bowl of ice and continue stirring until sauce is cool. Refrigerate until serving time.

TEXAS PEACH ICE CREAM

George Washington was our first Founding Father to indulge in ice cream, reportedly spending $200 on the frozen dessert in a single summer. Thomas Jefferson so enjoyed the French version of ice cream that he brought the recipe back to America in 1789. Dolley Madison's meals at the White House also concluded on a cold sweet note, adeptly described by one delighted guest:

Last night I was bid by our President to the White House, and it was a most unusual affair. Mrs. Madison always entertains with Grace and Charm, but last night there was a sparkle in her eye that set astir an Air of Expectancy among her Guests. When finally the brilliant Assemblage—America's best—entered the dining room, they beheld a Table set with French china and English silver, laden with good things to eat, and in the

Following a trip to the Orient, famed explorer Marco Polo reported on the Chinese "ices" that were made with milk. The Italians then introduced ice cream to the world, as soon as they learned how to utilize the ice from the mountains. However, the dessert was considered a luxury by Americans until 1900, when affordable ice cream makers were developed for home use.

The Johnsons preferred to use Texas peaches in making their own ice cream, so the fresh fruit was shipped up from their home state. Commercial ice cream had become commonplace, but old-fashioned homemade ice cream became popular again during the Johnson administration, as the public followed the example set by the First Family. Even the White House prescribes to the sage theory of Ralph Waldo Emerson: "We dare not trust our wit for making our house pleasant to our friends, and so we buy [or make!] ice cream."

Makes about 1 gallon

8 medium-size very ripe peaches	*6 eggs*
	6 egg yolks
1½ cups sugar	*3 cups half-and-half, cold*
2 tablespoons vanilla extract	*3 cups half-and-half, hot*

1. Dip peaches in boiling water for 2 to 3 seconds; transfer to a bowl of ice water and peel immediately. Cut in half, remove pits, and slice. (You should have about 4 cups.)

2. In a large bowl, combine sliced peaches with ½ cup sugar and the vanilla. Cover and let stand for 1 hour.

3. In another large bowl, beat eggs and yolks with remaining cup of sugar; add cold half-and-half, and mix with a wire whisk.

4. Slowly stir in the hot half-and-half. Blend well.

5. Transfer to the top of a double boiler; cook, stirring constantly, until mixture coats the spoon. Do not boil.

6. Strain the custard into a bowl. Let cool over a bowl of ice, stirring often.

7. Freeze in an ice cream maker, following the manufacturer's instructions. Add peaches just before ice cream becomes solid.

8. Freeze to desired consistency. Serve ice cream in individual serving bowls or cups garnished with fresh peach slices and whipped cream or topped with fresh raspberries and cold RASPBERRY SAUCE (page 29), if desired. Ice cream tastes best on the day it is made, but can be stored frozen in an airtight plastic or stainless steel container.

Luci insisted on having a layer of her favorite chocolate cake for the top of her traditional wedding cake. The newlyweds brought the chocolate "bride's cake" to their honeymoon retreat in the Bahamas. Luci also served her chocolate cake at her first-born son's very first birthday party, which was held in the Yellow Oval Room in the White House. Unfortunately, little Lyn set his little foot right down in the middle of the chocolate cake!

Luci found that she had to make a special effort to do any cooking while living at the White House. Although she liked to bake desserts and fix simple meals for her friends, Luci admitted that it was just too easy to have the food sent up to the Solarium from the White House kitchens. And since Luci was always so busy, especially during the hectic months before her wedding day, she found less time for baking and cooking as a White House resident. Luci made up for it later, as a housewife and new mother in Austin. Luci still enjoys the dense chocolate cake that helped to enrich her White House memories.

LUCI'S CHOCOLATE LAYER CAKE

Makes one 9-inch, 2-layer cake

3 squares (3 ounces) unsweetened chocolate	1 teaspoon vanilla extract
1 stick (½ cup) butter	1 cup milk, at room temperature
1 cup sugar	3 egg whites, at room temperature
3 egg yolks	A pinch of cream of tartar
2 cups flour	ROYAL ICING
2 teaspoons baking powder	
¼ teaspoon salt	

1. Preheat oven to 350°F. Grease two 9-inch layer pans and dust lightly with flour.

2. Melt chocolate in a double boiler over hot water. Let cool.

3. In a large mixing bowl, cream butter with sugar; beat in egg yolks one at a time.

4. Mix in melted chocolate.

5. Sift together flour, baking powder, and salt.

6. In a small bowl, mix vanilla with milk; gradually add to chocolate mixture, alternately with dry ingredients, stirring in a small amount at a time. Beat until batter is smooth.

7. In a clean, dry bowl, beat egg whites with cream of tartar until stiff. Fold into batter.

(con't)

Centre high on a silver platter, a large shining dome of pink Ice Cream.

Yet even in the 1800s, America's passion for ice cream was tempered somewhat by recognition of the caloric consequences. The 1887 edition of The White House Cook Book *included the following advice as one of the "Small Points on Etiquette": "The stout woman . . . should shun champagne. She should hate ice cream."*

8. Pour into prepared pans and bake on middle shelf of preheated oven for 25 minutes; cake is done when it shrinks slightly from sides of pans and a toothpick inserted in the center comes out clean. Let cool for 5 minutes.

9. Turn layers out onto wire racks to cool completely before frosting with ROYAL ICING, and serve à la mode with vanilla, chocolate, or TEXAS PEACH ICE CREAM (page 32), if desired. The cake can also be prepared as a single layer by baking for 40 minutes in a 13 × 9 × 4-inch deep cake pan, if desired.

ROYAL ICING

Makes 4 cups

Perhaps the most famous White House hostess, Dolley Madison was well-known for her receptions, which were then referred to as "levées." She often served hot bouillon laced with sherry and a slice of her own Dolley Madison cake. The buxom First Lady was proud of her sweet tooth, and one of her credos was "I derived my pleasure from my indulgence."

*4 egg whites, at room
    temperature
Juice of 2 lemons
2 teaspoons light corn syrup
7 cups confectioners' sugar*

1. In a large mixing bowl, blend egg whites with lemon juice and corn syrup. Beat with a wire whisk until stiff.
2. Gradually add confectioners' sugar, beating constantly until smooth.
3. Use icing at once, or cover with a damp cloth and keep cool to prevent premature hardening.

LYNDA AND LUCI'S BROWNIES

When Lynda's husband was sent to do duty in Vietnam, she mailed him "care packages" with brownies she had baked in the Family Kitchen at the White House. Luci, too, filled a huge canister with her own home baking to accompany her husband on his tour of duty. The sisters shared recipes, as well as mutual concerns and many fun times as White House residents.

Luci has shared their recipe for brownies, along with her best wishes: "The brownies have been super successes with little ones and 'true loves' alike. I hope they add to your pleasant memories."

Makes sixteen 2-inch squares

1 stick (½ cup) butter
1 cup sugar
3 squares (3 ounces)
   unsweetened chocolate

2 eggs
1 cup chopped pecans
¾ cup flour
1 teaspoon vanilla extract

1. Preheat oven to 350°F. Grease an 8 × 8-inch square pan.
2. Melt butter in a small saucepan, pour into a mixing bowl, and stir in sugar.
3. Melt chocolate over low heat in the small saucepan, add to butter-sugar mixture, and blend well.
4. Add eggs and nuts, stirring until well blended.
5. Gradually add flour, blending thoroughly. Stir in vanilla.
6. Pour into prepared pan, and bake in preheated oven for 30 minutes, or until knife inserted in center comes out clean. Remove pan and cool on wire rack before cutting into squares.

When their father was Vice-President, Lynda and Luci were invited to their first State Dinner at the White House, held in honor of the President of Sudan. Mrs. Kennedy knew how much of a thrill it would be for the two girls to dine at the White House in the company of important politicians and glamorous film stars. Actually, the experience served as a pleasant introduction to their future roles as regular hostesses at White House parties and official functions.

Macaroons are small, round cookies that were invented in Italy but popularized in France. In the eighteenth century, it was customary in many French convents for the nuns to bake macaroons. While they are prepared today in a variety of sizes and textures, macaroon fans are divided into two main camps: those who prefer their cookies thin and crisp and those who like them soft and chewy.

President Johnson liked his macaroons soft and chewy. These cookies were among the final recipes prepared for the Johnsons during their stay in the White House. The Johnsons left the White House on January 20, 1969, waving and smiling at the devoted staff standing on the steps of the First Families' home.

PRESIDENT JOHNSON'S CHEWY MACAROONS

When a senator facetiously remarked, "Wonder who lives there?" Calvin Coolidge, known for his dry wit, provided a realistic appraisal of White House life by answering, "No one. They just come and go." Many of the former occu-

Makes 30 cookies

2 egg whites, at room
   temperature
A pinch of salt
½ cup sugar

1 cup sweetened shredded
   coconut
½ teaspoon vanilla extract

pants of the White House enjoyed the sweets of the day, such as the Almond Macaroons from the 1887 edition of The White House Cook Book:

Half a pound of sweet almonds, a coffee cupful of white sugar, the whites of two eggs; blanch the almonds and pound them to a paste; add to them the sugar and the beaten whites of eggs; work the whole together with the back of a spoon, then roll the mixture in your hands in balls about the size of a nutmeg, dust sugar over the top, lay them on a sheet of paper at least an inch apart. Bake in a cool oven to a light brown.

1. Preheat oven to 325°F. Lightly grease several baking sheets.
2. Beat egg whites with salt until stiff.
3. Gradually beat in sugar until stiff, shiny peaks form. Fold in coconut and vanilla.
4. Drop by teaspoonfuls onto prepared sheets; leave ample space (1½ to 2 inches) between spoonfuls to allow cookies to spread evenly while baking.
5. Bake on middle shelf of preheated oven for 20 minutes, or until golden brown. Do not overcook.
6. Cool cookies on wire racks before serving. Store in an airtight container in the refrigerator. Remove from refrigerator an hour before serving to allow cookies to warm to room temperature.

SPECIAL EVENT RECIPES

NACHOS

Even though the American public seemed to believe that the Johnsons dined on Texas-style food on a daily basis, the family typically reserved tacos, chalupas, and nachos for dinner parties and special events. The Johnsons liked to share their own regional cooking with guests from all over the country—and from all over the world —but especially enjoyed serving Tex-Mex food to guests from their home state. So when the Johnson girls got married, they each added a down-home favorite to the menus for their bridesmaids' parties.

While the bachelor party convened at a Redskins football game, Luci Johnson hosted a party for her bridesmaids in the White House Solarium. Steaming nachos adorned a long buffet table decorated with yellow flowers. Lynda's bridesmaid party was held in the Yellow Oval Room, where miniature chalupas were included on the hors d'oeuvre trays.

This recipe is only a rough guideline. Adjust proportions of ingredients according to individual needs and tastes—from single or double servings of very cheesy, very spicy nachos to party platters of lightly garnished tortilla chips.

Vegetable oil   *Grated cheddar cheese*
Corn tortillas   *Diced jalapeño peppers*

1. In a deep skillet, heat 3 inches of oil over medium-high heat until very hot.
2. Cut tortillas into quarters and fry until brown and crisp on both sides.
3. Drain thoroughly on paper towels and transfer to baking sheets.
4. Sprinkle each tortilla chip with cheese and hot peppers.
5. Broil for 1 to 2 minutes, or until the cheese is bubbling. Serve at once, with salsa, if desired.

CHILI CON QUESO

Chili con Queso is a great dish to serve to a crowd, and the Mexican-style dip is smooth and tasty when prepared properly. We found that Ro-Tel brand Tomatoes and Green Chilies from Texas yielded the best results, so we always used this product in preparing Chili con Queso for special events at the White House.

The Johnsons were friendly and gregarious, and they enveloped the White House in a warm, convivial atmosphere. Even the State Dinners and other formal functions seemed relaxed and enjoyable. The aura of the White House had been transformed by this Texan family from formal French to informal Western American. So when

I arrived at the White House in February 1966, I was honored to be able to contribute to this pleasurable and productive administration. I rapidly honed my skills with Tex-Mex cuisine, as Eric Sevareid acknowledged on the *CBS Evening News* after I had prepared my first Annual Congressional Reception at the White House:

> At the buffet table they were served steamship round of beef, shrimp, chili con queso, chicken Mexicana, ham on hot biscuits, plus candies, pastries, and nuts. Dancing followed. Today the President flew off to Texas, serene in the knowledge that Congress will give him no more trouble for a while. The rule is, to take liberties with Harry Truman's famous maxim— if you can't stand Texas cooking, get out of the kitchen. That is what the French chef hired by the Kennedys did a few weeks ago. . . . The new chef, who presided over the table last night, is Swiss, a people who have demonstrated their capacity to survive through a thousand years of war and sweet chocolate. He quickly learned that four things temporal are held inviolate in Texas—women, states' rights, a cattle brand, and chili. His chili with cheese last night was reported by survivors as first class.

About 3 cups, to serve 6 to 8

One 10-ounce can Ro-Tel tomatoes with green chilies, or one 10-ounce can tomatoes, chopped, plus 1 tablespoon chopped jalapeño pepper

1 pound American cheese
Warm tortilla chips

1. In the top of a double boiler, mix tomatoes and chilies with cheese.
2. Cook over hot water for an hour, stirring often, until thick and creamy. Serve at once with warm tortilla chips.

The tall, handsome Marine who led the White House guard when Lynda Johnson lived in the White House was Charles "Chuck" Robb. By Labor Day of 1967, the couple had announced their plans to marry. The wedding was to be held in the White House in only three months' time. Luci's wedding reception had been held in the White House the summer before, but the actual ceremony was conducted at the National Shrine of the Immaculate Conception in Washington, D.C. Lynda and Chuck chose to hold their wedding ceremony in the East Room, with a reception afterward in the State Dining Room and under a pink-lined heated tent on the adjoining terrace.

During the week before the wedding, Mrs. Johnson's press secretary held daily briefings for hundreds of reporters hungry for any tidbit of wedding plans that could be set into print. This served as a great opportunity to test out my hors d'oeuvres on the hardworking journalists, who enthusiastically endorsed my Lobster Barquettes and the other items that were included in the wedding reception buffet.

LOBSTER BARQUETTES

Makes 24 barquettes

3 tablespoons butter
2 tablespoons finely minced
  shallots
2 cups finely minced lobster
  meat
1 cup CREAM SAUCE
1 tablespoon dry sherry
24 oval 2½-inch prebaked
  pastry shells (barquettes)

1 cup heavy cream, whipped
1 cup CHEF HALLER'S
  HOLLANDAISE SAUCE
A pinch of cayenne pepper
2 to 3 tablespoons grated
  Parmesan cheese

1. Melt butter in a large sauté pan, add shallots and sauté until golden brown.

2. Remove from heat and add lobster, CREAM SAUCE, and sherry; mix together gently.

3. Place prebaked barquettes on baking sheets. Fill each three-quarters full of lobster mixture.

4. In a mixing bowl, fold whipped cream into Hollandaise sauce; season with cayenne pepper. Spread evenly over lobster-filled barquettes (1–2 tablespoons on each).

5. Sprinkle tops with cheese. Broil for 1 minute, or just until sauce bubbles and browns slightly; serve at once.

Sherry is an important
flavoring ingredient in many
White House recipes.

(FRANCIS MILLER, LIFE MAGAZINE, © TIME INC.)

CREAM SAUCE

Makes 1 cup

1 tablespoon butter
1 tablespoon flour
¾ cup milk, scalded
⅛ teaspoon nutmeg

A pinch of salt
A pinch of freshly ground
  white pepper

1. In a small saucepan over low heat, melt butter, whisk in flour, stirring constantly, and work into a roux. Let cook for a minute or two; do not boil.
2. Gradually add scalded milk, stirring with the wire whisk, and bring to a boil.
3. Reduce heat, and simmer for several minutes, until thickened.
4. Add seasonings, and simmer for 5 minutes. Cool slightly before use.

CHEF HALLER'S HOLLANDAISE SAUCE

Hollandaise sauce is a very rich sauce that includes egg yolks and butter and is served with egg dishes, fish, and cooked vegetables. There are two basic methods for preparing Hollandaise sauce: the traditional way described below, and the easy way described in countless current cookbooks. When I am in the kitchen, I do not choose to take the easy way out. But the busy part-time cook/full-time executive or homemaker may elect to prepare a simple version of this classic recipe. Either way, it is important to use a heavy saucepan, reduce the vinegar and seasonings all the way to bring out a piquant flavor, and to keep the sauce warm (90°F to 95°F) until use.

The classic recipe for Hollandaise Sauce was first recorded in the nineteenth century by Antonin Carême, the founder of classic French cookery. Carême is remembered for his extraordinarily decorative cuisine and as the author of a number of works devoted to the theory and practice of cooking. Crowned as "the Cook of kings and the King of cooks," Carême was the private chef for King George IV (when he was the Prince Regent in England), the Czar Alexander, Princess Bagration and Lord Steward, and Baron de Rothschild when his table was regarded as the best in all of Europe. Carême is credited by today's chefs as having created architectural confectionery and many classic sauces.

In 1986, I was honored to receive the Carême Medal, which is awarded each year by the American Culinary Federation for "cu-

Rose Haller and her son share a
proud moment after the American
Academy of Chefs awards Chef
Haller a Gold Medal.
(© 1968 DIE TAT)

linary achievements." Like Carême in his day, I have had the great
honor of preparing meals for kings and other VIPs, including five
of America's Presidents and their families.

Makes 2 cups

Juice of 1 lemon
24 white peppercorns, crushed
2 tablespoons tarragon vinegar
½ teaspoon chopped fresh
   tarragon

2 tablespoons water
4 tablespoons cold water
6 egg yolks
1 pound CLARIFIED BUTTER
½ teaspoon salt

1. In a heavy copper or stainless-steel 1½-quart saucepan, mix
lemon juice, peppercorns, vinegar, tarragon, and the 2 tablespoons
of water; boil over medium-high heat until fully reduced.

2. Remove from heat and add the 4 tablespoons of cold water.
Beat in the egg yolks.

3. Transfer to the top of a double boiler and cook over low heat
for 4 minutes, stirring constantly with a wire whisk, while increasing the heat gradually.

4. Beat over high heat until thick and creamy. (This will take
about 4 minutes.) Remove from heat and continue to beat until
lukewarm.

5. Using a wire whisk, slowly stir in CLARIFIED BUTTER; add salt.

6. Strain through fine cheesecloth and use at once, or keep warm
(90°F to 95°F) until ready to use. If allowed to get too cold or too
hot, the sauce will separate. If the sauce becomes too thick, add 1
to 2 tablespoons hot water to prevent it from separating. To avoid
undesirable browning, be sure to use CLARIFIED BUTTER, which is
the key to high-quality sautéed dishes, butter sauces, basting, and
baking. Milk sediments in unclarified butter will turn brown and
burn very rapidly when butter is heated, resulting in a speckled
appearance and a bitter flavor. Clarified butter does not burn as
readily, and yields a more attractive and better-tasting result. Since
it is pure fat, clarified butter will keep for weeks in the refrigerator.

Makes 1½ cups

CLARIFIED BUTTER

1 pound butter

1. In a heavy-bottomed saucepan, simmer butter over low heat for 20 to 30 minutes until the butterfat is clear and the milk sediment has settled. (Do not overheat, or butter will turn dark and bitter.)
2. Let stand for 1 hour. Pour off clarified butter into a plastic container, discarding the milky solid.
3. Let cool, then store, covered, in the refrigerator.

Ham-Stuffed Biscuits are a delicious way to use leftover ham. We served the dish at a number of functions during the Johnsons' White House years, including Lynda's wedding reception. Leftovers were served that evening as part of a post-wedding buffet.

HAM-STUFFED BISCUITS

SPECIAL EVENT RECIPE

Makes 24 biscuits

1 tablespoon butter
¼ medium onion, finely diced
1 garlic clove, finely minced
1 pound cooked ham, diced
1 tablespoon chopped fresh parsley

A pinch of thyme
½ cup CREAM SAUCE (page 41)
24 HOT BISCUITS (page 7), split

1. In a cast-iron skillet, melt butter, sauté onion and garlic until golden brown.
2. Add ham and seasonings; stir in CREAM SAUCE and keep warm.
3. Arrange open biscuits on serving platter(s). Place a heaping teaspoonful of ham stuffing in the center of each biscuit, close gently, and serve at once.

CRAB BISQUE

Crab Bisque was a popular menu item at the special luncheons given by President Johnson and his wife. Hot Crab Bisque was the first course at a 1967 White House dinner held by the President in honor of General William C. Westmoreland, then commander of the American forces in Vietnam. As First Lady, Mrs. Johnson often served crabmeat bisque at her monthly luncheons in honor of women of achievement in various fields.

Mrs. Johnson held her "Women Doers'" and Senate Ladies' Luncheons in the Family Dining Room on the state floor of the White House. She also introduced the practice of providing some type of entertainment at the Senate Ladies' Luncheons. At one of these luncheons, Mrs. Johnson displayed White House memorabilia, including eleven sets of presidential china. Sometimes a simultaneous "stag" luncheon was hosted by the President in the State Dining Room or upstairs in the President's Dining Room. Mrs. Johnson usually varied the menu for the coinciding luncheons slightly in order to suit the diverging tastes of the guests. The ladies' menus typically included lighter dishes and a fancy dessert, while the meals served at the President's luncheons featured simple, substantial foods. Timing two such meals sometimes proved to be tricky!

Serves 10

½ cup vegetable oil
½ cup butter
10 fresh crabs (about 12 ounces each), halved
6 shallots, peeled and quartered
2 garlic cloves, peeled and crushed
1 red bell pepper, diced
1 green bell pepper, diced
1 cup diced carrots
1 cup diced celery
1 cup chopped white leeks
Juice and grated peel of 1 lemon
½ cup warm brandy
2 tablespoons tomato paste
¾ cup rice flour, or all-purpose flour

3 tomatoes, peeled, seeded, and diced
1½ quarts fish stock
2 cups dry white wine
Tied cheesecloth "spice bag," containing 24 black peppercorns, 1 teaspoon chopped fresh thyme, 1 teaspoon chopped fresh rosemary, and 1 teaspoon chopped fresh marjoram
½ pound cooked lump crabmeat
1 cup heavy cream
A pinch of cayenne pepper
1 tablespoon salt

1. In a 6-quart saucepan, heat oil and butter; sauté fresh crabs for 3 to 4 minutes, until pale red in color.

2. Add shallots, garlic, peppers, carrots, celery, leeks, and lemon juice and peel. Cover, and simmer for 5 minutes.

3. Add warm brandy, light with a match, and flame quickly, shaking pan, until the flames die out.

4. Stir in tomato paste and rice flour; mix well. Add diced tomatoes.

5. Stir in fish stock and wine. Add the spice bag and bring to a boil.

6. Cover, and simmer over low heat for an hour, stirring occasionally.

7. Strain through cheesecloth or a fine metal strainer.

8. In the top of a double boiler, reheat bisque directly over low heat.

9. Break cooked lump crabmeat into small pieces and add to bisque. Stir in cream, cayenne, and salt.

10. Bring bisque just to the simmering point; do not boil. Remove from heat.

11. Keep bisque hot until serving time by setting top of double boiler over hot water. Serve with JEFF'S GEORGIA-STYLE CHEESE STICKS or topped with PARMESAN CROUTONS.

CHESAPEAKE CRABMEAT MOLD

Also listed on White House menus as Crabmeat Salad Ring and Crabmeat Salad Mold, this dish became a favorite first course for President Johnson. However, the first time it was served, the President pushed his dish aside and remarked, "Take the rest home to your wife." He was half serious! Once this seafood lover realized that the dish really had a nice light-yet-spicy crab flavor, President Johnson became a crabmeat mold fan and often requested seconds.

This seafood mold was served at a number of special functions during the Johnson administration, including the State Dinner held in honor of the Prime Minister of Barbados. The formal dinner was set up in the beautiful Rose Garden just outside the Oval Office. President Johnson was the first to host a State Dinner in the scented garden, always a risky business since sudden weather changes could cause surprises: No one likes crabmeat salad soaked from the sky!

When President and Imelda Marcos visited the White House in 1966, they were served Crabmeat Salad Mold as a first course at the

State Dinner held in their honor. Dessert was a pineapple-lime sherbet ring garnished with blueberries and dubbed Glace Imelda. The Johnsons' social secretary initiated the practice of personalizing the menus by naming dishes for the guests of honor or their homeland.

Crabmeat Salad Mold was also served when the Johnsons' new china collection was first used at a State Dinner in honor of Prime Minister Gorton of Australia. The gift of an anonymous donor, the 216-piece set was the creation of Mrs. Johnson, in collaboration with Tiffany and Company, designer Van Day Truex, painter André Piette, and the Castleton China Company, to meet the need for a matched set that could serve over 140 guests. Until then, guests at large dinner parties were served on a hodgepodge of plates from the collection of presidential china. The seafood salad looked terrific on the new cream-colored china bordered by wildflowers, a reflection of Mrs. Johnson's special interest in environmental preservation and the beautification of America.

Serves 10

1½ pounds lump crabmeat
¼ cup finely minced shallots
½ cup horseradish, well
   drained
1 cup mayonnaise
1 cup chili sauce
1 tablespoon Worcestershire
   sauce
10 drops of Tabasco sauce

1 tablespoon finely chopped
   fresh chives
1 tablespoon unflavored gelatin
¼ cup dry sherry
5 hard-boiled egg yolks,
   pressed through a sieve
5 large black olives, sliced into
   rings
Fresh parsley sprigs

1. In a large mixing bowl, pick over crabmeat carefully and remove any pieces of shell. Add shallots, horseradish, mayonnaise, the chili, Worestershire, and Tabasco sauces, and chives; blend well.

2. In the top of a double boiler, dissolve gelatin in sherry over hot water. Fold into crabmeat mixture.

3. Spoon into a 9-inch round cake pan, and refrigerate for at least 2 hours.

4. To unmold, set pan in hot water for 5 or 6 seconds; unmold onto a round serving platter.

5. Spread sieved yolks over top and decorate with olive rings. Line base with sprigs of parsley. Serve with melba toast or JEFF'S GEORGIA-STYLE CHEESE STICKS (page 240).

Sometimes the White House staff is asked to do the impossible. So we do it, even if we have to work all night. In the spring of 1967, President Johnson hosted a last-minute luncheon for 140 people, and the staff was notified just 24 hours in advance. Since we usually have several weeks to prepare for official functions, such short notice was disconcerting, to say the least.

Emergency sessions of the United Nations General Assembly had been called, and President Johnson recognized the international importance of hosting a White House meal in honor of the visiting diplomats. In spite of the last-minute invitation, the 4 VIPs —Danish Prime Minister Jens Otto Krag, Italian Prime Minister Aldo Moro, Italian Foreign Minister Emintare Fanfani, and British Foreign Minister George Brown—were all able to attend. The other 136 guests were invited by phone.

The menu needed to be practical and possible, a simple but elegant meal that could be prepared in a single day's work. Seafood and fresh fruit are abundant in Washington in the spring, and a cold consommé can be made quickly and served in cups that have been chilled overnight. The staff remained calm, and the luncheon was a success, as the President acknowledged in a memo he sent to me the very next day.

SEAFOOD NEWBURG

Serves 10

½ cup butter	2 cups diced cooked lobster
2 tablespoons minced shallots	2 cups cooked tiny shrimp
2 garlic cloves, finely minced	2 cups cooked bay scallops
2 tablespoons flour	¼ cup dry sherry
1 tablespoon paprika	4 egg yolks
2 cups hot LOBSTER COURT BOUILLON	1 cup heavy cream

A pinch of cayenne pepper

1. Melt butter in a large sauté pan. Add shallots and garlic and sauté until golden brown.
2. Stir in flour and paprika.
3. Add hot bouillon and stir until smooth. Add cayenne pepper.
4. Stir in seafood and bring to a simmer. Add sherry and remove from heat.
5. Blend egg yolks with cream, and gently stir into sauce.
6. Transfer to the top of a double boiler; keep warm until serving time. Serve hot, with steamed rice.

LOBSTER COURT BOUILLON

Makes 2 quarts

Tied cheesecloth "spice bag," containing 24 black peppercorns, 1 bay leaf, ½ teaspoon chopped fresh tarragon, ½ teaspoon chopped fresh thyme, and ½ teaspoon chopped fresh marjoram
1½ quarts water
1 cup cider vinegar
1 cup dry white wine
½ cup coarsely diced carrots
½ cup coarsely diced onions
1 large leek, white part only, chopped
Sprig of parsley
¼ lemon
2 tablespoons salt
Two 2-pound fresh lobsters

1. Tie peppercorns and herbs in cheesecloth bag.
2. In a deep pot, combine all ingredients except lobsters and bring to a boil. Boil for 5 minutes.
3. Add lobsters, cover, and simmer for 10 minutes.
4. Remove from heat and let stand for 10 minutes.
5. Remove lobsters and chill in refrigerator (it is easier to remove the meat from the shell once the lobster is cold). Strain court bouillon and reserve.

TEXAS-STYLE BARBECUED RIBS

After announcing that he would not be seeking reelection, President Johnson hosted a party on the White House lawn to thank over 200 friends for their support. Since a majority of the guests were from the Johnsons' home state, the party was a Texas-style barbecue. The ribs were prepared by Walter Jetton, "The Barbecue King" from Fort Worth. He did a terrific job and I was most impressed with the results. His barbecue sauce avoided all of the common flaws (oversweetening, overcooking, excessive thinning), and by serving the sauce separately, he also avoided drying out the meat. The ribs were tender and juicy, and very delicious (yet the cost was only $1.80 per serving!). The Barbecue King charcoal-broiled the ribs in a giant pit, then transferred the meat to stainless steel canisters where it finished cooking on its own heat. The hungry guests helped themselves to the hot juicy ribs, dipping the meat into side dishes of barbecue sauce. I had long been curious to see just how Texas-style barbecues are conducted. This professional production will long stand out in my mind as one of the more strikingly successful White House parties.

The Johnson administration was noted for barbecues, but it was the *quality* of the food served—rather than the number of events conducted—which was the real reason for this reputation. In fact, although they were the first family to conduct a cookout at the White House, the Johnsons did not host very many barbecues in D.C. Instead, they entertained friends, fellow politicians, and foreign dignitaries at big barbecues held at the LBJ Ranch. At one such party, held in honor of West German Chancellor Ludwig Erhard, the 400 guests were served from chuck wagons and dined at long tables covered with red-checked tablecloths.

Serves 6

6 to 10 pounds lean pork ribs   1 cup white wine
3 tablespoons dry mustard   3 to 4 cups BARBECUE SAUCE

1. Preheat oven to 350°F.
2. Boil ribs in a large pot of salted water for 5 minutes; drain well. Arrange in a large baking pan.
3. Mix mustard with wine and coat ribs with the mixture, using a pastry brush.
4. Brush ribs with BARBECUE SAUCE. Bake on middle oven shelf, turning often and brushing with additional sauce, for 45 minutes to 1 hour. Pork is done when meat pulls easily from the ribs. Serve with hot beans and cold beer.

BARBECUE SAUCE

Makes 1 quart

2 teaspoons butter   1 cup chili sauce
1 large onion, chopped   2 cups catsup
1 green bell pepper, chopped   1/4 cup Worcestershire sauce
2 garlic cloves, chopped   1 bay leaf
1 cup cider vinegar   12 black peppercorns
1/4 cup brown sugar   Fresh parsley sprig

1. In a sauté pan, melt butter; sauté chopped vegetables until slightly browned.
2. Transfer to a large saucepan and mix in remaining ingredients.
3. Bring to a boil and simmer for 1 hour. Strain.

LBJ Ranch

DINNER

Sherry   Split Pea Soup

                      Supreme of Pheasant
Beaulieu Cabernet   Rice Deganya
Sauvignon
                    Green Beans Amandine
                    Zucchini Niçoise

                        Salad Greens
                            Paté
Almaden
Blanc de Blancs
              Macédoine of Fresh Fruits au Kirsch

L B J Ranch
Sunday, January 7, 1968

POTATO WHITE HOUSE

When James Webb resigned as the Director of the National Aeronautics and Space Administration (NASA) in 1968, President Johnson awarded him the nation's highest civilian honor, the Presidential Medal of Freedom. A dinner was held to honor 23 *Apollo* astronauts and their recently resigned boss, along with such dignitaries as Charles Lindbergh. The menu included Potato White House.

Prior to the White House dinner, the astronauts joined the President in the Treaty Room, where they signed a document to commemorate the occasion. Lindbergh added his signature, encouraged by the President, who noted that "The Lone Eagle" was actually America's first astronaut. When Lindbergh had returned from Paris after his solo flight across the Atlantic some 40 years earlier, President Calvin Coolidge had welcomed him with a White House dinner.

Most of the 140 guests at the award dinner had worked in the space program, which President Johnson had helped to launch. The entertainment following the meal included a presentation by Sarah Caldwell's Opera Company of Boston, a whimsical science fiction comedy appropriately entitled "Voyage to the Moon."

Serves 6

6 large Idaho baking potatoes, scrubbed well
3 tablespoons butter
3 slices bacon, chopped
½ cup onions, finely diced
3 egg yolks
¾ cup sour cream
1 tablespoon chopped fresh chives
1 teaspoon salt
A pinch of freshly ground white pepper
⅛ teaspoon nutmeg
2 tablespoons grated Parmesan cheese
½ teaspoon paprika

1. Bake potatoes in a 375°F oven for about an hour, or until a sharp knife can be inserted easily in their centers.
2. Melt butter in a small sauté pan, add bacon, and brown lightly.
3. Add onions, and sauté until golden brown.
4. Split baked potatoes in half lengthwise, and scoop the insides into a mixing bowl; reserve 6 of the empty potato shells.
5. Purée the potato. Add the bacon and onions, egg yolks, sour cream, and chives, and mix thoroughly; season with salt, pepper, and nutmeg.
6. Spoon this mixture into the 6 reserved potato shells; if desired, potato can be piped into the shells through a fluted pastry tube.
7. Mix cheese with paprika, and sprinkle over stuffed potatoes.
8. Bake on middle shelf of a 375°F oven for 20 minutes, or until golden brown. Serve at once.

RÖSTI

When I first arrived at the White House in February 1966, noted food columnist Craig Claiborne predicted in his *New York Times* food column that, "in months to come those who dine at the White House may feast not only on French cuisine but also on the likes of Gruyère ramequins, rösti potatoes, émincé of veal, and zugertorte au Kirsch." Indeed, I have prepared many of the specialties of my homeland for White House guests, and they do seem to enjoy the Swiss dishes.

On one of General William C. Westmoreland's temporary returns from Vietnam, President Johnson held a luncheon in his honor. The menu included *Rösti*. After the general was appointed as Army Chief of Staff, he dined regularly in the White House: President Johnson established the "Tuesday Lunch Group" specifically for setting policy on the Vietnam war, so General Westmoreland and the other Chiefs of Staff had lunch every week with the President and his Secretary of Defense. This somber group met weekly in the President's Dining Room, where we tried to sustain their energy levels with hearty luncheon dishes. Despite his position of power and the immense pressure he was under, General Westmoreland always took the time to be pleasant, thanking the White House staff for the meals and cordial service. The Swiss are known for their simple but substantial midday meals, so the "Tuesday Lunch Group" sampled a variety of dishes from Switzerland.

Serves 6

6 medium-size Maine boiling
   potatoes, scrubbed
1 tablespoon butter
1 tablespoon vegetable oil

1 teaspoon salt
⅛ teaspoon freshly ground
   white pepper

1. Boil potatoes in salted water for 20 minutes, or until a sharp knife can be inserted easily in their centers. Drain, and refrigerate overnight.
2. Peel potatoes and grate coarsely.
3. In a sauté pan, heat butter with oil. Spread potatoes evenly in the pan; season with salt and pepper.
4. Cook the potatoes over low heat without stirring. When brown, turn over in one piece (like a crêpe) to brown the other side.
5. Slide onto a serving platter and serve at once, as an accompaniment to sausages, or pork chops. Variations include *Rösti Jurassienne,* made with smoked bacon and Gruyère cheese, *Rösti mit*

Apfel, containing grated apples, and *Rösti mit Eier,* topped with a fried egg.

President Johnson was a pleasure to cook for because he was an appreciative eater and had a hearty appetite. Even at the formal meals and State Dinners, the President ate his share with gusto. He was exceptionally enthusiastic about Eggplant Niçoise, which he found to be light, yet more filling—and flavorful—than plain, steamed vegetables.

Luci also liked the stuffed eggplant, and complimented me when it was included on the menu for a State Dinner given in honor of the King and Queen of Thailand. As we watched a fireworks display out on the White House lawn, she commented, "Sometimes food looks nice yet isn't so tasty, but your dinner looked good and was delicious!" Whether for a small private dinner or a huge banquet, I made sure that the food served at the White House was always both attractive and tasty.

Entertainment following the State Dinner for Thailand's head of state included a jazz band, because the King played the saxophone and was an admitted jazz buff. Guests included well-known jazz musicians Stan Getz and Duke Ellington, with whom the King was able to have a lengthy discussion about their common interest.

EGGPLANT NIÇOISE

Serves 6

2 large eggplants
3 tablespoons vegetable oil
1 medium-size onion, diced
2 garlic cloves, chopped
2 teaspoons salt
¼ teaspoon freshly ground
    black pepper
1 tablespoon chopped fresh
    parsley

6 drops of Tabasco sauce
4 tomatoes, peeled and seeded,
    or one 14½-ounce can whole
    tomatoes, drained
½ cup bread crumbs
½ cup grated Parmesan cheese
A pinch of paprika

1. Preheat oven to 350°F.
2. Split eggplants in half lengthwise and gently scoop out the pulp without puncturing the skin; dice pulp.
3. Lightly brush insides of empty eggplant shells with oil and place in an ungreased baking dish, cavities up. Bake for 10 minutes, or until slightly softened.

4. In a nonstick frying pan, heat remaining oil, add onion and garlic and sauté until golden brown.

5. Add diced eggplant, salt, pepper, parsley, Tabasco sauce, and tomatoes; simmer for 10 minutes.

6. Combine the bread crumbs and cheese and fold half into the eggplant mixture. Spoon evenly into the baked shells. Sprinkle with the remaining crumb-cheese mixture and a dash of paprika.

7. Bake on middle shelf of a 375°F oven for 20 to 25 minutes, or until golden brown. Serve at once, as an accompaniment to beef or lamb, or as a vegetarian-style entrée.

TARRAGON DRESSING

The secrets to a fine salad dressing are to mince any shallots, onion, and garlic very fine and to dress the salad at the very last minute. Salad greens should always be washed, drained, and well dried before use. My three favorite vinegars include red wine, cider, and tarragon; I find the flavor of plain white vinegar unsatisfactory for salad dressings. At the White House, we use olive oil in certain dressings, and vegetable oil for others. For some salads, special oils, such as avocado or poppy seed, can provide unusual and interesting flavors.

During the Johnson administration, the menus emphasized economy and simplicity, even for State Dinners. Soon after I arrived at the White House in 1966, the Johnsons began to serve only domestic wines at special functions. American embassies throughout the world were encouraged to follow suit and serve American champagnes and wines exclusively. This practice not only cut costs, but demonstrated national pride as well.

When President Johnson held a State Dinner in honor of the Shah of Iran in 1967, the traditional toast—with domestic champagne—recognized the Shah's absent wife: The President acknowledged that his administration "champions beauty in all its forms." This toast also referred to the natural beauty of fine foods and fine wines, as illustrated by the menu served to the Shah and his guests.

Makes 2 cups

4 shallots, finely minced
1 garlic clove, finely minced
2 tablespoons finely chopped
  fresh tarragon
1/2 teaspoon freshly ground
  white pepper
Juice of 1 lemon

1 tablespoon Dijon-style
  mustard
2 egg yolks
1/3 cup red wine vinegar
1/2 teaspoon Tabasco sauce
1 1/2 cups olive oil

1. In a blender, combine all ingredients except olive oil; blend at high speed for 10 seconds.

2. With blender running at low speed, gradually add oil; then cover and blend at high speed for 10 seconds. (You can also make the dressing by hand in a mixing bowl using a wire whisk.) Keep dressing in the refrigerator unless used immediately. Serve over Bibb lettuce or other salad greens.

A successful salad relies on a perfect blend of oil and vinegar, as well as a harmonious mixture of salad greens. A salad should always be dressed with due regard to accompanying wines and cheeses. I developed this light dressing when I first arrived at the White House, and it has remained popular throughout the succeeding administrations for both family use and at State Dinners and other special functions.

When King Faisal al Saud of Saudi Arabia visited the White House, however, he did not sample my salad dressing. In fact, citing a gastrointestinal condition, he consumed only the food prepared by his own Royal Chef! He attended the State Dinner held in his honor accompanied by the turbaned chef and three royal waiters: Each carried a black briefcase, from which they withdrew the King's four-course dinner, which included chopped lamb and yogurt. His entourage did enjoy the State Dinner, but their wine goblets were filled with juice, since Muslims do not drink alcohol. The White House always researches the culinary predilections and dietary restrictions of foreign visitors prior to designing the menus. But the King of Saudi Arabia was the only guest of honor who never ate a morsel off my menu!

Fortunately for my ego, there has always been enthusiastic feedback following the State Dinners. One fan, Julia Child, visited the White House for the first time during the Johnson administration. The famous French chef hosted a televised State Dinner held to honor Prime Minister Sato of Japan, including a visit "behind the scenes" in the White House kitchen. The generous Mrs. Child described the salad as "salad as it should be—but rarely is. Lots of good oil in the dressing . . . not too much strong vinegar . . . perfectly seasoned." She sang the praises of the entire State Dinner menu, exclaiming, "The good news about good food at the White House should be trumpeted far and wide." We have continued to

CHEF HALLER'S WHITE HOUSE DRESSING

this day the friendship that began during the preparation of that dinner.

Makes 2 cups

4 shallots, finely minced
1 garlic clove, finely minced
1 tablespoon Worcestershire
　sauce
1 teaspoon salt
⅛ teaspoon freshly ground
　black pepper

Juice of 1 lemon
1½ tablespoons Dijon-style
　mustard
½ cup red wine vinegar
1 cup olive or vegetable oil

1. In a blender, place all ingredients except oil; blend at high speed for 10 seconds.

2. With the blender running at low speed, gradually add oil; then cover blender and blend at high speed for 10 seconds. (You can also make the dressing by hand in a mixing bowl using a wire whisk.) Store dressing in the refrigerator, but serve at room temperature; shake well before using. Serve on garden salads, endive and watercress, or other mixed greens.

WHITE HOUSE PINK FRUIT PUNCH

SPECIAL EVENT
RECIPE

This sparkling punch has been served as a nonalcoholic alternative to the traditional champagne at many White House parties and receptions. The cranberry juice imparts a pretty pink hue, which made the punch popular with the Johnson girls. At both of their weddings, large frosted crystal bowls enticed the guests to appease their thirst with the sweet, light White House Pink Fruit Punch.

Since Luci was married on a hot August day, cold drinks were appreciated at the reception held in both the East Room and the State Dining Room. Over 700 guests and some 200 press people toasted the newlyweds after the ceremony, which had been seen by an estimated 55 million television viewers. Luci was the first President's daughter to be married in Washington since 1914, and the American public was overjoyed. In the months preceding the wedding, Luci received around 3,000 letters each week, many from fellow teenagers wishing her happiness and offering her advice. I responded to thousands of requests for wedding reception recipes, and assisted an uncertain number of brides-to-be in replicating Luci's wedding reception buffet.

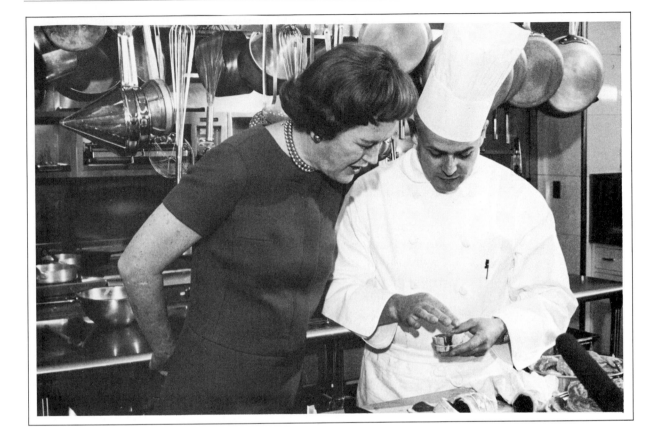

Since Lynda's wedding was the second time around for the White House staff, we were a little less stressed and a bit better prepared. A wedding in the White House is just the same as a wedding anywhere else: It is a real production that requires a great deal of advance planning and last-minute preparation. But the wedding of a President's daughter must be near-perfect, and it must take place without a hitch. Both of the Johnson girls' weddings were pronounced by all attendees and observers as impeccable. Perhaps of most importance, both brides loved their weddings and White House receptions, and each buffet passed with flying colors the close inspection of a critical father-of-the-bride, President Johnson.

"French Chef" Julia Child consulting with Chef Haller behind the scenes during a televised State Dinner in honor of Prime Minister Sato of Japan.

Serves 12 to 16

1 quart orange juice
2 cups pineapple juice
1½ quarts cranberry juice

1 quart ginger ale
Block of ice

1. In a large punch bowl, mix together fruit juices; chill.
2. Just before serving, add ginger ale and stir.
3. Add ice. (Ice cubes make punch difficult to serve; use larger blocks of ice instead.) Ladle punch into pretty punch glasses, and garnish with orange slices, if desired.

FLOWERPOT SUNDAES

SPECIAL EVENT RECIPE

Luncheon

Gardeners' Soup

Krug
Pinot Chardonnay   Coast of Maine Lobster
Parkside Asparagus
Window Box Tomatoes

Almaden
Blanc de Blancs   April Flower Pot

Demi-tasse

The White House
Thursday, April 27, 1967

This cute little creation was a hit at the bridesmaid parties hosted by Luci and Lynda Johnson. Mrs. Johnson also liked the sweet look and light taste of these miniature sundaes served in tiny flowerpots. The dessert also proved perfect for Mrs. Johnson's Beautification Luncheons, which she hosted regularly at the White House in the Family Dining Room for the staff and a volunteer board who were developing the Beautification Program. Mrs. Johnson considered the term "beautification" trivial and cosmetic-sounding; actually her project grew into a major nationwide effort to keep America beautiful. Mrs. Johnson focused at first on the capital city, where Pennsylvania Avenue was lined with azaleas, 2 million daffodils were planted, and cherry trees were added to the Hains Point waterside area. The Highway Beautification Act was passed, and the White House sponsored a Conference on Natural Beauty to discuss the conservation of scenic wilderness, improvements in building and highway design, increased park space for cities, and pollution control. With her husband's confidence and encouragement, Mrs. Johnson succeeded in her efforts to be a productive rather than ornamental addition to the White House. She inspired her staff to follow suit, and supported us in our efforts to please the First Family and their many guests.

Makes 12

12 *clean clay flowerpots (about*
   3 inches in diameter)
SPONGE CAKE *(page 107)*
1½ *cups vanilla ice cream*
¾ *cup chocolate ice cream*

MERINGUE
6 *plastic drinking straws, cut*
   into 3-inch lengths
12 *fresh flowers of the season*

1. Line bottom of each flowerpot with a ¼-inch round of SPONGE CAKE.
2. Top cake with a heaping tablespoon of vanilla ice cream and spread evenly; repeat with chocolate ice cream and another layer of vanilla ice cream. Freeze until shortly before serving.

3. Using a pastry bag fitted with a #6 star tip, pipe MERINGUE over the tops in a circular pattern.

4. Bake at 425°F on upper oven shelf for 1 to 2 minutes to brown the meringue. Place a length of straw in the center of each sundae and insert a fresh flower and serve at once.

MERINGUE

Makes 6 cups

6 egg whites, at room
   temperature
A pinch of salt

A pinch of cream of tartar
1½ cups sugar
A few drops of vanilla extract

1. Beat egg whites with salt and cream of tartar until soft peaks form.

2. Gradually add sugar, beating constantly; beat until stiff peaks form.

3. Fold in vanilla. Use at once.

Meringue-topped Flowerpot Sundaes provide a dainty ending to a White House luncheon.

LUCI'S WEDDING CAKE

Alice Roosevelt Longworth, the daughter of President Theodore Roosevelt, attended Luci Johnson's wedding. She had been married in the White House herself 60 years earlier, with a breakfast reception for nearly 700 guests served in the State Dining Room. "Princess Alice" thoroughly enjoyed being in the spotlight as Teddy Roosevelt's most popular offspring. As a teenager living in the White House, Alice smoked cigarettes, drank cocktails, wore riding breeches, and kept a pet snake named Emily Spinach. Songs were written about "Princess Alice" and parties were given in her honor. Her frustrated father once announced, "I can do one of two things; I can be the President of the United States, or I can control Alice." When Alice Roosevelt married Representative Nicholas Longworth, the menu served at their White House reception breakfast included croquettes, pâtés, salads, assorted sandwiches, and ice

Luci's wedding cake was a masterpiece designed by White House pastry chef Ferdinand Louvat and decorated by New York pastry chef Maurice Bonté. The 300-pound cake was baked in 7 separate layers that were adorned with 60 crystalline flowers that Bonté had made by hand. Each of the 6 tiers of light-yellow fruit cake was topped with a tier of crystalline arches framing crystalline lilies-of-the-valley. The top layer was Luci's favorite chocolate cake—the "bride's cake," which the newlyweds brought along on their honeymoon. Fresh lilies-of-the-valley replaced the traditional bride and groom statuettes. Bonté had painstakingly created the crystalline decorations from granulated sugar, pulled like taffy and hand-formed into delicate petals, leaves, archways, and other designs. Due to the immensity of the wedding cake (the bottom tier was almost 3 feet in diameter), we assembled the final cake just before the reception: Moveable tables bearing the unfrosted layers were wheeled to the East Room, where the cake was assembled, frosted, and decorated. Louvat was assisted in this arduous task by Bonté, and I provided a helping hand as well. The wedding cake was an obvious success; the guests "oohed and ahhed" and ate every last crumb. Louvat had baked miniature summer fruit cakes that were packed in little gift boxes for each guest to take home as a delicious keepsake of Luci Johnson's memorable White House wedding reception.

Makes an 8-inch, 2-layer cake

½ cup seedless white raisins
Brandy
1¾ cups cake flour
1 teaspoon baking powder
¼ teaspooon salt
½ cup butter
¾ cup sugar

5 egg whites
¾ cup chopped candied
    pineapple
1 cup chopped walnuts
½ teaspoon almond extract
½ teaspoon vanilla extract

1. Cover raisins with brandy and let stand in refrigerator overnight.
2. Preheat oven to 300°F. Line two 8-inch cake pans with greased paper and grease the sides.
3. Mix together flour with baking powder and salt; sift.
4. In a large mixing bowl, cream butter. Gradually add sugar, and cream until light and fluffy.
5. Beat in egg whites one at a time.

6. Drain raisins; add to batter with pineapple, walnuts, and extracts.

7. Add dry ingredients to batter a little at a time, beating after each addition; blend until smooth.

8. Pour cake batter into prepared pans and bake in preheated oven for 1¼ hours, or until toothpick inserted in center comes out clean. Cool on wire racks before frosting with SEVEN-MINUTE ICING.

cream molded into hearts, wedding bells, and wedding rings, plus petits fours, wedding cake, champagne, punch, lemonade, and coffee. If this sounds like an imposing meal, consider the following breakfast menu, which was served at Nellie Grant's White House wedding reception in 1874:

SOFT SHELL CRABS ON TOAST
GÂTEAUX GARNIS DE CRABES ET CHAMPIGNONS
CROQUETTES OF CHICKEN WITH GREEN PEAS
COTELETTES D'AGNEAU
ASPIC DE LANGUES DE BOEUF
WOODCOCKS AND SNIPES ON TOAST
BROILED SPRING CHICKEN
SALAD
STRAWBERRIES WITH CREAM
CHARLOTTE RUSSE
BROQUES EN BOUCHE
CORBEILS GLACÉS À LA JARDINIÈRE
GÂTEAUX DE TROIS FRÈRES
NESSELRODE PUDDING
BLANCMANGE
FRUITS GLACÉS
ICE CREAM
WATER ICES
SMALL CAKES
BRIDE'S CAKE
ROMAN PUNCH
COFFEE

SEVEN-MINUTE ICING

Makes 2 cups

1½ cups sugar
5 tablespoons cold water
¼ teaspoon salt

¼ teaspoon cream of tartar
2 egg whites
1 teaspoon lemon extract

1. In the top of a double boiler, mix together all ingredients except lemon extract. Cook over rapidly boiling water, beating constantly at high speed with an electric hand mixer, until stiff peaks form, for about 7 minutes.

2. Remove from heat, add lemon extract, and beat for another minute. Let cool slightly before icing cake (not too long, or icing will harden).

LYNDA'S WEDDING CAKE

The only President to be wed in the White House was Grover Cleveland. On June 2, 1886, a 21-year-old college student from Buffalo married her guardian, a 49-year-old bachelor who was also the President of the United States. Frances Folsom became the "Lady Di" of her day, with constant public attention to all of her doings. Even Frances's hairstyle was dubbed "à la Cleveland," and became the rage with American women.

Three pastry chefs were involved in the creation of Lynda's masterful wedding cake. Ferdinand Louvat was still the pastry chef at the White House, but his serious illness required recruitment of outside help. Clement Maggia, the noted pastry chef from the exclusive Greenbriar Hotel in West Virginia, designed the 5-layer pound cake. Maggia labeled the cake his "crowning achievement," but died of a heart attack only 3 days prior to the wedding and so was unable to see the completion of his impressive production.

Another pastry chef from the Greenbriar, Eric Crane, helped to decorate the 6-foot-high cake, which was set on an oval table in the East Room of the White House and hidden behind a screen until after the wedding ceremony was concluded. Lynda and her new husband, Captain Charles Robb, filed happily out of the East Room under an arc of military swords and, while the guests enjoyed the buffet held in the State Dining Room, the East Room was transformed from chapel to celebration room. The screen was withdrawn to reveal the towering white cake adorned with pulled sugar birds. As the orchestra tuned up for some lively dance numbers, the chilled champagne began to flow. When Lynda struggled to cut the beautiful cake with the traditional but awkward military sword, the groom and the President lent her a hand. Wedding guests again included Alice Roosevelt Longworth, who had struggled to cut her own wedding cake with a military sword nearly 62 years before.

A happy Lynda Johnson
with her future husband,
Captain Charles Robb.

A 21-gun salute followed a wedding ceremony conducted in the Blue Room, and music was provided by a band led by John Philip Sousa. The bride sent her guests home with "cake to dream on," each slice encased in satin, boxed in lace, and tied with satin bows. The cake was iced with "plain frosting in accordance with the wish of the President," as reported by the newspaper accounts of the day. Yet, there was certainly nothing "plain" about America's first celebrity wedding. The 1887 edition of The White House Cook Book *provided the following recipe for "Bride's Cake," an old-fashioned "cake to dream on":*

Cream together one scant cup of butter and three cups of sugar; add one cup of milk, then the beaten whites of twelve eggs; sift three teaspoonfuls of baking powder into one cup of cornstarch mixed with three cups of sifted flour and beat in gradually with the rest; flavor to taste. Beat all

Makes two 9 × 5-inch loaves or two 9-inch layers

3 sticks (½ cups) butter,
   softened
2 cups confectioners' sugar
8 eggs, at room temperature

3 cups plus 3 tablespoons sifted
   cake flour
¼ teaspoon ground mace
Finely grated peel of 1 lemon

1. Preheat oven to 325°F. Lightly grease two 9 × 5-inch loaf pans or two 9-inch layer pans.

thoroughly, then put in buttered tins lined with letter paper well buttered; bake slowly in a moderate oven. A beautiful white cake. Ice the top. Double the recipe if more is desired.

2. In a large mixing bowl, cream butter until light and fluffy.
3. Gradually add sugar and beat well.
4. Add eggs one at a time, beating after each addition.
5. Mix in flour, mace, and lemon rind and blend until smooth.
6. Divide batter between prepared pans and bake on lower shelf of preheated oven for 50 minutes, or until toothpick inserted in center comes out clean. (After 15 minutes baking time, loaves can be split with a sharp knife to allow air to escape and to create the characteristic center split; make a clean slit ¼-inch deep and around 6 inches in length along the top of each loaf.) Turn out of pans and cool on wire racks before icing.
7. Frost cooled cakes with ROYAL ICING (page 34), if desired, or serve plain, with whipped or ice cream.

THE CANAPÉ BIRTHDAY CAKE

SPECIAL EVENT RECIPE

This unique party platter is an invention I introduced when I was Executive Chef at the Sheraton-East Hotel in New York City. At cocktail parties and receptions, the simulated cake was a real conversation piece and quite breathtaking to behold.

When I was hired as Executive Chef for the White House, a press reception was held upon my arrival. I served my special canapé cake, which was the simplest way to demonstrate some of my culinary skills. I believe that cooking is an art, and a good cook must have feeling and finesse. Mrs. Johnson also believed that cooking is a fine art, so she treated the chef as an artist. Thus, it is easy to understand why I was inspired to create so many beautiful dishes during the Johnson administration, including the "yellow rose of Texas," a pretty garnish carved from the humble turnip. Vegetable flowers can be used to enhance the beauty of any hors d'oeuvre tray, including this elaborate canapé "cake."

The base of this dish is a Styrofoam circle eight to ten inches in diameter and shaped like a two-layer cake. The "cake" is draped with nonpoisonous plant leaves called galax leaves (which resemble lily pads with the stems removed and are available at most florists) that have been thoroughly washed and well dried. A variety of bite-size canapés are then attached to the "cake." The result is an edible visual delight.

Any number and type of cold canapés can be used to create The Canapé Brithday Cake, so long as the choices are all bite-size and can be readily fastened with toothpicks. (A canapé is any appetizer that can be eaten out of hand and without the use of fork or spoon, thus leaving one hand free for holding a cocktail.) I usually created my "cake" with around 300 of the following canapés:

· ham rolls filled with horseradish and cream cheese
· roast beef rolls also filled with horseradish and cream cheese
· cheese puffs

A small version of the Canape Birthday Cake boasts fresh shrimp and other hors d'oeuvres.
(COURTESY: RINGIER DOKUMENTATIONSZENTRUM, ZURICH)

· fresh medium-size shrimp
· fresh lobster, in bite-size pieces

A side dish of Cocktail Sauce or Sauce Rémoulade (page 213) should be served if shrimp and/or lobster are included in the "cake." Sometimes I served a canapé cake composed entirely of fresh shrimp.

Serves 50 to 150

Styrofoam "cake," 8 to 10 inches in diameter and about 6 inches high
Galax leaves to cover "cake," cleaned and stemmed

300 assorted bite-size canapés
300 decorative toothpicks

1. Cover Styrofoam "cake" with galax leaves and staple in place.
2. Spear the canapés with toothpicks and carefully insert each toothpick into the Styrofoam; space the canapés as evenly and attractively as possible. Refrigerate until serving time.

(FRANCIS MILLER, <u>LIFE</u> MAGAZINE, © TIME INC.)

THE
NIXON FAMILY

The Nixons'
Light Luncheon Plates

Nixon Family Favorite Entrées

Nixon Family Favorites
On~the~Side

Nixon Family Favorite Desserts

Special Event Recipes

THE NIXONS'
LIGHT LUNCHEON
PLATES

For department heads at the White House, a change in the administration always elicits a certain amount of anxiety, especially for the Executive Chef. When the Nixons moved into their new home, the arrival of a new Chief Usher, who replaced the well-respected J. B. West, created additional pressure for the kitchen staff. Fortunately, it was a smooth transition (and Mr. West enjoyed a farewell luncheon with his wife in the Main Kitchen, before retiring to write his best-selling memoirs). Even more fortunately, the kitchen staff was immediately reassured that their positions would all be retained with the new administration. Phew!

A few weeks before their arrival, the Nixons sent advance men to the White House to discuss the new First Family's needs, likes and dislikes, and life-style. With the departure of the Johnsons' family cook, my job included full responsibility for the family menus, in addition to the State Dinners and other official White House functions. After six months of double-duty, the understanding new Chief Usher recognized the need to hire an assistant chef to help me.

During this hectic period, I was relieved to discover that the advice of the Nixons' advance men proved accurate in the kitchen: The new First Family liked simple American foods and ethnic dishes. With full responsibility for the many meals served at the White House, it was a relief to be asked to prepare simple salads as lunchtime fare—especially on days with an evening reception for 500 or a fancy formal dinner to honor a king or prime minister.

Snowball Salad, like most of the Nixons' lunchtime salad selections, was a quick and easy family favorite. This salad can be exceptionally refreshing as a light summer luncheon plate, and is best when topped with freshly grated coconut.

SNOWBALL SALAD

Serves 4

¼ cup shredded coconut
4 heads of Bibb lettuce, washed
   and well dried
3 ripe pears, peeled, cored, and
   sliced into 6 sections
3 oranges, peeled and sectioned

12 large strawberries, washed
   and stemmed
24 ripe black cherries, washed
   and pitted
1 pint lemon sorbet

1. To use fresh coconut: Warm the coconut in a moderate oven for 20 to 30 minutes to soften the shell. Pierce the "eyes" with an ice pick or screwdriver and drain out the milk, which can be reserved for use in sauces or drinks. Crack the shell by tapping gently with a hammer and pry out the coconut meat, paring the flesh from the shell. Grate and toast lightly, if desired. The extra effort of wrestling with fresh coconut yields worthwhile flavor results.

2. Arrange lettuce on individual serving plates.

3. Divide pear and orange sections evenly among the plates, alternating in a circular pattern with the strawberries and cherries; leave the center of each plate open.

4. Center a scoop of lemon sorbet on each plate. Sprinkle with coconut, and serve at once.

WESTERN WAY SALAD

Thomas Jefferson, who attributed his longevity to a diet rich in vegetables, was an avid salad eater. In his gardens at Monticello, Jefferson grew five different varieties of endive, a wide

The entire First Family was partial to dishes made with fresh produce from California and Florida, including ripe avocadoes, and Mrs. Nixon was especially fond of salads made with avocado.

The inclusion of California avocadoes, or "alligator pears," gives this salad a "Western" touch. These leather-skinned avocadoes are typically available in the marketplace from January through April. In the summertime, Mrs. Nixon liked a salad in which slices of the smooth-skinned Florida avocado were alternated with fresh grapefruit sections to make a light luncheon plate.

Since she was naturally slim, Mrs. Nixon never had to count calories too carefully. But she was very conscious of her diet and chose to eat healthful meals. She was always appreciative of the variety of nutritious luncheon salad plates available on the White House family menus.

Serves 6

1 large head escarole, washed
   and well dried
Two 4- to 6-ounce cooked
   chicken breasts, boned and
   skinned
2 ripe avocadoes, peeled
2 medium-size tomatoes

3 hard-boiled eggs, quartered
6 slices bacon, cooked crisp
   and drained
½ cup crumbled blue cheese
1 tablespoon chopped fresh
   parsley
POPPY SEED DRESSING

1. Shred the escarole into a large serving bowl.

2. Slice cooked chicken into julienne strips and arrange on the escarole in a circular pattern.

3. Use a sharp knife to cut each avocado in half; to remove pit, tap with knife blade and twist out. Slice each half into 6 strips and arrange between chicken strips.

4. Cut each tomato into 6 wedges and arrange alternately with egg quarters on the lettuce bed in the same circular pattern.

5. Crumble crisp bacon and sprinkle over salad with the crumbled blue cheese.

6. Sprinkle with parsley and refrigerate briefly until serving time. Serve with HOT BISCUITS (page 7). POPPY SEED DRESSING can be added just before serving, or served on the side.

array of lettuce, thirty kinds of peas, and a host of other produce. Perhaps due to this early President's influential example, Americans at that time were already aware of the healthfulness of vegetable salads. In the 1887 edition of The White House Cook Book, *the section on "Medicinal Food" advised:*

We might go through the entire list and find each vegetable possessing its especial mission of cure, and it will be plain to every housekeeper that a vegetable diet should be partly adopted, and will prove of great advantage to the health of the family.

Makes 1½ cups

POPPY SEED DRESSING

2 egg yolks
1 teaspoon dry mustard
Juice of 1 lemon
½ teaspoon salt
4 twists freshly ground black
   pepper

1 garlic clove, finely minced
4 drops of Tabasco sauce
¼ cup cider vinegar
¾ cup poppy seed oil
½ teaspoon poppy seeds

1. In a blender, combine all ingredients except for poppy seed oil and poppy seeds; blend at high speed for 10 seconds.

2. With blender running at low speed, gradually add oil; cover and blend until consistency is creamy. (You can also make the dressing by hand in a mixing bowl using a wire whisk.)

3. Add poppy seeds and use at once, or refrigerate.

PANAMANIAN SHRIMP PLATE

During the humid Washington summers, the Nixons preferred luncheon menus built around cold foods. They enjoyed cold soups like gazpacho, cold cucumber and other mousses, cold poached salmon, and especially cold seafood plates. With cold shrimp and crab, the Nixons liked a special red cocktail sauce made with catsup. However, the Nixons preferred the Panamanian-style shrimp plate, served with a rather unusual sauce to enhance the flavor of the cold seafood.

The Nixons were also fond of another cold seafood dish, the Mississippi Platter, which was made with fresh tuna or shrimp, lobster, and crab served on a bed of iceberg lettuce and garnished with sliced hard-boiled eggs and tomatoes, radish roses, and crisp coleslaw. They also liked the Alligator Pear Princess, avocado stuffed with lobster salad and garnished with asparagus tips. As the Executive Chef at the Hotel Hampshire House in New York City, I had included these cold seafood plates on my summer menus. The acclaim these salads received at the time convinced me that they would be a success as summertime dishes for the Nixons' White House luncheons.

Opposite page: First Lady Pat Nixon is clearly pleased to be visiting the White House kitchen.

Serves 4

1 head Romaine lettuce, washed and well dried

4 ripe papayas, peeled, halved, and seeded

24 large (about 1 pound) shrimp, boiled and peeled

6 lemon wedges

Fresh parsley sprigs

¾ cup CURRY MOUSSELINE

1. Arrange lettuce leaves on a large serving platter or individual salad plates.

2. Cut papaya halves lengthwise into thin, even slices. Arrange on serving plate in a spokelike pattern, leaving centers open.

3. Put shrimp in centers and garnish with lemon wedges and parsley. Serve chilled, with CURRY MOUSSELINE and whole-grain crackers or JEFF'S GEORGIA-STYLE CHEESE STICKS (page 240) on the side.

CURRY MOUSSELINE

Makes 1½ cups

1 tablespoon curry powder

4 tablespoons dry white wine

3 egg yolks

2 tablespoons lemon juice

1 teaspoon salt

¼ cup cider vinegar

1 cup vegetable oil

½ cup heavy cream, whipped

1 teaspoon paprika

1. In a small saucepan, mix curry powder with wine, using a wire whisk. Cook over medium heat to reduce wine by half; transfer to a mixing bowl and let cool.

2. Add egg yolks, lemon juice, salt, and vinegar; mix well with the wire whisk.

3. Gradually add vegetable oil, continuing to whisk, until sauce thickens. Fold in whipped cream.

4. Spoon into a sauceboat, sprinkle with paprika, and serve at once.

PEPPERONI SALAD

Throughout history, both the popularity and content of salads have varied with the times. The original Chef's Salad, for example, was tossed at New York's Ritz-Carlton in the early 1900s by Chef Louis Diat. His creation included smoked ox tongue and watercress. Today's popular versions might include any variety of leftover meats, cheeses, and vegetables—but rarely ox tongue—depending on the chef. During Chef Diat's era, The White House Cook Book provided some guidelines that would still guarantee good results with most any chef's salad:

Everything in the make-up of a salad should be of the freshest materials, the vegetables crisp and fresh, the oil or butter the very best, meats, fowl, and fish well cooked, pure cider or white wine vinegar—in fact, every ingredient first class, to insure success.

As an avid fan of spectator sports, President Nixon was especially fond of football. The well-known football coach George Allen, then head coach for the Washington Redskins, was a regular on the guest list for White House functions. President Nixon liked to lunch on this spicy Pepperoni Salad, which I developed during his administration, while watching an occasional Redskin game on television. It later became a favorite of football fans President Ford and his son Jack. It is best to use very fresh Italian pepperoni, either the peppery-hot pork-and-beef variety or one of the hot-and-sweet types.

I do not know if the President was watching television when I appeared as a mystery guest on the popular game show *To Tell the Truth.* I was able to stump the panel, who cast their votes for the two talented imposters posing as French chefs. (For those in the know, my Swiss nationality was the key to my secret identity.) The most memorable aspect of my appearance on the show was the floppy chef's hat supplied by the wardrobe department. The supposed "toque" was so droopy that I refused to appear on television looking like a pizza chef! I can still recall the frantic stagehands inserting cardboard in my toque just minutes before air time. The producers all knew *my* line by then, both in the kitchen and out: Do it right or not at all.

Serves 4

1 head red-leaf lettuce, washed and well dried	*¼ pound mozzarella cheese, julienned*
1 pound pepperoni sausage, peeled and cut into 1½-inch strips	*A pinch of salt*
	¾ cup RED WINE VINEGAR DRESSING
1 cup julienned red bell pepper	*4 hard-boiled eggs, quartered*
1 medium-size Bermuda onion, peeled and slivered	*Sprigs of fresh parsley*
	Italian bread
1 cup peeled and julienned white radish	

1. Arrange lettuce on serving plates.
2. In a mixing bowl, combine pepperoni with sliced vegetables and cheese. Sprinkle with salt and mix well.
3. Add RED WINE VINEGAR DRESSING and mix thoroughly.
4. Spoon into center of each lettuce bed; garnish with egg quarters and parsley, and serve at once, with toasted Italian bread. Serve extra dressing in a sauceboat on the side.

RED WINE VINEGAR DRESSING

Makes 1½ cups

1 egg yolk
¼ cup red wine vinegar
Juice of 1 lemon
1 teaspoon Dijon-style mustard
4 twists freshly ground black
    pepper
2 sprigs fresh oregano,
    chopped, or ¼ teaspoon
    dried

1 garlic clove, finely minced
½ teaspoon Worcestershire
    sauce
¾ cup vegetable oil

1. In a blender, combine all ingredients except vegetable oil; blend well.

2. With the blender running at low speed, gradually add the oil, until the dressing is thickened. (You can also make the dressing by hand, using a wire whisk.)

3. Use at once, or keep refrigerated in a covered jar and shake well before serving.

PRESIDENT NIXON'S DIET SPECIAL

Even as a resident of the White House, where lavish meals and daily stress can promote weight gain, President Nixon was able to maintain his marriage weight from some thirty years earlier. His success in long avoiding undesirable weight gain was due to a combination of self-discipline and common sense: President Nixon ate small portions, avoided snacking, and made up for immoderate eating at gourmet State Dinners with light menus for subsequent meals.

The social schedule at the White House invariably included many evening receptions and dinners, so President Nixon often requested a light luncheon tray served in his office. A cottage cheese plate became his regular noontime meal, served with Rye Crisp and sometimes fresh fruit in season. Occasionally the cottage cheese was served with a tropical fruit plate composed of grapefruit, oranges, bananas, and pineapple. Or the cottage cheese might be served along with strawberries, bananas, and melon balls in a pineapple boat. President Nixon also liked fresh peaches, papayas, and mangoes.

If the President ever doused his cottage cheese with catsup, I never saw him, and doubt that he did. Yet the rumored "recipe" became rather popular with the dieting American public. In fact, a

President Nixon was not the only moderate eater to head the nation's top household. President Kennedy had a small appetite, which often had to be whetted with a few favorites, such as homemade fish chowder or fresh whipped cream. President Chester Arthur ate very small meals, such as a hurried "continental" breakfast while dressing (a roll with a bit of cheese and cof-

fee), a meatless luncheon, and supper consisting of either mutton chops and ale or rare roast beef and claret. Abraham Lincoln, however, earned the distinction of possessing the smallest presidential appetite. Often satisfied with a simple dinner of fruit salad, cheese, and crackers, his repeated requests for such plain fare annoyed the First Lady, especially when she had planned an elaborate dinner.

cottage-cheese-and-catsup "diet plate" actually appeared on some "chic" restaurant menus!

Serves 1 weight watcher

*Lettuce leaves, washed and
   well dried
1 large scoop low-fat cottage
   cheese
3 to 4 Rye Crisp crackers
1 hard-boiled egg, cut in
   wedges*

½ fresh tomato, cut in wedges

*¼ cucumber, thinly sliced
¼ green pepper, seeded and
   thinly sliced
   or
¼ fresh pineapple, diced
½ fresh peach, peeled and
   sliced
¼ fresh papaya, peeled and
   sliced*

1. Arrange lettuce on individual serving plate.
2. Mound cottage cheese in the center, and set crackers around edges; encircle with vegetables or fruits. Plain cottage cheese can also be enlivened with a variety of other fresh vegetables, raw or lightly steamed, and fruits, fresh or canned (without added sugar).

NIXON FAMILY
FAVORITE ENTRÉES

NEW ENGLAND
BOILED DINNER

Family menus for the Nixons included all-American fare. For breakfast, the President liked fresh fruit, wheat germ with nondairy creamer, and coffee, while his wife and daughters substituted toast for the cereal. The whole family liked light luncheons, often salads or cold plates served with a glass of milk and a slice of quick bread (such as date-nut or banana). Desserts were typically reserved for special family occasions and meals attended by guests.

Family dinner menus followed Mrs. Nixon's preferred pattern: meat or chicken, potato or pasta, vegetables and/or salad, dessert by request. A first course was waived—except for the family's favored Baked Grapefruit and occasionally a fresh fruit cup or clams on the half shell. Desserts, if any, consisted of fruits native to California and Florida. Dinner was served promptly at 6:00 P.M., unless the Nixons had warned the kitchen about a delay. My staff always appreciated this courtesy.

One of the Nixons' favorite dinner meals was the boiled corned beef and cabbage dish popular in the Northeast. Though neither the President nor his wife hailed from New England, their enthusiasm for this dish was indicative of their taste for simple fare.

Serves 6

2 pounds corned beef	1 head cabbage, washed and
2 pounds pointe de boeuf (top	cut into 6 wedges
butt)	6 medium-size fresh red beets,
1 tablespoon salt	washed, tops removed
1 bay leaf	12 small red Bliss potatoes,
3 small onions, peeled	scrubbed
3 medium-size carrots, peeled	HORSERADISH SAUCE
and halved	

1. In a large saucepan, cover corned beef with 1½ quarts of water; bring to a boil, cover, and simmer for 1½ hours, or until tender. Keep warm in the broth until serving time.

2. In a deep pot, cover *pointe de boeuf* with 1 quart of cold water; bring to a boil, skimming off any froth.

3. Add salt and bay leaf, and simmer gently for 30 minutes.

4. Add onions and carrots, cover, and simmer for 20 minutes; remove vegetables and continue to cook for 25 minutes more, or until beef is tender.

5. In a large sauté pan, cover cabbage wedges with the broth from the corned beef; bring to a boil, cover, and simmer for 20 minutes.

6. Cook beets in boiling water for 30 minutes, or until tender; drain.

7. Cook potatoes in boiling water for 10 minutes, or until tender; drain.

8. Slice the cooked meats and arrange in the center of a large, deep serving platter; surround with the cooked vegetables. Pour the hot broth from the boiled beef over the dish just before serving. The potatoes can be served separately, in a bowl lined with a linen napkin. Serve with HORSERADISH SAUCE on the side.

The Franklin D. Roosevelts liked corned beef and other simple American dishes, and their housekeeper insisted that the Roosevelts' favorite meals were no more elaborate than those served daily in a typical American home. During Woodrow Wilson's administration, dinners were even more simple, since the war necessitated stark menus, typically "meatless and wheatless." As food administrator during World War I, Herbert Hoover approved the following simple recipe for "Warbread," to help Americans economize on the use of wheat and—since it could replace an entrée—meat:

Warbread—1 cup rye meal, 1 cup graham flour, ½ cup flour, 1 teaspoon cream of tartar, 1 teaspoon baking soda, 1 teaspoon salt, ¼ cup molasses, 1⅛ cup sour milk, 1 egg, 2 tablespoons melted shortening, ½ cup raisins. Mix dry ingredients, add molasses, sour milk, well-beaten egg, shortening, and raisins cut in pieces. Mix thoroughly and bake in a greased pan.

HORSERADISH SAUCE

Makes 1½ cups

2 tablespoons butter
2 tablespoons flour
1 cup hot beef broth (from the
    boiled beef)
½ cup milk
A pinch of salt

A pinch of freshly ground
    white pepper
A pinch of nutmeg
2 tablespoons freshly grated or
    bottled, well drained
    horseradish

1. Melt butter in a 1-quart saucepan, add flour, and mix well with a plastic or wooden spoon; cook until the mixture bubbles.
2. Add the beef broth, stirring with a wire whisk until smooth.
3. Add milk and bring to a boil; add salt, pepper, and nutmeg.
4. Boil over medium heat for 1 to 2 minutes, stirring constantly, until thickened.
5. Remove from heat and stir in horseradish; serve in a sauceboat.

BRAISED SWISS STEAKS

Up until World War II, a regional vote-gathering ritual was the "New York Beefsteak." The dinner drew constituents with a traditional menu, including celery, radishes, olives, and scallions; crabmeat cocktails; skewered lamb or pork kidneys; grilled steaks with Worcestershire butter; baked Idaho potatoes; and plenty of cold beer.

Mrs. Nixon's first food order at the White House was a relatively simple one, but it caused a furor in the kitchen. On the evening of the President's inauguration, Mrs. Nixon phoned the Main Kitchen to order the First Family's first White House dinner: four steaks (for the President, daughters Tricia and Julie, and Julie's husband, David Eisenhower), and "just a bowl of cottage cheese," to be sent up to Mrs. Nixon's bedroom as she dressed for the Inaugural Balls.

The kitchen had been warned about the First Family's fondness for steak, so a selection of prime cuts was already on hand. But no one had alerted the White House about the Nixons' penchant for cottage cheese. On Inaugural Day in Washington, shopping can prove difficult, as the city is in a turmoil with the influx of hundreds of thousands of visitors who attend the inaugural ceremony and the parades, balls, and celebrations that follow. Picking up a container of cottage cheese was no easy task.

An adventurous member of the kitchen crew volunteered to drive a White House limo around the upturned city in search of cottage cheese. Fortunately, the mission was a success. After that night, cottage cheese was always on hand in the White House.

Chef Haller gives a butler's tray one last check before it leaves the Main Kitchen.

(© DICK SWANSON)

Serves 6

2 tablespoons butter

1 large onion, thinly sliced

3 garlic cloves, finely minced

Six 10-ounce steaks, from top round

1 teaspoon salt

½ teaspoon freshly ground black pepper

2 tablespoons flour

2 tablespoons vegetable oil

1 teaspoon chopped fresh thyme, or ½ teaspoon dried

1 bay leaf

2 cups beef stock

2 cups julienned carrots, leeks, and celery, in equal proportions

1 cup chopped fresh parsley

1. Melt butter in a large sauté pan, add onion and garlic and sauté until golden brown. Set aside.

2. Season steaks with salt and pepper, and dredge lightly with flour.

3. Heat oil until very hot in a cast-iron skillet, add steaks and sear quickly on both sides.

4. Transfer steaks to the large sauté pan; add thyme and bay leaf.

5. Pour in beef stock, cover, and simmer slowly for 1 hour.

6. Turn steaks over, cover with julienned vegetables and simmer for 20 minutes more. Keep warm until serving time.

7. Arrange steaks on a deep serving platter; spoon broth and vegetables onto each steak, and sprinkle with parsley. Braised Swiss Steaks can be prepared in advance, as the steak keeps well without loss of taste or appearance.

DOUBLE SIRLOIN STEAKS IN HERB SAUCE

All of the Nixons enjoyed steak, but the President and his son-in-law David Eisenhower were the most enthusiastic fans of the Double Sirloin. The President preferred his steak cooked medium-rare and lightly seasoned, while the rest of the family liked light sauces. This dish suited everyone's tastes, as the sauce is not too rich. The flavor is derived more from the herbs than from the fat.

At Mrs. Nixon's request, sauces served to the First Family were reduced in fat content. Most sauces can be made in less caloric forms, and it is a myth that all sauces are "fattening." Portion size is important, too. A sauceboat or *saucière* can be helpful in controlling the amount of sauce added to dishes. Most cooks agree that a successful dish requires less sauce, because it has ample flavor of its own.

After enjoying his first White House steak dinner, President Nixon came into the kitchen to thank me in person. David Eisenhower was always pleased with the steaks, and with the rest of the food served to him as a White House guest. He once remarked, "Y'know, Chef, having dinner here is like eating in one of New York's finest French restaurants." It is that sort of heartfelt thanks from satisfied "customers" that makes a chef's job worth all the effort.

President Nixon also liked to be served steak in the rustic atmosphere of the presidential retreat, Camp David, or on the presidential yacht, the *Sequoia*. He also enjoyed steak in the elegant White House, even for his own birthday meal.

Serves 6

Three 2-pound sirloin steaks, 2 inches thick
3 tablespoons olive oil
3 garlic cloves, minced
2 shallots, minced
1 tablespoon chopped fresh rosemary, thyme, and
marjoram, in equal proportions
A pinch of salt
A pinch of freshly ground black pepper
¼ cup HERB SAUCE

1. Arrange steaks in a glass or stainless steel pan for marinating.
2. Mix oil with garlic, shallots, herbs, salt, and pepper. Brush generously on both sides of steaks, cover with plastic wrap, and marinate in the refrigerator for 2 hours or longer.
3. Using the back of a knife, lightly scrape the marinade from both sides of steaks.

4. Under a hot broiler, sear steaks on both sides until very brown; broil for 15 minutes for medium-rare steaks, or to desired degree of doneness, turning occasionally.

5. Let steaks stand for 5 minutes before slicing. Slice diagonally into thick strips (around 2 inches wide), arrange on a serving platter, and pour HERB SAUCE over all. Serve with steamed rice or any type of potato, and a garden salad. The HERB SAUCE gives the steaks both flavor and shine.

HERB SAUCE

Makes ¼ cup

3 tablespoons butter
1 tablespoon BROWN SAUCE, or
    substitute ½ bouillon cube
    dissolved in 2 tablespoons
    red wine
1 teaspoon chopped parsley

1 teaspoon chopped chives
3 twists freshly ground black
    pepper
1 teaspoon Worcestershire
    sauce

1. In a small saucepan, heat butter with brown sauce. (If using bouillon cube, reduce mixture to 1 tablespoon before adding butter.)
2. Add rest of ingredients and mix well, using a wire whisk.
3. Pour into a sauceboat and serve at once.

BROWN SAUCE

Makes 2 quarts

4 pounds veal bones
¼ cup vegetable oil
1 cup coarsely chopped onions
4 garlic cloves, crushed
1 cup peeled and coarsely
    chopped carrots
1 cup coarsely chopped celery
¼ cup flour
2 cups dry white wine
2 quarts hot veal stock or
    chicken stock
1 large leek, white part only

Fresh parsley sprig
Tied cheesecloth "spice bag,"
    containing 24 black
    peppercorns, 2 cloves, 1 bay
    leaf, 1 teaspoon fresh
    rosemary or ¼ teaspoon
    dried, 1 teaspoon fresh
    thyme (or ¼ teaspoon dried),
    and 1 teaspoon fresh
    marjoram (or ¼ teaspoon
    dried)

1. Preheat oven to 375°F.

2. Chop veal bones into small 1½-inch square pieces.

3. In a large cast-iron skillet, heat oil; add bones and brown on all sides, stirring constantly.

4. Transfer skillet to lower shelf of preheated oven. Bake for 20 minutes, stirring occasionally, until bones are well browned.

5. Add onions, garlic, carrots, and celery; roast for 10 minutes, until vegetables are lightly browned, stirring occasionally. Remove from oven.

6. Transfer bones into a stockpot and drain off fat.

7. Stir flour into the browned vegetables and cook for a minute, stirring constantly.

8. Add wine and bring to a boil, stirring constantly until all crusty pieces have dissolved. Transfer into the stockpot.

9. Add hot stock and bring to a boil over medium-high heat.

10. Tie leek and parsley sprig together using fine string; add to stockpot with cheesecloth spice bag containing remaining ingredients.

11. Set cover slightly ajar and simmer over low heat for at least 4 hours, stirring occasionally; if sauce reduces too much, add more hot stock.

12. Strain sauce through cheesecloth. Let stand for 30 minutes.

13. Skim fat from the top of the sauce before use. To store, cool completely; refrigerate in a covered container. Freeze sauce unless used within 2 to 3 days.

FAMILY-STYLE MEAT LOAF

In the eyes of the American public, barbecued beef was supplanted by mundane meat loaf when the Nixons replaced the Johnsons in the nation's First Home. Although the Presidents' personal tastes have often been exaggerated, President Nixon was quite fond of his wife's meat loaf, and meat loaf appeared about once a month on the family dinner menus. As soon as the public became aware of this fact, the White House was inundated with inquiries for the recipe that so pleased a presidential palate.

To ease my burden, Mrs. Nixon's meat loaf recipe was printed on White House stationery to be sent in response to the thousands of requests. This proved to be such a convenient and time-saving method for the White House kitchen to share certain recipes with the ever-curious public that a number of the Nixons' favorite recipes for simple, inexpensive, all-American dishes were printed on special stationery. Although the Family-Style Meat Loaf was the most common of the 100 to 150 weekly requests, other recipes that proved popular with the public included Mrs. Nixon's Continental Salad with Sesame Seed Dressing, Tricia's Chicken Divan, Tricia's Chicken Imperial, Julie's Spanish Eggs, Mrs. Nixon's Chestnut and Apple Stuffing, Apricot Nut Bread, Ham Mousse, and Barbecued Chicken.

President Truman's wife Bess was a popular First Lady, respected by the American public as a down-to-earth woman who was less interested in politics than in family and household affairs. One of her favorite recipes was for Small Meat Loaf—to serve eight. Perhaps a "Big Meat Loaf" would have served the entire household, a considerable undertaking in a home the size of the White House.

Serves 6

*2 tablespoons butter
1 cup finely chopped onions
2 garlic cloves, minced
3 slices white bread
1 cup milk
2 pounds lean ground beef
2 eggs, lightly beaten
1 tablespoon salt
4 twists freshly ground black pepper
1 tablespoon chopped fresh parsley
½ teaspoon dried thyme
½ teaspoon dried marjoram
2 tablespoons tomato purée
2 tablespoons bread crumbs*

1. Grease a 13 × 9-inch baking pan.
2. Melt butter in a sauté pan, add onions and garlic and sauté until just golden. (Do not brown.) Let cool.
3. Dice bread and soak in milk.
4. In a large mixing bowl, mix beef by hand with sautéed vegetables and bread pieces. Add eggs, salt, pepper, parsley, thyme, and marjoram, and mix by hand in a circular motion.
5. Turn into the prepared pan and pat into a loaf shape, leaving at least 1 inch of space around the edges to allow fat to run off.
6. Brush top with tomato purée and sprinkle with bread crumbs. Refrigerate for 1 hour to allow the flavors to penetrate and to firm up the loaf.
7. Preheat oven to 375°F.
8. Bake on lower shelf of preheated oven for 1 hour, or until meat is cooked through. Pour off the accumulated fat several times while baking and after meat is fully cooked. Let stand on wire rack for 5 minutes before slicing.

IRISH STEW

President Nixon's father was of Scottish and Irish ancestry, and his mother was of German, English, and Irish heritage. With Irish lineage on both sides of the family, it is not surprising that some of the President's favorite foods were Irish specialties. Although lamb was not one of his favorite meats, President Nixon was very fond of an Irish stew made with cubes of lean lamb. And the President adored dumplings.

One of Mrs. Nixon's favorite entrées was a simple broiled lamb chop. She also enjoyed this lamb stew, served with vegetables and steamed dumplings. Fina Sanchez, the Nixons' family cook in California and Florida, shared the recipe so that the dish could be included regularly on White House family dinner menus.

During Tricia's courtship with husband-to-be Ed Cox, she once requested a picnic supper from the White House kitchen that included the stew. Perhaps she realized that Irish stew could be the way to a man's heart.

Serves 6

2 pounds lean shoulder of
  lamb, cubed
2 Idaho baking potatoes,
  peeled and sliced
3 leeks, white parts only, sliced
2 medium-size onions, peeled
  and sliced
3 garlic cloves, minced
2 stalks celery, peeled and
  chopped
1 tablespoon salt

¼ teaspoon freshly ground
  white pepper
1 bay leaf
1 tablespoon Worcestershire
  sauce
24 pearl onions, peeled
2 medium-size carrots, peeled
  and julienned
STEAMED DUMPLINGS
1 tablespoon chopped fresh
  parsley

1. In a large sauté pan, cover lamb cubes with cold water; bring to a boil and blanch meat. Remove meat to a colander to drain.

2. Rinse out the sauté pan; add potatoes, leeks, sliced onions, garlic, and celery. Top with blanched lamb.

3. Add water to cover, and the salt, pepper, and bay leaf.

4. Cover and simmer for 50 minutes, or until meat is tender. Do not overcook.

5. Use a long sharp fork to transfer lamb to a deep casserole dish; keep warm.

6. Remove the bay leaf. In a blender or food processor, purée the vegetables; add Worcestershire sauce.

7. Spoon vegetable purée over lamb; keep warm.

8. In a saucepan, bring 1 quart water to a boil; add pearl onions, cover, and simmer for 5 minutes. Add carrots, and simmer for 5 minutes more.

9. Spoon onions and carrots around the edges of the lamb casserole. Ring STEAMED DUMPLINGS evenly around the rim of the stew.

10. Sprinkle with parsley, and serve at once with a Caesar salad or other green salad.

STEAMED DUMPLINGS

Makes 12

2 cups flour
1 tablespoon baking powder
A pinch of sugar
½ teaspoon salt
½ cup vegetable shortening

1 egg
½ cup milk
1 tablespoon chopped fresh
parsley

1. Sift together flour, baking powder, sugar, and salt.

2. Add shortening and mix thoroughly by hand.

3. In a large mixing bowl, beat egg with milk; add parsley. Quickly stir in the flour mixture, working by hand to make a smooth, pastelike dough.

4. Turn out onto a lightly floured board, and shape dough by hand into a large cylinder. Slice into rounds of 1-inch thickness.

5. Use a vegetable steamer set over boiling water to steam dumplings for 5 to 7 minutes; add to stew at once.

SPAGHETTI AND MEATBALLS

Italian dishes were always a favorite on the Nixons' family dinner menus, with lasagna a close second to spaghetti. Since the Nixons liked beef, meatballs and/or meat sauce always adorned their pastas. Warm Italian bread, a green salad, and a good red wine typically rounded out the meal. This ethnic menu was reminiscent of their early years of marriage, when the Nixons often celebrated with a spaghetti dinner: Mrs. Nixon would cook up a pot of pasta, while her young husband tossed the salad and uncorked the wine.

The Nixons also enjoyed other ethnic fare, including Chinese and Mexican food. At one of President Nixon's favorite restaurants near his San Clemente home, the menu once featured "The Presi-

*Italian immigrants intro-
duced spaghetti to America,
but pasta was not very
widely accepted until after
the turn of the century,
when Russian durum wheat
was used to make the semo-
lina. Thomas Jefferson
brought back a spaghetti-
making machine from Italy,
after he traveled throughout Europe in 1784 as the
American minister to
France. However, spaghetti
did not become a popular
menu item at the White
House until relatively recently, once it was established as one of America's
favorite ethnic specialties.*

dent's Choice," a meal consisting of the items served at a party held there by President Nixon during his first term, including beef enchiladas and refried beans. For his thirtieth wedding anniversary, President Nixon requested a Mexican meal that included beef tacos with hot sauce. Such simple ethnic foods were popular with the entire Nixon family, but spaghetti was always the number-one favorite.

The secret to a great spaghetti sauce is adequate cooking time. The richest, most favorful sauces are allowed to simmer over low heat for hours, until the aromatic herbs fully season the tomato-meat mixture. In my own home, my wife (who is American and was never trained in the culinary arts) makes a delicious spaghetti dinner, now that she knows the key to a successful tomato sauce. A great sauce can mean the difference between an ordinary pasta dish and a favorite—in any home.

Serves 6

2 tablespoons olive oil

3 garlic cloves, minced

Two 15-ounce cans whole tomatoes, or 6 fresh tomatoes, peeled and seeded

One 3-ounce can tomato paste

One 15-ounce can tomato sauce

1 cup dry red wine

1 bay leaf

1 teaspoon sugar

1 teaspoon salt

24 MEATBALLS

1 tablespoon chopped fresh basil, or 1 teaspoon dried

1 tablespoon vegetable oil

12 ounces spaghetti

½ cup grated Parmesan cheese

1. Heat oil in a large saucepan, add garlic, and sauté for only a few seconds. (Do not brown.)

2. Chop tomatoes coarsely and add to the saucepan with their juice; add tomato paste, tomato sauce, wine, bay leaf, sugar, and salt.

3. Bring to a boil, stirring constantly.

4. Simmer for 30 minutes to reduce by about 1 cup, or until thickened.

5. Add MEATBALLS and basil; cover, and simmer slowly for 45 minutes, stirring gently from time to time.

6. In a large pot, add vegetable oil to 2 quarts of salted water and bring to a full boil. Add spaghetti and cook until *al dente*, about 7 minutes.

7. Drain spaghetti and arrange on a large serving platter. Top with MEATBALLS and sauce, sprinkle with cheese, and serve at once with a tossed green salad and warm garlic bread.

MEATBALLS

Makes 24

1 tablespoon butter
½ cup finely chopped onions
2 garlic cloves, finely minced
¾ pound lean ground beef
¼ pound lean ground pork
1 cup bread crumbs
½ cup grated Parmesan cheese
1 egg, lightly beaten

½ cup heavy cream
4 twists freshly ground black
    pepper
1 tablespoon Worcestershire
    sauce
1 teaspoon salt
1 tablespoon chopped fresh
    parsley

1. Melt butter in a large nonstick sauté pan, add onions and garlic and sauté until just golden. Let cool.

2. In a large mixing bowl, mix together ground beef and ground pork by hand; add sautéed vegetables and the remaining ingredients, and mix by hand in a circular motion.

3. Roll into approximately 24 plum-size balls.

4. Sauté the meatballs in the nonstick sauté pan, browning evenly on all sides; drain on paper towels before adding to the simmering tomato sauce.

PRESIDENT NIXON'S POLENTA CASSEROLE

A traditional Northern Italian dish, polenta is a porridge or mush made from cornmeal. Polenta can be served plain as a side dish, fried into fritters and baked in sauce as a main dish, or sweetened to be eaten as dessert. In Italy and Switzerland, polenta is still prepared the old-fashioned way: The cornmeal is made in a *paiuolo*, a tinned copper kettle with a handle for hanging over an open hearth. Proper cooking necessitates continuous stirring for about an hour using a *mescola*, a wooden spoon with a tapered point. As the cornmeal cooks down, the polenta pulls away from the sides of the pot, leaving a crispy crust that is considered a special treat for children or the weary cook.

In Switzerland, freshly cooked polenta is served straight from the pot, and only leftovers are made into fritters and served in casseroles. In the Nixon White House, however, a sauced polenta was preferred to the plainer version. Once the family cook, Fina Sanchez, had explained the President's favorite recipe for polenta, the dish was always served as a hearty entrée of baked cornmeal patties in a savory tomato-meat sauce.

The native American version of polenta was called cornpone, from the Indian apone or "barefoot bread." The 1887 edition of The White House Cook Book offered a recipe for "Southern Corn Meal Pone":

Mix with cold water into a soft dough one quart of southern corn meal, sifted, a teaspoonful of salt, a tablespoonful of butter or lard melted. Mold into oval cakes with the hands and bake in a very hot oven in well-greased pans. To be eaten hot. The crust should be brown.

Serves 6

1 quart beef bouillon
¼ teaspoon freshly ground
  white pepper
1 tablespoon butter
1 cup yellow cornmeal

1 tablespoon vegetable oil
4 tablespoons grated Parmesan
  cheese
2 cups MEAT SAUCE

1. In a 2-quart saucepan, mix bouillon with pepper and butter; bring to a boil.

2. Add cornmeal, stirring with a wire whisk, and cook over low heat for 10 minutes or until thick.

3. Cover and simmer over very low heat for 20 minutes, stirring often with a plastic or wooden spoon.

4. Brush a baking sheet with oil and spread out the polenta evenly, about ½-inch thick. Sprinkle with 3 tablespoons of the cheese.

5. Let cool slightly; then chill in refrigerator for at least 1 hour, or until firm to the touch.

6. Use a cookie cutter to make twelve 2-inch rounds.

7. Arrange rounds in a buttered casserole dish. Spoon on MEAT SAUCE, and sprinkle with remaining tablespoon of cheese.

8. Bake on middle shelf of preheated 375°F oven for 30 minutes.

9. Serve topped with MEAT SAUCE as an entrée, with a green salad. For a plainer version to serve as a side dish, stop after step 3 and serve the thickened cornmeal mixture with butter and grated cheese.

MEAT SAUCE

Makes 4 cups

2 tablespoons butter
1 cup finely chopped onions
2 garlic cloves, finely minced
1½ pounds lean ground beef
1 tablespoon salt
1 teaspoon freshly ground
  black pepper

1 teaspoon dried oregano
1 bay leaf
1 cup dry red wine
1 cup peeled, seeded, and
  chopped fresh tomatoes
One 15-ounce can tomato sauce

1. Melt butter in a large saucepan, add onions and garlic and sauté lightly.

2. Add meat, salt, pepper, oregano, and bay leaf; cook over medium-high heat to brown meat lightly.

3. Add wine, tomatoes, and tomato sauce; cover, and simmer over medium heat for 45 minutes, stirring often.

4. Skim fat from the top and remove bay leaf. Keep warm until use; extra sauce can be kept covered in the refrigerator.

The rising cost of food during the Nixon administration forced most American families to stretch their household budgets. In the White House, where one eye is always on the economy, instructions were given to stretch the domestic food budget as much as possible. State Dinners and other official functions were less vulnerable to economic sanctions, but the Nixons requested extra budgeting with their own family meals. These tended to be easy on the budget anyway, but were adjusted to emphasize less expensive chicken and fish dishes instead of costly cuts of beef.

Fortunately, the Nixons liked poultry dishes. In fact, some of Mrs. Nixon's and Tricia's favorite recipes included chicken. Mrs. Nixon liked CHICKEN AND MUSHROOM CRÊPES (page 126), a hot chicken salad, *Backhendl* (the unusual Viennese fried chicken), and *Pojarski de Volaille* (ground chicken patties, breaded and fried). Tricia favored casserole-type chicken dishes such as Chicken Divan, Chicken à la King, and Chicken in Suprême Sauce served with steamed rice.

President Nixon preferred plain chicken, baked or broiled in a low-fat manner. He also liked a few of the richer recipes, such as CHICKEN CORDON BLEU (page 186). Other family favorites included the ever-popular CHICKEN POT PIE (page 352), a Chinese-style recipe for chicken with walnuts (page 94), and old-fashioned Chicken Fricassee.

In considering White House menus from the past twenty-plus years, chicken really stands out as the most common family dinner entrée. Even though they have access to the finest foods, the First Families usually opt for affordable, practical meals, just like most American families.

CHICKEN FRICASSEE

At one point during Franklin D. Roosevelt's lengthy administration, the White House attempted to comply with the national wartime plan for food conservation. The New York Times *quoted Eleanor Roosevelt at the time as remarking, "Making the servants help me do my saving has not only been possible but highly profitable." The President teased her in a note: "All I can say is your latest newspaper campaign is a corker and I am proud to be the husband of the Originator, Discoverer, and Inventor of the New Household Economy for Millionaires."*

"Let's Try That Recipe Once More"

(COPYRIGHT © 1971 BY HERBLOCK IN THE WASHINGTON POST)

Serves 6 to 8

Two 3-pound frying chickens
2 teaspoons salt
¼ teaspoon freshly ground
*   white pepper*
¼ cup flour
5 tablespoons butter
1 cup dry white wine
1 to 2 cups chicken stock

¼ pound tiny onions, peeled
1 garlic clove, finely minced
½ pound tiny button
*   mushrooms, washed*
Juice of ½ lemon
1 cup heavy cream
1 tablespoon chopped fresh
*   parsley*

1. Cut each fryer into 10 pieces: quarter the breasts, separate legs from thighs, and leave wings whole.
2. Season chicken pieces with salt and pepper; dredge with flour.
3. In a medium-size saucepan, melt 4 tablespoons of the butter; brown chicken pieces a few at a time on both sides. Drain off fat and return all the chicken pieces to the pot.
4. Add wine and just enough chicken stock to cover. Bring to a boil; cover, and simmer for 10 minutes.
5. In a nonstick sauté pan, melt the remaining butter; sauté onions for 2 minutes. Add garlic and sauté for 1 minute more. Continue to cook until all the liquid has evaporated.
6. Add mushrooms and lemon juice; cook until liquid is completely reduced.
7. Add cream and bring sauce to a boil.
8. Turn the chicken pieces and pour the cream sauce over; simmer for 10 minutes. Transfer chicken to a deep serving platter and keep warm. (Since the chicken breasts will cook more rapidly than the legs and thighs, you may want to remove them earlier.)
9. Continue cooking sauce over medium heat to reduce to about 4 cups.
10. Pour sauce over chicken, sprinkle with chopped parsley, and serve at once, with pasta, noodles, or rice.

PRESIDENT NIXON'S DIET CHICKEN WITH HERBS

President Nixon, like the other four Presidents I have served as Executive Chef at the White House, was conscious of his diet and careful with his weight. Presidents Ford and Carter elected to stay in shape through rigorous exercise, while Presidents Johnson, Nixon, and Reagan depended more on dietary restrictions. During each of the five administrations, the White House physician warned the incumbent to be wary of pernicious weight gain. For anyone in such a stressful position, a subtle increase in weight can easily become an undesirable side effect, especially when rich, tempting foods are continually available at the mandatory social and official functions.

The Nixons encouraged the White House kitchen to experiment with creative low-calorie versions of standard recipes. At the informal family dinners, low-fat variations of chicken, fish, and certain meat dishes were often found on President Nixon's plate. The President became fond of a few such recipes, notably a light chicken dish flavored with fresh herbs. In fact, the little herbarium on the third floor of the White House was rejuvenated during the Nixon administration, so that some of the President's favorite herbs (thyme, tarragon, chives, and parsley) could be available fresh at all times.

On the rare occasions when he did indulge, President Nixon consumed his very favorite, very rich foods, such as BEEF STROGA-NOFF (page 10), Beef Wellington (filled with duxelles of mushrooms, onions, and goose liver) and the similar Filet de Boeuf Prince Albert (filled with foie gras instead), Duckling á l'Orange, Duckling Montmorency, and Duckling Bigard, as well as Homard à l'Américaine (lobster sautéed in oil and tomatoes, a dish of Provençal origin despite the name).

Serves 1 dieter

One 4 to 6 ounce whole chicken
    breast, boned and skinned
A pinch of salt
A pinch of freshly ground
    white pepper
1 garlic clove, peeled

½ teaspoon fresh thyme, or a
    pinch of dried
½ teaspoon fresh oregano, or a
    pinch of dried
1 teaspoon vegetable oil
Juice of 1 lemon

1. Season chicken lightly with salt and pepper.

2. Mince garlic with thyme and oregano, and rub into chicken breast.

3. Heat oil in a nonstick sauté pan, add chicken and brown on both sides.

4. Add lemon juice, cover, and simmer for 5 minutes; turn chicken, and simmer for 5 minutes more.

5. Remove from heat and let stand, covered, for 5 minutes. Transfer chicken to a serving platter or individual plate, top with pan juices, and serve at once, with steamed rice or plain pasta. (President Nixon liked this simple dish served with a garnish of fresh watercress, which he ate along with the herb-flavored meat.)

MRS. NIXON'S CHINESE WALNUT CHICKEN

Politically active First Lady Eleanor Roosevelt was not always available for White House menu planning. Her husband grew tired of dining on "chicken six times in a single week," and complained that the food served at the White House was all "plain fare, plainly prepared." President Franklin D. Roosevelt once sent his wife a letter in which he joked, "I'm getting to the point where my stomach positively rebels, and this does not help my relations with foreign powers. I bit two of them today."

President Nixon will long be admired for his advances in foreign policy, perhaps most notably for opening up U.S. relations with the People's Republic of China. In 1972, he was the first U.S. President to visit China, where the two governments agreed to broaden their scientific, cultural, and trade relationships. As a historic gesture of friendship, China donated two giant pandas, Ling-Ling and Hsing-Hsing, to the National Zoo.

China has also provided America with a passion for Chinese cuisine. President Nixon was fond of authentic Chinese dishes, both the lightly seasoned fare of Northern China and the hotter foods that characterize Hunan and Szechuan cuisine. Tricia preferred the more Americanized versions of Chinese food such as egg rolls and chow mein.

Mrs. Nixon liked chicken, and one of her favorite recipies was a Chinese-style chicken dish made with walnuts. When she first described the dish to a group of journalists, Mrs. Nixon referred to the recipe as "a favorite of Henry's." The press assumed that the dish was a Peking specialty, brought back by presidential adviser Henry Kissinger. The dish was actually from a recipe created by a different Henry, that is, the presidential chef.

Serves 6

1½ cups quartered walnuts
½ cup walnut oil
12 fresh water chestnuts, peeled and julienned, or one 8-ounce can, drained
¼ pound fresh bamboo shoots, julienned, or one 8-ounce can, drained
3 stalks celery, julienned
1 large onion, peeled and thinly sliced

1 small head Chinese cabbage, washed, drained, and shredded
3 tablespoons soy sauce
2 tablespoons cornstarch
2 teaspoons salt
1½ pounds chicken breasts, boned, skinned, and julienned
½ cup chicken broth
¼ cup dry sherry

1. In a small saucepan, cover walnuts with cold water and bring to a boil; cook for 3 minutes to remove bitter flavor. Drain and set aside.

2. Heat 1 tablespoon of the oil in a small sauté pan, add water chestnuts and bamboo shoots and sauté for 2 minutes. Set aside.

3. In a large skillet, heat another tablespoon of the oil; sauté celery and onion for 3 minutes. Add cabbage, and sauté for 5 minutes more or until vegetables are tender-crisp.

4. Stir in water chestnuts and bamboo shoots; drain the vegetables on paper towels and transfer to a mixing bowl.

5. Add walnuts to skillet and sauté until browned; mix half with the vegetables and reserve the rest.

6. Add remaining oil to the skillet and heat.

7. In a medium-size mixing bowl, blend soy sauce with cornstarch and salt until smooth, dip in chicken strips to coat, and sauté in the hot oil for 3 minutes or until tender.

8. Add broth and sherry; bring to a boil, stirring constantly.

9. Fold in sautéed vegetables, and cook for 2 to 3 minutes, until the mixture is thickened and heated through.

10. Spoon into a deep serving platter; sprinkle with remaining walnuts, and serve at once, with steamed rice.

Foreign diplomacy begins at home, whether at the White House or abroad.

FINA'S FLORIDA-STYLE FISH

George Washington was reportedly fond of fish, but his preference was probably due to his inability to chew tough cuts of meat. The first President of the United States had notoriously poor teeth, suffering so much from toothaches that all of his teeth were pulled before he reached sixty years of age. Contrary to the common myth, George Washington's dentures were not wooden, but the plate made for him by a silversmith was so ill-fitting that he could barely close his lips and found it difficult to smile. (This feature was exaggerated in the famous portrait saved from a flaming White House by First Lady Dolley Madison.) Yet Washington was actually a pleasant person with a fine sense of humor, who reportedly enjoyed good company, good wine, and good food—so long as he could chew it, that is.

When the Nixons first arrived at the White House, a typed sheet of menu suggestions was sent down to the Main Kitchen, including the helpful instructions to "Ask Fina or Manolo to describe their method of cooking fish." Fina and her husband, Manolo Sanchez, were refugees from Cuba who had worked in the Nixons' households since their arrival in America in the 1960s. When the Nixons lived in the White House, the Sanchez couple served as the personal maid and butler, and relinquished their cooking duties to the White House kitchen staff. Fortunately for all of us, Fina and Manolo were generous with their culinary suggestions. The Nixons' favored fish turned out to be prepared just like most of their favorite foods, that is, in a very simple manner: The Sanchez recipe called for marinating the fish first in fresh lemon and lime juice, then baking.

Some type of fish dish was included on the Nixons' family dinner menus at least once a week.

Serves 4

Four 6- to 8-ounce red snapper fillets
Juice of 1 lemon
Juice of 2 limes
1 teaspoon salt
¼ teaspoon freshly ground white pepper

2 tablespoons olive oil
2 tablespoons bread crumbs
¼ teaspoon paprika
4 lemon wedges

1. Marinate fillets in juice of lemon and limes for 2 hours.
2. Preheat oven to 375°F. Brush a broiling pan with vegetable oil.
3. Season the fillets with salt and pepper, and transfer to the prepared pan.
4. Brush fish with olive oil; mix together bread crumbs and paprika, and sprinkle over fillets.
5. Bake in preheated oven for 15 minutes, or until golden brown and firm to the touch. Serve at once, garnished with lemon wedges and the juices from the broiled fish spooned over, if desired. President Nixon liked simple fish dishes like this one served with fresh watercress and tiny boiled potatoes.

The Nixons were satisfied with such simple meals that the White House kitchen could have served eggs for dinner. In fact, one of the Nixons' favorite Sunday night suppers was a simple Western omelet made with diced green pepper, onions, and ham. They also liked a Spanish-style egg dish made with poached eggs and a spicy tomato sauce. And President Nixon—as we discovered rather suddenly—was especially fond of his Spanish Omelet.

During the first month of his administration, President Nixon occasionally appeared in the White House kitchen to praise the staff and the food. One quiet Sunday evening, he took the kitchen by surprise when he dropped in to make a special request. Home alone for dinner, President Nixon had a sudden hankering for a Spanish omelet.

Realizing that it is not good to keep the President of the United States waiting, the kitchen was under a bit of pressure to quickly create a Spanish-style sauce. Fortunately, an omelet can be made rather rapidly, and our last-minute Spanish Omelet was a success. From then on, there was always a container of Spanish Sauce on hand in the White House kitchen, just in case.

PRESIDENT NIXON'S SPANISH OMELET

When Herbert Hoover became President, he was a millionaire with gourmet appetites, and he was soon recognized as setting the finest table in the history of the White House. Yet one of his favorite dishes was the simple omelet. President Hoover's favorite omelet recipe was included in a cookbook written by his personal cook entitled Mr. Hoover Asked for Some More. *The Franklin D. Roosevelts preferred their eggs scrambled. On Sunday nights, Eleanor often scrambled eggs in a chafing dish, while President Roosevelt mixed drinks for their guests.*

Serves 1

1 teaspoon butter	½ cup warm SPANISH SAUCE
3 eggs, at room temperature	1 tablespoon chopped fresh
A pinch of salt	parsley
A pinch of freshly ground	Fresh parsley sprig
black pepper	

1. Heat butter in an 8-inch nonstick frying pan.
2. Break eggs into a small mixing bowl, and season with salt and pepper; beat well.
3. Pour into hot pan and cook over low heat for 1 minute.
4. Use a plastic or wooden spoon to stir eggs, while gently moving the pan in a circular motion, for 1 to 2 minutes, or until the eggs begin to puff up around the edges.
5. Spoon the warm SPANISH SAUCE into the center of the eggs and sprinkle with the chopped parsley; continue cooking for 1 minute, or until the bottom of the omelet is firmly set.
6. Tip pan and use a fork to fold the omelet in half. Lift out with a spatula, and turn upside-down onto a serving dish.
7. Garnish with parsley sprig, and serve at once, with toasted whole-grain bread, warm rolls, or CORN BREAD (page 277).

SPANISH SAUCE

Makes 2 cups

2 tablespoons olive oil
½ cup thinly sliced onions
2 garlic cloves, minced
1 cup julienned green bell
*　pepper*
2 medium-size tomatoes, or
*　1 cup drained canned*
*　tomatoes, diced*

1 bay leaf
Juice of 1 lemon
½ teaspoon salt
A pinch of sugar
6 drops of Tabasco sauce

1. Heat oil in a 1-quart saucepan, add onions and garlic and sauté for 3 minutes, or until golden brown.
2. Add green pepper, cover, and simmer for 2 minutes.
3. Add diced tomatoes; stir in remaining ingredients.
4. Bring to a boil, stirring constantly; simmer for 10 minutes, stirring often.
5. Remove from heat; discard bay leaf. Use at once, or store refrigerated in a covered jar.

NIXON FAMILY
FAVORITES ON-THE-SIDE

PRESIDENT NIXON'S BAKED POTATO

The Nixons' personal maid, Fina Sanchez, spent some time in the White House kitchen demonstrating how to prepare the President's favorite recipe for baked stuffed potatoes. The weight-conscious President was able to enjoy this special side dish on a regular basis because, contrary to popular belief, potatoes are not fattening. A plain potato is naturally low in fat and calories—until it is slathered with butter, dolloped with sour cream, or French-fried in oil, that is. Mrs. Nixon was also fond of potatoes, so the family dinner menus included potatoes in a low-fat form at least once a week.

The best potatoes for baking purposes are the large white varieties generically labeled as Idaho potatoes. The sweeter red-skinned potatoes are also delicious baked, but an Idaho potato is preferable for stuffing. Mashed potatoes can be made from most varieties, including the common brown Maine potatoes.

In his younger days, President Nixon was reportedly fond of mashing potatoes. According to his mother, Hannah Milhous Nixon, "He was the best potato masher one could wish for. Even in these days, when I am visiting Richard and Pat in Washington, or when they visit me, he will take over the potato mashing. My feeling is that he actually enjoys it." The President would have been more than welcome to help out in the White House kitchen, but we prepared his potatoes for him, just the way he liked them.

As early as 1719, Irish settlers brought "spuds" (named after the spades used to dig potato trenches) to America. However, the potato was not widely accepted in this country for another hundred years. When Thomas Jefferson first cultivated potatoes on his farm in Virginia, the much-maligned tuber was still considered dangerous to eat. By the time President Jefferson moved into the White House, however, potatoes had finally been accepted as healthful, tasty, and suitable even for the First Family's table.

Serves 2

2 medium-size Idaho baking potatoes, scrubbed	*A pinch of freshly ground white pepper*
1 tablespoon butter	*A pinch of nutmeg*
¼ teaspoon salt	*¼ cup hot milk*

1. Bake potatoes on middle shelf of 375°F oven for about 50 minutes, turning once, until crispy outside and fork-tender inside.

2. Remove the potatoes from the oven and slice off the top third of each. Scoop out the flesh from the sections into a small mixing bowl. Set the bottom shells aside, and discard the tops.

3. Mash the potato with butter, salt, pepper, and nutmeg. Add milk gradually, beating with a wire whisk.

4. Fill the potato shells with the mashed potato mixture and return to the oven for 5 minutes, or until piping hot. Serve at once. For added color and flavor, sprinkle the stuffed potatoes with grated Parmesan cheese, chopped parsley, or paprika before final baking.

JULIE'S NATIVE CORN PUDDING

The early American colonists survived their first harsh winter in New England with the help of the Indians, who taught them how to grow their native corn. The yellow kernels have been warmly welcomed on America's dinner plates ever since, and many dishes made with corn have proven popular in America's homes, from the White House on down. While serving as America's first minister to France, Thomas Jefferson grew corn in his garden in Paris. His immediate successor as President, James Madison, was often served spoonbread, a specialty of his popular wife, Dolley. President Herbert Hoover reportedly enjoyed corn in a cream soup, while New Englanders Calvin Coolidge and John Kennedy preferred corn muffins. "Rough Rider" Theodore Roosevelt ate cornmeal in the form of Indian pudding. His relatives, the Franklin D. Roosevelts, ate fried cornmeal mush for break-

Corn Pudding has appeared on family dinner menus during each of the past five administrations. All of the First Families seemed to enjoy the very plain, very simple corn dish. In fact, plain and simple corn sticks, corn bread, corn chowder, and corn on the cob have also been all-time favorites at the White House.

Julie Nixon Eisenhower occasionally helped to plan the Nixons' family dinner menus. For a brief period of time, Julie attempted to introduce her family to "health foods." Corn Pudding was one of the more popular choices. Some of her other suggestions were not so well received, such as the recipe she once requested from a cookbook written by the well-known nutrition guru Adelle Davis, who was eventually disparaged by the scientific, medical, and nutrition communities for the vast amount of misleading information offered in her best-selling books. The palatability of most "health food" recipes, though, can be improved with culinary improvisation. Julie's healthful Corn Pudding is a true White House recipe, that is, nutritious in content yet undeniably delicious as well.

Serves 6

One 16-ounce can whole kernel corn

One 16-ounce can cream-style corn

2 tablespoons sugar

A pinch of salt

A pinch of freshly ground white pepper

2 tablespoons melted butter

4 eggs

1 cup warm milk

1. Preheat oven to 350°F. Generously butter a 1½-quart baking dish.

2. In a mixing bowl, combine whole kernel and cream-style corn with sugar, salt, pepper, and melted butter.

3. In a separate bowl, beat eggs; add warm milk and beat well. Pour over corn mixture, and blend thoroughly.

4. Pour into prepared baking dish and set in a shallow pan of water.

5. Bake on middle shelf of preheated oven for 35 minutes, or until firm and golden brown. Do not overcook. Serve warm with pork chops, baked ham, or barbecued spareribs.

Julie Nixon shares a favorite cookbook with Chef Haller.

fast. The 1887 edition of The White House Cook Book *described Corn Pudding as "a Virginia dish," but provided some universal advice in the "Small Points on Table Etiquette": "Green corn should be eaten from the cob; but it must be held with a single hand."*

President Nixon was a world traveler and an adventurous eater, so there were few dishes served in the White House with which he was not familiar. However, he was pleased to be intoduced to the then-uncommon Chinese cabbage, which I prepared in a low-fat manner to suit the President's dietary preferences.

Also known as napa cabbage and bok choy, Chinese cabbage is actually a member of the mustard family and has a mild flavor. The Nixons liked their vegetables plain, cooked briefly and seasoned lightly. Thus, the crispy Chinese cabbage was readily accepted, and became a regular addition to the Nixons' family dinner menus. It was second in popularity only to zucchini, President Nixon's favorite vegetable. A low-calorie zucchini dish was also prepared for the first family using the same low-fat recipe.

The Nixons usually drank ice water with dinner, and served dry wines when joined by guests. President Nixon was alone in his love of low-fat buttermilk, however. He often enjoyed a cold glass just before bed.

LOW-CALORIE CHINESE CABBAGE

Serves 6

Buttermilk was a favorite drink of Presidents Truman and Carter, but it was served in the White House even before the turn of the century. The 1887 edition of The White House Cook Book *extolled (and exaggerated) the health benefits of "Buttermilk as a Drink," and prescribed the beverage (without any medical evidence) for the treatment of numerous health disorders ranging from constipation to diabetes and liver disease: "Buttermilk, so generally regarded as a waste product, has latterly been coming somewhat into vogue, not only as a nutrient, but as a therapeutic agent."*

4 slices bacon
1 cup finely shredded onions
2 garlic cloves, finely minced
1 to 2 heads Chinese cabbage, shredded (about 8 cups)
1 teaspoon salt
⅛ teaspoon freshly ground white pepper
1 small red bell pepper, seeded and cut in thin strips
1 tablespoon soy sauce
1 tablespoon chopped fresh chives

1. Cut bacon slices crosswise into thin strips; in a large sauté pan, brown the strips over medium heat.
2. Add onions and garlic; sauté for 2 minutes, or until onion is transparent.
3. Add cabbage, salt, pepper, and red pepper strips. Sauté, stirring with a spatula, until steaming hot but still crisp, about 5 minutes. Stir in soy sauce.
4. Transfer to a deep serving platter, sprinkle with chives, and serve at once, with steamed rice and broiled chicken or fish for a low-fat, low-calorie meal.

BAKED GRAPEFRUIT

The Nixons did not usually include a first course in the family dinner menu, but they did enjoy clams on the half shell on special occasions, and fresh fruit from Florida or California on a regular basis. Baked Grapefruit was one of the Nixons' regular first courses, and sometimes they requested a rum-flavored version to be served as a dessert.

Growing up in California, President Nixon had long enjoyed the citrus fruits cultivated in his home state. The California grapefruit has a higher natural sugar content, so is considered the best variety for eating plain or as Baked Grapefruit. Florida grapefruit is good for squeezing into juice, and both types can be used in fruit salads.

One of Mrs. Nixon's favorite recipes was an unusual jelled Continental Salad made with grapefruit sections and sliced beets. It is the citrus flavor—simultaneously sweet and tart—that allows grapefruit to be included in a surprising variety of food combinations.

In French, grapefuit is called *pamplemousse,* from the Asian fruit called *pummelo* or *pomelo.* According to an old legend, the first *pummelo* was brought West from the East Indies in 1696 by a British sailor, Captain Shaddock, so the fruit was long known as "Shaddock." How grapefruit received its present name is unknown, but it may have been derived from the grapelike way these fruits grow, that is, in scattered bunches.

Unlike the tasty grapefruit so popular in America today, the earlier fruit was very bitter and required heaping amounts of sugar to make it edible. By 1900— when Teddy Roosevelt set his sights on the White House—botanists had developed a sweeter, more acceptable grapefruit. First Families have been able to enjoy the bittersweet citrus fruit ever since.

Serves 1

1 large grapefruit	*1 large strawberry*
1 teaspoon honey	*2 to 3 fresh mint leaves*
1 tablespoon brown sugar	

1. Slice off top third of grapefruit. Remove center core and separate sections with a serrated knife for easy eating.
2. Spread surface of grapefruit with honey and sprinkle with sugar.
3. Place under broiler, turning to heat evenly, until glaze is bubbly (about 5 minutes).
4. Garnish center with fresh strawberry and mint leaves. Serve at once. (To serve as a dessert, add 1 teaspoon of dark rum to the honey; after cooking grapefruit until glaze is bubbly, dust top with confectioners' sugar and heat for an additional minute before serving.)

In the history of the United States, probably no other bread has enjoyed greater popularity than the simple all-American biscuit. The recipe for biscuits is basic, but a variety of added ingredients can give new flavors to the light rolls, including fruit juices, chopped herbs, grated cheese, and maple syrup or other sweeteners.

In earlier, more active days, American farmers and laborers often shunned bread in favor of heaping platters of hot biscuits at every meal. Biscuits can be bun-size or tiny, the size of a silver dollar.

SEQUOIA ORANGE BISCUITS

The dough can be leavened and allowed to rise like yeast rolls, or measured out in spoonfuls and baked (dropped biscuits), even pounded with a mallet so they puff up on heating (beaten biscuits). Whatever the form, biscuits should be prepared as rapidly as possible and handled as little as possible.

Whenever members of the First Families traveled aboard the presidential yacht or spent time away at Camp David, their meals were prepared by Navy personnel. Over the years, the First Families have reported that the Navy "grub" was always excellent, especially appreciated because of the outdoor activity and travel that heightens appetites. One of the specialties served by the Navy cooks is homemade biscuits. In July 1970, Prince Charles and Princess Ann lunched aboard the presidential yacht, the *Sequoia*: Orange Biscuits were served, specially prepared by Navy cooks for the Nixons and their royal guests.

Makes 12 to 16

2 cups flour
1 teaspoon salt
4 teaspoons baking powder
Finely grated rind of
  1 medium-size orange

3 tablespoons butter, softened
Juice of 1 orange
½ cup sour cream

1. Preheat oven to 400°F.
2. Sift together flour, salt, and baking powder. Add orange rind.
3. Use a pastry cutter to cut the butter into the dry ingredients. Add orange juice and sour cream; blend lightly.
4. Turn onto a lightly floured board and roll out to ¾-inch thickness.
5. Use a 2-inch cutter to make 12 to 16 rounds; arrange on nonstick baking sheets, leaving 2 inches between the rounds.
6. Bake on middle shelf of preheated oven for 8 minutes, or until biscuits rise about ½ inch and the tops are lightly browned.
7. Cool on wire racks or serve hot, with butter and orange marmalade for breakfast, or plain for an unusual dinner roll.

Mrs. Nixon adored bananas, so there was always a bunch on hand in the White House. Fortunately, any overripe fruit was not wasted because, like many American families, the Nixons loved home-made banana bread. The Nixons liked apricot-nut and date-nut quick breads, too, but banana bread was always their number-one choice, especially with Julie and her husband, David Eisenhower.

From a chef's point of view, it was highly gratifying to serve meals at the White House to a guest like young David Eisenhower. A hearty eater, David was always a polite and enthusiastic diner. During the Nixon administration, Julie and David spent many of their weekends at the White House. And as a child, David had been a regular guest at the White House when his grandfather was the President. Even then, David was a grateful diner and a chef's delight. After his eighth birthday, David sent President Eisenhower's French chef a thank-you note for preparing all of the party fare, which he pronounced "very, very, very, very good."

NIXON-EISENHOWER BANANA BREAD

A wholesome, all-American couple, Julie and David Eisenhower first met as eight-year-olds, while attending President Eisenhower's second inauguration. The daughter of the Vice-President and the grandson of the President did not see each other again until they were freshmen at neighboring colleges in Massachusetts. One month before the Nixons moved into the White House, Julie and David were wed in a private ceremony. Julie wore the same blue garter worn by Mamie when she married Lieutenant Dwight Eisenhower on July 1, 1916.

Makes 2 loaves

1 stick (½ cup) butter, softened
1 cup sugar
3 eggs
3½ cups flour
4 teaspoons baking powder

2 teaspoons salt
3 very ripe medium-size
   bananas, puréed
1½ cups chopped walnuts

1. Preheat oven to 325°F. Grease two 9 × 5-inch loaf pans and dust lightly with flour.
2. Cream butter with sugar in a large mixing bowl.
3. Beat in eggs one at a time, mixing well after each addition.
4. Sift together flour, baking powder, and salt. Fold into egg mixture.
5. Fold in banana purée and chopped nuts.
6. Divide batter evenly between prepared pans, filling each slightly more than half full. Smooth tops, using a plastic spatula.
7. Bake in preheated oven for 40 minutes, or until top is golden brown and toothpick inserted in center comes out clean. Cool on wire racks before removing from pans and slicing to desired thickness.

NIXON FAMILY
FAVORITE DESSERTS

BAKED ALASKA
FLAMBÉ

When America's first minister to France returned home in 1789, he shared a new and elaborate French recipe with his dinner guests, and eventually with the rest of the country. The rich French ice cream was served in Thomas Jefferson's special way, scooped into individual balls, each wrapped in a warm crust of pastry. Thus, Thomas Jefferson "invented" Baked Alaska, some 150 years before anyone else considered serving cold ice cream as a hot dessert.

An old-fashioned fancy dessert, Baked Alaska is still a popular way to present ice cream. The Nixons were fond of the flamed dessert, although such sweets were included on family menus only when guests were expected for dinner. The Nixons liked the meringue and sponge cake shell to envelop a triple combination of vanilla and pistachio ice cream and raspberry sorbet.

Baked Alaska Flambé may be regarded as the dish that most resembles the White House itself: The flaming white dessert can be an impressive sight in a darkened dining room, just like the brilliant white mansion illuminated at night by bright flood lights. In fact, the practice of spotlighting the White House was first implemented during the Nixon administration.

Serves 10

One 9-inch layer SPONGE CAKE, preferably 3 to 4 days old
¾ cup brandy
¼ cup SUGAR SYRUP
1 pint pistachio ice cream, softened
1 pint raspberry sorbet, softened
1 pint vanilla ice cream, softened

10 egg whites, at room temperature
¼ cup confectioners' sugar
2½ cups granulated sugar
1 cup hot water
1 teaspoon vanilla
Candied fruit (optional)

1. Cut SPONGE CAKE into 9 × 4-inch rounded oblong and set in a foil-lined baking pan. Slice remaining cake into very thin slivers and set aside.

2. Mix ¼ cup of the brandy with the SUGAR SYRUP; use a pastry brush to coat the oblong sponge cake with some of the syrup.

3. Spread the pistachio ice cream evenly on top of the sponge cake. Top with an even layer of raspberry sorbet, and then a layer of vanilla ice cream.

4. Cover the ice cream completely with the cake slivers and press firmly in place; brush with more of the SUGAR SYRUP. Freeze until serving time.

5. Just before serving, make an Italian meringue: In a clean, dry bowl, beat the egg whites with confectioners' sugar until stiff. In a saucepan, mix the granulated sugar with hot water and bring to a boil; cook until syrup reaches the soft ball stage (235°F on a candy thermometer). Pour hot syrup gradually into the stiff egg whites in a very thin stream, beating constantly. Beat in vanilla and continue beating until very stiff.

6. Preheat oven to 425°F. Remove ice cream cake from freezer.

7. Use a metal cake spatula to spread meringue evenly over the ice cream cake. (For a more decorative effect, use a pastry bag fitted with a star tube and filled with more of the meringue to create fluted swirls across the top; garnish with colorful candied fruit.)

8. Bake on middle shelf of preheated oven for 5 to 6 minutes, or until golden brown; turn the pan around once to brown evenly, and watch carefully to prevent burning.

9. Flame by warming the remaining ½ cup of brandy and pouring around the outer edges of the dessert; light with a match, and serve at once.

SPONGE CAKE

Makes one 9-inch layer

4 eggs, separated, at room
  temperature
½ cup confectioners' sugar

Grated peel of 1 lemon
⅞ cup (14 tablespoons) cake
  flour

1. Preheat oven to 325°F. Brush a cake pan with butter and dust lightly with flour.

2. In a mixing bowl, beat egg yolks with sugar and lemon rind until fluffy.

3. In a clean, dry bowl, beat egg whites until stiff; fold into yolks. Fold in flour.

4. Pour into prepared pan and bake on lower shelf of preheated oven for 30 minutes, or until golden brown and firm to the touch. (A toothpick inserted in the center should come out clean.)

5. Remove and let stand for 5 minutes before turning out onto a wire rack to cool.

SUGAR SYRUP   Makes 1 cup

⅓ cup sugar   *1 cup warm water*

1. In a small saucepan, mix sugar with warm water and bring to a boil.
2. Simmer for 5 minutes, to reduce by one-quarter.
3. Strain syrup into a small container. (Syrup keeps well under refrigeration.)

MACADAMIA NUT SOUFFLÉ

American Presidents have had varied appetites, and some were not very disciplined with their diets. Grover Cleveland reportedly weighed around 250 pounds, and was very fond of rich foods and domestic beers. William Taft weighed between 300 and 350 pounds while residing in the White House, and his wife had an enormous bathtub installed, designed specifically to fit "Big Bill." Ulysses S. Grant was not a thin president either, which is not surprising considering that his memorable White House meals included as many as 29 courses.

President Nixon loved the taste of macadamia nuts. A sweet soufflé flavored with the rich nuts and served with a light Kirsch sauce became one of his favorite White House desserts. Since the Nixons also loved ice cream, it seemed apropos to devise a recipe for homemade macadamia nut ice cream, to be served with a dollop of freshly whipped cream. As the family's cook in California, Fina Sanchez had to convince a local market to keep several pints of macadamia nut ice cream in stock to satisfy the Nixons' occasional urges to splurge. On a very special occasion, the Nixons' dessert menu might include one or the other of these desserts.

Serves 4 to 6

4 tablespoons butter   *A pinch of salt*
½ cup flour   *A pinch of cream of tartar*
1 cup hot milk   *⅓ cup granulated sugar*
4 egg yolks   *¾ cup finely ground roasted*
4 drops vanilla extract   *macadamia nuts*
6 egg whites, at room   *Confectioners' sugar*
*   temperature*

1. Preheat oven to 350°F. Brush the inside of a 1½-quart soufflé dish with soft butter and sprinkle with granulated sugar.
2. Melt butter in a 1-quart saucepan, add flour, and work into a roux. Cook briefly over low heat to get rid of the raw taste of the flour.
3. Add hot milk and stir with a wire whisk until smooth.
4. Cook for 1 minute, stirring constantly with a plastic or wooden spoon. Remove from heat and let cool slightly.

5. Add egg yolks one at a time, mixing until smooth; stir in vanilla.

6. In a mixing bowl, beat egg whites with salt and cream of tartar until soft peaks form; add the granulated sugar gradually, beating constantly until very stiff.

7. Add about one-fifth of the stiff egg whites to the egg yolk mixture and blend until smooth; transfer to a mixing bowl.

8. Fold in the rest of the egg whites and the ground nuts.

9. Pour into prepared mold to about ½ inch from the rim.

10. Bake on middle shelf of preheated oven for 35 minutes, or until golden brown and puffed 1½ to 2 inches above the rim. Dust with confectioners' sugar and serve at once, plain or with a sauceboat of CRÈME ANGLAISE AU KIRSCH.

CRÈME ANGLAISE AU KIRSCH

Makes 2 cups

5 egg yolks
½ cup sugar
1 cup cold milk

1 cup hot milk
½ teaspoon vanilla extract
1 tablespoon Kirsch

1. In the top of a double boiler, mix egg yolks with sugar using a wire whisk.

2. Add cold milk and blend with the wire whisk until smooth.

3. Stir in hot milk; cook slowly over medium heat, stirring with a plastic or wooden spoon, for about 7 minutes, or until almost at the boiling point. Custard should be smooth and coat the spoon.

4. Remove double boiler from heat and stir over a bowl of ice until cool.

5. Stir in vanilla and Kirsch; strain before serving.

MACADAMIA NUT ICE CREAM

Makes 1½ quarts

1 cup sugar
10 egg yolks
2 cups cold half-and-half
2 cups hot half-and-half

1½ cups macadamia nuts,
 lightly toasted and coarsely
 ground
2 tablespoons Kirsch (optional)

1. In a large mixing bowl, blend sugar with egg yolks and cold half-and-half.

2. Stir in the hot half-and-half, using a wire whisk.

3. Transfer to the top of a double boiler and cook, stirring con-

stantly with a plastic or wooden spoon, until the mixture coats the spoon. Do not boil.

4. Remove double boiler from heat; set in a bowl of ice and stir until cooled. Strain.

5. Add nuts and, if desired, flavor with Kirsch.

6. Freeze in an ice cream maker, following the manufacturer's directions, until ice cream reaches the desired consistency. Serve with whipped cream, if desired. Store in the freezer.

APPLE CHARLOTTE

A charlotte is a lovely French dessert that is piled high in a lined mold: Charlotte Russe is made with Bavarian cream set in a lining of ladyfingers and served cold; fruit charlottes are made with sweetened fruits set in a bread lining and are served warm. Apple appears to have been the original flavor and still reigns as the favorite, but charlottes can be prepared using a variety of fruits, including apricots, peaches, pears, and plums.

Pomme is French for apple, but a number of spherical foods have also been called by either of these names: *pommes de terre* are earth apples, better known as potatoes; the pomegranate is also called the Chinese apple; in Italy, the golden apple or *pomo d'oro* eventually became the "*pomodoro*," or tomato, known to the French as the *pomme d'amour*, or "love apple." And then there is the pineapple, the inedible Adam's apple, even New York's Big Apple.

During my apprenticeship in Switzerland, one of the dishes I had to prepare for an important exam was an Apple Charlotte. Although I had never made the dish before, the three chefs who graded me were quite pleased and awarded me the top score.

Apple Charlotte is delicious topped with a warm fruit sauce, such as applesauce or Apricot Sauce. At the small dinner parties served in the Family Dining Room, the Nixons liked to offer guests a pretty, high-scoring dessert such as fruit charlotte, especially this Apple Charlotte served with warm Apricot Sauce and Sweet Whipped Cream.

Serves 8 to 10

16 slices firm white bread,
    crusts removed
2 sticks (1 cup) butter, softened
1 cup seedless white raisins
½ cup dry white wine
2½ pounds tart green apples,
    peeled, cored, and thinly
    sliced

1 teaspoon cinnamon
Grated peel of 2 lemons
¾ cup sugar
½ cup APRICOT SAUCE
2 cups SWEET WHIPPED CREAM

Charlotte Russe was a favorite dessert on President Polk's White House dinner menus. Perhaps a sweet dessert was one of their only indulgences, as the strict Polks banned drinking, dancing, and card playing in the White House. President McKinley was a more lively entertainer, and his 8- to 12-course White House meals often ended with Chantilly Charlotte, flavored with "essence of violets." Desserts served at President Johnson's very lively dinner parties included Charlotte Monticello, a Charlotte Russe spiked with an orange-flavored liqueur such as Cointreau or Grand Marnier.

1. Preheat oven to 350°F.
2. Cut bread into 2 × 3-inch strips, and brush generously with soft butter.
3. Line the sides of a Charlotte mold evenly with about one-third of the bread strips, overlapping them slightly.
4. Cut remaining bread strips diagonally in half to make triangular shapes. Line the bottom of the Charlotte mold with most of the bread triangles in a spokelike pattern.
5. Mix raisins with wine.
6. Melt the remaining butter in a nonstick sauté pan, add the apples and sauté with cinnamon and grated lemon, until tender.
7. Add the sugar, raisins, and wine. Cook over high heat for 10 minutes, stirring occasionally.
8. Pour into the bread-lined Charlotte mold; cover top evenly with the remaining bread triangles.
9. Bake on lower shelf of preheated oven for 50 minutes to 1 hour, until the Charlotte is firm and the top crust is lightly browned; if top layer becomes too brown before the Charlotte is fully baked, cover with foil.
10. Let cool for 30 minutes on wire rack before unmolding onto a deep serving platter. Serve with bowls of warm APRICOT SAUCE and SWEET WHIPPED CREAM.

APRICOT SAUCE

Makes 1½ cups

1 cup dried apricots
1 cup warm water

1 cup hot water
¼ cup sugar

1. Soak apricots in warm water for 1 hour. Transfer to a saucepan.
2. Add hot water and sugar, and bring to a boil.
3. Cook over medium heat for 20 minutes. Let cool slightly.
4. Purée in blender, and serve warm.

SWEET WHIPPED CREAM

Makes 2 cups

1 cup very cold heavy cream
4 teaspoons sugar

2 drops vanilla extract

1. In a cold mixing bowl, whip cream with sugar and vanilla until very stiff.
2. Refrigerate until serving time.

BOSTON CREAM PIE

Boston Cream Pie is not really a pie per se, but a custard-filled cake topped with an apricot glaze and coated with chocolate fondant that was first created at the famous Parker House hotel in Boston. The sponge cake layers are made especially light in order to prevent the custard from extruding. Yet eating the dessert still tends to be a somewhat messy affair, so Boston Cream Pie has earned a reputation for being a lunch counter dessert. However, the Nixons liked to serve their guests the custard cake in spite of the sloppy reputation, and the cream-filled dessert was always a hit at the White House.

Other "messy" desserts served to the Nixons' White House guests included frosted coconut cake, cream-topped angel food cake, and juicy apple, blueberry, and strawberry pies. The Nixons also liked to offer guests an old-fashioned version of Boston Cream Pie called Martha Washington Cream Pie. With sticky red currant jelly spread between the cream-filled cake layers and a dusting of confectioners' sugar on the top, this "pie" was perhaps the messiest dessert served at the White House. And it was always a hit as well.

Opposite page: A private dinner with the President, the Vice-President, their wives, and guests.

Rich Sponge Cake

Makes three 9-inch "pies"

1¼ cups sugar
10 eggs, at room temperature
1 teaspoon vanilla extract

3 cups sifted cake flour
1 stick (½ cup) butter, melted
  and cooled to lukewarm

1. Preheat oven to 350°F. Grease three 9-inch cake pans and dust lightly with flour.
2. In a mixing bowl, beat together sugar and eggs until thick and fluffy; add vanilla.
3. Gradually fold in flour and melted butter.
4. Divide batter evenly among the prepared pans.
5. Bake on lower shelf of preheated oven for 20 minutes, or until golden brown and firm to the touch.
6. Let cool completely on wire racks before removing cakes from pans.

Custard Cream

1 cup cold milk
3 tablespoons flour
5 tablespoons cornstarch
¾ cup sugar
4 egg yolks

1 cup hot milk
1 teaspoon vanilla extract
¾ cup heavy cream, whipped
  stiff

1. In a mixing bowl, combine cold milk with flour, cornstarch, sugar, and egg yolks. Beat together with a wire whisk until smooth.
2. Add hot milk, stirring constantly with the wire whisk. Transfer to a heavy saucepan.
3. Bring to a boil over medium heat, stirring constantly with the wire whisk; as custard thickens, stir constantly with a plastic or wooden spoon.

4. Boil for 1 minute, add vanilla, and remove from heat. Transfer to a mixing bowl and chill over ice, stirring occasionally. Refrigerate for 2 to 3 hours.

5. Whisk stiffly whipped cream into very cold custard. Keep refrigerated.

Apricot Glaze

1 cup apricot jelly or strained   2 tablespoons water
   apricot preserves

1. In the top of a double boiler placed over boiling water, mix jelly with water.

2. Stir until melted, and keep warm.

Chocolate Fondant

1½ cups confectioners' sugar   A pinch of cream of tartar
½ cup hot water   2 ounces semisweet chocolate

1. Sift 1 cup of the confectioners' sugar into a small mixing bowl.

2. Stir in hot water and cream of tartar.

3. Transfer to a stainless steel saucepan; boil until mixture forms a thin, clear syrup, about 5 minutes.

4. Stirring with a wooden spoon, add remaining confectioners' sugar until mixture coats the spoon.

5. In the top of a double boiler, melt chocolate; add to fondant.

6. Keep fondant at 90°F until use to preserve maximum brilliance; refrigerate extra for later use.

To assemble Boston Cream Pie:

1. Split the cold sponge cakes in half lengthwise, using a long serrated knife.

2. Divide custard cream evenly among the cakes; spread evenly onto the bottoms and gently replace the tops.

3. Use a pastry brush to spread a thin layer of apricot glaze on top of each cake.

4. Spread tops evenly with chocolate fondant, using a metal cake spatula.

5. Return pies to cake pans to maintain structure; refrigerate for 1 hour or more.

6. When fondant has hardened, cut each pie into 6 to 8 wedges.

Even before the turn of the century, "messy" cream pies were served in the White House. To properly prepare the less-practiced diner, the 1887 edition of The White House Cook Book *advised as one of the "Small Points on Table Etiquette": "A cream cake should always be eaten with knife and fork, never bitten." In addition to a recipe for Boston Cream Pie, the old cookbook included a similar recipe for Washington Pie, with another sensible suggestion:*

In the summertime, it is a good plan to bake the pie the day before it is

Key limes were brought over to Florida and the Caribbean by sixteenth-century Spanish and Portuguese explorers. Key limes are not cultivated on a large scale because the yield tends to be too small to grow them profitably on a commercial basis. Most of the Key lime trees grow wild along the Florida Keys, the hundred-mile stretch of islands off the southernmost tip of the state. The locations of the few commercial groves in existence have been kept secret in order to guard against Key lime poachers.

Authentic Key Lime Pie is not really green in color, but yellowish. This is because the Key lime is actually a tiny yellow fruit. Most lime pies are prepared with the more common Persian lime, a larger and greener fruit. Key limes are typically sold only in markets near where they are grown.

President Nixon grew so fond of the Key lime pie served at a hotel restaurant he frequented on Key Biscayne that Mrs. Nixon requested the recipe from the hotel chef. Since fresh Key limes were not available in Washington, bottled Key lime juice was substituted for the fruit. Another delicious version of lime pie, which was usually prepared with the more common Persian limes, became one of Mrs. Nixon's favorite desserts to serve to White House dinner guests. The recipe yields a lime chiffon pie, which is like a lime mousse in a baked pie shell. For Key lime pie lovers who cannot find Key lime juice or extract, Mrs. Nixon's Florida Lime Pie is a more accessible substitute. A few drops of green food coloring can be added to the lime juice if desired.

MRS. NIXON'S FLORIDA LIME PIE

Makes one 9-inch pie

1 cup sugar	1 teaspoon grated lime rind
1/4 teaspoon salt	4 egg whites, at room
1 package (1/4 ounce) unflavored	temperature
gelatin	1 fully baked 9-inch PIE CRUST
1/4 cup water	(page 18)
1/2 cup lime juice	SWEET WHIPPED CREAM (page
4 egg yolks	112)

1. In the top of a double boiler, combine 1/2 cup sugar with the salt, gelatin, and water.

2. In a small bowl, combine the lime juice with the egg yolks; stir into the gelatin mixture in the double boiler, using a wire whisk.

3. Cook for about 7 minutes, or until gelatin dissolves and mixture thickens.

4. Remove from heat and stir in lime rind.

(con't)
wanted; then when cool, wrap around it a paper and place it in the ice box so as to have it get *very* cold; *then serve it with a dish of fresh strawberries or raspberries. A delicious dessert.*

Refrigerated in order to protect the filling, cream pies can be safe desserts as well.

5. Place pan in a bowl of ice water, stirring occasionally as mixture cools.

6. In a large clean, dry bowl, beat egg whites until stiff; gradually add the remaining ½ cup of sugar, beating constantly.

7. Fold cooled lime mixture into stiff egg whites, using a plastic spatula.

8. Turn into prebaked pie shell and refrigerate for several hours, or until set. Cover pie with SWEET WHIPPED CREAM and keep refrigerated until serving time.

TRICIA'S CHOCOLATE CHIP COOKIES

The following anecdote may explain why President Nixon was so disciplined with his diet, and especially restrained about desserts: On May 8, 1952, Richard Nixon gave a successful speech in New York for an annual fund-raising dinner given by the Republican party. After he received a standing ovation, young Nixon shook hands with Governor Dewey, who told him, "That was a terrific speech. Make me a promise: don't get fat, don't lose your zeal, and you can be President some day."

After the pastry chef learned that Tricia Nixon often craved cookies, the White House kitchen was continually stocked with several different kinds of freshly baked treats. Some of the White House specialties included almond cookies and hazelnut cookies, mini eclairs and mini cream puffs, fresh fruit tartelettes, petit fours of various types, brownies, and chocolate chip cookies. Tricia delighted in sampling everything baked by the White House pastry chef, whom she always described with enthusiasm as "just excellent!"

A naturally petite young woman, Tricia was fortunate to escape the weight-watching woes suffered by many of her peers. She was also a chef's delight, openly pleased with the food served at the White House. Tricia once hosted a lively Masked Ball, and sent a sweet note of thanks to the White House kitchen a few days later.

Makes 50 cookies

1½ sticks (¾ cup) butter, softened	1 teaspoon baking soda
¾ cup sugar	1 tablespoon water
1 egg	1 teaspoon vanilla extract
1 egg white	2½ cups cake flour
1 teaspoon salt	8 ounces semisweet chocolate chips

1. Preheat oven to 350°F. Grease baking sheets and dust lightly with flour.

2. In a mixing bowl, cream butter with sugar. Beat in egg, egg white, and salt.

3. In a small bowl, dissolve soda in water; add to batter, and stir in vanilla.

4. Stir in flour until well-blended.

5. Fold in chocolate chips; do not overmix.

6. Drop by teaspoonfuls onto prepared baking sheets; leave 1½ inches between cookies to allow for spreading.

7. Bake on lower shelf of preheated oven for 15 minutes, or until golden.

8. Let cool on wire racks before serving; store in an airtight container.

Brownies prepared in slightly different versions have been enjoyed by each of the First Families I have served in the White House. Like chocolate chip cookies, the chocolate-flavored bar cookie is an all-American favorite, popular with people of all ages and from all walks of life.

Sequoia Brownies are rich and chewy, made with chopped walnuts and thickly iced with chocolate frosting. Named after the presidential yacht, the brownies were often served to the Nixons and their guests as they cruised the Potomac. When Prince Charles and Princess Anne had lunch aboard the *Sequoia* during their visit to Washington in July 1970, Sequoia Brownies were on the menu.

President Nixon eloquently described the pleasures of dining aboard the *Sequoia* after his final cruise on August 5, 1974: "Out on the river the evening was beautiful. The breeze off the water stirred the sultry air, and we sat on the topdeck watching the sunset." Certainly, a homemade brownie savored in the relaxed atmosphere of a sunset river cruise can taste better than almost anything else.

Makes 16

2 squares (2 ounces) unsweetened chocolate	1 teaspoon vanilla extract
1 stick (½ cup) butter	½ cup sifted flour
1 cup sugar	1 cup chopped walnuts
2 eggs	BROWNIE FROSTING

1. Preheat oven to 325°F. Grease an 8-inch square pan and dust lightly with flour.

2. Melt chocolate in the top of a double boiler set over hot water, and let cool.

3. Cream butter with sugar; add eggs and beat well.

SEQUOIA BROWNIES

The Kennedys enjoyed cruising on the presidential yacht almost as much as they liked eating chocolate. President Kennedy's younger brother Robert was designated as the clan's most devoted chocolate fan. President Kennedy preferred light desserts such as angel food cake or fresh strawberry tarts. But he liked to tease his brother by joking with journalists about Bobby Kennedy's "favorite dessert": chocolate cake with chocolate frosting, served with chocolate ice cream and chocolate sauce!

4. Blend in melted chocolate, vanilla, and flour; stir in nuts.

5. Pour into prepared pan and bake in preheated oven for 35 minutes. Let cool completely on wire rack before icing with BROWNIE FROSTING; cut into 16 even squares. Serve with vanilla ice cream and/or whipped cream, if desired.

BROWNIE FROSTING

Makes enough to frost 2 batches

1 square (1 ounce) unsweetened chocolate
1½ cups sugar
1 tablespoon corn syrup

A pinch of salt
½ cup milk
2 tablespoons butter
1 teaspoon vanilla extract

1. Melt chocolate in the top of a double boiler, set over hot water.

2. Stir in sugar, syrup, salt, and milk. Cook over low heat until sugar dissolves and reaches the soft ball stage (235°F on a candy thermometer).

3. Remove from heat; mix in butter, and cool until just warm (110°F).

4. Add vanilla and beat to spreading consistency.

5. Frost brownies and let set before cutting into squares. Frosting can be kept for several weeks if refrigerated in an airtight container.

TRICIA'S FANCY NAPOLEONS

The Napoleon is a popular American pastry composed of several thin layers of puff paste that are cut in rectangular strips and layered with custard cream. The layers are lightly spread with an apricot glaze to prevent the custard and the white fondant from seeping into the pastry. The top is decorated with wavy lines of chocolate icing in the familiar pattern that characterizes the Napoleon. This rich, pretty pastry was named after Napoleon Bonaparte, emperor of France during the early part of the nineteenth century. However, the pastry has always been called "mille-feuille" in France, which means a thousand layers—a slight exaggeration, to be sure.

Tricia was very fond of Napoleons and other sweets. For her wedding reception, she selected seven different pastries to be served with the Lady Baltimore wedding cake.

Makes 12

Follow recipe on page 346 through step 9. **Puff Paste**

1. Preheat oven to 400°F. Moisten baking sheet with water.
2. Roll out puff paste to ⅛-inch thickness and cut into 3 long strips, each 4 × 16 inches. Arrange strips on wet sheet and let set for at least 20 minutes; use a fork to prick the puff paste thoroughly.
3. Bake in preheated oven for 15 minutes, or until crisp and golden brown; turn each layer around at least once while cooking to brown evenly. Let cool.
4. Using a serrated knife, cut each strip into four 4 × 4-inch squares.

Follow recipe under BOSTON CREAM PIE *(page 112).* **Custard Cream**

Follow recipe under BOSTON CREAM PIE *(page 112).* **Apricot Glaze**

1½ cups confectioners' sugar   *A pinch of cream of tartar*   **White Fondant**
½ cup hot water

1. Sift 1 cup of the confectioners' sugar into a small mixing bowl. Stir in hot water and cream of tartar.
2. Transfer to a stainless steel saucepan; boil until mixture forms a thin, clear syrup, about 5 minutes.
3. Stir with a wooden spoon, and add remaining confectioners' sugar until mixture coats the spoon.
4. Keep fondant at 90°F until use to preserve maximum brilliance.

Follow recipe under BOSTON CREAM PIE *(page 112).* **Chocolate Fondant**

To assemble the pastry:
1. Brush 4 squares of pastry with a very thin coat of apricot glaze; spread a thick layer of custard cream on each and top with another pastry square.
2. Brush second layer of each pastry with apricot glaze; add another thick layer of custard cream to each, and place the final 4 pastry squares upside down atop each pastry to form a smooth surface.

3. Brush tops of pastries with apricot glaze and spread evenly with a coating of white fondant. Use a paper funnel to squeeze on the chocolate fondant, drawing 3 thin lines down the length of each pastry top.

4. Use a sharp knife to cut through the fondant lines crosswise at 1-inch intervals, creating the decorative wavelike pattern characteristic of Napoleons.

5. Keep chilled until serving time.

SPECIAL EVENT RECIPES

BAKED OYSTERS WHITE HOUSE

Every Friday during the Nixon administration, the White House kitchen submitted a menu plan for the following week to Mrs. Nixon for her approval. The menus for impending State Dinners, however, had to be planned several weeks in advance. Mrs. Nixon was usually pleased with the proposed menus and made few changes. President Nixon selected the wines to complement both the informal family meals and the formal dinner menus.

The White House wine cellar offered President Nixon a good selection of excellent wines. He generally preferred French wines, but included a variety of wines on the White House menus. The President liked German wines with fish, California red wine with meat, and a French champagne with dessert. At some special events, only American wines were served.

French cuisine prevailed on the menus for the Nixons' State Dinners. Unlike the more casual Johnson family, the Nixons preferred the decorum of "white tie" dress, receiving lines, and full pomp and circumstance. Their White House state dinners reverted to the formality of the Eisenhower administration and the classic menu style of the Kennedy era.

French foods tend to make a nice presentation, which is an important aspect of any official White House function. When Great

Britain's Secretary of State for Foreign and Commonwealth Affairs was the Nixons' honored guest at the White House, the State Dinner menu included a number of classic French dishes: *Paillettes dorées* (French cheese sticks), Beef Wellington stuffed with duxelles and French goose liver, and a *Sauce Périgueux* made with French truffles.

Baked Oysters White House, the first course served at the State Dinner in honor of Sir Alec Douglas-Home, is actually an American dish. The recipe is a slight variation on the classic Oysters Rockefeller, a popular dish that was created in 1899 by Chef Jules Alciatore of Antoine's Restaurant in New Orleans. Long a favorite of the Nixons, Oysters Rockefeller was their dish of choice when the President took his young wife to Antoine's to celebrate their very first wedding anniversary.

By some accounts, Oysters Rockefeller was named as such because the dish is so rich, like the famous New York family. But perhaps the dish should have been called "Oysters Casanova" after the famous lover, who once referred to oysters as "a spur to the spirits and to love." State Dinner guests have been almost as romantic in their praise of the popular Baked Oysters White House.

Serves 6

3 *dozen fresh oysters*	2 *tablespoons Worcestershire*
3 *tablespoons butter*	*sauce*
3 *tablespoons minced shallots*	4 *tablespoons Pernod*
2 *garlic cloves, finely minced*	1 *cup warm (95°F)* BÉARNAISE
3 *cups cooked fresh spinach,*	SAUCE
finely chopped, or defrosted	½ *cup warm (95°F) fish*
frozen, well drained	VELOUTÉ SAUCE
1 *teaspoon salt*	A *pinch of cayenne pepper*
A *pinch of freshly ground*	¾ *cup heavy cream, whipped*
white pepper	*Sprigs of fresh parsley*
A *pinch of nutmeg*	*Lemon wedges*

1. Remove top shells from oysters and broil for 3 minutes, or until oysters are slightly shrunken and lightly firmed. Do not overcook. Keep warm.

2. Arrange empty oyster shells in a foil-lined baking pan and set aside.

3. Melt butter in a saucepan, add shallots and garlic and sauté until golden brown.

4. Add spinach, and season with salt, pepper, nutmeg, and Worcestershire sauce.

5. Cook over medium heat, stirring constantly, for 3 minutes, or until mixture is heated through. Remove from heat.

6. Stir in Pernod.

7. Preheat oven to 425°F.

8. Gently mix the warm BÉARNAISE SAUCE with a thick fish VELOUTÉ SAUCE (they should be at equal temperature—about 95°F—to prevent separating). Add cayenne pepper. Fold whipped cream into the sauce.

9. Place a spoonful of the hot spinach mixture on each oyster shell. Top each with a cooked oyster, and press firmly in place.

10. Cover each oyster with a spoonful of sauce, and bake in preheated oven for 5 minutes, or until golden brown.

11. Serve at once on a napkin-lined serving platter and garnish with sprigs of fresh parsley and lemon wedges.

BÉARNAISE SAUCE

SPECIAL EVENT RECIPE

Makes 2 cups

¼ cup white wine vinegar
¼ cup dry white wine
Juice of ½ lemon
12 black peppercorns, crushed
12 white peppercorns, crushed
1 tablespoon minced shallots
1 teaspoon dried tarragon

2 tablespoons cold water
5 egg yolks
1½ cups CLARIFIED BUTTER
    (page 43), warmed to 95°F
½ teaspoon salt
1 tablespoon minced fresh
    tarragon leaves

1. In a small saucepan, combine vinegar with wine; stir in lemon juice, black and white peppercorns, shallots, and dried tarragon.

2. Bring to a boil over medium-high heat; simmer until reduced to 2 tablespoons of liquid.

3. Remove from heat and stir in cold water. Strain through cheesecloth into the top of a double boiler.

4. Stir in egg yolks, and whip for 1 minute to blend well, using a wire whisk.

5. Set pan over *simmering* water; continue to stir with the whisk.

6. Cook for 5 minutes, stirring constantly, until sauce is thickened and smooth. Do not overheat or eggs will curdle.

7. Remove pan from heat and continue stirring for 2 minutes as sauce cools.

8. Gradually stir in warm butter, mixing with the whisk until butter is well absorbed and sauce appears thick and creamy.

9. Stir in salt and fresh tarragon. Keep warm until use in the top of the double boiler set over warm water.

VELOUTÉ SAUCE

Makes 1 cup

2 tablespoons plus 1 teaspoon
   butter
2 tablespoons plus 1 teaspoon
   flour
1 cup hot fish, chicken or veal
   stock

A pinch of freshly ground
   white pepper
A pinch of nutmeg

1. Melt butter in a small saucepan, add flour, and mix well to make a roux. Cook over low heat for 2 minutes, stirring constantly.

2. Add hot stock, bring to a boil, and stir with a wire whisk until smooth.

3. Add pepper and nutmeg and simmer over low heat for 10 minutes. Strain sauce before use.

NEW ENGLAND CLAM CHOWDER

It is always a thrill to receive an engraved invitation to a White House party or reception. Regular guests report that the excitement does not diminish with repeated visits, but is rekindled each time the President, First Lady, and honored guests descend the White House staircase to the sound of trumpets playing "Ruffles and Flourishes" and "Hail to the Chief."

For the White House kitchen, the trumpets sound out an important signal. After the President leaves the main stairway to start the receiving line, the Head Butler calls the kitchen so that our timing is exact. The food served at a State Dinner must be transported up a flight of stairs from the Main Kitchen to the Family Dining Room, a room adjoining the State Dining Room that serves as private dining room for small official functions. The room can also serve as a butler's pantry when easy access to the State Dining Room is needed. Hot food must remain hot, and cold food must stay cold. In the White House, a beautifully planned menu could be a disaster if the timing were less than perfect.

White House luncheons also require proper planning and perfect timing by the kitchen staff. President Nixon hosted a number of formal and informal luncheons at the White House. The Chowder and Marching Society, a Republican social group organized by young House members in 1949, once met for lunch at the White House. Even this politically experienced group was visibly moved by the honor of dining in the White House.

The first course served to the club members was—quite appropriately—clam chowder. Chowder received its name from *la chaudière,* the enormous copper pot used in the old French fishing villages: The returning fishermen would toss in part of their catch for a community feast in celebration of their safe return from the sea. New Englanders have always prepared clam chowder with milk, while Manhattan clam chowder has a thin, milk-free broth that includes tomatoes. The Maine legislature once considered a bill that would actually have banned mixing milk with tomatoes! Obviously, New Englanders take their clam chowder seriously.

Serves 6

2 dozen fresh clams, shucked
3 cups clam juice
½ cup finely diced salt pork
1 cup finely diced onions
2 cups finely diced potatoes
2 tablespoons flour

2 cups heavy cream
6 twists freshly ground white
  pepper
2 teaspoons chopped fresh
  parsley

1. In a saucepan, boil clams in clam juice for 3 minutes; remove clams and let cool slightly. Strain broth through cheesecloth and keep warm.

2. Separate the soft part of the clams from the hard part; dice clams very fine.

3. In a large pot, simmer salt pork over low heat for 5 minutes; add onions and sauté until transparent.

4. Add the diced soft clams and diced potatoes, cover, and simmer for 5 minutes.

5. Stir in diced hard clams. Add flour and stir gently with a plastic or wooden spoon.

6. Add most of the hot clam broth. (Do not use the clam juice from the bottom of the pot, which may contain sand.) Bring to a boil and cook for 5 minutes.

7. Stir in cream and pepper and bring to a boil. Remove from heat.

8. Sprinkle with parsley. Serve chowder at once, in mugs or ceramic bowls, with soda crackers or Saltines crumbled on top.

As Secretary of State from 1973 to 1977, Henry Kissinger was a regular guest at State Dinners and other official White House functions. During the Nixon administration, Dr. Kissinger often joined the President for working luncheons, sometimes with visiting dignitaries from foreign countries or key members of the President's staff. The impressive Map Room was a favored dining spot for such luncheons.

Henry Kissinger also served as President Nixon's National Security Advisor. In 1973, Dr. Kissinger was awarded the Nobel Peace Prize after the Peace Agreement was signed in Paris to mark the end of U.S. involvement in Vietnam. Dr. Kissinger was instrumental in working toward detente with the Soviet Union, easing tensions in the Middle East, and resuming diplomatic relations with Egypt and Syria.

Like many of the world leaders served by the White House kitchen, Dr. Kissinger was a sophisticated diner, yet easy to please. As a White House guest, Dr. Kissinger seemed to favor the French menus served by the Nixons. I, too, prefer French cuisine, because it is so enjoyable to prepare and so attractive to present. We also concurred in our appreciation of creamy luncheon broths, like this delicious Chicken Velvet Soup.

CHICKEN VELVET SOUP

SPECIAL EVENT RECIPE

Serves 6

1 quart strong chicken stock, cold
1 cup heavy cream
4 egg yolks

½ cup heavy cream, whipped stiff
1 teaspoon chopped fresh chives

1. In a large saucepan, heat 3 cups of the chicken stock with the cream. Do not boil.
2. In a stainless steel bowl, beat egg yolks with the remaining cup of cold stock, using a wire whisk.
3. Add hot stock to the egg mixture, beating constantly with the wire whisk. Transfer to the saucepan.
4. Bring just to a boil over medium heat, stirring constantly with the wire whisk.
5. Pour into 6 heated mugs or bowls; top each with a dollop of

whipped cream and a sprinkling of chopped chives. Accompany with JEFF'S GEORGIA-STYLE CHEESE STICKS (page 240) or toasted slices of herbed French bread.

CHICKEN AND MUSHROOM CRÊPES

As First Lady, Mrs. Nixon carried on the refurbishing project that Mrs. Kennedy had initiated to restore to the White House the authentic furnishings of the early nineteenth century. Mrs. Nixon completed the redecoration of fourteen rooms, including the Map Room, the Oval Office, the Cabinet Room, and the President's Bedroom. Mrs. Nixon was also able to amass one of the finest collections of American art ever displayed in the White House.

Like her predecessors, Mrs. Kennedy and Mrs. Johnson (and her successors Mrs. Ford, Mrs. Carter, and Mrs. Reagan), Mrs. Nixon was a crêpe fan. She was especially fond of the thin pancakes filled with a rich chicken and mushroom mixture. In Thomas Jefferson's time, the recipe was known as "Filled Pannequaiques."

Mrs. Nixon often included crêpes—with the chicken-mushroom filling or an equally rich crabmeat one—on the menus for the special luncheons she hosted at the White House for those involved in the First Lady's White House projects and for the Senate wives.

Serves 6 as an entrée, 12 as an hors d'oeuvre

Twelve 6-inch CRÊPES
2 tablespoons butter
1 tablespoon minced shallots
2 garlic cloves, finely minced
1 cup diced fresh mushrooms
Juice of 1 lemon
½ teaspoon salt
⅛ teaspoon freshly ground
white pepper
2 tablespoons dry sherry
1 tablespoon Worcestershire
sauce

2 cups diced cooked chicken
1 tablespoon chopped fresh
parsley
2 cups warm (95°F) VELOUTÉ
SAUCE *(page 123), made with*
chicken stock
½ cup warm (95°F) CHEF
HALLER'S HOLLANDAISE SAUCE
(page 41)
1 cup heavy cream, whipped
2 tablespoons grated Parmesan
cheese

1. Butter a large oval ovenproof platter; set aside with crêpes.

2. Melt butter in a sauté pan, add shallots and garlic and sauté until golden brown.

3. Add mushrooms, lemon juice, salt, and pepper, and simmer until liquid has evaporated.

4. Stir in sherry and Worcestershire sauce. Mix in diced chicken and chopped parsley.

5. Fold in 1 cup of the warm VELOUTÉ SAUCE; remove from heat.

6. Spoon this filling evenly into the centers of each of the crêpes and roll up.

7. Place the crêpes, seamless side up, close together on the prepared platter; keep warm.

8. Gently mix the remaining cup of warm VELOUTÉ SAUCE with the HOLLANDAISE SAUCE (they must be the same temperature to keep the sauce from separating).

9. Fold in whipped cream.

10. Spoon sauce evenly over crêpes, sprinkle with cheese, and broil for 1 minute; turn platter around and broil for another minute or so, or until crêpes are evenly browned. Serve at once.

CRÊPES

Makes about 12 crêpes

3 eggs
⅓ cup milk
⅓ cup chicken stock
⅓ cup flour
⅛ teaspoon salt

A pinch freshly ground white pepper
A pinch nutmeg
2 tablespoons melted butter

1. In a small bowl, beat eggs with milk and stock.

2. Place the flour in a mixing bowl; pour in egg mixture, stirring with a wire whisk until smooth.

3. Add the salt, pepper, nutmeg, and melted butter and blend well. Let batter rest for 30 minutes.

4. Brush the inside of a 6-inch crêpe pan or well-seasoned iron skillet with butter and set over high heat. Pour in just enough batter to coat the pan, tilting to spread evenly. Cook for about 1 minute, or until lightly browned. Flip and brown the other side, for 30 seconds or so. (The second side will be spottier in color than the first, which is the "right" or outer side when the crêpe is filled.)

5. Repeat until all the batter is used up, wiping the pan clean with a towel and brushing with additional butter as needed. Keep the finished crêpes covered and warm in a low oven.

SUPRÊME OF SEAFOOD NEPTUNE

The most challenging culinary event of my twenty-plus years at the White House was the sit-down dinner for 1,300 American POWs given during the Nixon administration. The White House kitchen had grown accustomed to serving formal dinners for up to 200 guests with efficiency and expediency, but a sit-down dinner for over 1,000 special visitors presented a real challenge. President Nixon referred to the event as "a tremendous success," but I would have to describe it as an organizational triumph.

The South Lawn of the White House was ablaze with bright orange and yellow striped tents. The largest tent measured 100 × 180 feet in size, even longer than the White House, and held 130 tables for 10 and a center stage. There were 2 smaller service tents adjoining the big tent on either side, each set up to serve 650 as efficiently as possible. Each service tent housed huge portable food warmers, and outside each was a refrigerated military truck plus 2 aluminum Army canoes filled with ice and hundreds of bottles of champagne.

The most pressing concern for the kitchen was to ensure that the service was very fast and very smooth. In order to serve 1,300 seated guests a hot meal, the 130 platters had to be transported from tent to table in seconds. The regular White House staff of 6 butlers had to be augmented with 100 extra waiters, and the kitchen borrowed china, crystal, and silver from a local caterer. We also "borrowed" the Pentagon, where the 90 quarts of strawberries were puréed in a giant blender, and the Washington Hotel, where the 1,300 pounds of beef were roasted in restaurant-size ovens. Everyone seemed eager to help us honor the brave Prisoners of War with a memorable White House party.

The POWs and their families were invited to an open tour of the White House, followed by the sit-down dinner and entertainment by a roster of stars that included Bob Hope, Sammy Davis, Jr., John Wayne, Jimmy Stewart, Phyllis Diller, and Irving Berlin. The meal was planned to suit the tastes of servicemen, so a seafood dish was served before the platters of roast beef. Preparation of the first course was especially demanding since we chose to decorate the 130 molds with 1,300 peeled and glazed cherry tomatoes, 1,300 peeled and glazed shrimp, 1,300 individual rings of hard-boiled egg, and 1,300 sprigs of fresh parsley. The pastry chef decorated the 130 strawberry soufflés with swirls of whipped cream just minutes before serving. A masterpiece of culinary creativity and coordination, the entire meal was served with perfect precision and eaten with visible delight by the 1,300 honored guests.

The program for the POW dinner was inscribed with President Nixon's inspiring request: "Let us resolve anew to be worthy of the sacrifices they have made." The President was equally magnanimous in expressing his gratitude for the sacrifices made by the kitchen staff in contributing to this historic event.

Serves 6 as an entrée, 12 as a first course

1½ cups mayonnaise
2 tablespoons minced shallots
¼ cup horseradish, well
   drained
¾ cup chili sauce
1 teaspoon salt
A pinch of freshly ground
   white pepper
1½ teaspoons Worcestershire
   sauce
6 drops Tabasco sauce
2 envelopes unflavored gelatin
   (½ ounce)

¼ cup white wine
2 cups lump crabmeat
1 cup cooked bay scallops
2 cups cooked tiny shrimp
10 large shrimp, cooked and
   peeled
10 cherry tomatoes
Fresh parsley sprigs
10 to 12 hearts of palm spears
1 large green bell pepper, finely
   minced
2 tablespoons VINAIGRETTE

1. In a large mixing bowl, combine mayonnaise with shallots, horseradish, chili sauce, salt, pepper, Worcestershire sauce, and Tabasco sauce; blend until smooth.

2. In the top of a double boiler, melt gelatin in wine over hot water and stir into the sauce. Fold in crabmeat, scallops, and tiny shrimp. (If frozen seafood is used, drain well on paper towels.)

3. Spoon into a 1½-quart ring mold and chill for several hours or overnight, until firm.

4. Immerse mold in hot water for several seconds, then turn ring out onto a serving platter. Garnish top with whole shrimp, cherry tomatoes, and sprigs of parsley.

5. Arrange hearts of palm spears in the center of the ring. Sprinkle with minced green pepper, and spoon on VINAIGRETTE. Serve at once.

VINAIGRETTE

Makes ½ cup

2 tablespoons cider vinegar
Juice of ½ lemon
1 teaspoon Dijon-style mustard
1 teaspoon finely minced
  shallots

1 garlic clove, finely minced
A pinch of salt
4 twists freshly ground black
  pepper
¼ cup olive oil

1. In a small bowl, blend all ingredients except oil, using a wire whisk.
2. Slowly add oil, blending constantly until thick and smooth. Use at once, or keep refrigerated and whisk briskly before use.

ALL-AMERICAN BURGER

As First Lady, Mrs. Nixon organized an evening entertainment series that was presented at the White House. Each program featured a celebrated figure from the world of music, comedy, or theater, such as Johnny Cash, Glen Campbell, or Red Skelton. When Sammy Davis, Jr., sang for the first time at a White House program, he admitted that he had fulfilled a lifelong dream. Yet when he was given the opportunity to order whatever he chose to eat following his White House performance, the talented singer requested a simple "burger"—with "the works." And he so enjoyed the all-American sandwich that he autographed a program for his grateful fan, the White House chef.

Hamburgers have become an American tradition, practically a staple in a nation where fast food is the norm. In its original form, a hamburger was eaten like a steak and referred to as a "hamburg-steak." Encased in a soft bun, the ground beef sandwich became the burger that spawned the billion-dollar fast-food industry. At one time, in fact, President Nixon's brother owned a chain of restaurants that featured the popular "Nixonburger."

Hamburgers made with lean ground beef often appeared on the family's dinner menus, as well as on informal party menus. In fact, one of the largest events held during the Nixon administration featured burgers for 4,000. After the huge picnic, given by the First Family for the White House staff and their families, both the President and Mrs. Nixon sent thank-you notes to the kitchen staff.

Serves 1

*5 to 6 ounces freshly ground
  lean chuck
A pinch of salt
A pinch of freshly ground
  black pepper*

*1 teaspoon vegetable oil
Hamburger bun*

1. Form meat into a large, thick patty.

2. Season with salt and pepper.

3. In a cast-iron skillet, heat oil until very hot; sauté beef patty until brown on both sides. Do not overcook (no more than 5 minutes for medium rare).

4. Drain on paper towels.

5. Serve at once on a lightly toasted hamburger bun, plain or with a choice of condiments—classics include catsup, mustard, relish, and lettuce leaves, and sliced tomato, onion, and pickle. Burgers can also be topped with bacon strips (not crisp), chili (beanless), guacamole, and a variety of cheeses including blue, cheddar, jack, or the traditional American slices. Chopped onions mixed with the ground beef can also help to moisten the meat and enhance the flavor of the burger.

SAMMY DAVIS, JR.

has been a star of the theatrical profession from birth. He began as a determined, energetic boy from Harlem, working with his father and uncle, Will Mastin. Success came to the Will Mastin Trio on a cross-country night club tour in 1946. When his father and uncle decided to retire, Mr. Davis became an entertainer in his own right.

Mr. Davis' list of achievements is remarkable. He has recorded over 30 albums. His single recordings have sold over 16 million copies and six of these, including *"I Gotta' Be Me"* and *"What Kind of Fool Am I?"*, have become standard favorites. This year saw his first Gold Record, *"Candy Man."* He has appeared on every major nationally televised musical show and is the only star to have made a guest appearance on *"All In the Family"*; the segment received the highest ratings in the history of television. Mr. Davis made his debut on Broadway in *"Mr. Wonderful"* which was followed shortly by *"Golden Boy."* He starred in the movie version of *"Porgy and Bess."*

Not only is Mr. Davis known as an outstanding entertainer, but he is also known for his tireless efforts to aid the underprivileged and share his joy in living with those who are less fortunate. He appears in sixty benefit performances a year. He has been given the highest award of the NAACP, the Alan Bernstein award for cancer research, and honored by the Friars Club and the American Legion.

FRIED SHRIMP WITH COCONUT

Even though I had presided over the cuisine for the wonderful weddings of Luci and Lynda Johnson, I did not find that the extra experience eased the pressure in preparing for Tricia Nixon's wedding reception. White House weddings are expected to be perfect, so the food served also has to be perfect.

Due to inflated food prices, the White House had curtailed unnecessary extravagances in the kitchen. Even for the wedding of his own daughter, President Nixon practiced what he preached by setting an economical example for the nation. For Tricia's wedding reception, the food was served in a buffet with a limited number of dishes and without exotic fare such as caviar. However, the buffet menu overcame in creativity and beauty whatever was lost in budgeting.

Tricia had a penchant for Polynesian-style cuisine. To suit her tastes, the wedding menu submitted weeks before the event included an Oriental-style shrimp dish made with freshly grated coconut. Intrigued by the unusual dish, Tricia requested a taste test prior to the all-important buffet. Fried Shrimp with Coconut was served with the First Family's dinner one evening, and became an immediate family favorite. The dish was introduced to the public for the first time on Tricia Nixon's wedding day.

Only one item on Tricia's buffet menu had been served at a Johnson wedding: The miniature shishkebabs had been so well received at Lynda's reception that Tricia readily agreed with my suggestion that the little skewers of meat be served at her own buffet. Shishkebab is not popular in the White House kitchen, however, because preparation is labor-intensive and time-consuming, especially with 400 guests (Tricia's) or 700 (Lynda's).

Concern had been great over a continuous drizzle on the day of the wedding. Fortunately, the rain held off for the 12-minute ceremony so that the couple was wed as planned, outside in the Rose Garden, where the breathtaking beauty was amplified by the addition of a profusion of flowers.

Hundreds of the eleven different kinds of hors d'oeuvres and the seven types of pastry adorned the long State Dining Room table. Thirty-five formal butlers served domestic champagnes and chilled fruit punch to the excited guests after the wedding ceremony had ended.

Serves 4

2 pounds large raw shrimp
  (about 16)
½ cup flour
1 teaspoon salt
¼ teaspoon freshly ground
  white pepper
4 eggs

A pinch of cayenne pepper
1½ cups coarsely shredded
  unsweetened coconut
1 cup CLARIFIED BUTTER (page
  43)
6 lemon wedges
Fresh parsley sprigs

1. Peel shrimp, leaving fantails intact; slit top side open just wide enough to devein.

2. In a shallow bowl, mix flour with salt and white pepper.

3. In a separate bowl, beat eggs well with cayenne pepper.

4. Dredge each shrimp lightly in flour, dip in egg, and roll in coconut.

5. In a large nonstick sauté pan or cast-iron skillet, heat ½ cup CLARIFIED BUTTER; fry half of the shrimp for 2 minutes on each side, or until golden brown.

6. Remove shrimp to drain on paper towels and wipe pan clean.

7. Heat the remaining ½ cup CLARIFIED BUTTER; fry the rest of the shrimp and drain on paper towels.

8. Arrange hot shrimp on a serving platter. Garnish with lemon wedges and sprigs of parsley, and serve at once, with steamed rice and a sauceboat of SAUCE MAYONNAISE PIQUANT.

SAUCE MAYONNAISE PIQUANT

Makes 1¼ cups

3 tablespoons mango chutney
1 teaspoon Worcestershire
  sauce
3 drops Tabasco sauce

Juice of ½ lemon
1 cup mayonnaise
1 teaspoon chopped fresh
  chives

1. In a small bowl, mix chutney with Worcestershire sauce, Tabasco sauce, and lemon juice. Add mayonnaise and blend well.

2. Add chives and stir. Serve at once, or keep refrigerated in a covered container.

ARTICHOKES SAINT-GERMAIN

As in most American households, it is not easy to keep a secret for very long in the White House. On one occasion, however, the Nixons invited an important guest to dinner at the White House and successfully kept the visitor's identity a secret right up until the time of arrival. The staff knew that the guest was a VIP because Mrs. Nixon had requested a classical menu with a French accent several days in advance. The Maître D' brought in special French wines, and a beautiful meal—including elegant Artichokes Saint-Germain—was prepared on the designated date. Yet, up until a few hours before serving time, we had no idea just who was to be the guest of honor.

At 5:00 P.M., the Maître D' shared the secret, which he had just discovered: The Nixons would be dining at 7:00 P.M. with Mrs. Jacqueline Kennedy and her two children, 13-year-old Caroline and 10-year-old John. The Nixons had invited the Kennedy family to a private viewing of the White House portraits of President and Mrs. Kennedy, freshly hung on the walls of the Lower Hall. This was the first visit to the White House for Mrs. Kennedy since her sorrowful departure in 1963.

At Mrs. Kennedy's request, no one—not the press, the public, or the White House staff—was informed of the former First Lady's impending visit. Thus, on the evening before the public unveiling of Aaron Shikler's impressive portraits, Mrs. Kennedy and her children were able to examine the paintings privately, before joining the Nixon family for a pleasant dinner in the Family Dining Room.

As First Lady, Mrs. Kennedy had set precedents with her own creative menus and unusual ideas for entertainment. During the Kennedy administration, the State Dinners were informal but glamorous, and the meals were simple but of fine French design. The menu that the Nixons served to Mrs. Kennedy was chosen accordingly.

While the parents sipped after-dinner coffee, Tricia and Julie took Caroline and John on a tour of their former home. At this time, I was notified that the President wanted me to join him in the Diplomatic Reception Room. The White House is typically too discreet to invite staff members to meet honored guests, so I was quite surprised to have the honor of meeting the Nixons' special dinner guest.

As elegant and gracious as ever, Mrs. Kennedy extended her hand and thanked me for "a delicious dinner." President Nixon, ever the waist watcher, chimed in, "But the soufflé was very rich." However, none of the diners seemed to have let this fact interfere with their appetites, and the entire meal was a definite success.

Serves 6

½ pound dried split peas
6 large fresh artichokes
½ cup flour
Juice of 2 lemons
2 tablespoons olive oil
1 large Idaho baking potato,
   peeled and thinly sliced

4 tablespoons butter, softened
A pinch of freshly ground
   white pepper
A pinch of nutmeg
2 egg yolks
½ cup heavy cream

1. Soak peas in 3 cups of water for 4 hours, drain, and rinse under cold water. Set aside.

2. Cut off artichoke stems and remove outer leaves to expose artichoke bottoms; use a sharp knife to peel off the woody surface of each artichoke bottom.

3. Slice off tops of artichokes so that each bottom is left with a ¾-inch-high layer of leaves.

4. Mix together the flour and 1½ quarts cold water; carefully wash the artichoke bottoms in this solution.

5. Bring 1½ quarts of salted water to a boil, and add lemon juice and oil; boil artichoke bottoms for 10 minutes with cover slightly ajar. Remove from heat and let cool in the water.

6. In a covered saucepan, mix drained peas with sliced potato and 1 teaspoon salt. Add 2 cups of water and cook slowly for ½ hour, or until potato is tender.

7. Purée pea-potato mixture in a blender or food processor, and transfer to a large mixing bowl.

8. Stir in butter, using a wire whisk. Add pepper and nutmeg; beat in egg yolks.

9. Beat in cream a little at a time, until mixture is the consistency of thick whipped potatoes.

10. Preheat oven to 375°F.

11. Use a pastry bag fitted with a large (#8) star tip to fill artichoke bottoms with pea purée in a rosette design.

12. Place filled artichokes in a greased 9-inch round pan, and bake on middle shelf of oven for 10 minutes, or until thoroughly heated. Serve at once.

BIBB LETTUCE SALAD WITH MONTICELLO DRESSING

Bibb lettuce, which is named after the Kentucky agronomist who developed it, is the undisputed king of the salad greens. Also known as Kentucky limestone lettuce, Bibb is recognized even by the most critical French chefs as a high-quality lettuce. The tiny heads yield buttery leaves that can form the base of a fine American salad.

Mrs. Nixon favored Bibb lettuce, so the family menus often included Bibb salads, as did many State Dinners. The flavor of Bibb lettuce melds well with chives, so dressings containing chives are best served with these salads. Two of the Nixons' favorites included Chive Dressing, which is cool and light, and the White House special Monticello Dressing, which is flavored with bacon as well as chives. Since Bibb lettuce wilts very easily, dressings should be added at the last minute or served on the side.

The Kentucky salad green has been served at White House dinners as diverse as the State Dinner for Leonid Brezhnev and the ninetieth birthday party for Theodore Roosevelt's daughter. Alice Roosevelt Longworth was a great wit and raconteur, especially in her later years when she cared even less than ever about the ramifications of her straightforward, outspoken demeanor. Nearing ninety, Alice commented candidly on her friend, First Lady Mrs. Nixon: "I wish she wouldn't call people 'kiddo.' She called *me* 'kiddo' just the other day, and frankly I can't stand it."

Mrs. Nixon requested a birthday cake for Alice's party, iced with white fondant and lettered in light green to match the grape and melon vacherin. Fortunately, the lettering spelled out HAPPY BIRTHDAY ALICE, not KIDDO.

Serves 4

3 firm heads Bibb lettuce
¼ cup cider vinegar
½ teaspoon salt
6 drops of Tabasco sauce
1 teaspoon Dijon-style mustard
Juice of 1 lemon
6 twists freshly ground black pepper

1 teaspoon finely diced red bell pepper
¾ cup sunflower oil
½ teaspoon chopped fresh chives
3 slices crisp bacon, crumbled
1 hard-boiled egg, chopped

1. Separate leaves from lettuce heads carefully and soak in very cold water until crisp; drain. Wash lettuce leaves thoroughly and dry on paper towels or in a salad spinner.

2. In a metal mixing bowl, stir together vinegar, salt, Tabasco sauce, mustard, lemon juice, ground pepper, and diced pepper, using a wire whisk.

3. Gradually add oil, beating constantly, until dressing is thickened. Add chives and stir.

4. Transfer dry lettuce leaves to a large mixing bowl. Add ¼ cup of the dressing and toss lightly using salad forks. (Extra salad dressing may be kept for several days in the refrigerator, but it should be served at room temperature.)

5. Divide salad among 4 individual salad plates. Sprinkle with crumbled bacon and chopped egg, and serve at once.

A happy birthday to First Lady Pat Nixon from the East Wing staff.

PARKER HOUSE ROLLS

Parker House Rolls are elegant yeast rolls that were originally created at the elegant Parker House hotel in Boston. The delicate Parker House Roll can be distinguished by the classic design: The dough is folded off-center to create rolls with uneven tops. Mrs. Nixon and her elder daughter Tricia were especially fond of hot, buttery Parker House Rolls.

Reserved for special dining occasions, Parker House Rolls were included on the dinner menu when Prince Charles and his sister Princess Anne visited the White House in July 1970. Tricia and Julie designed an all-American menu for the royal siblings' first night as the Nixons' honored guests. The private dinner was served in the Family Dining Room to the four young people and Julie's husband, David Eisenhower, while the President and Mrs. Nixon entertained the American ambassador to Great Britain, Walter Annenberg, and his wife upstairs in the President's Dining Room. Later that evening, a dance was held outside the White House. Some 600 guests blanketed the South Lawn, where music drifted through the soft summer air and fireworks streaked the starlit sky. A full moon helped to illuminate the elaborate buffet table, laden with late-night fare to appease appetites awakened by hours of dancing.

The Prince of Wales and his sister enjoyed several other outdoor events on their first visit to the capital city, including a luncheon cruise aboard the presidential yacht *Sequoia,* and a picnic at the presidential retreat Camp David. Touring about in the hot humidity of Washington can drain even a young visitor's energy. Thus the menus were planned to provide cooling nourishment as well as an introduction to typical American foodstuffs. On their final night in the White House, the menu was catered to appeal to British tastes with a cold beef platter that is often served as a summer supper dish in England.

Upon his departure, Prince Charles made a point of thanking the White House staff for their hospitality. After greeting us in the Diplomatic Reception Room, Prince Charles inquired where I had learned "to cook so exquisitely." Surprised to learn of my Swiss heritage, the Prince explained that he had noted a French accent to the White House meals. When I told him of my training in the French-speaking areas of Switzerland, Prince Charles complimented me once more, this time stating in French that the food served at the White House was, well, *magnifique*!

Prince Charles compliments
Chef Haller on his cooking—
"Magnifique!"

Makes 24

½ cake (½ ounce) yeast, or 1½   *1 teaspoon salt*
  teaspoons dry yeast   *1 teaspoon sugar*
¾ cup warm water (105°F to   *2 tablespoons butter*
  115°F)   *3 cups bread flour*
½ cup scalded milk

1. Dissolve yeast in ¼ cup warm water.
2. In a large mixing bowl, combine the remaining water with scalded milk, salt, sugar, and 1 tablespoon butter; blend well.
3. Add yeast. Add flour, one cup at a time. Mix dough with a dough hook or turn out and knead by hand until dough is smooth and elastic. (This will take about 5 minutes.)
4. Cover bowl with a damp cloth and let rise in a warm place until doubled in bulk, about 1 to 1½ hours.

5. Shape dough by hand into twenty-four 2-inch balls, and arrange in a single layer in a buttered baking dish, cover, and let rise in a warm place for 30 minutes, or until balls are doubled in size. Let remaining tablespoon of butter soften.

6. Using the floured handle of a wooden spoon, press each ball through the center until almost cut in half. Brush the crease with a little of the soft butter, and press halves together like a purse; repeat with each roll.

7. Let rise again until doubled in bulk. Preheat oven to 400°F.

8. Bake on middle shelf of preheated oven for 15 minutes, or until golden. Serve warm. (If desired, tops may be brushed with melted butter after baking for a golden sheen.)

MRS. NIXON'S BLUEBERRY MUFFINS

Mrs. Nixon loved hot yeast rolls and quick breads, so she readily fell in love with the homemade blueberry muffins served at the White House. She enjoyed the freshly baked muffins served warm for breakfast, with her light salad plates for lunch, and sometimes in place of hot rolls at dinner. Chock-full of plump berries, Mrs. Nixon's Blueberry Muffins also proved popular with guests at special White House functions.

While living in the White House, the Nixons hosted ecumenical Sunday services each week in the East Room. A stand-up brunch in the State Dining Room followed the service. Silver trays of warm blueberry muffins adorned the long dining room table, along with fresh-baked brioches and sweet rolls, hot coffee, and freshly squeezed orange juice.

The Nixons also arranged for some special overnight guests to have an engraved breakfast menu left in their bedrooms, so that they could select their own White House breakfasts in advance. Blueberry muffins proved a popular choice with many houseguests.

Mrs. Nixon's Blueberry Muffins were also served at one of the largest sit-down meals ever prepared at the White House, which was served to one of the oldest groups ever to dine at the White House. In 1969, the annual fall project for the General Federation of Women's Clubs encouraged members to invite lonely elderly neighbors into their own homes for holiday meals and cheer. As the honorary chairperson that year, Mrs. Nixon, joined by co-hosts Tricia, Julie and David Eisenhower, and Mamie Eisenhower, set the pace by hosting a Thanksgiving dinner for 270 elderly individuals living in area nursing homes and homes for the aged.

Individual plate service replaced the customary platters used for serving White House guests. The food was dished out in advance and kept in special plate warmers. Shaky hands and sensitive palates appreciated the pre-portioned and not-too-hot turkey dinner plates set before each guest. The menu, too, was designed with older eaters in mind. Gravy helped to soften the lightly seasoned stuffing, and the sweet potatoes were puréed. My own recipe for cranberry sauce provided a tart relish with finely grated orange peel. The White House pastry chef prepared his smooth pumpkin pie for dessert, a fine recipe of which he was especially proud. And the blueberry muffins were also a hit.

Makes 18 to 24

2 cups flour
2 teaspoons sugar
2½ teaspoons baking powder
½ teaspoon salt
1 egg

1 cup milk, at room
   temperature
¼ cup butter, softened
1 cup fresh blueberries, or
   frozen, thawed, and drained

1. Preheat oven to 400°F. Grease twenty-four 2-inch muffin cups and dust lightly with flour (or use paper muffin cup liners).
2. Sift together flour, sugar, baking powder, and salt.
3. In a mixing bowl, beat egg until foamy, and blend in milk and softened butter; fold into dry ingredients just enough to moisten flour. Do not beat. (Overmixing results in flat, heavy muffins.)
4. Fold in blueberries.
5. Spoon into prepared tins, filling each three-quarters full.
6. Bake on middle shelf of preheated oven for 20 to 25 minutes, or until golden brown and a toothpick inserted into center of muffin comes out clean.
7. Let cool for a few minutes on wire racks before removing from muffin tins. Serve warm. Freeze extra muffins or store in an airtight container; reheat in a 350°F oven for several minutes just before serving.

SOUFFLÉ AU GRAND MARNIER

On a number of occasions during my twenty-plus years at the White House, I was asked to create a special dish for an important State Dinner or other official function. Since President Nixon was very fond of soufflés, I devised some dessert soufflés of unusual flavors to please his honored guests.

When Prince Juan Carlos of Spain brought his beautiful Greek wife, Princess Sophia, to the White House, I developed a special soufflé in their honor, made with puréed strawberries (wild strawberries provide the best flavor, when available), flavored with strawberry liqueur, and garnished with poached strawberries.

But the President's favorite dessert soufflé was one made with orange-flavored liqueur and topped with a light, sweet wine sauce. The popular Soufflé au Grand Marnier with Sauce Sabayon was served to Tito (Josip Broz), the President of Yugoslavia, at the State Dinner hosted by the Nixons in 1971. A few days later, I received a nice letter in praise of the dessert from the Chief of Protocol, Emil Mosbacher, Jr.

To make a perfect soufflé, the recipe must be accurate and followed exactly. To serve a perfect soufflé, proper timing is essential. However, the real key to success with soufflés is to learn by doing, that is, by cooking hundreds of them.

When the Nixons held a birthday party at the White House for Mamie Eisenhower, the menu included Soufflé au Grand Marnier. Everyone seemed impressed with the perfect birthday soufflé, especially the guest of honor. On the morning after the party, I answered the phone when Mrs. Eisenhower called the kitchen to request her breakfast. Realizing that she had the "soufflé chef" on the line, Mrs. Eisenhower asked, "How is it possible to serve a soufflé in the first floor dining room that was made in the ground floor kitchen that is still perfectly puffed?" Mrs. Eisenhower was not satisfied with my honest response, according to the butler who brought her breakfast up soon after. She told the butler, "Your chef is smart. He doesn't want to tell his secret for soufflés. He simply tells people that it comes with *experience*."

Serves 4 to 6

4 tablespoons butter	6 egg whites, at room
½ cup flour	temperature
1 scant cup hot milk	A pinch of salt
4 egg yolks	A pinch of cream of tartar
3 tablespoons Grand Marnier	⅓ cup granulated sugar
4 drops vanilla extract	Confectioners' sugar

1. Preheat oven to 350°F. Brush the inside of a 1½-quart soufflé dish with soft butter and sprinkle with granulated sugar.

2. Melt butter in a 1-quart saucepan, add flour, and work into a roux. Cook for a minute or two to remove the raw taste of the flour.

3. Add hot milk and stir with a wire whisk until smooth.

4. Cook for 1 minute, stirring constantly with a plastic or wooden spoon; remove from heat and cool slightly.

5. Add egg yolks one at a time, mixing until smooth; stir in Grand Marnier and vanilla.

6. In a clean, dry mixing bowl, beat egg whites with salt and cream of tartar until soft peaks form; add the granulated sugar gradually, beating constantly until very stiff.

7. Add around one-fifth of the stiff egg whites to the egg yolk mixture and blend until smooth; transfer to a mixing bowl.

8. Fold in the rest of the egg whites. Do not overmix.

9. Pour into prepared dish, and fill to ½ inch from the rim.

10. Bake on middle shelf of preheated oven for 35 minutes, or until golden brown and puffed 1½ to 2 inches above the rim. Dust with confectioners' sugar and serve immediately with a sauceboat of SAUCE SABAYON or warm APRICOT SAUCE, if desired.

SAUCE SABAYON

Makes 1 quart

6 egg yolks

1 cup dry white wine

2⅛ cups confectioners' sugar

1. In a stainless steel bowl, beat yolks with wine and sugar.

2. Transfer to the top of a double boiler and continue to beat over hot water until creamy. Keep warm.

3. Pour into a sauceboat and serve at once.

TRICIA'S WEDDING CAKE

Towering some 7 feet in height, Tricia's wedding cake was dubbed by the press at the time as "Washington's newest monument." The giant Lady Baltimore cake was prepared in 6 layers of graduated size, with a bottom tier that measured 5 feet in diameter and had to be baked in 8 specially designed cake pans. The bottom layer alone could have fed the 400 reception guests.

The 6 foot 10 inch cake was set on a low table and topped with a pulled sugar gazebo that added almost another foot of height. The gazebo, a miniature version of the one in the White House Rose Garden, replaced the traditional figurines of the bride and groom. Filled with cherry blossoms, it drew much admiration for the artistic designer, pastry chef Maurice Bonté.

Mr. Bonté was familiar with White House weddings since he had assisted in the preparation of Luci Johnson's wedding cake. Some three weeks prior to Tricia's wedding, Chef Bonté began working on the many pulled sugar decorations which would adorn the big cake. The French pastry chef transformed granulated sugar into flowers and shooting stars, lovebirds and wedding rings. On the day before the wedding, Chef Bonté carefully transported his fragile creations by station wagon from his New York apartment to the White House. Maurice Bonté, who eventually opened his own pastry shop in Manhattan (Patisserie Bonté), donated his skilled assistance to the White House weddings for the pure pleasure of contributing to the perfection of a historical event.

Assisted by White House pastry chef Heinz Bender, Mr. Bonté and I assembled the grand cake in the high marble foyer of the Northern Hall. The cake was frosted in advance to maintain moistness, but the final decorations took several hours and were not completed until just hours before the ceremony. The result was one of the most magnificent works of confectionary art that I have ever seen.

Tricia and her new husband used a special cake knife to slice the delicate cake. Four hundred extra slices had been encased in tiny decorative boxes so that each guest could bring home a "dream cake" souvenir. Some of the well-known guests to enjoy Tricia's special wedding cake included Red Skelton, J. Edgar Hoover, Ralph Nader, George Bush, Art Linkletter, and three former White House brides: Luci Johnson Nugent, Lynda Johnson Robb, and Alice Roosevelt Longworth. Asked whether the ceremony brought back any memories, the ever-candid Mrs. Longworth replied, "It didn't bring back one goddam memory—after sixty-six years it's a whole new world."

Makes one 6-layer, 8-inch cake or two 3-layer cakes

2 sticks (1 cup) unsalted butter   *4 teaspoons baking powder*

2 cups sugar   *4 cups sifted flour*

1 cup milk   *1 teaspoon almond extract*

10 egg whites, at room   ROYAL ICING *(page 34)*
  temperature

1. Preheat oven to 350°F. Grease six 8-inch layer pans; dust with flour.

2. In a large mixing bowl, cream butter with sugar until very light and smooth.

3. Add milk a little at a time; beat well after each addition.

4. In a clean, dry bowl, beat egg whites until stiff.

5. Sift baking powder with flour; add to batter alternately with stiff egg whites, folding well after each addition. Fold in almond extract.

6. Pour into prepared pans and bake in preheated oven for 25 minutes, or until toothpick inserted in center comes out clean. Turn out and let cake cool completely on wire racks before frosting with ROYAL ICING. (The frosting will help keep the cake moist and fresh tasting.)

With the assistance of her new husband, Tricia Nixon Cox cuts the cake.

Maurice Bonté performs the delicate task of decorating the top tier of Tricia's wedding cake.

White House employees are unusual in their nonpartisan devotion as they seek to fulfill the needs of the incumbent First Family. We are loyal to the presidency, but we try not to get involved in the politics. However, there have been times when we are forced to deal directly with the ramifications of national politics.

On the morning of August 9, 1974, I arrived at the White House at 6:00 A.M. for the breakfast shift. As I stepped away from the second-floor elevator on my way to the kitchen in the First Family's quarters, I noticed President Nixon standing in the West Hall outside of the Family Kitchen. He was still in his pajamas, but he seemed full of energy. The President shook my hand when I approached him, and stated in a candid manner, "Chef, I have dined all over the world but your food is the best."

After I thanked him, President Nixon followed me into the kitchen. He ordered a special breakfast for himself, more substantial than his usual morning meal of wheat germ and coffee. The President asked a butler to serve what was to be his final White House meal in his favorite room, the Lincoln Sitting Room. When the President finished eating his poached egg and hash, Alexander Haig entered the room bearing a sheet of paper with a single typed sentence: "I hereby resign the Office of the President of the United States." President Nixon signed his resignation, to be delivered at 11:35 A.M. to the American public and the rest of the world.

PRESIDENT NIXON'S FAREWELL BREAKFAST

At 10:00 A.M., President Nixon bid good-bye to his staff. Around 250 employees and friends gathered in the East Room to hear the President's farewell address, which included an unforgettable acknowledgment of the White House staff:

> This house for instance, and I was thinking of it as we walked down this hall, and I was comparing it with some of the great houses of the world that I have been in. This isn't the biggest house . . . This isn't the finest house . . . But this is the best house. It's the best house because it has something far more important than numbers of people who serve, far more important than numbers of rooms, or how big it is. Far more important than numbers of magnificent pieces of art. This house has a great heart, and that heart comes from those who serve.

It was especially sad to watch the President wave good-bye to the White House from the ascending helicopter. As the staff stood outside on the White House lawn, waving to the departing President, I think we were all in a state of shock. Certainly, none of us had ever expected to have to bid farewell so abruptly to a family we had served for almost 6 years.

Serves 1

1 tablespoon butter	*¼ cup chopped stewed*
2 tablespoons chopped onion	*tomatoes*
1 garlic clove, minced	*4 twists freshly ground black*
⅓ cup cooked diced potatoes	*pepper*
½ cup cooked diced corned	*4 drops of Tabasco sauce*
beef	*1 POACHED EGG*

1. Melt butter in a cast-iron skillet, add onion and garlic and sauté until golden brown.

2. Add potatoes and corned beef, mix well, and sauté over medium heat for 10 minutes.

3. Add tomatoes, pepper, and Tabasco sauce; mix well. Cook for 10 minutes, stirring gently, until brown on all sides.

4. Using a spatula, mold the hash into an omelet shape and brown evenly on both sides. Avoid cooking hash too rapidly; it should dry out as it crisps up. Turn out onto a breakfast plate.

5. Using a slotted spoon, transfer POACHED EGG to center of hash; press the bottom of the spoon into the hash to form a nest for the egg, and turn egg over onto the hash with the smooth side facing up. Serve at once.

2 cups water　　　　　*1 egg*　　　　　POACHED EGG
1 tablespoon white vinegar

1. In a small saucepan, bring water to a gentle boil. Add the vinegar.
2. Break the egg and gently slide it into the water. Let simmer for 3 minutes, taking care that the egg does not stick to the bottom of the pan.
3. Carefully remove the egg with a slotted spoon and let drain for a few seconds on paper towels. Use a small, sharp knife to cut away any fuzzy strands of egg white and serve at once.

THE
FORD FAMILY

*The Fords'
Breakfast Favorites*

*Ford Family Favorite
Soups, Salads, and Sandwiches*

Ford Family Favorite Entrées

Ford Family Favorite Desserts

Special Event Recipes

THE FORDS'
BREAKFAST FAVORITES

The culinary habits of America's First Family can serve to illustrate the old maxim, "You are what you eat." President Gerald Ford, for example, possessed certain personal qualities that were similar to the properties of the diet he followed: "Jerry" Ford was unpretentious, honest, wholesome, hearty, and all-American. His straightforward and good-natured approach to his new role demonstrated to the American public that the presidency need not be private and impersonal. All of the Fords proved to be candid, open, and willing to share family life in the White House with an ever-interested American audience.

In 1974, America was prepared to trade political pomp and glory for public confidence and stability. Americans were tired of uncertainty and longed to renew public faith in government. Outgoing President Nixon told his Vice-President, "I know the country is going to be in good hands with you in the Oval Office." Less than 30 minutes after Nixon resigned, Gerald Ford was sworn in as the thirty-eighth President of the United States. Chief Justice Warren E. Burger conducted the brief ceremony, held in the East Room of the White House instead of at the Capitol in order to ensure a private, uneventful inauguration. The new President reassured America that he aimed "to replace the national frown with a national smile." And from one coast to the other, America heaved a national sigh of relief.

At the White House, a change in administration usually requires some time for the regular staff to adjust. The Ford family was so friendly and so easygoing that the White House rapidly became warm and relaxed. The White House staff heaved a collective sigh of relief.

The President really enjoyed life—and food—in the White House. Six feet tall, with a trim, muscular physique maintained by an athletic life-style, President Ford had a healthy appetite and

GOLDEN BROWN WAFFLES WITH STRAWBERRIES AND SOUR CREAM

Waffles were sold in the streets of Europe as far back as the twelfth century. When Thomas Jefferson returned to America from Holland, he brought back a waffle iron so that he could enjoy the crisp batter cakes at home in Monticello. His daughter's 1824 cookbook, The Virginia Housewife, included their recipe for "Rice Woffles":

Boil two gills of rice quite soft, mix with it three gills of flour, a little salt, two ounces of melted butter, two eggs beaten well, and as much milk as will make it a thick batter—beat it till very light, and bake it in woffle irons.

President Ford demonstrates for
the press just how he likes his
English muffins.
(COURTESY: GERALD R. FORD LIBRARY)

simple tastes. For breakfast, the President usually consumed
an energy-rich high-carbohydrate meal that included freshly
squeezed orange juice, a piece of fresh fruit such as melon, one or
two toasted English muffins with margarine and jam, and hot tea.
Sunday breakfast was always a special meal in the Fords' home,
however, with the President's favorite: Golden Brown Waffles
served with "the works"—strawberries and sour cream.

These light, delicious breakfast cakes are best served piping hot,
crisp on the outside and soft on the inside. The Fords preferred
their Sunday waffles served with fresh strawberries and sour cream
in place of the more conventional butter and maple syrup. They
are delicious served either way.

Makes 6 waffles

1¾ cups cake flour
3 teaspoons baking powder
½ teaspoon salt
2 tablespoons confectioners'
   sugar
1½ cups milk, at room
   temperature
½ teaspoon vanilla extract

3 egg yolks
5 tablespoons melted butter
3 egg whites, at room
   temperature
1 pint fresh strawberries,
   lightly dusted with
   granulated sugar
1 pint sour cream

1. Into a large mixing bowl, sift together flour, baking powder, salt, and sugar. Using the back of a wooden spoon, make a deep well in the center of the dry ingredients.

2. In a separate mixing bowl, combine milk, vanilla, egg yolks, and melted butter. Pour rapidly into the center of the dry ingredients, and combine quickly, using a wire whisk.

3. In a clean, dry bowl, beat the egg whites until stiff but not dry. Fold into batter.

4. Transfer batter to a pitcher for easy pouring.

5. Heat a waffle iron to medium-hot temperature. Pour in batter until grid is two-thirds full.

6. Close the lid of the waffle iron and bake for 4 minutes, or until steam stops emerging and waffle is golden brown. Remove gently, using a fork. (Waffles should not stick to a well-seasoned iron, but if they do, add a little melted butter to the batter, not to the iron.)

7. Repeat baking process to make 5 more waffles. Serve hot, accompanied by bowls of sweetened strawberries and sour cream, or a pitcher of maple syrup and a crock of whipped butter.

The Fords were open-minded and flexible, amenable to new ideas and adaptable to life in the White House. Like their easygoing parents, the Ford children—Mike, age 24; Jack, age 22; Steve, age 18; Susan, age 17—rapidly made life in the White House relaxed and fun for everyone, including the kitchen staff.

The Family Quarters was kept well stocked with tennis rackets and ski equipment, golf clubs and sneakers, balls and bicycles to meet the needs of the athletic Fords and their guests. Many of the Fords' visitors replenished their energy supplies at the White House dining tables. Cautioned by their thoughtful parents against

STEVE'S FRENCH TOAST

making excessive demands on the staff, the young Fords often prepared breakfast and snacks for themselves and their friends.

Since Susan was still in high school when the Fords moved into the White House, she became a regular at the dining table. Mike was newly married and lived in Massachusetts, where he attended theology school. He brought his pretty wife, Gayle, to the White House for holiday repasts. Jack was a college student in Utah, but he lived in the White House after graduation. And until Steve left for a year of ranch life out West, he was a constant caller in the White House kitchen. An active and growing teenager, his favorite between-meal refrain was, "Is there anything to eat, Chef?" The White House kitchen was always prepared to satisfy the healthy appetites of hungry young folks.

One of Steve's favorites was French toast. He often prepared a plateful for himself on mornings he was home for breakfast in the White House. French toast was also included on the family's breakfast menu on occasion.

Known as *pain perdu* (or "lost bread") in France, this dish was originally devised as a means of utilizing dried-out French bread. Soft on the inside and crisp on the outside, hot French toast can be served with a variety of toppings. Some French toast fans prefer to sweeten the puffy bread with honey or maple syrup, fruit jams or jellies, or juicy berries such as fresh strawberries. Others enjoy their French toast lightly buttered and sprinkled with black pepper or ground nutmeg. Steve's French Toast was lightly dusted with confectioners' sugar and glazed under the broiler. The Fords preferred their French toast served with a pitcher of pure Vermont maple syrup.

Serves 1 to 2

¼ *loaf French bread*	*4 tablespoons butter*
2 eggs	*1 tablespoon confectioners'*
½ *cup light cream*	*sugar*

1. Use a serrated bread knife to slice French bread diagonally into four 1-inch thick slices.

2. In a shallow bowl, beat eggs with cream until fluffy. Soak bread slices on both sides in this mixture.

3. In a cast-iron skillet, melt butter over medium heat; do not brown. Add bread slices and brown on both sides.

4. When toast is well-browned and puffy, transfer to paper towels to drain.

5. Transfer toast to an ovenproof serving platter. Sprinkle with confectioners' sugar.

6. Set under medium-hot broiler for 2 seconds to glaze; serve hot with whipped butter and maple syrup, or less-traditional toppings such as honey, strawberry jam, or MRS. JOHNSON'S PEACH PRESERVES (page 8).

President Ford was in excellent physical condition, probably the most athletic president since Theodore Roosevelt. An avid skier, tennis player, and golfer, President Ford also followed a daily exercise regimen: He arose early each morning to spend 15 to 20 minutes on calisthenics and weight lifting, and he ended every work day with thirty minutes of laps in the White House pool. Rain or shine, in the storms of winter and the humid Washington summer, President Ford took his daily swim before dinner in the thermoregulated pool behind the White House.

An indoor pool had been built during Franklin D. Roosevelt's first term, funded by the pennies donated by America's school children to help the President stay healthy. Since the pool had been converted into a press room during the Nixon administration, funds to build a new outdoor swimming pool were donated during President Ford's first months in office. America has long recognized the importance of keeping the President physically fit.

According to the White House physician, Rear Admiral William M. Lukash, the daily swim was essential for President Ford because "in his case, it seems to be a tonic and invigorates him after a long day." The President himself joked, "Fifteen minutes in the pool is worth two martinis."

Gerald Ford had realized early in life the many benefits provided by sports. A star football player in high school and college, Ford was drafted by two professional football teams after leading the University of Michigan Wolverines into two Big Ten championships. Even though he chose law school and politics over a career in professional football, he maintained an avid interest in athletics. And his rigorous exercise habits had long necessitated an adequate food intake to meet his caloric needs.

President Ford was always careful to eat well on those mornings

GOLFER'S BREAKFAST SPECIAL

Theodore Roosevelt is considered the most physically versatile President ever to occupy the White House. As a youngster, Teddy built up his physique in a home gym installed by his father. He learned to box and wrestle, he practiced judo and was an avid horseman, he climbed the Matterhorn and hunted big game in Africa. However, another healthy and physically active President, Thomas Jefferson, once summarized what remains the general consensus on choice of exercise for overall health: "Of all exercises, walking is best."

when he planned to play a few sets of tennis or rounds of golf. One of his favorite breakfasts for such physically active days was dubbed the "Golfer's Special" by the White House kitchen: a plate of fried eggs, crisp bacon, and toasted English muffins.

Since the Fords did not have any problems with elevated blood cholesterol levels, Dr. Lukash allowed a moderate intake of eggs. Mrs. Ford preferred her morning eggs boiled, served with rye toast and tea. The President liked his eggs fried sunny-side up, and he loved the crisp bacon served alongside.

One morning when the President was dining alone before playing golf, the butler requested extra slices of bacon for him as a special treat. After President Ford had eaten all six slices, the butler commented, "Y'know, Chef, the President really likes that bacon. You had better cook up another six slices." I was happy to oblige.

Serves 1 golfer

2 *slices bacon*
2 *eggs*
1 *tablespoon butter*

1 *English muffin, split*
2 *teaspoons butter or*
    margarine

1. In a nonstick sauté pan, cook bacon very slowly until crisp; drain on paper towels.

2. Carefully break eggs into a small bowl; do not rupture yolks.

3. Melt butter in a well-seasoned frying pan, gently slide in eggs, and fry over medium heat for 3 to 4 minutes, or until egg whites are solid in appearance. (For best results when frying eggs, use a well-seasoned frying pan reserved for that purpose; do not wash the pan with soap and water, but clean well after each use with a kitchen towel. Professional fry cooks often keep their frying pans in their lockers to ensure that they are not used by anyone else for any other purpose.)

4. Lightly toast muffin. Spread each half with 1 teaspoon of butter or margarine; brown quickly under hot broiler.

5. Slide fried eggs onto a serving plate. Add toasted muffin and crisp bacon, and serve at once, with a pot of hot tea or café au lait, plus freshly squeezed orange juice.

MRS. FORD'S SPECIAL SCRAMBLED EGGS

Mrs. Ford was a friendly, charming, natural person. As the nation's First Lady, she was frank and open, expressing special interest in women and their issues at home and in the workplace. At one point during her husband's administration, Mrs. Ford was rated as the most popular First Lady in the history of the United States. The reasons for her immense appeal were aptly summarized in a citation she received from the University of Michigan: "She combines an assertive position on women's rights with a dedication to family values and ties. She has become widely admired for her courage, compassion, and commitment to common sense."

Mrs. Ford was committed to following a sensible diet. Her typical breakfast consisted of fresh fruit, toast, and tea. On occasion, she liked to include some type of eggs. A rich version of simple scrambled eggs, served atop fresh tomatoes, was one of her favorite special breakfasts.

Serves 8

8 large fresh tomatoes
Salt
A pinch of freshly ground
    black pepper
1 dozen eggs
¼ teaspoon freshly ground
    white pepper
2 cups warm (95°F) LIGHT
    CREAM SAUCE

3 tablespoons butter
1 cup warm (95°F) CHEF
    HALLER'S HOLLANDAISE SAUCE
    (page 41)
¼ cup grated Parmesan cheese
8 fresh parsley sprigs

1. Use a sharp knife to slice off stem and top of each tomato. Remove seeds with a small melon ball scoop.

2. Grease a shallow baking dish and line with tomatoes, cut side up; season with a pinch of salt and black pepper.

3. In a large mixing bowl, beat eggs with ½ teaspoon salt and the white pepper. Add 1½ cups of the warm CREAM SAUCE, and beat well, using a wire whisk.

4. Melt butter in a large nonstick skillet, pour in the eggs and scramble over medium heat, stirring constantly, until slightly solidified but not firm.

5. Use an ice cream scoop to divide scrambled eggs evenly among the tomatoes.

6. Mix warm HOLLANDAISE SAUCE with the remaining ½ cup of

warm CREAM SAUCE; spoon over eggs. Sprinkle tops with grated cheese.

7. Broil for 1 to 2 minutes, or until bubbling hot.

8. Transfer to a large serving platter. Garnish each with a parsley sprig, and serve at once.

LIGHT CREAM SAUCE

Makes 2 cups

2 tablespoons butter
2 tablespoons flour
2 cups hot milk
½ teaspoon salt

A pinch of freshly ground
   white pepper
A pinch of nutmeg

1. In the top of a double boiler, melt butter directly over heat; add flour, and work into a roux. Cook briefly over low heat, stirring constantly.

2. Add hot milk gradually, stirring constantly with a wire whisk.

3. Add seasonings and bring to a boil; cook for 10 minutes over low heat, stirring often.

4. Set top of double boiler over warm water to keep warm (not hot) until use.

PRESIDENT FORD'S GERMAN APPLE PANCAKE

Gerald Ford was an amiable President with an unusually fine sense of humor. In such an important position, with the ever-present public scrutiny, it is essential to be able to find some humor amidst all of the stress. President Ford and his family maintained a healthy attitude toward each other and the public during their stay in the White House.

The Ford family also maintained a healthy life-style. All of the Fords enjoyed breakfast, which provided the energy required for a full day's work—in and out of the public eye. The entire family joined the President in his enthusiasm for the hearty breakfast dish we called the German Apple Pancake.

Serves 2

3 eggs
¼ cup milk
A pinch of salt
¼ cup flour
1 large apple (McIntosh, if
   available)

1 teaspoon cinnamon
4 tablespoons sugar
4 tablespoons butter

In Thomas Jefferson's time, pancakes were called "batter cakes." Often eaten as dessert, the cakes were stacked in a pile, layered with maple syrup, and cut into wedges like a pie. Pancakes have actually been popular since the Middle Ages, when they provided a tasty way to use up certain foods prior to the Lenten fasts. The Germans have long enjoyed their Omeletten, *a thick pancake wrapped around warm fruit and traditionally served as a simple supper dish.*

1. Preheat oven to 375°F.
2. In a small mixing bowl, beat eggs with milk. Whisk in salt.
3. Measure flour into a large mixing bowl. Add egg mixture, and whisk batter until smooth.
4. Peel and quarter apple, and core with a small sharp knife. Cut each quarter into very thin slices, and place in a small bowl.
5. Mix cinnamon with sugar. Sprinkle half of the cinnamon-sugar over sliced apple.
6. Melt butter in a 12-inch cast-iron skillet, add apple slices and sauté for 1 minute, until lightly browned and tender.
7. Pour in batter and cook over medium heat for 1 minute, until bottom is lightly browned.
8. Transfer skillet to middle shelf of preheated oven. (If you are using a pan with a plastic handle, cover the handle with aluminum foil before transferring to oven.) Bake for 5 minutes, or until pancake is puffed.
9. Return skillet to top of stove and cook over medium heat for 2 minutes, or until bottom of pancake is golden brown.
10. Use two metal spatulas to fold pancake in half and transfer to an ovenproof serving platter. Sprinkle with remaining cinnamon-sugar.
11. Place under broiler for 1 minute to glaze. Serve at once.

MRS. FORD'S HOMEMADE TOASTING BREAD

Prior to moving into the White House, the Ford family had never had a home with more than eight rooms. For the preceding twenty years, "home" was their modest four-bedroom house in Alexandria, Virginia. When Ford was appointed Vice-President, the family was reluctant to leave their beloved neighborhood for the stately Victorian mansion that had been designated as their new home.

Until 1974, the Vice-President and his family always resided in their own home. In 1966, Congress obtained authorization to build a special residence for use by the Vice-President. However, it was not until Ford's Vice-Presidency that the mansion on the grounds of the U.S. Naval Observatory, the former home of the Chief of Naval Operations, was located and approved. Before renovations on the gracious old house could be completed, the Fords became White House residents instead.

Betty Ford gave the spacious 132-room mansion a familiar, home-like environment. She rearranged the First Family's living quarters to resemble the comfortable style of their previous homes. The President's Bedroom was transformed into a den, complete with family photos and President Ford's favorite leather lounge chair. The Fords really liked living in the White House, which President Ford jokingly referred to as "the best public housing I've ever seen."

To further enhance the homey atmosphere, the fresh aroma of home-baked bread wafted through the White House almost every morning. Mrs. Ford requested that the kitchen serve bread baked fresh each day from her own special recipe. The White House kitchen prepared two to six loaves at a time so that the Fords always had freshly baked bread on hand for morning toast, luncheon sandwiches, and snacks at any time.

Mrs. Ford's recipe yields a dense white bread that is perfect for toasting. A self-leavening bread, the recipe calls for a "starter," which ferments to create air bubbles, and eventually helps the bread to rise. We discovered through experimentation that the best results were attained when the self-leavening was boosted by the addition of a little yeast. The loaves resemble sourdough bread in appearance and texture. But they taste even better!

In 1880, President Rutherford B. Hayes named a commission to select a new site for the Naval Observatory, which was to be "free of obstructions on the horizon and from objectional vibrations from traffic." A year later, the President's commission recommended Pretty Prospect, a 72-acre estate in Georgetown Heights. Ten years later, Congress provided the funding to build a naval observatory, with a superintendent's house that was occupied by sixteen superintendents and sixteen Chiefs of Naval Operations prior to 1974. The carriage house behind what is now the Vice-President's home is a nostalgic reminder of the history of the estate, but currently serves to house the Vice-President's Secret Service men.

Makes 2 loaves

2 cups milk
½ cup white stone-ground
*   cornmeal*
2 teaspoons salt
1 tablespoon sugar
¼ cup shortening

1 package active dry yeast
¼ cup warm water
6 to 6½ cups sifted bread flour,
*   preferably a high-protein,*
*   high-gluten variety*

1. Heat 1 cup milk. Combine with cornmeal in a large mixing bowl. Cover the bowl, and let rest overnight in a warm place.

2. In a small saucepan, heat remaining 1 cup milk over medium heat until hot. Add to the cornmeal mixture with salt, sugar, and shortening.

3. Mix yeast with warm water; stir into cornmeal mixture, using a wire whisk.

4. Add flour 1 cup at a time, working first with a spoon, then by hand to achieve a smooth, elastic dough. (This will take about 5 minutes.) Turn out onto a lightly floured board.

5. Knead dough by hand, working outside edges in, for 5 minutes, in order to incorporate air into the dough. Return to the bowl.

6. Cover the bowl with a hot damp cloth and place in a warm spot for about 2 hours, or until doubled in bulk.

7. Turn out onto floured board; knead again, adding enough flour to make a smooth dough that does not stick to the board.

8. Use a sharp knife to divide dough into 2 equal loaves, and place each in a greased 9 × 5-inch loaf pan.

9. Cover with a hot damp cloth and let rise for 45 minutes, or until dough rises to a level even with the rims of the pans.

10. Preheat oven to 350°F.

11. Brush tops of loaves lightly with water. Use a long thin knife to slit tops down the middle; make each slit ¼-inch deep.

12. Bake on lower shelf of preheated oven for 40 minutes, or until golden brown and firm to the touch.

13. Turn loaves out onto wire racks; let cool completely before slicing. This bread tastes best toasted, and freezes well when wrapped tightly in plastic.

FORD FAMILY
FAVORITE SOUPS, SALADS,
AND SANDWICHES

NAVY BEAN SOUP

Gerald Ford served his country during World War II as an officer in the U.S. Navy. He was originally commissioned to work with other athletes as a "physical training instructor," to whip recruits into tip-top condition. Ford eventually became the assistant navigator on the *Monterey*, a ship that took part in virtually all of the battles in the South Pacific. When the war was over, Ford returned to civilian life and began practicing law in Grand Rapids, Michigan.

Although he served his country in active war duty, Ford escaped harm. He was equally fortunate as the President of the United States: In two assassination attempts, he walked away unscathed. Both incidents happened on trips to the West Coast, with the sec-

ond gun threat occurring just seventeen days after the first. When the unharmed President joined his wife at a California airport soon after the second close call, Mrs. Ford was still unaware of the most recent attempt on her husband's life. "Well," she asked breezily, "how did they treat you in San Francisco?"

President Ford once commented, "Presidents are sitting ducks. You might as well sit back and enjoy it," but he was referring to being a target of harmless jibes. As President, Ford served as a "sitting duck" for a number of comedians, most notably Chevy Chase and Johnny Carson. He handled the teasing well: He simply sat back and enjoyed it!

It is easy to understand why the White House staff found it so enjoyable to serve President Ford. After all, how many Americans would describe their own lives the way President Ford appraised the time he spent in the White House:

> I never felt better physically. I never had a clearer mind. I never enjoyed an experience more. The truth is, I couldn't wait to start the day. . . . I really enjoy getting up every morning, looking at the schedule, seeing what the problems are. I don't long for the end of the day.

For over sixty years, a special bean soup has been served to Washington politicians who dine in the Senate restaurant. Controversy over the origin of the recipe has existed for many years, but Senate Bean Soup is always prepared with white Michigan navy beans. And the recipe always yields a thick, delicious soup, said to fully energize even the weariest politicians.

Makes 2 quarts

1½ cups dried navy beans
4 tablespoons butter
1 cup finely diced onions
4 garlic cloves, finely minced
1 cup finely diced celery
1 cup finely diced carrots
1 pig's knuckle
Tied cheesecloth "spice bag," containing ¼ teaspoon thyme, ¼ teaspoon marjoram, and 1 bay leaf

6 twists freshly ground black pepper
2 quarts hot water
2 teaspoons salt
2 tablespoons chopped fresh parsley

1. In a deep bowl, cover dried beans with cold water. Let soak overnight.

2. Melt butter in a 4-quart soup pot, sauté onions and garlic for 5 minutes, until transparent. Do not brown.

3. Stir in diced celery and carrots. Cover, and simmer for 5 minutes.

4. Drain navy beans and add to soup pot.

5. Wash pig's knuckle and add to soup pot. Add spice bag and pepper.

6. Pour in hot water and bring to a boil. Add salt, cover, and simmer over medium heat.

7. Cook for 2 hours, stirring occasionally. Skim froth from top as necessary.

8. Remove pig's knuckle and dice the meat; add meat to the hot soup.

9. Just before serving, skim any froth from the top. Add chopped parsley, and serve hot, with toasted French bread or HOT BISCUITS (page 7).

MARTHA WASHINGTON'S CRAB SOUP

As a young man, George Washington married widow Martha Custis, and they settled with her two children at majestic Mount Vernon. One of the outstanding Virginia estates, the Washingtons' farm was self-sufficient; they baked their own bread from grain that they grew on their land and ground in their own mill and made all their own food. When George Washington became America's first President, he hired a

Betty Ford was a very patriotic First Lady, always partisan to American arts and crafts, wines and foods. At State Dinners, the works of American artists and craftspeople decorated the White House, while the guest list included American poets, writers, dancers, and performing artists. During the Ford administration, only American wines were served at the official functions. Menus featured all-American favorites and regional dishes, such as Strawberry Short-cake and Maryland Crabcakes.

Mrs. Ford pored over menus and recipes from the collections of former First Ladies, and she enjoyed reading about the culinary exploits of early administrations. On certain occasions, Mrs. Ford was able to integrate presidential history into the Ford administration's special events.

In the spring of 1975, a historic recipe was received by the White House kitchen, along with the following memo: "Attached is a recipe for Martha Washington's Crab Soup which was served at the Senate Wives' Red Cross Luncheon recently. Mrs. Ford really liked it and thought you might like to try it sometime."

With a few adjustments, we were able to reproduce the crab soup to Mrs. Ford's satisfaction. The delicious soup became a favorite on the Ford family's dining table. The Fords often requested a simple luncheon of soup and homemade bread. The hot crab soup, served with slices of MRS. FORD'S HOMEMADE TOASTING BREAD (page 162), made a savory light luncheon meal.

Serves 6

1 tablespoon butter
5 teaspoons flour
3 hard-boiled eggs, sieved
Grated rind of 1 lemon
A pinch of salt
A pinch of freshly ground
    white pepper

4 cups milk
½ pound cooked crabmeat
½ cup heavy cream
½ cup dry sherry
A dash of Worcestershire Sauce

1. In a 2-quart saucepan, combine butter, flour, sieved eggs, lemon rind, salt, and pepper.

2. In a separate saucepan, bring milk to a boil; remove from heat.

3. Gradually pour the hot milk into the egg mixture, stirring with a wire whisk.

4. Add crabmeat, and cook over low heat for 5 minutes; do not boil.

5. Add cream and remove from heat. Stir in sherry and Worcestershire sauce and serve piping hot.

steward to "provide genteel dinners, and give aid in dressing them." Washington was pleased at first with the steward, whom he regarded as "an excellent cook," but was eventually forced to fire the fellow for stealing food and wine! This was certainly a foolish mistake to make while working for a President who "could not tell a lie"!

The menu for the Fords' first family dinner in the White House—prime rib, parsleyed new potatoes, green beans, salad, and ice cream—served as a reliable indicator of the meals that would follow. The Fords preferred plain all-American food, simple dishes that were hearty and nutritious. For the family's first White House dinner, the kitchen staff was careful to cater to President Ford's personal preferences from start to finish.

Since he was very active physically, President Ford had rarely experienced undesirable weight gain. However, an intense travel schedule during his vice-presidency had interfered with Ford's regular exercise routine. As soon as the Fords arrived at the White House, the President's physician, Dr. William Lukash, advised him to shed the extra pounds he had gained and outlined the basics of the reduction regimen for the public: "I set a limit on the amount of food that the President should eat each day, and the White House chef sees that he gets no more than that."

The White House allowed the press to publish a week of dinner menus served to the dieting President, to illustrate the sensible, safe weight-loss plan. Designed to suit the President's personal

PRESIDENT FORD'S BOSTON LETTUCE SALAD WITH RED ONIONS

tastes, the White House diet plan was both palatable and sensible, emphasizing portion control and balance. A similar calorie-controlled menu can be devised in any home.

After about a month in the White House, President Ford successfully shed the fifteen pounds he had gained as a peripatetic Vice-President. For the remainder of his term, he maintained his weight within a healthful range, and he continued to eat sensibly and exercise regularly.

For the calorie conscious, salads serve as a dietary staple. President Ford enjoyed a sizable green salad with dinner. A wise way to fill up without consuming excessive calories or fat, White House salads are prepared with a variety of fresh greens and very light dressings. President Ford preferred a salad made with crisp Boston lettuce and finely sliced red onion, tossed with a small quantity of a peppery French dressing. One need not reside in the White House in order to emulate his healthful eating habits and overall life-style.

Serves 6

2 heads Boston lettuce
2 small red onions, peeled and
  finely sliced
2 tablespoons chopped fresh
  chives

A dash of salt
½ cup SPICY FRENCH DRESSING

1. Gently separate lettuce leaves; cut large leaves in half.
2. Wash leaves twice in very cold water to crisp; drain thoroughly in a colander or lettuce spinner.
3. Arrange crisp leaves in a large salad bowl. Sprinkle with sliced oinons and half of the chopped chives; sprinkle with salt.
4. Add dressing slowly; toss gently for 1 minute.
5. Sprinkle with remaining tablespoon of chives, and serve at once, in the salad bowl or on individual serving plates.

SPICY FRENCH DRESSING

Makes 2 cups

2 tablespoons finely minced shallots

2 tablespoons finely chopped Anaheim peppers (large, mild chili peppers)

2 garlic cloves, finely minced

1 tablespoon dry mustard

1 teaspoon Worcestershire sauce

2 egg yolks

1 teaspoon salt

6 twists freshly ground black pepper

¼ cup red wine vinegar

Juice of 1 lemon

1 cup vegetable oil

1. In a blender, combine all ingredients except vegetable oil; blend at high speed for 10 seconds.

2. With blender running at low speed, gradually add oil; then cover blender and blend at high speed for 10 seconds. (Dressing can also be mixed by hand, using a wire whisk.) Refrigerate in a covered jar, if not using at once.

MRS. FORD'S CORNED BEEF ON RYE SANDWICH

Mrs. Ford was a gracious and well-liked First Lady who earned the admiration of the nation for her willingness to be open and outspoken. Although she was not an activist like Eleanor Roosevelt and Lady Bird Johnson, Betty Ford was a model wife and mother with a contemporary outlook on women's rights and social issues. Hesitant at first about serving as America's First Lady, Mrs. Ford discovered that she loved her life in the White House.

Natural and down-to-earth, Mrs. Ford wore comfortable clothes —"I think I can be well-dressed without designer clothes"—and she always appeared attractive and self-assured. Her poise was partly due to her training as a dancer; she began dance lessons at age eight, taught dancing by age fourteen, and studied dance professionally upon graduating from high school. Mrs. Ford was very pleased when her idol and teacher, Martha Graham, was honored in 1976 with the Presidential Medal of Freedom.

Mrs. Ford was tall and always trim, with little need to count calories. A light eater, she was careful to see that her diet—and the diet of her active family—was healthful and well balanced. Mrs. Ford included fibrous whole-grain breads in her diet, and she was fond of sandwiches served on hearty rye bread. She often had a lean meat sandwich for lunch while living in the White House.

Makes 4 sandwiches

½ cup finely shredded cheddar
   cheese
4 tablespoons cream cheese
1 tablespoon Dijon-style
   mustard
2 tablespoons chopped sweet-
   and-sour pickles
1 tablespoon finely chopped
   fresh parsley

1 tablespoon finely chopped
   onion
8 slices fresh rye bread
16 very thin slices cooked
   corned beef
4 twists freshly ground white
   pepper
Tomato wedges
Boston lettuce hearts

1. In a small mixing bowl, mix shredded cheese with cream cheese until smooth.

2. Add mustard and chopped pickles, parsley, and onion; mix well.

3. Divide evenly among bread slices; spread evenly on each slice.

4. Cover 4 of the bread slices with 4 slices of corned beef each; give each a twist of pepper before topping with the remaining 4 slices of bread.

5. Slice each sandwich in half. Serve with tomato wedges and lettuce hearts for garnish.

JACK'S REUBEN SANDWICH

In 1956, when Jack Ford was four years old, the Reuben won first prize in the National Sandwich Contest. The recipe was submitted by a waitress from Omaha; she named it after Mr. Reuben Key, who created the Reuben at a weekly poker game held at the home of her employer. The prize-winning sandwich grew in popularity, and by the time Jack Ford arrived at the White House, the Reuben was an all-American favorite.

When his father was the President of the United States, Jack was a college student at Utah State. As a forestry major, Jack worked as a park ranger between semesters. He did manage to spend some time in the White House, however, which he enjoyed immensely. Jack even invited several of his idols to join him for lunch at the White House, including ex-Beatle George Harrison and tennis star Chris Evert.

Like all of the Fords, Jack felt at home in the White House. Sometimes he would wander into the kitchen to fix himself a sandwich for a quick lunch or a snack. There was always a good supply

The First Lady has traditionally supported her husband in his demanding position as the President of the United States. In certain circumstances, her role has expanded beyond that of White House hostess. When President Woodrow Wilson suffered a stroke during his second term in office, his wife met with government officials, summed up national issues, and brought presidential decisions to her husband's bedside. During the administration of Rutherford Hayes, the press joked about the influential role of his First Lady: "In the absence of his wife, Mr. Hayes is acting President."

Mrs. Ford enjoyed hosting parties at the White House, including outdoor dinners when the weather was mild.

of cold sliced meats and fresh bread on hand so that the active Fords could get a fast refueling at any time.

One of Jack's favorite snacks was a Reuben Sandwich. Although rye bread is traditional, Jack often substituted pumpernickel or Mrs. Ford's Homemade Toasting Bread, baked fresh each day in the White House kitchen. There was always crisp, well-drained sauerkraut on hand, and lean corned beef, which Jack sliced very thin. Jack preferred his sandwich made with Emmenthaler cheese and plenty of mustard. He usually grilled his Reuben until the bread had browned and the cheese was melted. A New York deli could not have improved on Jack's Reuben Sandwich!

Since Jack was a busy, independent young man, he did not always join his family for dinner. The White House butlers were confused at first, and always set a place for Jack, wondering when he would appear. Finally, President Ford reassured the kitchen staff that Jack was quite capable of meeting his nutritional needs on his own; we followed his good-natured advice to let Jack "do his own thing."

When Jack did join his family for meals at the White House, he was very enthusiastic about the food. At the end of the Fords' first year in the White House, Jack interrupted his sandwich-making one day to inform me, 'Y'know Chef, I haven't had a bad meal here yet." When I told him that he was not going to get a "bad" meal in the White House, Jack responded that, wherever one may be, "there has to be a bad meal once in a while." Jack was pleased to discover that, in this instance, he was quite mistaken.

Makes 4 sandwiches

8 slices rye or pumpernickel bread
8 teaspoons Dijon-style mustard
1 cup sauerkraut, well drained

8 slices Swiss cheese
16 very thin slices cooked corned beef
2 tablespoons CLARIFIED BUTTER (page 43)

1. Heat an electric griddle to 375°F.
2. Spread each bread slice with 1 teaspoon of mustard.
3. Top 4 of the bread slices with ¼ cup sauerkraut each.
4. Top each of the remaining 4 bread slices with 2 slices of cheese and 4 slices of corned beef.
5. Brush hot griddle with CLARIFIED BUTTER. Use a metal spatula to transfer bread slices to the hot griddle; heat until bread is lightly

browned on the underside. (To toast quickly, cover sandwiches with a sheet of aluminum foil. If a griddle is not available, use a nonstick sauté pan with a cover.)

6. Carefully fold each of the 4 meat-topped bread slices over onto the 4 sauerkraut-topped slices; press together gently.

7. Continue grilling until evenly browned on both sides. Remove sandwiches from the griddle when they are well-browned and cheese is melted.

8. Transfer to individual serving plates. Cut each sandwich in half and serve at once, with potato chips and dill pickle spears.

President Ford meets with son Jack's special luncheon guest, ex-Beatle George Harrison.
(COURTESY: GERALD R. FORD LIBRARY)

STEVE'S CHICKEN 'N' PICKLES SANDWICH

President Calvin Coolidge was known for his frugality and dry wit. After daily walks with his Secret Service guard, Coolidge would prepare sandwiches for the two of them in the White House pantry. Careful to slice the Vermont cheese evenly and to make the two sandwiches exactly equal in size, the President once commented, "I'll bet no other President of the United States ever made cheese sandwiches for you." When the guard agreed, President Coolidge cracked, "I have to furnish the cheese, too."

When Gerald Ford was appointed President in 1974, his youngest son was a recent high school graduate. Like the rest of his family, Steven Ford immediately became the object of intense media attention. Steve was able to handle his new role with maturity beyond his years. Perhaps his positive experience with the media at that time helped to influence Steve's decision later on to embark on an acting career.

While he was living in the White House, Steve decided to postpone college in favor of experiencing ranch life out West. He learned how to ride broncos and rope calves, and he eventually entered the rodeo circuit. This led to a minor role in a movie about rodeo life, which in turn resulted in a permanent position as the star of a daytime television series. I have watched Steve on television several times, and I think he is terrific.

Before Steve left to pursue his career, the staff very much enjoyed having him at the White House. A pleasant and friendly young man, Steve prepared his own breakfast each morning in the White House kitchen and often wandered in to make himself a quick lunch or snack. Like his brother, Jack, Steve was especially fond of sandwiches served on Mrs. Ford's Homemade Toasting Bread. His favorite concoction was a cold chicken sandwich made with mayonnaise and chopped dill pickles.

When Steve left in search of the fine future that lay ahead of him, the White House staff was rooting for him, yet we were genuinely sorry to see him go.

Makes 4 sandwiches

¼ teaspoon fresh thyme, or a pinch of dried	1 tablespoon vegetable oil
½ teaspoon chopped fresh parsley	3 tablespoons mayonnaise
1 garlic clove, minced	3 tablespoons chopped dill pickles
1 teaspoon salt	8 slices freshly baked bread, toasted (see MRS. FORD'S HOMEMADE TOASTING BREAD, page 162)
¼ teaspoon freshly ground white pepper	
1 large whole chicken breast	4 leaves crisp iceberg lettuce

1. Preheat oven to 350°F.

2. Blend chopped herbs and garlic with salt and pepper. Rub some into chicken breast; reserve extra.

3. In a cast-iron skillet, heat oil over medium-high heat; brown chicken breast on both sides.

4. Roast chicken in preheated oven for 25 minutes, basting twice.

5. Refrigerate cooked chicken to cool rapidly.

6. Cut cold chicken breast into very thin slices, using a long, sharp knife.

7. Mix mayonnaise with chopped pickles and spread evenly on each of the 8 bread slices.

8. Arrange sliced chicken on 4 of the bread slices; top the remaining 4 slices with lettuce leaves.

9. Sprinkle chicken slices with reserved seasoning. Put bread slices together to make 4 sandwiches.

10. Slice each sandwich in half and serve, or wrap tightly and refrigerate until serving time. Serve sandwiches with MATCHSTICK POTATOES or potato chips.

Steve Ford was a popular White House resident and an active participant in the Ford administration.
(COURTESY: GERALD R. FORD LIBRARY)

MATCHSTICK POTATOES

Serves 4

2 quarts vegetable oil

4 large Idaho baking potatoes, peeled

A pinch of salt

4 twists freshly ground white pepper

1. In a deep fryer or Dutch oven, heat oil to 350°F.
2. Cut potatoes into thin spears (¼ × 5 inches).
3. Fry potatoes in a basket in hot oil until tender, about 5 minutes; do not brown. Let drain.
4. Raise heat to 375°F.
5. Fry potatoes quickly in the hot oil until golden brown and crisp, about 3 minutes. Drain well on paper towels.
6. Season with salt and pepper. Serve hot.

FORD FAMILY FAVORITE ENTRÉES

SUNDAY ROAST WITH OVEN-ROASTED VEGETABLES

The Ford family's choice of menus was dubbed "Michigan gourmet," that is, hearty, healthy and unpretentious. When the Fords first arrived at the White House, the kitchen staff was informed that the family was easy to please at the dining table and would welcome almost anything we served, as long as portion sizes were not excessive—for reasons of both economics and weight control. The menu for Sunday dinner, however, was a long-established tradition in the Ford home: Mrs. Ford's Sunday Roast.

The Ford family practiced a Sunday ritual; church in the morning, a big brunch afterward (with waffles and strawberries), and in the evening, a dinner of Mrs. Ford's rib roast. No matter where his work carried him over the years—out on the campaign trail, to the capital, or somewhere in their home state of Michigan—Gerald Ford always attempted to get home to his family on Sundays. Living in the White House actually enabled the President to enjoy quiet Sundays with his family on a more regular basis.

During the rest of the week, family dinner favorites included other hearty home-style dishes such as spareribs with sauerkraut, spaghetti and meatballs, burgers wrapped in bacon, liver and onions, and various casseroles. Dinner was typically served with a lightly cooked vegetable and a tossed salad. The Fords usually skipped a first course and included dessert only by request, for which the White House kitchen kept plenty of fresh fruit and ice cream on hand.

In the Ford home, the dinner table served as an open forum for family discussions. The family always had plenty of different ideas and opinions to share along with their home-style meal.

Family life in the White House has always been an aspect of the presidency of utmost interest to the American public. Almost every event that occurs in the life of the First Family, no matter how inconsequential, becomes an object of national interest. At the core of American politics is the home of an American family, after all. The White House embodies domestic life carried on in the midst of world affairs. Franklin D. Roosevelt, who resided in the White House longer than any other President, noted, "I never forget that I live in a home owned by the American people." America has long owned the White House, but its residents have always held America's hearts.

Serves 6

6 *pounds rib roast*
3 *garlic cloves, pressed*
3 *tablespoons salt*
2 *teaspoons freshly ground black pepper*
2 *tablespoons vegetable oil*
6 *small (1-inch diameter) onions, peeled*
12 *baby carrots, peeled*

12 *small Maine boiling potatoes, peeled*
6 *small white turnips, peeled*
1 *bay leaf*
Fresh parsley sprig
1 *cup dry red wine, preferably Burgundy*
1 *cup beef bouillon*
A bunch of fresh watercress

1. Preheat oven to 375°F.

2. Rub rib roast with garlic. Season with salt and pepper.

3. In a large roasting pan, heat oil over medium-high heat; slowly brown roast on both sides.

4. Turn roast bone side up and transfer to lower shelf of preheated oven; roast for 45 minutes.

5. Remove pan from oven and drain off excess fat. Gently turn roast over.

6. Surround roast with onions, carrots, potatoes, and turnips; add bay leaf and parsley.

7. Roast on lower shelf of oven for 30 minutes (for medium-rare meat), occasionally basting meat and vegetables; remove vegetables when lightly browned and fork tender (they will cook faster than the roast) and keep warm in a covered casserole.

8. Remove roast and let stand for 15 minutes on a carving board.

9. Drain fat from roasting pan. Add wine and bouillon, and simmer over medium heat to reduce to 1½ cups; strain.

10. Use a long, sharp knife to carve roast into thin slices; arrange on a serving platter.

11. Surround sliced meat with warm vegetables; pour a little of the strained "jus" (pan juices) over all.

12. Garnish platter with watercress. Serve at once, with a sauceboat of the remaining "jus."

SWEET-AND-SOUR STUFFED CABBAGE

Cabbage dishes have long been appreciated at the White House, and sauerkraut has served as a favorite side dish for several First Families. President James Buchanan (1857–1861) was partial to simple sauerkraut, a sharp contrast to the fanciful party fare that typically graced his elaborate dining tables. Warren G. Harding (1921–1923) was also a fan of sauerkraut, especially served with his favored knockwurst. President Franklin D. Roosevelt (1933–1945) was so fond of sauerkraut with pigs' knuckles that he once served it to an esteemed White House guest, British Prime Minister Winston Churchill. The candid statesman later admitted that the pickled cabbage

One of President Ford's favorite vegetables was cabbage. He especially enjoyed Braised Red Cabbage, so this side dish usually appeared on the family dinner menu once a week, typically served with spareribs or pork chops. Sometimes sauerkraut was substituted. On other occasions, green cabbage leaves were stuffed with ground meat and rice, and served as an entrée.

Like the ubiquitous stuffed peppers, cabbage rolls, containing various fillings and accompanied by a number of different sauces, have appeared in various forms in a number of different cuisines. In Italy, *Cavolo Imbottito* is cabbage leaves stuffed with spinach, beef, and grated Romano cheese. The Polish cabbage rolls are known as *Golumpki* and contain potatoes and kasha, whereas the Germans' *Kohlrouladen* substitutes rolled oats. The Fords preferred a plain pork, beef, and rice filling, enlivened by a pungent Sweet-Sour Sauce.

Serves 4

1 large head green cabbage
¼ pound pork sausage
½ pound ground beef
1 teaspoon salt
A dash freshly ground black pepper
1 teaspoon dried thyme
6 drops of Tabasco sauce
¼ cup cooked rice, well-drained

1 tablespoon chopped fresh parsley
1 tablespoon butter
½ cup finely chopped onion
1 garlic clove, minced
1 egg
1½ cups SWEET-SOUR SAUCE

1. Halve cabbage through the stem. Wash in cold water.

2. Bring 3½ quarts of salted water to a boil, add cabbage, set cover slightly ajar, and simmer for 15 minutes; drain.

3. Peel off 8 outer leaves; spread them on wax or freezer paper, and top each with 1 or 2 inner leaves.

4. Preheat oven to 350°F.

5. In a mixing bowl, combine sausage and ground beef with salt, pepper, thyme, Tabasco sauce, cooked rice, and chopped parsley.

6. Melt butter in a small sauté pan, add onion and garlic and sauté for 3 to 4 minutes, or until golden brown. Add to meat mixture.

7. Add egg and mix well by hand.

8. Use an ice cream scoop to center equal amounts of stuffing on cabbage leaves.

9. Use a metal spatula to transfer each stuffed leaf to the center of a spread-out linen napkin. Gather napkin around cabbage and squeeze tightly to form closed cabbage rolls.

10. Form the cabbage rolls one by one, and place in a single layer in a 9 × 12-inch casserole dish. Bake on middle shelf of preheated oven for 15 minutes; remove from oven.

11. Spoon over 1 cup of SWEET-SOUR SAUCE. Cover with aluminum foil and return to oven for 30 minutes; remove from oven and remove foil.

12. Spoon over remaining ½ cup of SWEET-SOUR SAUCE. Bake, uncovered, for 30 minutes, or until cabbage is fork tender; remove from oven.

13. Let stand for 10 minutes to allow cabbage rolls to fully absorb the flavor of the sauce.

14. Transfer to a deep serving platter. Serve hot, with additional sauce, if desired.

might have proven acceptable, had it not been for "those damned pigs' knuckles leering at me."

SWEET-SOUR SAUCE

Makes 2½ cups

4 slices bacon
2 garlic cloves, minced
½ cup beef bouillon
¼ cup brown sugar
¼ cup cider vinegar

1 tablespoon prepared mustard
6 twists freshly ground white pepper
1½ cups strained chili sauce

1. Cut bacon slices crosswise into thin strips.

2. In a small sauté pan, brown the bacon over medium-high heat.

3. Add garlic and sauté for 1 minute; do not brown.

4. Add bouillon, sugar, vinegar, mustard, and pepper. Bring to a boil and let simmer for 5 minutes.

5. Add chili sauce and simmer for 5 minutes more. Store extra sauce in the refrigerator in a covered jar.

Betty Ford drops by the kitchen to
give the staff a personal thank-you.

BRAISED PORK CHOPS

The Fords liked very lean pork chops simmered in red wine and
served midwestern-style with braised red cabbage and apples.
When they were first married, however, Betty Ford prepared pork
chops casserole-style with stewed tomatoes, which she once
claimed was then just about the only entrée she knew how to cook:
"Those pork chops, and hamburgers, were my entire repertoire."
By the time the Fords arrived at the White House, however, Mrs.
Ford was highly skilled in meal preparation, specifically in cooking
the dishes her family preferred. Mrs. Ford readily shared with
the White House kitchen staff the recipes for Ford favorites.
We quickly discovered that we, too, could please the family's
palates.

As long as it is not overcooked, pork is naturally very tender. It
is best to buy the center loin and request that it be cut into chops,
in order to avoid pockets of hidden fat. Pork chops are best braised,
as broiling and pan-frying can dry out the meat. The Pennsylvania

Shakers are famous for their pork chops served with cabbage. In Italy, the same dish is the popular *Castatelle di Maiale con Cavolo.*

Apples and other cooked fruits enhance the naturally sweet flavor of red cabbage. Red wine or red wine vinegar helps to retain its pretty color. The French sometimes add brown sugar and chestnuts to *choux rouges,* while the Bavarian version includes chopped bacon. Plain Braised Red Cabbage can be spiced up by the addition of cloves, caraway, and other seasonings. President Ford requested that braised red cabbage be served on a regular basis at the White House, prepared the way midwesterners prefer. No problem there.

President James Buchanan reportedly favored pork served with pickled cabbage. Buchanan was the sole American president who served his full term as a bachelor. So President Buchanan's lovely 25-year-old niece served as his hostess in the White House, where her charm and beauty were said to have inspired the popular tune "Listen to the Mockingbird." Grover Cleveland, the only other bachelor elected President, was wed during his term in office. When President Cleveland's daughter was born, America was inspired to name a candy bar in her honor, the still-popular Baby Ruth.

Serves 6

1 teaspoon salt
¼ teaspoon freshly ground
   white pepper
6 pork chops, 1 inch thick
2 garlic cloves
1 tablespoon mixed fresh
   thyme, rosemary, and
   oregano, or 1 teaspoon dried

3 tablespoons flour
Grated rind of 1 lemon
3 tablespoons butter
1½ cups dry red wine
A bunch of fresh watercress

1. Mix salt and pepper; season pork chops on both sides.
2. Press garlic and mix with herbs; rub into pork chops on both sides.
3. Mix flour with lemon rind and spread on a plate; dredge pork chops on both sides.
4. In a heavy sauté pan, melt butter over medium-high heat, and brown pork chops for 5 minutes on each side.
5. Add half of the wine, cover, and simmer slowly for 20 minutes.
6. Turn pork chops over; add remaining ¾ cup wine and simmer, covered, for 30 minutes more, or until fork tender.
7. Arrange pork chops on a deep serving platter. Strain pan juices over chops.
8. Garnish platter with watercress. Serve very hot, with BRAISED RED CABBAGE.

BRAISED RED CABBAGE

Serves 6

8 strips bacon, thinly sliced
1 tablespoon vegetable oil
2 large onions, finely sliced
2 small heads red cabbage, shredded
2 apples, peeled and sliced
1 tablespoon salt

A pinch of freshly ground white pepper
¼ teaspoon nutmeg
A pinch of cinnamon
1 tablespoon sugar
2 cups dry red wine

1. In a 6-quart pot, heat bacon with oil over medium heat. Add onions, cover, and simmer for 8 minutes, stirring occasionally (do not brown onions).

2. Add half of the shredded cabbage; cover with apple slices, and top with remaining cabbage.

3. Add salt, pepper, nutmeg, cinnamon, and sugar. Pour wine over all.

4. Cut a circle of wax paper the same diameter as the pot; place over cabbage and anchor with a heatproof plate about the same size. Cover pot, and simmer for 15 minutes.

5. Remove coverings, and stir carefully with a long fork until well blended.

6. Cover and cook over low heat for 15 minutes; stir again with the fork.

7. Cover, and cook for 15 minutes more, or until juice is almost completely reduced. Serve hot.

SAUTÉED VEAL CHOPS AND MUSHROOMS

Veal is a mild-flavored meat that has not always been well liked by Americans, because of the inferior quality of the veal available commercially in the United States. Until quite recently, American veal came from older calves fed on grass or grain. In Switzerland, young calves have always been fed fresh milk and slaughtered early in life, and Swiss veal has long been a very popular, high-quality meat—firm and smooth, fine-grained, and mother-of-pearl white with a slight pinkish tinge. American veal tended to be less smooth, tough, and typically darkened in color to a reddish hue. Fortunately, tender milk-fed veal is now sold commercially in the United States, too, and veal has recently become a popular meat here, as it has long been in Switzerland and other parts of Europe.

As an apprentice chef at the Park Hotel in Davos, Switzerland, my first meal included veal chops. I can still recall how delicate and flavorful the meat was, and how pleased the head chef was with my final results. Even as a young chef in training, I understood the importance of high-quality meat and proper preparation techniques.

The best method to ensure a tender veal dish is to cook the meat very gently, even if the cut is from a milk-fed calf. Veal can be simmered in liquid to minimize shrinkage, and combined with vegetables to enhance the flavor. Most veal dishes should be prepared just before serving so that the meat does not have a chance to toughen up. An easy, flavorful way to prepare veal is to simmer lightly seasoned veal chops in butter and wine, and top with sautéed mushrooms. The Fords were very fond of this dish, especially with Noodle Pudding on the side.

Noodle Pudding is a German dish, a custard made with pasta and topped with grated cheese. As an unusual replacement for potatoes or rice, Noodle Pudding is a tasty accompaniment to pork, chicken, or veal dishes. A special Ford family recipe, Noodle Pudding was first introduced at the White House at Mrs. Ford's request. This interesting side dish became a popular menu item for the subsequent First Families as well.

Serves 6

1 teaspoon salt	*4 tablespoons butter*
¼ teaspoon freshly ground white pepper	*1 cup dry white wine*
	SAUTÉED MUSHROOMS
6 large loin veal chops (¾-inch thick)	*1 tablespoon chopped fresh parsley*
2 tablespoons flour	

1. Mix salt with pepper; season veal chops on both sides.

2. Spread flour on a plate; dredge chops on both sides.

3. In a large sauté pan, melt butter over medium-high heat, add the veal chops and brown for 5 minutes on each side.

4. Add half the wine, bring to a boil, cover, and simmer for 20 minutes.

5. Turn veal chops over. Add the remaining ½ cup of wine and cover.

6. Simmer for 20 minutes more, or until fork tender; keep warm.

7. Just before serving, transfer chops to a deep serving platter. Spoon on SAUTÉED MUSHROOMS, and garnish each chop with 2 of the button mushrooms.

8. Pour the hot pan juice over all, sprinkle with chopped parsley, and serve at once with warm NOODLE PUDDING.

Attentive preparation is essential to
get the best from a fine cut of meat.

(© DICK SWANSON)

SAUTÉED MUSHROOMS

Serves 6

12 *fresh button mushrooms,*
   washed
2 *tablespoons butter*
1 *tablespoon minced shallots*
2 *garlic cloves, finely minced*
1 *pound fresh mushrooms,*
   washed and thinly sliced

1 *teaspoon salt*
¼ *teaspoon freshly ground*
   white pepper
Juice of 2 lemons

1. Remove stems from button mushrooms. Slice stems; keep tops whole.

2. Melt butter in a small sauté pan, add shallots and garlic and sauté until golden brown.

3. Add button mushroom caps, sliced stems, and mushroom slices.

4. Add salt, pepper, and lemon juice; simmer for 7 minutes, or until liquid is completely reduced. Use at once.

Serves 6   **NOODLE PUDDING**

8 ounces flat noodles

3 eggs

1 cup milk

½ cup half-and-half

6 twists freshly ground white
  pepper

¼ teaspoon nutmeg

1 teaspoon salt

2 tablespoons Saltine cracker
  crumbs

2 teaspoons grated Parmesan
  cheese

2 tablespoons melted butter

1. Preheat oven to 325°F. Butter inside of a 6 × 10-inch casserole dish.

2. Cook noodles in 3 quarts of boiling salted water for 8 minutes; drain well.

3. In a mixing bowl, beat eggs with milk, half-and-half, pepper, and nutmeg, using a wire whisk.

4. Stir in salt and cooked noodles.

5. Pour into prepared pan. Sprinkle with cracker crumbs, grated cheese, and melted butter.

6. Set casserole dish in a shallow pan of water. Bake on middle shelf of preheated oven for 35 to 40 minutes, or until golden brown and firm to the touch.

7. Serve hot, from the casserole.

CHICKEN CORDON BLEU

Chicken has been a popular entrée with each of the five administrations I have served. Mrs. Ford was fond of chicken dishes, and she requested that the family dinner menus include other types of fowl as well. It was satisfying to be able to explore a variety of recipes using capon, duck, quail, and squab, as well as turkey and chicken. President Ford's favorite turned out to be Chicken Cordon Bleu. On occasion, the President even asked for a second helping.

Chicken Cordon Bleu is made with boneless breast of chicken, stuffed with finely diced ham and Swiss cheese. In France, the title of "cordon bleu" was an honor bestowed on "a female cook or chef of great distinction." The original cordon bleu was a medal suspended from a dark blue ribbon, awarded to women who were able to pass a special exam administered by the French government between 1578 and 1830. In 1895, the Cordon Bleu Cooking School opened in Paris. Successful graduates still command much respect all over the world.

Serves 6

Six 6-ounce chicken breasts,
   boned and skinned
2 tablespoons butter
2 tablespoons flour
¾ cup hot milk
¼ teaspoon salt
A pinch of freshly ground
   white pepper
A pinch of nutmeg
6 tablespoons finely diced
   Gruyère cheese
4 tablespoons finely diced
   cooked ham

1 tablespoon chopped fresh
   parsley
½ cup flour
2 eggs, beaten with a pinch of
   salt and white pepper
2 cups fresh French bread
   crumbs
½ cup CLARIFIED BUTTER (page
   43)
Fresh parsley sprigs

1. From each chicken breast, remove the small fillet. Wrap the small fillets in aluminum foil and flatten by pounding with a wooden mallet.

2. Use a sharp knife to cut a pocket in each chicken breast: On each side of the indentation left from the small fillet, make a long slit about ¼-inch deep (do not pierce through breast); gently pull the center strip away from the breast to reveal the pocket.

3. In a saucepan, melt butter over low heat, add flour, and work into a roux. Cook for 2 minutes, stirring constantly.

4. Stir in hot milk, salt, pepper, and nutmeg, and bring to a boil. Cook over low heat, stirring, until very thick; let cool.

5. When sauce is almost cold, fold in diced cheese and ham and chopped parsley.

6. Divide evenly among the chicken breast pockets. Press a flattened fillet over each stuffed pocket.

7. Carefully roll each stuffed breast in flour, dip in beaten egg mixture, and gently roll in fresh bread crumbs.

8. Transfer chicken breasts to a casserole dish. Refrigerate for 1 hour.

9. Preheat oven to 375°F.

10. In a cast-iron skillet, heat clarified butter over medium-high heat; sauté chicken breasts, stuffed side down, until golden brown. Carefully turn to brown other side.

11. Return sautéed chicken breasts to casserole dish. Bake in preheated oven for 10 minutes.

12. Arrange on a serving platter and garnish with sprigs of parsley. Serve at once, with a rice salad and a hot green vegetable.

A stuffed refrigerator is many a cook's primary problem each time the Thanksgiving holiday has passed. At the White House, it is very unusual to have leftovers, as we are careful to prepare all meals according to exact calculations. However, it is sometimes desirable to plan for extra food to use in special recipes and for snacks. The Fords liked to have leftovers on Thanksgiving for both of these purposes.

There are a number of interesting ways of using up the leftovers: turkey soup, turkey salad, turkey tetrazzini, turkey à la king, and the traditional turkey sandwich all can be embellished with unusual ingredients such as wild rice or spinach pasta, artichokes and asparagus, capers, and truffles. There is nothing redundant, for example, about a turkey club sandwich made with bacon, avocado, and jalapeño cheese, served on fresh sourdough bread with a generous slathering of hot mustard.

Perhaps the most challenging way to use up holiday leftovers is to create an interesting casserole. Turkey casserole recipes abound, and most can be elaborated on with delicious results. *Cacerola de Paro*, for example, is a South American turkey casserole made with

BAKED TURKEY CASSEROLE

The first Thanksgiving dinner held at the White House was during the administration of James K. Polk, America's eleventh President. The newspapers of the day reported on the event and predicted more holiday dinners in years to come: "The President had some friends to dinner—this new idea of a Thanksgiving in Washington was well observed and gave such general satisfaction as to lead to the dedication that it will be an annual custom hereafter."

pimientoes, olives, onions, and capers and seasoned with Spanish paprika.

The Fords were very fond of my own recipe for turkey casserole, a country-style dish made with smoked Virginia ham. This dish can serve as a creative way to use up leftover ham, as well as some of the extra turkey from a hearty holiday repast.

Serves 6 to 8

4 tablespoons butter
2 medium-size green peppers, julienned
6 tablespoons flour
3 cups hot chicken stock
1 pound cooked turkey, julienned
¼ pound smoked Virginia ham, julienned
1 tablespoon chopped fresh parsley

2 teaspoons Worcestershire sauce
A pinch of salt
A pinch of freshly ground white pepper
1 cup milk
10 ounces thin noodles
6 Saltine crackers, crushed
2 tablespoons grated Parmesan cheese

1. Melt butter in a 3-quart saucepan, add green pepper strips and sauté for 5 minutes.
2. Add flour and stir well.
3. Add hot stock and bring to a boil. Cook for 5 minutes, or until smooth; stirring constantly.
4. Add julienned turkey and ham, chopped parsley, Worcestershire sauce, salt, and pepper. Bring to a boil.
5. Gradually add milk, stirring gently. Simmer for 5 minutes.
6. Preheat oven to 375°F. Butter inside of a shallow casserole dish.
7. Cook noodles in 2 quarts of boiling salted water for 7 minutes; drain well.
8. Spread noodles in prepared pan. Spread turkey mixture evenly over noodles.
9. Sprinkle with cracker crumbs and grated cheese.
10. Bake on middle shelf of preheated oven for 20 minutes, or until heated through and lightly browned on top. Serve warm, with a green salad or tomatoes vinaigrette.

While living in the White House, the Fords tried to set a good example for the nation's households in the battle against inflation. To economize in the kitchen, Mrs. Ford eliminated the first course from the family dinner menus and cut back on the desserts. President Ford requested that the sugar bowl be removed from the dining table as a symbol of their support for public protest against inflated sugar prices. Mrs. Ford also attempted to renew consumer interest in less costly meats and nonmeat entrées, including basic casserole dishes.

Mrs. Ford asked the White House Kitchen staff to please "shop as carefully as they would for their own families." Each Monday, the First Lady reviewed my suggested menus for the following week's meals. Sometimes she would offer her own suggestions for simple, inexpensive family dinners such as tuna casserole or stuffed peppers. When she publicly endorsed such dishes as "a good way to stretch a dollar," her press secretary explained, "As a Congressional wife rearing four children, Betty Ford learned a lot about household economy. When she talks about stuffed green peppers as one way to stretch hamburger, she knows what she's talking about." And when Betty Ford requested a tuna casserole from the White House kitchen, she also knew what she was talking about!

The Ford family preferred plain cooking but welcomed creative elaborations on their basic menus, and they found that they enjoyed an unusual variation on the typical tuna noodle casserole in which shells were substituted for noodles and a light curry sauce replaced the thick cream sauce. To save dollars in the dining room, the creative cook who caters to open-minded dinner guests need not sacrifice one cent's worth of eating enjoyment.

CURRIED TUNA CASSEROLE

During the Truman era, "convenience foods" were catching on with the increasingly hurried and harried consumer. For women who were working outside of the home, time-saving meals and short-cut kitchen concepts began to grow popular. First Lady Bess Truman was admired by the public as a model homemaker. One of her favorite recipes, which she shared with her fellow housewives, was for a quick and easy tuna noodle casserole.

Serves 6 to 8

6 tablespoons butter
2 tablespoons minced shallots
2 garlic cloves, minced
2 medium-size red peppers, julienned
4 tablespoons flour
2 tablespoons curry powder
3 cups hot chicken stock
1 cup hot milk
6 twists freshly ground black pepper

1 tablespoon Worcestershire sauce
A pinch of salt
10 ounces small pasta shells
2 cups drained tuna
¼ cup dry sherry
6 Saltine crackers, crushed
2 tablespoons grated Parmesan cheese

1. Preheat oven to 375°F. Butter inside of a 2-quart casserole dish.
2. Melt butter in a 2-quart saucepan, add shallots and garlic and sauté lightly for 1 minute. Do not brown.
3. Stir in red pepper strips and sauté for 2 minutes.
4. Stir in flour and curry powder; cook, stirring constantly, until flour is well absorbed.
5. Add hot stock and bring to a boil; stir until smooth.
6. Add hot milk, pepper, Worcestershire sauce, and salt. Bring to a boil and simmer for 5 minutes; keep warm.
7. In a large pot of boiling salted water, cook pasta for 7 minutes, drain well, and transfer into the prepared casserole dish.
8. Flake tuna into small pieces and spread evenly over the shells.
9. Slowly pour over the sherry, then top with the warm sauce. Sprinkle with cracker crumbs and grated cheese.
10. Bake on middle shelf of preheated oven for 30 minutes, or until heated through and lightly browned on top. Serve warm, with hearts of palm, cold asparagus, or other vegetable vinaigrette.

LOBSTER FOO YUNG

Occasionally, the Fords requested an ethnic dish, usually a popular one like ravioli or lasagna. The Fords were especially fond of the interesting flavors and textures of Chinese-style stir-fry dishes. So they enjoyed an occasional Oriental dinner featuring their favorite: shrimp or lobster foo yung.

Egg foo yung is actually a Chinese-style omelet made with eggs and shredded vegetables, spiced with soy sauce, and topped with a light gravy. Diced pork, poultry, or seafood can also be included in the omelet patties. Foo yung may be quick-cooked in a wok in the traditional Chinese manner, or fried in hot oil in a cast-iron skillet. Served with rice, a foo yung dinner makes a well-balanced and nutritious meal that is light yet satisfying.

After a very rich State Dinner or an elaborate buffet was served at the White House, the Fords preferred to each lightly on the following day. Breakfast would consist of fruit juice, toasted home-made bread—with English muffins for the President—and tea. Lunch would be light, too, usually soup and bread or a cottage cheese plate. Dinner was also a light meal, and egg dishes often suited the Fords' evening menu needs. An omelet or foo yung was a frequent choice, served with rice, a tossed salad, and hot tea.

Serves 6

10 eggs
2 cups cooked shredded lobster
1 cup shredded celery
1 cup shredded Chinese black
   mushrooms, fresh or
   reconstituted
½ cup shredded onions

1 tablespoon salt
6 twists freshly ground black
   pepper
2 tablespoons dry sherry
6 tablespoons vegetable oil
FOO YUNG SAUCE

Martha Jefferson Ran-dolph's cookbook, The Vir-ginia Housewife, included a number of entries in Thomas Jefferson's own handwriting, such as his "Chinese Mode of Boiling Rice." Published in 1824, some of the sage observa-tions offered in the old cookbook are still appropri-ate today, such as: "The government of a family bears a Lilliputian resem-blance to the government of a nation."

1. Break eggs into a large mixing bowl; do not beat. Stir in shred-ded lobster, celery, mushrooms, and onions.

2. Stir in salt, pepper, and sherry. Mix batter well.

3. In a large cast-iron skillet, heat 2 tablespoons of the oil. Spoon one-third of the batter into the hot skillet to form 4 thick pancakes, each 4 to 5 inches in diameter, and fry over medium-high heat until golden-brown on both sides, about 2 minutes per side; drain on paper towels.

4. Heat 2 more tablespoons of the oil and fry 4 more pancakes; repeat once more to fry a final 4 pancakes.

5. Arrange the 12 pancakes on a serving platter, and serve at once with hot FOO YUNG SAUCE and steaming FRIED RICE.

FOO YUNG SAUCE

Makes 1¼ cups

1 cup chicken broth
1 tablespoon catsup
1 tablespoon soy sauce

1 tablespoon cornstarch
2 tablespoons dry sherry
2 tablespoons water

1. In a small saucepan, bring broth to a boil. Add catsup and soy sauce.

2. In a small bowl, combine cornstarch with sherry and water. Add to hot broth, and stir with a wire whisk.

3. Bring to a boil, and simmer briefly; serve hot.

FRIED RICE

Makes 4 cups

4 cups cooked rice
2 eggs
2 teaspoons salt

1 teaspoon dry sherry
1 tablespoon minced scallion
4 tablespoons vegetable oil

1. Place cooked rice in a large mixing bowl. Break eggs over rice.
2. Add salt, sherry, and minced scallion. Mix thoroughly, using a wooden spoon.
3. In a cast-iron skillet, heat vegetable oil; add rice and cook over medium heat, stirring occasionally, for 8 to 10 minutes, or until rice is heated through and no longer sticks together. Serve hot.

FORD FAMILY
FAVORITE DESSERTS

LEMON SPONGE PUDDING

At President Ford's State Dinners, a fine dessert was always served, and any array of assorted pastries was often made available at other official White House functions. But in private, the Fords usually confined their after-dinner sweets to family celebrations and special occasions when guests were dining with them.

One of the Fords' few dessert requests was for an old-fashioned lemon-flavored pudding. Popular in the 1800s, Lemon Sponge Pudding was once a light sponge cake coated with lemon sauce and turned out onto a warm serving platter. The modern-day version is less cakelike, now a feather-light pudding flavored with fresh lemon and steamed or baked. On cooling, the top of the pudding becomes spongy.

Lemon Sponge Pudding is plain yet versatile, delicious served with a variety of toppings. A well-strained black raspberry sauce enlivens the light dessert, and other fruit toppings—either warm or cold—are also tasty. The Fords preferred their special pudding served plain, or topped with a rich Rum-Raisin Sauce when calorie counting was conquered by an urge to splurge.

Serves 6 to 8

1 cup flour
2 cups sugar
2 cups cold milk
4 egg yolks
¼ teaspoon salt
Grated rind of 2 lemons

¾ cup lemon juice
2 tablespoons melted butter
4 egg whites, at room
  temperature
1 to 2 tablespoons
  confectioners' sugar

1. Preheat oven to 375°F. Butter inside of a 2-quart casserole dish.

2. In a 3-quart mixing bowl, combine flour with sugar. Stir in cold milk, using a wire whisk.

3. Add egg yolks, salt, lemon rind and juice, and melted butter; stir with the wire whisk.

4. In a clean, dry bowl, beat egg whites until stiff; fold into egg-yolk mixture.

5. Pour into prepared pan. Bake on middle shelf of preheated oven for 25 minutes, or until golden brown and fluffy.

6. Dust with confectioners' sugar and serve warm: At the dining table, spoon into individual dessert dishes and serve with RUM-RAISIN SAUCE, RASPBERRY SAUCE (PAGE 29), or other fruit topping. The pudding is also delicious served cold, with or without whipped cream.

Puddings in various forms and flavors have been favored by a number of First Families, including the Trumans. Dubbed by the press as "The Three Musketeers," President Truman and his wife were very close to their college-age daughter, Margaret, and the three ate most every meal together. The tight-knit Truman family concurred on a fondness for puddings, especially chocolate. President Truman was also a fan of "Ozark Pudding" made with apples and nuts, topped with all-American vanilla ice cream.

RUM-RAISIN SAUCE

Makes 2 cups

1½ cups water
½ cup seedless raisins
¼ cup sugar
A pinch of salt

2 tablespoons butter
1½ teaspoons flour
2 tablespoons dark rum

1. In a small saucepan, combine water with raisins, sugar, and salt.

2. Bring to a boil; simmer syrup for 10 minutes.

3. In a separate saucepan, melt butter, add flour, and work into a roux.

4. Gradually add the hot syrup to the roux, stirring constantly.

5. Bring to a boil and simmer for 3 minutes. Remove from heat.

6. Stir in rum. Serve warm.

WHITE HOUSE HOLIDAY FRUIT CAKE

Martha Washington's "Rich, Black Great Cake" is the most famous recipe from the First Lady's "receipt book." Although Mrs. Washington swore by a British cookbook—written by a man under the pen name of Hannah Glass—her own recipe for "Great Cake" became an American classic. American history books recorded Martha Washington's fruit cake recipe as "written out for her by granddaughter Martha Custis, datemarked Mount Vernon":

Take 40 eggs and divide the whites from the yolks and beat them to a froth then work four pounds of butter to a cream and put the whites of eggs to it a spoon full at a time till it is well worked then put four pounds of sugar finely powdered to it in the same manner then put in the youlks of eggs and 5 pounds of flower and 5 pounds of fruit. 2 hours

Fruit cake is distinctly British in origin, but became an American holiday custom during the eighteenth century. Known as "Great Cake," the special liquor-soaked dessert was reserved for the winter holidays. Sugar was a very expensive luxury, so the term "Great" might not have referred to taste or size, but to the cost of these choice cakes.

A rich, dense cake made with dried fruits and nuts, fruit cake is flavored with brandy or rum and allowed to age for at least one month. Contents can vary, depending on the cook's preferences. The White House Holiday Fruit Cake has long been based on a single reliable recipe, and "Great Cakes" have adorned holiday tables for every administration I have served. However, the fruit cakes have varied slightly from year to year as each pastry chef has added his personal touch.

Each Christmas season, White House Holiday Fruit Cakes are served at the many parties hosted by the First Family. Approximately 200 fruit cakes must be prepared in the White House kitchen in order to feed the thousands of holiday guests at celebrations for the staff, special family dinners, Congressional balls, and parties for the press.

The Fords also liked to give homemade fruit cakes to special friends as holiday gifts. A home cook should find this recipe for four loaves to be a practical quantity for gift giving and easy preparation using home kitchen equipment.

Makes 4 loaves

2 pounds golden raisins
1 pound diced mixed candied fruit
½ pound diced candied pineapple
½ pound currants
1½ cups pecan or walnut pieces
2 cups dry sherry
2 cups brandy
1½ cups white cornmeal
8 sticks (2 pounds) soft butter
4 cups light brown sugar
8 cups flour
18 eggs, at room temperature

1 tablespoon vanilla extract
1 teaspoon almond extract
1 teaspoon nutmeg
1 tablespoon cinnamon
1 tablespoon salt
½ cup honey
¼ cup light corn syrup
¼ cup molasses
5 teaspoons baking powder
4 tablespoons apricot jelly or strained apricot jam
1 tablespoon water
½ cup WHITE FONDANT (page 119)
1 tablespoon dark rum

1. In a large mixing bowl, cover raisins, diced candied fruit, currants, and nuts with sherry and brandy; let soak for 24 hours.

2. One hour before preparing cake batter, stir cornmeal into brandied fruit and nuts. (This will prevent them from sinking to the bottom of the cakes.)

3. In a large mixing bowl, cream butter with sugar. Add half the flour and mix well.

4. Beat in eggs one at a time; stir in vanilla and almond extract, nutmeg, cinnamon, and salt.

5. Stir in honey, syrup, and molasses; mix thoroughly.

6. Sift remaining 4 cups of flour with baking powder; stir into batter.

7. Fold brandied fruit and nuts into batter.

8. Preheat oven to 350°F. Grease four 9 × 5-inch loaf pans, and line each with brown paper.

9. Divide batter evenly among prepared pans. Bake on lower shelf of preheated oven for 30 minutes.

10. Reduce heat to 325°F; bake for 1 hour more, or until tops are brown and firm to the touch and a toothpick inserted near the center comes out clean.

11. Let pans cool on wire racks for 10 minutes.

12. Turn cakes out onto racks; do not remove brown paper.

13. In a small saucepan, mix apricot jelly or jam with water. Simmer until smooth, stirring constantly. Keep glaze warm. In a separate saucepan, combine the fondant with the rum and place over low heat, stirring, until the mixture is smooth. Use a pastry brush to coat tops of cakes with the warm apricot glaze, then with the warm sugar-rum glaze. (This adds sheen and flavor, while sealing in moisture.)

14. When cakes are cold, wrap tightly in plastic. Let cakes age in the refrigerator for at least one month before serving. Leave on the brown paper during the aging process to hold the cakes firm, while allowing excess oils to seep out. To serve, use a long serrated knife to slice cakes while still cold.

will bake it add to it half an ounce of mace and nutmeg half a pint of wine and some fresh brandy.

MRS. FORD'S CHOCOLATE ANGEL FOOD CAKE

Holiday cakes —including the traditional gingerbread house—have always been popular at the White House.

The President and his four offspring were avid skiers, swimmers, and tennis players. Like their father, the Ford boys played high school football. In her younger days, Betty Ford had practiced dance and had even studied professionally under the legendary Martha Graham. Later, as a busy Congressional wife and eventually First Lady, Mrs. Ford found the time to take long brisk walks.

Despite their physically active life-styles, the Fords did not exhibit excessive or insatiable appetites. The family diet was quite moderate, with rich dishes and second helpings limited to infrequent occasions. The rare dessert requested for family dinners was typically very light. Once in a while, Mrs. Ford liked to serve her active family an airy angel food cake.

An American creation, angel food cake is a light sponge-type cake made with well-beaten egg whites and fine cake flour. Weight-

conscious Americans appreciate the relatively low caloric value of this delicious dessert. Unlike most cakes, angel food cake is sweet but not high in fat. Even the chocolate-flavored cake is relatively low in fat content because cocoa is used rather than fat-rich chocolate made with cocoa butter.

The Ford family's housekeeper occasionally prepared a fancy version of Mrs. Ford's regular recipe by spreading the angel food cake with chocolate frosting, topping it with whipped cream, and freezing until serving time. The rich rendition was reserved for birthdays and other special family occasions when the Fords' diet conservatism would be temporarily cast aside.

James Monroe, America's fifth president, was tall, athletic, and an avid horseman, just like his predecessors George Washington and Thomas Jefferson. However, America's second President, John Adams, was short and stout. He reportedly felt particularly self-conscious around Washington and Jefferson. Adams's son inherited his father's physical stature and political career, but the sixth President of the United States was more like Monroe, Washington, and Jefferson in his lifelong commitment to physical training: Even at the age of fifty-six, John Quincy Adams reportedly took daily swims in the Potomac of up to 1½ hours.

Makes one 10-inch cake

1 cup plus 2 tablespoons cake flour	1 tablespoon lemon juice
¼ teaspoon salt	1 tablespoon water
¼ cup cocoa powder	1¼ teaspoon cream of tartar
1½ cups sugar	1 teaspoon vanilla extract
12 egg whites, at room temperature	1 teaspoon almond extract

1. Preheat oven to 350°F.
2. Sift flour three times with salt, cocoa powder, and half the sugar.
3. In a mixing bowl, beat egg whites with lemon juice, water, and cream of tartar until almost stiff, using an electric mixer.
4. Beat in the remaining ¾ cup sugar, vanilla, and almond extract; continue beating until stiff.
5. Sift one-third of the cocoa mixture over the egg whites; fold in gently, using a rubber spatula. Repeat two more times to add in the remaining cocoa mixture.
6. Spoon batter into an ungreased 10-inch tube pan. Bake on lower shelf of preheated oven for 45 minutes, or until cake springs back when touched lightly on top.
7. Turn upside down on wire rack to cool; cake will gradually loosen from the pan as it cools.
8. Turn over onto a serving platter, or store in an airtight cake tin. Serve plain, dusted with confectioners' sugar, or frosted with a light chocolate icing. Cake is also delicious topped with whipped cream and garnished with chocolate shavings.

MIKE'S CHOCOLATE-ORANGE CAKE

Cake has long served as a ceremonial dessert, used to end special meals on a memorable note. Successful cake baking requires attention to detail, accuracy in measuring ingredients, utilization of proper pans, and a constant oven temperature. It may have proven difficult to produce a successful Chocolate Cake using the recipe from the 1887 edition of The White House Cook Book:

One-half cup butter, two cups sugar, three-quarters of a cup sweet milk, two and one-half cups flour, whites of eight eggs, one teaspoonful of cream of tartar, one-half teaspoonful soda; bake in shallow pans. For the frosting— take the whites of three eggs, three tablespoonfuls of sugar and one tablespoonful of grated chocolate to one egg; put the cake together with the frosting, then frost the top of the cake with the same.

Michael Gerald Ford, the eldest of the Fords' offspring, was in his mid-twenties during the Ford administration. During the time his father was in the White House, Mike attended a theological seminary in western Massachusetts. He planned to work with high school and college students as a minister and counselor. While his father was Vice-President, Mike married Gayle Brumbaugh, a fellow college student from Wake Forest. With her blonde, wholesome good looks, Gayle fit in well with the all-American Fords.

When Mike and Gayle came "home" for the holidays or special family celebrations, the White House kitchen always tried to cater to their personal preferences. The young couple liked to indulge in their favorite desserts on these special occasions. Mike introduced an unusual cake one year, served to the Fords to help celebrate Gayle's birthday. The recipe combined the rich flavor of chocolate with the citrus tang of orange, and made an impressive presentation when ablaze with birthday candles. Mike's Chocolate-Orange Cake is perfect for any family's birthday celebrations.

Makes one 9-inch, 2-layer cake

3 oranges	½ teaspoon salt
2 sticks (1 cup) butter, softened	1 cup milk, at room
2 cups sugar	temperature
3 eggs	3 ounces semisweet chocolate
3 cups flour	ORANGE ICING
2 teaspoons baking powder	CANDIED ORANGE PEEL

1. Preheat oven to 350°F. Grease two 9-inch cake pans; dust lightly with flour. Grate peel of 3 oranges. Set aside.

2. In a large mixing bowl, cream butter with sugar until light and fluffy.

3. Add eggs one at a time, beating until smooth.

4. Sift flour with baking powder and salt.

5. Alternately add dry ingredients and milk to creamed mixture in thirds, mixing until batter is smooth after each addition.

6. Melt chocolate in the top of a double boiler. Remove from heat.

7. Transfer one-third of the batter into the top of the double boiler and gently mix with the melted chocolate.

8. Stir the orange peel into the remaining yellow batter. Divide evenly between the prepared pans.

9. Spread chocolate batter evenly over the orange-flavored batter; do not mix.

10. Bake on middle shelf of preheated oven for 25 to 30 minutes, or until firm to the touch. A toothpick inserted near the center should come out clean.

11. Let pans cool on wire racks for 10 minutes. Turn out on racks to cool completely before frosting.

12. Finish peeling 2 of the oranges. Slice and arrange over one layer; top with the second layer.

13. Frost top and sides of layer cake with ORANGE ICING and sprinkle top with CANDIED ORANGE PEEL. Refrigerate cake for 1 hour before serving. To slice cleanly, dip a cake knife in hot water before cutting each piece of cake.

ORANGE ICING

Makes about 2 cups

1 stick (½ cup) unsalted butter, softened
4 cups confectioners' sugar, sifted
¼ cup milk

Grated peel of 1 orange
2 drops orange food coloring (optional)
2 tablespoons Cointreau (optional)

1. In a large mixing bowl, cream butter until light and fluffy.

2. Add sugar 1 cup at a time, alternating with 1 tablespoon of milk; mix until smooth.

3. Add grated orange peel and whip until very fluffy; whip in food coloring and/or Cointreau, if desired.

4. Frost top and sides of a 2-layer cake with a thin coating of the icing. Fill a pastry bag fitted with a small star tube with remaining icing and decorate the top in an attractive manner; sprinkle with CANDIED ORANGE PEEL.

CANDIED ORANGE PEEL

2 oranges

1 to 2 tablespoons confectioners' sugar

1. Set oven at lowest temperature possible.

2. Peel the oranges, and cut orange peel as thin as possible into very fine julienne.

3. In a small saucepan, boil orange peel slivers in 1 cup water for 3 minutes.

4. Strain; dry slivers on paper towels.

5. Transfer slivers to a cake pan, and dust generously with sugar, using a shaker to ensure a thin, even coating.

6. Dry in preheated oven, stirring occasionally, for 1 hour, or until sugar is crystallized.

7. Keep candied peel in an airtight container until use.

SUSAN'S STRAWBERRY SHORTCAKE

When Queen Elizabeth visited the Franklin D. Roosevelts, an all-American meal was served. The menu included the popular dessert, Strawberry Shortcake. President Roosevelt was not the first White House resident to favor this dessert, however. In fact, the 1887 edition of The White House Cook Book *included this recipe:*

Make a rule of baking powder biscuit, with the exception of a little more shortening; divide the dough in half; lay one-half on the molding-board (half the dough makes one short-cake), divide this half again, and roll each piece large enough to cover a biscuit

For Susan Ford, living in the White House turned out to be teen heaven. A senior in high school, Susan brought her friends home to bowl in the White House bowling alley, invited her beaus to view popular films in the White House movie theater, and held parties in the third-floor Solarium. Her bright yellow bedroom in the Family Quarters was filled with schoolbooks, plants, and photos taken by Susan after she picked up some pointers from one of the White House photographers.

Active and athletic, Susan was tall and strong, like her father and brothers. When the President started watching his weight at the suggestion of the White House physician, Susan began to be more careful in her own dietary habits, limiting herself to moderate portions. Since desserts were served only on special occasions, Susan was able to stay in shape at the White House.

Susan's favorite treat was an old-fashioned all-American sweet, Strawberry Shortcake, which can be prepared with either a rich pastry dough or a delicate genoise, as in this recipe. The cake is sliced in half and filled with fresh strawberries and sweetened whipped cream, then topped with additional whipped cream and garnished with glazed whole strawberries.

President Ford was very fond of fresh strawberries. When in season, they were kept on hand in the White House to serve plain or in fruit salads. On those rare occasions when father and daughter really felt the urge to splurge, a special Strawberry Shortcake would be whipped up in the White House kitchen.

Makes one 10-inch cake

6 eggs, at room temperature	*3 pints fresh strawberries*
1 cup granulated sugar	*1 pint heavy cream, very cold*
Grated peel of ½ lemon	*1 teaspoon vanilla extract*
1 cup flour, sifted	*¼ cup confectioners' sugar*
1 stick (½ cup) butter, melted	*½ cup currant jelly*

1. Preheat oven to 375°F. Butter a 10-inch cake pan; dust lightly with flour.

2. In a mixing bowl, beat eggs with the granulated sugar until fluffy. Transfer to the top of a double boiler.

3. Set over hot water and continue beating until doubled in bulk and thickened, about 7 minutes.

4. Remove from heat. Continue beating until cooled. Fold in grated lemon peel.

5. Fold in one-third of the sifted flour; fold in one-third of the melted butter.

6. Repeat twice to fold in remaining flour and butter. Do not overmix batter.

7. Pour batter into prepared pan. Bake on lower shelf of preheated oven for 20 minutes, or until top is golden brown and firm to the touch and a toothpick inserted near the center comes out clean.

8. Let pan cool for 10 minutes on a wire rack.

9. Turn cake out onto wire rack and let cool completely. Wrap tightly in plastic, and refrigerate overnight.

10. Wash strawberries and remove stems; towel dry.

11. Reserve several smaller berries for garnish. Slice the rest.

12. In a cold mixing bowl, whip cream with vanilla. Fold in confectioners' sugar and beat until very stiff.

13. Use a long serrated knife to slice cold cake in half horizontally.

14. Spread the bottom layer with whipped cream (¼-inch thick) and top with sliced strawberries. Top with a thin layer of whipped cream and cover with the other cake layer, cut side down.

15. Frost entire cake with a thin layer of whipped cream, leaving enough to use for decoration. Garnish top with the small strawberries.

16. In a small saucepan, melt currant jelly. Use a pastry brush to glaze the decorative strawberries with the warm jelly.

17. Fill a cold pastry bag with the remaining whipped cream; use a small (#4) star tip to decorate the top and sides of the cake.

18. Refrigerate cake until serving time.

tin, or a large-sized pie tin; spread soft butter over the lower one and place the other on top of that; proceed with the other lump of dough the same, by cutting it in halves, and putting on another tin. Set them in the oven; when sufficiently baked take them out, separate each one by running a large kitchen knife through where the cold soft butter was spread. Then butter plentifully each crust, lay the bottom of each on earthen platters or dining-plates; cover thickly with a quart of strawberries that have been previously prepared with sugar, lay the crusts on the fruit. If there is any juice left, pour it around the cake. This makes a delicious shortcake. Peaches, raspberries, blackberries and huckleberries can be substituted for strawberries. Always send to the table with a pitcher of sweet cream.

PRESIDENT FORD'S BUTTER PECAN ICE CREAM

President Warren G. Harding died suddenly during his administration, which had become the center of much controversy and the focal point for an unpleasant political scandal. When the calm, cool, and candid Vice-President inherited the President's position, America heaved a national sigh of relief. Supreme Court Justice Oliver Wendell Holmes, Jr., spoke for the country when he evaluated the new Coolidge administration: "While I don't expect anything very astonishing from it, I don't want anything astonishing."

According to Betty Ford, the President's favorite food was ice cream. While he lived in the White House, President Ford confirmed this and demonstrated that his favorite flavor was, without a doubt, butter pecan. To keep the President happy, there was always plenty of Butter Pecan Ice Cream available in the White House freezers.

President Ford was disappointed when he lost the 1976 election, albeit by a very slim margin, because he really enjoyed serving the United States as President. The Fords had watched the election returns up in the Family Quarters with a small group of their close friends, including Joe Garagiola and Pearl Bailey. The kitchen sent up hot and cold hors d'oeuvres to help keep spirits high.

After the Fords had acknowledged the election results, the White House was quiet and still. There was no visible crying, no sign of anger, no outpouring of emotion. The Fords and their friends and supporters accepted America's decision with aplomb. That's the way it was.

When he was appointed President, Ford had promised the American public: "In all my public and private acts as your President, I expect to follow my instincts of openness and candor with full confidence that honesty is always the best policy in the end." President Ford wanted to be remembered for restoring public confidence in America and in the presidency. The aura of the Ford administration was one of honesty and candor; its relaxed motto was, "This is not the time for change." The atmosphere at the White House reflected the President's and the nation's calm, and it was indeed a happy time. When it became time for a change, the White House staff was truly sorry to say farewell to a fine First Family.

Makes 1½ quarts

4 whole eggs   *1 quart half-and-half*
4 egg yolks   *1 teaspoon vanilla extract*
¾ cup sugar   *1½ cups BUTTER PECANS*

1. In a large mixing bowl, beat eggs with yolks and sugar.
2. Add half the half-and-half and mix with a wire whisk.
3. In a saucepan, heat the remaining 2 cups of cream to the boiling point; slowly stir into the egg mixture.
4. Transfer to the top of a double boiler. Cook, stirring constantly, until mixture coats the spoon; do not boil.

5. Let cool over a bowl of ice, stirring often.

6. Add vanilla and BUTTER PECANS.

7. Place in an ice cream freezer and freeze to desired consistency, following manufacturer's instructions. Store in the freezer in an airtight plastic or stainless steel container.

BUTTER PECANS

Makes 1½ cups

3 tablespoons sugar

3 tablespoons butter

1¼ cups large pecan pieces

1. In a small nonstick sauté pan, brown sugar over low heat.

2. Stir in pecans; mix until nuts are well coated. Remove from heat.

3. Stir in butter and mix thoroughly.

SPECIAL EVENT RECIPES

EGGS BENEDICT

With the arrival of the Ford family, a friendly air settled over the White House. The staff found it easy to relax around the First Family, and the atmosphere in the White House was natural and personal, as in any large home with a big family. On those days when a party is planned, the White House always pulsates with preparations, but the calm aura of the Ford administration made even the special events flow smoothly.

The Ford family was particularly fond of brunches, perhaps because of their informality. On her eighteenth birthday, Susan Ford hosted a small brunch up in the Solarium. Susan had really celebrated the occasion on the previous day, with a big bash out on the South Lawn: grilled hot dogs and burgers, soft drinks and draft beer, a beautiful birthday cake decorated to resemble a camera, and a live rock band for dancing. Susan called it "the best party in the world," and she took to heart the advice former First Teenager Alice Roosevelt Longworth gave to young White House residents: "Have a helluva good time."

President Ford hosted a brunch one year, a holiday football party held on Thanksgiving. The guest list included some of Ford's former teammates from the University of Michigan's champion football team. The President retained an avid interest in football and remained a loyal fan of his alma mater's Wolverines. He was also a big fan of brunch-style fare, including the classic Eggs Benedict.

According to culinary legend, Eggs Benedict was first created in 1760 for Pope Benedict XIII in the kitchens of the Vatican. The traditional recipe includes poached eggs and cooked ham on a toasted muffin, topped with a rich Hollandaise sauce. Because of the richness of the dish, Eggs Benedict has lost favor in recent years with fat and cholesterol-wary consumers. However, as a breakfast or brunch specialty for notable occasions, this timeless dish is still very much in demand. The menus for Susan's eighteenth birthday brunch and her father's Thanksgiving football brunch both included Eggs Benedict. Despite the differences in the guest lists, the classic egg dish was very well received on both occasions.

Serves 2

2 *English muffins*
4 *slices Canadian bacon,*
  broiled
4 POACHED EGGS (*page 149*)

1 *cup warm* CHEF HALLER'S
  HOLLANDAISE SAUCE (*page 41*)
4 *thin slices of truffle (optional)*

1. Split muffins in half. Toast to a golden brown.
2. Top each half with 1 slice of hot Canadian bacon.
3. Top each slice with 1 freshly poached egg.
4. Spoon a generous amount of warm hollandaise sauce over each egg, and garnish with a truffle slice. Serve at once.

To ensure the finest results in the kitchen, it is always best to start with the freshest possible ingredients. (© NATIONAL GEOGRAPHIC)

Luci and her future husband,
Patrick Nugent, reflect the style
of the Johnson era.

The new Mrs. Charles Robb on the arm of her husband.

President Nixon will long be remembered for opening up U.S.-Chinese relations—
and for introducing Americans to the treasures of Chinese culture.

President Nixon leads an applauding audience at the huge dinner,
held outside the White House, in honor of the POWs.

Bride Tricia Nixon enters the Rose Garden on the arm of her proud father.

The historic aura of White House rooms provides a special ambiance for private meetings and teas.

On the Carters' thirty-first wedding anniversary the household staff surprised the President and First Lady with the gift of an engraved silver tray.

(© JEFF CARTER/UNI PHOTO)

Twelve days before Halloween,
Amy Carter celebrates her
tenth birthday with friends
and a festive pumpkin cake.
(COURTESY: JIMMY CARTER LIBRARY)

The White House
kitchen is koshered
when dinner guests'
needs so dictate.

Christmas guests at the White House sometimes provide surprises along with holiday cheer.

Working lunches at the White House often blend cultures as well as cuisines.

Special parties and State Dinners are occasionally conducted in the outside elegance of the White House during the milder months.

Even for small private dinners, attention to details makes all the difference— at the White House or your house.

Susan Ford called her eighteenth-birthday celebration "the best party in the world."

Betty Ford loved everything about hosting parties, from all of the advance planning right through the final dancing. As First Lady, she always made a visible effort to make White House guests feel welcome, to relax and really enjoy themselves. Since she was always so nice to everyone, it was only natural to be nice to Mrs. Ford. And because she so loved parties, one way to be nice to Betty Ford was to hold a party in her honor.

President Ford held a surprise party for his wife to celebrate their first Valentine's Day in the White House. A simple buffet was served in the Family Quarters to fifteen couples. After dinner, everyone gathered in the West Hall and made toasts to love and romance. The White House pastry chef created a heart-shaped cake to help the celebrants enjoy the romantic holiday.

During their final weeks in the White House, the Fords hosted a number of farewell parties in order to thank their many friends and supporters. During the last few days of the administration, President Ford held a surprise party for his wife. After attending a private dinner in Georgetown, the Fords returned to the quiet White House, where the President suggested a final dance in the darkened East Room. Suddenly, more than a hundred friends joined the Fords for a twirl around the dance floor and a party to celebrate the reign of a well-loved First Lady.

CHINESE PEPPER STEAK

One of Betty Ford's first official requests as First Lady was that dancing follow all State Dinners. Humorist Art Buchwald had published a book entitled *I Never Danced in the White House*, so Mrs. Ford invited him to a state dinner and made sure to dance with him. He later sent Mrs. Ford a framed poster of the cover of his book, with "Never" crossed out! Art Buchwald also joked with me when he came through the kitchen on tour with the Fords' social secretary, "Hi, Chef! I've been reading about you for a while now in the newspapers. You're doing OK. But remember, whatever you see while you work here, be sure to keep it to yourself. One day it might be worth money to you."

The menu from the surprise Valentine's Day party included one of Mrs. Ford's favorites, an unusual variation on all-American pepper steak. Mrs. Ford's steak struck the public's fancy, so the White House printed her recipe on special White House stationery in order to meet the numerous recipe requests.

The Executive Chef keeps an eye on official functions from beginning to end.
(© DICK SWANSON)

Serves 6

2 pounds beef tenderloin, well trimmed

2 tablespoons vegetable oil

½ cup finely chopped scallions, white parts only

2 garlic cloves, finely minced

1 green bell pepper, julienned

1 red bell pepper, julienned

½ teaspoon salt

6 twists freshly ground black pepper

½ cup hot beef bouillon

½ cup dry sherry

1 tablespoon soy sauce

2 tablespoons cornstarch

1 tablespoon chopped fresh parsley

1. Remove all fat and gristle from tenderloin. Cut beef into strips 1½ inches long by ¼ inch thick.

2. In a cast-iron skillet, heat 1 tablespoon of the oil; sauté scallions, garlic, and pepper strips for 1 minute. Drain on paper towels.

3. Add remaining tablespoon of oil to the skillet and heat; sauté beef strips quickly over high heat to brown lightly. Add salt and pepper, and reduce heat.

4. Add hot bouillon and stir. Gently stir in sautéed vegetables, bring to a boil, and let simmer.

5. In a small bowl, combine sherry and soy sauce with cornstarch; pour over simmering pepper steak.

6. Continue simmering, stirring constantly for 1 to 2 minutes, or until sauce thickens.

7. Spoon into a deep serving platter, sprinkle with chopped parsley, and serve at once with steamed white or brown rice, or wild rice.

On October 15, 1948, Elizabeth Anne Bloomer married Gerald Ford in Grand Rapids, Michigan. The groom had rushed directly from campaigning to the simple ceremony, and his shoes were still muddy! This was a standard family joke with the Fords in the years to come. For their honeymoon, the young couple drove to a University of Michigan football game, then attended a campaign speech given by Governor Dewey. They returned to Grand Rapids right away to continue their own campaign for Ford's first congressional seat. They won.

Twenty-six years later, the Fords celebrated their wedding anniversary in the White House. A small group of friends joined them for a party buffet where several sculpted, heart-shaped fruit ices were unveiled. The menu also included one of Mrs. Ford's favorite

BEEF STEW WITH WALNUTS

SPECIAL EVENT RECIPE

dishes, a simple stew beefed up with walnuts. The recipe was requested so often from the White House kitchen that it was printed up on special stationery for ease in meeting the demand.

Serves 6

2 pounds lean stew beef, cubed	A pinch of thyme
1 teaspoon salt	A pinch of marjoram
½ teaspoon freshly ground black pepper	1 cup dry red wine
	2 cups beef bouillon
2 tablespoons vegetable oil	4 large carrots, cubed
2 large onions, peeled and cubed	4 stalks celery, cubed
2 garlic cloves, finely minced	2 medium-size green peppers, seeded and cubed
2 tablespoons flour	½ cup walnut halves

1. Season beef cubes with salt and pepper. In a cast-iron skillet, heat oil; brown beef cubes on all sides over high heat.

2. Add onions and garlic; sauté until golden brown.

3. Transfer to a saucepan or Dutch oven and set over medium heat.

4. Stir in flour; add thyme, marjoram, wine, and bouillon.

5. Cover, and simmer for 1 hour, stirring occasionally.

6. Add carrots, celery, and peppers; stir gently.

7. Cover, and simmer for 30 minutes, or until vegetables are tender.

8. Spoon into a deep serving dish. Sprinkle with nuts and serve at once, with steamed white or brown rice, or wild rice.

LOBSTER EN BELLEVUE

The most memorable social event of the Ford administration was the visit of Queen Elizabeth. During America's Bicentennial, the Queen of England and her husband Prince Philip came to the White House for the anniversary of America's Declaration of Independence from Britain. The visit marked the first trip to the United States that the royal couple had made in almost twenty years.

The Fords held the historic State Dinner out in the Rose Garden. A hundred-foot white canopy covered with pink Queen Elizabeth roses heralded the guests' arrival at the entrance to the fragrant garden. Japanese lanterns illuminated the two dozen round tables, each set for ten excited guests. Even at the White House, where

visits from heads of state have been countless, the presence of Queen Elizabeth aroused a special, almost magical feeling.

The petite Queen sparkled with animation—and with her exquisite diamond tiara and jewelry—as she offered a momentous toast to President Ford, and to the long friendship between his country and her own:

> Both our peoples believe in the world of the individual and the family, in the freedom of religion and expression, and in the right to change the government by the ballot box rather than the gun, perhaps the best definition of democracy . . . we have stood together on things that matter.

The President, handsome in the formal white tie attire so rarely seen during his administration, eloquently toasted the Queen, praising the Bicentennial celebration as "a great reaffirmation of American pride" and the royal visit as a "vivid reminder of the continuing vitality of our friendship and partnership in a noble endeavor."

Entertainment was provided by a young pop duo, the Captain and Tennille, and by comedian Bob Hope. Hope, who was born in Britain, had already given four command performances for the

Amid the pomp and pressures of the presidency, the Fords were able to enjoy a strong family life and some casual good times.
(COURTESY: GERALD R. FORD LIBRARY)

Royal Family. The Queen was also an admitted fan of television personality Telly Savalas, who was included on the guest list along with Barbara Walters, Helen Hayes, 92-year-old Alice Roosevelt Longworth, designer Bill Blass, Olympic skater Dorothy Hamill, baseball great Willie Mays, and Lady Bird Johnson.

To suit the impressive guest list, the menu had to offer food that was attractive and tasty, yet feasible for a party of 224. Lobster en Bellevue is delicious and elegant, the perfect dish to serve to a queen. Each large red lobster was mounted with medallions of the white tail meat and surrounded by pink lobster claws, all garnished with fine slices of black truffle. The tender saddles of veal were double loins, stuffed, rolled, and roasted, served with crisp rice croquettes in delicate hand-woven noodle baskets. The pretty peach ice cream bombes were molded around the seasonal fruit and decorated with fresh raspberries. Everything looked and tasted absolutely glorious.

Julia Child hosted a televised broadcast of the royal visit to share the event with the American public. Royal etiquette rules that the Queen is never photographed while eating, so the State Dinner was not televised while in progress. Instead, viewers were taken on a tour of the White House kitchen, where the dinner preparation was explained and the dishes to be served were displayed. Ms. Child informed the fascinated television audience, "It's a delicious menu and a sensible one, too. . . . He doesn't have a large staff at the White House, but he's a master at planning out in advance. . . . They're lucky to have him." Mrs. Ford was also generous in her praise for the contribution made by the White House kitchen during the Queen's visit.

Actually, I felt fortunate to have the opportunity to serve the Queen of England, and honored to prepare a fine dinner for America's Bicentennial celebration and to contribute to a historic event. Needless to say, the White House kitchen staff had to work extra-long hours to ensure that the meal for the Queen was fit for a queen!

One memorable "work break" occurred by chance on the night of the Fourth of July, just three days before the event. While the President and Mrs. Ford watched from the Truman Balcony of the White House, the Bicentennial fireworks display illuminated the Washington sky. By 10:00 P.M., the kitchen work was complete for the night, so I headed for home. My weary legs were forced to stand for an extra hour, however, because I found myself in the midst of an immense traffic jam: Cars, taxis, and pedestrians thronged the streets surrounding the White House, as the city joined the President in watching the beautiful fireworks exploding overhead. Exhilaration overcame my exhaustion, and for once I was pleased to be stuck in traffic. I joined many of my fellow Americans who were standing on their cars to watch the majestic and historic Bicentennial display.

Serves 8

One 4-pound fresh lobster
Six one-pound fresh baby
  lobsters
2 to 3 tablespoons mayonnaise
48 slices of truffle or black
  olive
48 pimiento rounds
1 cup peeled, diced apples
2 cups tiny peas, cooked and
  well drained
2 cups diced carrots, cooked
  and well drained

1 cup diced celery, cooked and
  well drained
A pinch of salt
A pinch of freshly ground
  white pepper
1½ cups thick HOMEMADE
  MAYONNAISE (page 250)
1 tablespoon Worcestershire
  sauce
2 lemons, sliced
A bunch of fresh parsley

1. In a lobster pot or other large kettle, bring 1 gallon of water to a boil. Add large lobster, cover, and simmer for 10 minutes.

2. Add baby lobsters and simmer for 10 minutes more.

3. Remove from heat and let stand for 10 minutes.

4. Remove lobsters and chill in refrigerator for several hours (it is easier to remove the meat from the shell once the lobster is cold).

5. When well-chilled, remove claws from the baby lobsters. Crack claws and remove meat; discard claw shells.

6. Remove lobster tails from shells in one piece: turn lobster on its back and slice along both sides of the tail; remove the thin skin covering the tail meat, and gently pull the tail meat out of the shell.

7. Using a very sharp knife, slice the lobster tails on the slant into thin disks, or "medallions"; the large lobster tail should yield 12 medallions, the baby lobster tails 6 medallions each.

8. Clean out innards from the large lobster; set empty shell in the center of a large serving platter.

9. Arrange larger medallions in an overlapping row up the back of the large lobster shell; hold each medallion in place with a dot of mayonnaise.

10. Top each medallion with a truffle or olive slice and a pimiento round.

Betty Ford was an enthusiastic hostess during her tenure as First Lady—and she always took time to thank her staff for their hard work. (COURTESY: GERALD R. FORD LIBRARY)

11. In a mixing bowl, season diced apples and cooked vegetables with salt and pepper. Add the MAYONNAISE and Worcestershire sauce, and mix gently to coat well.

12. Spoon vegetable salad around the large lobster shell.

13. Arrange the smaller medallions and the claw meat from the baby lobsters on top of the vegetable salad. Top each medallion with a truffle or olive slice and a pimiento round.

14. Garnish platter with lemon slices and sprigs of fresh parsley. Chill for several hours before serving. Serve very cold, with cold SAUCE RÉMOULADE.

SAUCE RÉMOULADE

Makes 2½ cups

2 tablespoons drained, minced sour gherkin pickles

2 tablespoons drained, minced capers

1 tablespoon minced fresh chervil, or 1½ teaspoons dried

1 tablespoon minced fresh tarragon, or 1½ teaspoons dried

1 tablespoon chopped fresh parsley

1 teaspoon anchovy paste

¼ teaspoon salt

A pinch of freshly ground white pepper

1 tablespoon Dijon-style mustard

1½ cups mayonnaise

½ cup sour cream

1. In a mixing bowl, combine pickles, capers, chervil, tarragon, and parsley.
2. Add anchovy paste, salt, and pepper; mix in mustard.
3. Fold in mayonnaise and sour cream.
4. Chill for several hours. Serve in a chilled sauceboat.

RED COCKTAIL SAUCE

To help celebrate their first Christmas in the White House, the Fords hosted a huge Congressional Ball. It was the first party for the legislative branch of Congress in four years, and the first in some six years for the entire Congress, so dozens of members had never attended a White House party. The nonpartisan celebration for 1,000 was a grand success.

Betty Ford planned White House parties to project the Fords' philosophy of minimal pomp and protocol. The Fords believed that even the most stately parties should be easygoing and fun for all. Their social functions also reflected the variety in American culture through the choice of entertainment, the guests, the menus, and the decor. With the Ford administration, there arrived a fine new spirit in White House entertaining.

For the Congressional Christmas Ball, the state floor of the White House was transformed into a holiday fairyland. A glorious crèche was set up in one corner of the East Room, while the rest of the expansive room was ablaze with bright poinsettias. The White House pastry chef's annual gingerbread house enlivened the State Dining Room, where a massive buffet adorned a room-length table.

A glittering Christmas tree illuminated the North Hall, and elicited a few quips from President Ford:

> That tree and I have a lot in common. Neither of us expected to be in the White House a little while ago. Both of us were a little green. Both of us have been put on a pedestal and—I will add this as a postscript—both of us have been trimmed a little.

The menu for the Christmas buffet included fresh seafood cocktails with jumbo shrimp and king crab on ice, served on such special occasions with a festive Red Cocktail Sauce.

Makes 1 quart

1 cup catsup
1 cup horseradish, well drained
2 cups strained chili sauce

5 drops Tabasco sauce
1 tablespoon Worcestershire
   sauce

1. In a mixing bowl, blend catsup with horseradish using a wire whisk.
2. Add chili sauce and whisk well.
3. Whisk in Tabasco sauce and Worcestershire sauce. Use at once, or keep refrigerated in a glass jar.

SAFFRON RICE PILAF

Some of the most beautiful, thrilling, and truly memorable social events held at the White House have been State Dinners. Whether the social tempo of the incumbent administration is ceremonial and tempered, or refined and sedate, or informal and lively, there is always an undercurrent of excitement associated with dining at the home of the President of the United States.

State Dinners always mean a lot of hard work, for the First Family as well as the White House staff. The President and the First Lady must be pleased with the entire event in every way, and they have to attend to the large group of important guests to ensure their satisfaction as well. The Fords were always delighted with the State Dinners served during their stay at the White House, and actually managed to enjoy themselves at these events.

Only a few of the Fords' state dinners were formal, and all were undeniably fun. For the first time, unmarried guests were able to bring their own dates for the evening instead of adhering to tradition by attending alone. The guest lists for State Dinners were compiled to include individuals from a wide array of fields: scientists and industrialists, artists and authors, union leaders and political followers, film stars and athletes. The menus for the Fords' State Dinners were short and simple, yet attractive and elegant. The dinner period was limited to just over an hour in order to leave enough time and energy for after-dinner dancing.

At the Fords' state dinner in honor of Yitzhak Rabin of Israel, Mrs. Ford coaxed the Prime Minister onto the dance floor. A very serious man and a tough negotiator, Rabin proved to be a pleasant dance partner. The menu served to the Prime Minister included his favored fish, accompanied by a flavorful saffron rice ring.

Saffron is an aromatic spice that originated in Asia and is currently cultivated in southern Europe. The most expensive spice on the market today, saffron is made from the dried stigmas of the purple-flowered saffron crocus. Since each flower only bears three stigmas, over four thousand flowers are required to produce a single ounce of the spice. Saffron has a musky smell and a golden color, and the spice imparts a distinctively fine flavor and hue to soups and desserts, curries and rice dishes. Fortunately for those who favor saffron, a little pinch can go a long way.

Saffron rice was served at several of the Fords' state dinners, as well as at Mrs. Ford's Senate Ladies' Luncheon. For official White House functions, Mrs. Ford liked to plan around a central theme. She often arranged to borrow impressive pieces of art and crafted works to highlight the motif, such as a collection of American-made silver, Steuben glass, or antique American Indian baskets. At her Senate Ladies' Luncheon, the American folk art theme was illustrated with folk dolls loaned by the Shelburn Museum in Vermont.

Serves 6 to 8

2 tablespoons butter
1 tablespoon finely minced
shallots
2 garlic cloves, finely minced
1½ cups long-grain rice
3 cups hot chicken stock

A generous pinch of saffron
1 bay leaf
1 teaspoon salt
¼ teaspoon freshly ground
white pepper

1. Melt butter in a 2-quart saucepan, add shallots and garlic and sauté for 3 minutes. Do not brown.
2. Add rice and mix well.

3. Add hot stock and bring to a boil.

4. Add saffron, bay leaf, salt and pepper; cover, and simmer over medium heat for 20 minutes, or until liquid is completely absorbed.

5. Remove from heat and let stand, covered, for 10 minutes; remove bay leaf. (Do not season cooked rice because consistency will turn mushy from excessive stirring and dish will taste unevenly seasoned.)

6. Transfer to a deep serving platter, and serve steaming hot.

During the bicentennial year, the White House kitchen was constantly busy. (WASHINGTON POST PHOTOGRAPH BY LINDA WHEELER)

Mrs. Ford collected recipes and menus from the meals served in the White House by some of the former First Ladies. To help celebrate America's Bicentennial, Mrs. Ford served a special dinner in honor of Thomas Jefferson. The old-fashioned American-style meal was designed to resemble the hearty dinners served 200 years earlier by Jefferson at his Virginia estate, before the White House had even been built.

Thomas Jefferson was an epicure, one of America's leaders in the introduction of new and exotic foods. Yet, his own dinner table at Monticello was usually laden with simple Southern staples such as fried chicken and country ham, grits and greens, corn bread and spoon bread. Moderate in his eating habits, Thomas Jefferson lived a long and healthy life. He made sure to leave room in his sensible diet for both the world's finest foods and America's most modest fare.

Spoon Bread has been a popular dish on America's tables since colonial times. Once served as an Indian porridge called "suppawn," Spoon Bread was also known as "batter bread." A light cornmeal soufflé, Spoon Bread has a custardlike consistency and a crusty top, so it is served and eaten with spoons. Similar to Italian polenta, Spoon Bread can be eaten plain, lightly buttered, or cooled, sliced and sautéed.

In Jefferson's kitchen at Monticello, batches of spoon bread were baked for the early-morning breakfasts, midday main meals, and late-night light suppers. Because they were so active physically, America's forefathers could afford to eat heartily. It is fun but impractical to reproduce historic menus for a weight-conscious modern-day family. Spoon bread, however, is an American classic that bears repeating by today's cooks.

SPOON BREAD

Serves 6 to 8

3 cups milk	*1 scant cup stone-ground white*
2 teaspoons salt	* cornmeal*
¼ teaspoon freshly ground	*3 eggs, well beaten*
* white pepper*	*3 teaspoons baking powder*
A pinch of nutmeg	*2 tablespoons soft butter*

1. Preheat oven to 350°F. Butter a shallow ovenproof dish.
2. In a 1½-quart saucepan, combine 2 cups of the milk with salt, pepper, and nutmeg; bring to a boil.

3. Stir in cornmeal, using a wire whisk; continue stirring over low heat until thick, about 5 minutes.

4. In a small mixing bowl, combine the remaining cup of milk with eggs and baking powder; stir into thickened cornmeal. Fold in soft butter.

5. Spoon into prepared pan. Set casserole dish in a shallow pan of water.

6. Bake on middle shelf of preheated oven for 30 minutes, or until top is golden brown and firm to the touch. Serve at once. Serve straight from the baking dish, "family style."

MUSHROOMS PROVENÇALE

In the unpredictable world of politics, more may be accomplished in a few hours at the dinner table than in many days spent around a conference table. For this reason, a significant number of impressive and extravagant meals are served in Washington. During my twenty-plus years as Executive Chef at the White House, the most concentrated period of such important dining events occurred during the celebration of America's Bicentennial.

The Spirit of '76 swept excitement across America and brought on an incredibly busy season for the White House kitchen. In July of that year, the White House hosted as many as two State Dinners a week! An immense white tent was installed in the Rose Garden, above round dining tables where as many as 240 guests were seated for each of the special dinners. A number of world leaders dined at the White House to help America celebrate the Bicentennial, including the Queen of England, the King and Queen of Spain, Chancellor Schmidt of Germany, the Prime Minister of Australia, the President of Finland, and the President of France.

The very first Bicentennial visit was made by Valéry Giscard d'Estaing, then President of France. At a beautiful State Dinner attended by 160 guests—including Clint Eastwood, Mickey Mantle, and Ann Landers—President Ford welcomed the guest of honor with a special toast, "both to express our gratitude for the assistance of France two hundred years ago and in the recognition of the continued important role which France and the United States must play as allies in the world today."

The following evening, a fête for 200 was held at the French embassy in honor of the Fords. French wines accompanied a fine foie gras, a stew of quail and lobsters served in delicate pastry nests, plus potato slices flavored with ham, five kinds of French cheese, and a molded sherbet made with fresh raspberries.

The menu from the Fords' dinner for President Giscard d'Estaing was similarly impressive. The salmon was poached in champagne, chilled, and glazed in aspic, and served on platters garnished with wedges of lemon, sprigs of fresh parsley, and rosettes of salmon mousse. The fillet was a delectable beef tenderloin prepared with a French inspiration, red wine laced with truffles. Another French creation, Mushrooms Provençale, made a savory side dish at this elegant meal. It is reasonable to surmise that much was accomplished across those two dinner tables!

Serves 6 to 8

2 pounds tiny fresh mushrooms
2 tablespoons butter
2 tablespoons minced shallots
2 garlic cloves, finely minced
Salt
Freshly ground white pepper

Juice of 1 lemon
2 large ripe tomatoes, peeled and seeded
1 tablespoon olive oil
1 tablespoon chopped fresh parsley

1. Rinse mushrooms lightly in cold water; drain well.
2. Melt butter in a sauté pan, sauté shallots until golden brown. Stir in minced garlic.
3. Add mushrooms, 1 teaspoon salt, ¼ teaspoon pepper, and lemon juice. Cook over high heat, stirring often, until liquid is evaporated.
4. Spoon mushrooms into an oval serving dish.
5. Slice tomatoes into julienne strips.
6. Heat oil in a small skillet, add tomato strips and sauté for 10 seconds. Season lightly with salt and pepper.
7. Top mushrooms with tomato strips. Sprinkle with chopped parsley and serve at once, as a side dish for broiled entrées such as filet mignon, lamb chops, fish or shellfish.

MOUSSE AU CHOCOLAT

Only a week after he was appointed President of the United States, Ford hosted the first State Dinner of his administration. It had been many months since the last State Dinner had been held in the White House. Even with less than a week to prepare dinner for 120 guests, President Ford's state dinner for the King of Jordan turned out to be a smooth success.

The Fords had hosted a dinner for King Hussein earlier that year, when President Nixon was traveling, and the previous experience eased the pressure. The Fords were grateful for an early opportunity to set their personal imprint on White House social events: like those that followed, their first State Dinner was relaxed, friendly, and fun for all.

King Hussein's religious convictions prohibited the inclusion of shellfish and alcoholic beverages on the state dinner menu. The absence of a pastry chef at the time precluded the inclusion of an elaborate dessert. And the lack of lead time necessitated a simple menu that could be rapidly and readily prepared. Fortunately, a cold first course and a cold Mousse au Chocolat for dessert were perfect for a hot summer evening, and three weeks' worth of food preparation was able to be condensed into one week of hard work. After their successful dinner, the Fords sent word to the White House kitchen that they were very pleased with our efforts as well as the food.

After-dinner dance music featured some of the Ford's favorite tunes, including "Betty Coed." Since the Fords had not yet moved into the White House, they left at midnight for their home in Virginia, with President Ford announcing, "I had a great time—wonderful. We love to dance. But I have to work; I'll be at the office at 8:00 A.M."

Once the Fords were settled in the Family Quarters at the White House, they could dance at official functions until as late as 1:00 A.M.—living upstairs made for an easy commute.

Serves 6 to 8

5 egg yolks
¼ cup sugar
1 cup scalded milk, cooled
   slightly
3 ounces sweet chocolate,
   grated

1 cup cold milk
1 cup very cold heavy cream
1 teaspoon vanilla

1. In a mixing bowl, beat egg yolks with sugar. Quickly stir in hot milk.

2. Stir in grated chocolate and cold milk.

3. Transfer to the top of a double boiler. Cook over low heat, stirring constantly, until mixture coats the spoon; strain.

4. Let cool over a bowl of ice, stirring occasionally with a wire whisk.

5. In a cold 2-quart mixing bowl, whip cream until stiff.

6. Add vanilla to cold chocolate mixture; add to whipped cream and fold with the wire whisk until blended.

7. Spoon into a chilled serving bowl. Refrigerate for 2 to 3 hours before serving. Decorate with additional whipped cream and chocolate shavings, if desired.

Betty Ford had been trained professionally as a dancer and was always fond of the fine arts. As First Lady, she paid special attention to the guest lists for the State Dinners and other official functions, taking care to invite dancers and singers, poets and playwrights, actors and artists. As an ex-football player and avid sports fan, President Ford enjoyed the company of athletes and others involved in professional sports. All this made for an interesting cross-section of guests.

The guest list for a dinner held by the Fords in honor of Prime Minister Harold Wilson of Great Britain included Cary Grant and Kirk Douglas, Saul Bellow and Margaret Truman Daniel, Warren Beatty and skier Billy Kidd. Guests at a state dinner for King Hussein of Jordan included Charlton Heston, Gloria Vanderbilt, champion race car driver Richard Petty, and world boxing champ Mohammad Ali. Washington Redskins football star Larry Brown sat next to Katharine Graham, owner of the *Washington Post*, at another of the Fords' official functions. Other well-known guests who were invited to dine with the Fords included Jack Paar, Alistair Cooke, Chad Everett, Ginger Rogers, Ralph Lauren, Estée Lauder, poet Rod McKuen, *Jaws* author Peter Benchley, baseball greats Hank Aaron and Johnny Bench, former football star George Blanda, boxer Joe Frazier, race car champion Mario Andretti, and golf pro Arnold Palmer.

When the Fords hosted a State Dinner in 1975 to honor President

PEACH MELBA

Anwar Sadat of Egypt, the guest list included Omar Sharif and Ernest Borgnine, Olympic gold medalist Bruce Jenner, and sports commentator Jim McKay. A last-minute guest was Pearl Bailey, who closed down her Boston performance of *Hello Dolly!* for the night in order to substitute for the scheduled entertainer who had fallen ill. The menu included Peach Melba, a classic dish named after another famous singer.

Nellie Melba was an Australian-born soprano who reportedly enjoyed eating peaches and ice cream. Famed chef Escoffier created a variation on Ms. Melba's favorite dish when the singer visited the London hotel where he worked: He lined a silver dish with a thick layer of the best vanilla ice cream, topped it with fresh peaches soaked in vanilla syrup, and covered it all with raspberry purée. Peach Melba is now known and loved the world over. The original recipe for Peach Melba does not include whipped cream, but used sparingly, the garnish improves the presentation of this classic dish.

Serves 6

6 medium-size very ripe peaches

1 quart vanilla ice cream

1 pint fresh raspberries, or one 10-ounce package frozen raspberries

4 tablespoons confectioners' sugar

¼ cup sliced almonds

1 cup very cold heavy cream

1. Peel peaches, slice in half, and remove pits. (To peel peaches, dip in boiling water for 2 to 3 seconds, transfer into ice water, and peel immediately. If peaches are not very ripe, poach for a few minutes in vanilla-flavored sugar syrup until tender; let cool before adding to ice cream.)

2. Scoop ice cream into 12 small scoops; set on a chilled serving platter or in chilled individual serving dishes, 2 scoops per dish.

3. Lightly press a peach half onto each scoop, cut side down. Freeze for 5 to 10 minutes, no longer.

4. Purée raspberries; mix with sugar.

5. Remove peaches from freezer. Spoon on raspberry sauce, and sprinkle with almonds.

6. In a chilled bowl, whip the cream until stiff. Use a chilled pastry bag fitted with a small (#4) star tip to decorate tops very delicately with the whipped cream. Serve at once.

The Ford family often hosted intimate dinners in the White House's smaller dining rooms.

IRISH COFFEE

Unlike even the best restaurants and the finest hotels, the White House kitchen has no "commercial" purposes; its sole aim is to elicit an expression of delight and satisfaction on every diner's face. The White House chef must learn how to take advantage of all that his unique position offers in order to please his many "customers" —premiers and prime ministers, kings and queens, politicians and military rulers, sports stars and movie stars, and the President of the United States.

When he dined at the White House, President Ford was one very satisfied "customer." Right through the final demitasse served at the very last State Dinner, the Fords were pleased with all of the meals prepared by the White House kitchen.

One pleasing way to end a fine dinner is to serve mugs of hot Irish coffee. Served after, with, or as a dessert, Irish coffee includes a shot of sweetened whiskey that is sipped through a layer of heavy cream. At a St. Patrick's Day State Dinner held in honor of the Prime Minister of Ireland, the menu concluded with this traditional drink.

President Ford enjoyed all of the holidays and other celebrations held at the White House. And the Fords demonstrated their gratitude to the White House kitchen staff for the sustenance provided during their brief and very pleasant stay. President Ford remarked that one reason he so enjoyed life in the White House was "the superior caliber of the permanent staff." And Mrs. Ford said, "Presidents come and go, but the people are the White House."

When the Fords were leaving the White House, Mrs. Ford stopped by the kitchen to thank me for all I had done to support her family and the Ford administration and make her role as First Lady both easier and more enjoyable. The Ford family made the work of the White House staff a pleasure as well as an honor, and I was very glad that I had the opportunity to assist them in serving a successful and satisfying term in the White House.

Serves 4

6 tablespoons heavy cream   ½ cup Irish whiskey
4 small sugar cubes   3 cups hot coffee

1. Whip cream until thickened but not stiff; chill.
2. Warm 4 Irish coffee mugs by rinsing in very hot water; dry thoroughly.

3. Place 1 sugar cube and 2 tablespoons whiskey in each warm glass. Use the back of a spoon to crush each cube against the side of the glass.

4. Pour ¾ cup hot coffee into each glass.

5. Slowly pour thickened cream over the back of a spoon held just above the coffee; cream should spread evenly over the top. Fill each glass to the brim with the cream. Do not stir.

6. Serve at once.

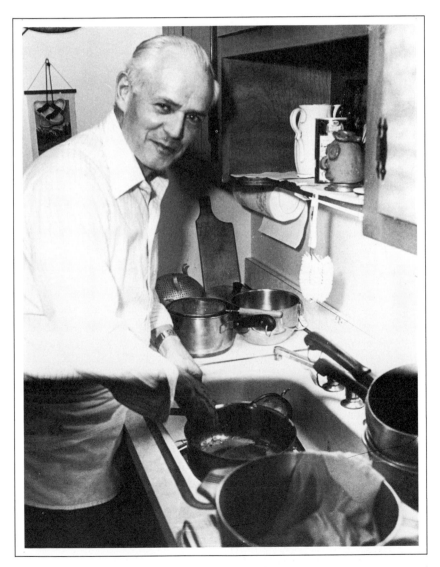

At home as at work, Chef Haller keeps his kitchen in spotless condition and in smooth working order.
(WASHINGTON POST PHOTOGRAPH BY HARRY NALTCHAYAN)

THE
CARTER FAMILY

Family Favorites from Plains

The Carters'
Favorite Soups and Salads

Carter Family Favorite Entrées

Carter Family Favorites
On~the~Side

Carter Family
Down~Home Sweets

Special Event Recipes

FAMILY FAVORITES
FROM PLAINS

To people from the South, "Southern-style cooking" means delicious food. Even though America's South covers a somewhat vague geographical area, most Southerners regard their home territory as a distinct country within a country. Bound together by a common attitude, Southerners place great value on tradition, including culinary and dining customs.

Even before they had settled into the White House, reports in the press began to highlight the Carters' Southern style of life. The public was forewarned that the White House would soon serve grits to guests. While New Englanders gasped and Midwesterners gagged, Southerners smiled with knowing satisfaction. In the Carters' home state of Georgia and the rest of the South, grits had long been an institution, a dish that Southerners were willing to share with full confidence of public acceptance.

Julia Child, the noted chef and public spokesperson for the culinary field, voiced strong support for the inclusion of Southern dishes on the Carters' White House menus: "I am all for trotting out American regional cooking for official visitors. We most certainly must act to preserve our culinary heritages, and what better way to encourage them than at the White House?"

The White House kitchen was in full agreement. As the Executive Chef for three previous Presidents, each from different parts of the country and with individual tastes and life-styles, I was accustomed to adjusting the White House menus to suit the First Families' needs. I had also developed a strong belief in the ability of the White House to set national trends. It was time for the rest of America to be able to experience the fine cooking and gracious dining that was customary in the South. And I had looked forward to the chance to learn some new Southern-style recipes and cooking techniques myself.

For the Carters' first breakfast in the White House, grits were included on the menu. A staple dish for the Carters and their

BAKED CHEESE GRITS

Calvin Coolidge was America's thirtieth, and possibly thriftiest, President. In order to save money, President Coolidge invited political leaders to the White House for breakfast, the least expensive meal for entertaining guests. To save time, the President sometimes had his hair trimmed while he ate breakfast, typically an inexpensive breakfast cereal made with cooked whole wheat and rye. A native of New England, President Coolidge liked corn finely ground into cornmeal and baked into his favorite corn muffins, which were included on the standard menu served at his "working breakfasts" in the White House.

(REPRINTED BY PERMISSION:
TRIBUNE MEDIA SERVICES)

Southern visitors, grits soon became standard fare for White House guests from all over the world. The White House kitchen had quickly realized that many of the Carters' distinguished visitors really expected to be served grits, and most were pleasantly surprised to discover that they actually liked the taste of the ground hominy dish.

Grits are made from hulled corn that has been washed and boiled into "hominy," a term derived from the Algonquin Indian *tackhummin,* which means to grind corn. Finely ground hominy is known as *cornmeal,* whereas the coarsely ground product is called *grits.* In the South, grits are typically eaten for breakfast, and as a side dish with other meals.

The key to preparing palatable grits is to avoid a watery product by cooking completely and stirring often. Grits taste delicious served hot with melted butter, or baked with a flavorful cheese. Leftover grits can be shaped into patties and fried to a golden brown, served plain or with maple syrup.

Although Rosalynn Carter feared that grits were "too fattening" for everyday eating, this high-carbohydrate grain is actually low in fat calories unless slathered with butter. President Carter liked grits baked with cheese, so the dish was often included on the family's weekend breakfast menu. The Carters' guests, however, wanted grits to be served on a more frequent basis.

Serves 6 to 8

4 cups chicken bouillon	2 cups grated sharp cheddar
1 cup enriched white hominy	cheese
grits	4 egg yolks
1 teaspoon Worcestershire	1/4 to 1/2 cup cold milk
sauce	4 egg whites, at room
1 stick (1/2 cup) butter	temperature

1. Preheat oven to 350°F. Grease inside of a 2-quart casserole dish.

2. Bring bouillon to a boil in a 2-quart saucepan; add grits gradually, stirring with a wire whisk.

3. Reduce heat and continue cooking, stirring vigorously, until mixture thickens.

4. Cover, and cook for 15 minutes, stirring often.

5. Remove from heat and add Worcestershire sauce, butter, and 1½ cups of the cheese, stirring until well blended.

6. In a small bowl, blend egg yolks with ¼ cup of milk. Pour into grits and mix thoroughly; add more milk if necessary, thinning to consistency of cream of wheat.

7. In a clean, dry bowl, beat egg whites until stiff. Fold into grits.

8. Pour into prepared baking dish. Sprinkle with the remaining ½ cup of cheese.

9. Bake on middle shelf of preheated oven for 30 minutes, or until fluffy and brown. Serve at once.

Every day for the first 25 years of her marriage, Rosalynn Carter arose before dawn to prepare a nourishing breakfast for her hard-working husband. Since Mrs. Carter preferred to sleep a bit later, these morning duties represented a loving sacrifice to a strong marriage. It was not until the Carters moved into the Governor's Mansion in Atlanta that Rosalynn discovered the truth about her early-rising husband: Jimmy Carter had not wanted to offend his devoted wife by telling her that he really preferred to breakfast later, starting the day with a simple glass of juice and a cup of coffee. Both of the Carters were a lot happier after their mutual disclosures, as Jimmy could then putter around the kitchen and prepare coffee before daybreak, while Rosalynn enjoyed sleeping until the sun was up.

COUNTRY HAM WITH REDEYE GRAVY

Thomas Jefferson was an ardent farmer, and the need for "agrarian democracy" was one of his personal and political philosophies. Thanks to his extensive travels and adventurous spirit, Jefferson was able to sample an international array of fresh foodstuffs. Although critic Patrick Henry insisted that President Jefferson "abjured his native victuals" in favor of imported cuisines while dining in the White House, America's third President supplemented the more elaborate fare of his French chef with real down-home cooking. President Jefferson served his many guests such simple Southern dishes as Virginia country-style ham and homemade biscuits, as well as plenty of locally grown vegetables. Jefferson even brought the governess from his Virginia estate to the White House to ensure that his favorite home-style dishes were prepared, including the hot fried apples he liked with his breakfast.

When the Carters lived in the White House, the President usually arose around 5:30 A.M., sipping on some freshly squeezed juice and hot coffee before heading for the Oval Office. After a few hours at his desk, President Carter was served a light breakfast, typically fresh fruit and buttered toast. The First Lady slept later than her husband, and enjoyed a light morning meal with their young daughter, Amy, at around 7:30 A.M. Before Amy sped off to elementary school and Mrs. Carter headed for her own office in the East Wing, they liked to share fruit juice, scrambled or poached eggs, and toast. Breakfast cereals were served alternately with the eggs, plus fresh fruit in season from time to time.

On most weekends, the Carters slept a little later and dined a bit more elaborately. The First Family especially enjoyed eating big Southern-style breakfasts after attending religious services on Sunday mornings. Classic Southern breakfasts include fried chicken or country ham, eggs and grits, biscuits or corn bread with butter and homemade preserves, and sometimes hot vegetables such as fried tomatoes or potatoes and cooked fruit such as fried apples. One of the Carters' favorite breakfast menus included Country-Style Ham with Redeye Gravy, scrambled eggs and baked grits, freshly baked Corn Bread, and hot Fried Apples.

Country-style ham is specially prepared in the rural areas of certain states, including Virginia and Georgia. Virginia's famous Smithfield hams come from hogs that are raised according to particular regulations, and the meat is specially cured to produce a very rich, salty and smokey, spicy type of ham. Other country-style hams tend to be leaner and less salty than the prized Smithfield ham; Georgia's country-style ham is usually sugar-glazed as well.

In the South, country ham is not served as a main course, but is sliced paper-thin and eaten as a first course or as an accompaniment to chicken or other fowl. Thicker slices of country ham topped with redeye gravy are a traditional Southern breakfast item. The unusual gravy is prepared with the drippings from the baked ham and is flavored with strong coffee. When the simmering gravy is ready, a telltale "red eye" is supposed to appear to the trained observer. Redeye gravy can add flavor to hot biscuits and grits as well as country-style ham.

Traditionally served with pork dishes, Fried Apples can be a delicious addition to a breakfast menu that features spicy slices of country ham, or as an accompaniment to an entrée such as grilled pork chops. Fried Apples are best served piping hot.

Serves 6

6 *slices country-cured ham,*   2 *tablespoons strong black*
    ½ *inch thick*   *coffee*
1 *cup boiling water*

1. In a large shallow baking pan, spread out ham slices and cover with cold water. Refrigerate for 3 hours.

2. Drain ham and blot dry with paper towels. Remove rind, using a small sharp knife.

3. In a cast-iron skillet, fry ham slices over medium heat; brown for 3 to 4 minutes on each side. Transfer to a heated serving platter.

4. Pour off all but about 2 tablespoons of fat from the skillet. Add boiling water, and simmer for 1 minute.

5. Use a metal spatula to loosen any small fragments of cooked ham from the bottom of the pan. Stir in coffee and simmer for 7 minutes to reduce by half.

6. Pour gravy over ham, and serve at once with hot FRIED APPLES.

Serves 6

FRIED APPLES

4 *large, tart, green cooking*   1 *teaspoon cinnamon*
    apples   4 *tablespoons butter*
4 *tablespoons light brown*
    sugar

1. Cut each apple into quarters, removing stem and core; cut each quarter into ⅛-inch thick slices.

2. Sprinkle with sugar and cinnamon, and mix to coat well.

3. Melt butter in a nonstick skillet, and sauté apples for 7 to 8 minutes, or until tender and lightly browned. Serve at once.

CORN FRITTERS

During the presidential campaign of 1800, Thomas Jefferson's rivals claimed that the candidate was unqualified since he had been "raised wholly on hoe-cake made of coarse-ground Southern corn, bacon and hominy. . . ." Jefferson rose above the campaign slurs, and eventually enlightened the national appetite with a variety of regionally grown foods. Thomas Jefferson also introduced a number of America's foodstuffs to European palates during his political travels abroad. As the American minister to the court of Louis XVI, Jefferson cultivated American produce in his garden in Paris, and surprised his dinner guests by serving some of his down-home favorites, including fresh ears of corn on the cob.

The Carter clan represented the new American extended family, a close group that spanned four generations. During the Carters' White House years, the constant flux of family members could have proven chaotic if the President and his wife had not been so well organized.

President Carter was extremely self-disciplined and unusually energetic, so he was able to set and achieve goals in many arenas, on personal and familial levels as well as national and international planes. Mrs. Carter was similarly self-directed and goal oriented, so she was an active First Lady both in and out of the White House.

The White House staff appreciated the First Family's disciplined life-style: Meals were served on time, menus were planned well in advance, and house guests were announced ahead of time. Yet the Carters were not at all rigid in their temperaments, but friendly and relaxed. In fact, President Carter appeared to be most comfortable when dressed informally in denim pants, plaid shirts, and work boots. He often welcomed guests to the White House with a wide grin and a friendly, "Hi! C'mon in."

The informal Southern hospitality of the Carters' White House years proved pleasurable for the kitchen staff. And during the Carter administration, the White House kitchen adopted a host of new recipes with a real Southern accent, including a significant number of dishes based on corn.

All grains were once called "corn," as the term referred to the presence of kernels. True corn was long known as "maize," and later as "Indian corn" in the forms found in the New World. While the early settlers' crops of European barley and wheat failed, Indian corn flourished and helped the new Americans to survive the harsh winter months. The colonists grew to appreciate just why the Indians referred to corn as "giver of life" and "she who sustains us." Corn was served at the first Thanksgiving celebration.

Corn is finely ground into cornmeal for use in a variety of regional dishes. Corn sticks and corn muffins are popular in the New England area, and Southern cooks serve cornmeal in corn pone and Corn Pudding. Corn Bread is popular in both locations (although somewhat different in appearance and flavor), and deep-fried fritters made with a cornmeal batter are also featured on menus in both North and South. For the Carter clan, hot Corn Fritters provided a frequent accompaniment to their informal family dinners, as well as an occasional treat served with their big weekend breakfasts.

Makes 12

6 *ears fresh corn, cooked and*
  cooled
2 *teaspoons sugar*
½ *teaspoon salt*
6 *twists freshly ground black*
  pepper
2 *tablespoons diced red bell*
  pepper

4 *egg yolks*
½ *cup flour*
4 *egg whites, at room*
  temperature
2 *cups vegetable oil*

1. Remove corn from cob: use a sharp kitchen knife to cut kernels off, then use the back of the knife to scrape the cob.

2. In a mixing bowl, combine corn kernels and scrapings with sugar, salt, pepper, and diced red pepper.

3. Stir in egg yolks, one at a time.

4. Fold in flour.

5. In a clean, dry bowl, beat egg whites until stiff. Fold into the batter.

6. In a large cast-iron skillet, heat oil over medium-high heat; gently drop in heaping tablespoons of the batter to make around 12 fritters.

7. Fry fritters to a golden brown, turning to cook evenly; allow 2 minutes frying time for each side so that fritters are puffed up and cooked through. (You may need to fry them in batches to avoid crowding the pan.)

8. Use a slotted spoon to transfer onto paper towels. Drain well, and serve hot with baked or SOUTHERN FRIED CHICKEN (page 261), or with pork chops. (For a breakfast dish, arrange cooked fritters on a baking sheet and dust with confectioners' sugar; glaze under a hot broiler for 1 to 2 minutes and serve at once, with honey or maple syrup if desired.)

RED BEANS AND RICE

In the time between an election and the beginning of a new administration, the White House staff must learn as much as possible about the life-style and eating patterns of the incoming First Family. When Jimmy Carter was elected as America's thirty-ninth President, the White House kitchen diligently studied up on Southern cuisine.

Although the Carters enjoyed many meals that were quite similar to those served to the previous First Families, the White House kitchen added a definite Southern accent to the Carter family

Thomas Jefferson could be regarded as the bravest gourmet to occupy the White House because he once risked his own life in order to please his nation's palate. While traveling in Italy, Jefferson was so impressed with a superior strain of rice that he smuggled some into the States by carrying the grains in his pockets. Jefferson introduced into the Carolinas this new type of rice that flourished in dry fields. At the time, exporting the grain from Italy was a crime punishable by death.

menus. For the most part, the Carters preferred simple, wholesome, down-home dishes. They were not "big eaters," but they were not "picky" about their food either. The Carters all appeared to enjoy whatever they were served while living in the White House.

Every Monday morning, I submitted to Mrs. Carter's office the proposed family menus for the following week. In adjusting each menu plan to suit her family's schedule and personal tastes, Mrs. Carter often took the time to describe a family favorite, so that the kitchen staff could prepare these dishes just the way the Carters liked them. One of the Carters' favorite Southern-style side dishes was "red and white," or Red Beans and Rice.

In the South, red beans and rice is typically served on Mondays, after a traditional Sunday dinner that includes baked ham. Kidney beans and white rice are eaten together, flavored with ham in the form of leftover ham bones or a pig's knuckle. A similar Southern dish is "Hoppin' John," made with black-eyed peas and rice flavored with leftover ham. Hoppin' John is traditionally served on New Year's Day, with a brand-new coin hidden in the pot as a guarantee of good fortune for the recipient.

Of course, coins were never buried in the Southern dishes served to the Carters and their guests. Yet the White House kitchen aimed to please pocketbooks as well as palates by emphasizing economical dishes that the First Family truly enjoyed. Red Beans and Rice was always a welcome addition to the Carter family's White House menus.

Serves 6

½ pound dried kidney beans
1 pig's knuckle
3 cups water
1 tablespoon salt
6 drops of Tabasco sauce
1 tablespoon Worcestershire sauce
3 tablespoons vegetable oil
1 cup chopped onions
4 garlic cloves, finely minced
1 cup diced celery
½ pound country-style ham, diced

¼ pound hot sausage, sliced ⅛ inch thick
½ pound smoked sausage, sliced ⅛ inch thick
2 bay leaves
A dash of salt
6 twists freshly ground black pepper
½ cup chopped fresh parsley
½ cup chopped celery leaves
2 cups warm cooked rice

1. Cover beans with cold water; let soak for 4 hours. Drain well.

2. In a 4-quart soup pot, combine pig's knuckle with water, salt, Tabasco sauce, and Worcestershire sauce. Add drained beans, bring to a boil, and let simmer over low heat.

3. Heat oil in a small sauté pan, add onions and garlic and sauté for 1 to 2 minutes, or until transparent. Add diced celery and sauté for 3 minutes.

4. Transfer sautéed vegetables to the soup pot. Cover, and continue simmering.

5. In a cast-iron skillet, sauté diced ham and sausage slices for 5 minutes to brown evenly. Drain well on paper towels, and add to the soup pot.

6. Add bay leaves, salt, and pepper. Set cover slightly ajar, and simmer for 2 hours, or until beans are very tender.

7. Remove bay leaves. Add chopped parsley and celery leaves, and serve at once over warm rice.

SALLY LUNN

Sally Lunn is a slightly sweetened bread or tea cake that originated in England and became popular in America's Southern homes. Named after an eighteenth-century woman from Bath, the original cakes were reportedly baked by the enterprising Miss Lunn, who then sold her fresh wares on the street corners of her hometown. Sally Lunn is still served at English-style "Hunt Breakfasts" and traditional "Southern Plantation Breakfasts." The hot, buttered tea cakes taste delicious with the foods that typically comprise these elaborate morning buffets, including eggs and grits, country-style ham, bacon and sausage, freshly baked biscuits, roasted game birds and English salmon, fresh fruits, the notoriously potent mint juleps, and plenty of hot coffee and tea.

Jimmy Carter was a Southerner of English descent. The Carters usually served Southern-style meals, sometimes with a glimmer of English influence. Mrs. Carter once defined her family's menu preferences as "the kind of cooking we have always had, the kind to which others who strayed away from the simple ways our forebears prepared food are now returning."

Sally Lunn can be prepared as a quick bread rather than a yeast bread, and the recipe is easily adapted to yield a tube cake, brownie-size squares, or small muffins. At the White House, Sally Lunn was prepared as a sliced yeast loaf, just the way the Carters liked it.

Eighteenth-century colonial cooks prepared a number of traditional English dishes, including tea-time delicacies such as trifle, fruit cake, and Sally Lunn. The 1887 edition of The White House Cook Book *offered two methods for preparing an English-style tea cake, an "unfermented" Sally Lunn and a longer recipe using the yeast-rising technique. The ingredients for the quick-bread version included: "... a piece of butter as large as an egg ... a quart of flour ... a tumbler of milk, two eggs, three tablespoonfuls of sugar, three tablespoonfuls of baking powder, and a teaspoonful of salt ... Eat warm with butter."*

The longer version advised:

Warm one-half cupful of butter in a pint of milk. Add a teaspoonful of salt, a tablespoonful of sugar, and seven cupfuls of sifted flour. Beat thoroughly, and when the mixture is blood-warm, add four beaten eggs and, last of all, half a cup of

As First Lady, Mrs. Carter devoted all of her time and energy to the First Family and the Carter administration. In addition to raising a young daughter and tending to the needs of an extended family, Mrs. Carter proved to be a special asset to her husband while living in the White House, just as she had during her years of successful involvement in the family peanut business. President Carter called his wife "the ultimate approach to my consciousness," and explained why: "There's very seldom a decision that I make that I don't first discuss with her ... she's got superb political judgment. She probably knows the human aspects of the American people and their relationship to the government better than I do."

To many Americans, Rosalynn Carter was the ultimate First Lady: She proved to be a hospitable and gracious hostess, a fine mother and grandmother, a supportive wife and a political asset, and a true inspiration to the many who admired her for what she represented and all that she achieved. For the White House kitchen staff, Mrs. Carter served as an inspiration for mastering the fine art of Southern cooking. We sharpened our skills to best serve the Carters in a manner befitting America's beloved First Lady.

Makes 1 round loaf

½ cup scalded milk	¼ cup lukewarm water
2 tablespoons sugar	2 eggs, beaten
2 tablespoons butter	2½ cups flour
1 package active dry yeast	2 tablespoons melted butter

1. In a large mixing bowl, combine hot milk with sugar and butter; let cool to lukewarm (105°F to 115°F).

2. In a small bowl, dissolve yeast in lukewarm water. Transfer to the mixing bowl, and stir to blend well.

3. Add beaten eggs. Add flour, and mix by hand to make a soft dough.

4. Transfer dough to a greased bowl; cover with a hot damp cloth, and place in a warm spot to let rise until doubled in bulk, approximately 2 hours.

5. Generously grease the inside of a 9-inch layer pan.

6. Punch dough down by hand. Transfer into the prepared pan and cover with a hot damp cloth; let rise again until doubled in bulk, approximately 1 hour.

7. Preheat oven to 350°F.

8. Bake loaf on lower shelf of preheated oven for 30 minutes, or

until top is golden brown and solid to the touch; brush top with melted butter several times during the baking period.

9. Turn bread out and let cool slightly on wire racks before slicing. Serve warm.

good lively yeast. Beat hard until the batter breaks in blisters. Set it to rise overnight. In the morning dissolve half a teaspoonful of soda, stir it into the batter and turn it into a well-buttered, shallow dish to rise again about fifteen or twenty minutes. Bake about fifteen to twenty minutes.

The cake should be torn apart, not cut. Cutting with a knife makes warm bread heavy.

First Lady Rosalynn brought her own special charm and Southern-style hospitality to the Carters' White House.

JEFF'S GEORGIA-STYLE CHEESE STICKS

The traditional recipe for cheese straws was provided in the 1887 edition of The White House Cook Book, *along with some rather quaint instructions: "... Roll out to the thickness of a silver quarter ... cut into strips about a third of an inch wide, twist them as you would a paper spill ... Serve cold, piled tastefully on a glass dish ..."*

The Carters' youngest son, Jeff, lived in the White House with his pretty wife, Annette. Jeff had graduated from George Washington University with a degree in geography and founded a consulting company for computer mapping. Both Jeff and Annette were skilled photographers, so they were able to record a pictorial history of the Carters' White House years.

Jeff and Annette were as personable as they were talented. They usually came into the White House kitchen to take snacks rather than photographs, and were always most pleasant and friendly. The young couple enjoyed entertaining their own friends at the White House, and they helped in planning out menus to suit their guests' tastes.

Jeff spent a considerable amount of time in the White House kitchen because he was very interested in food preparation. He often asked questions about menu items that had been served, and always informed the kitchen staff when a particular dish was a hit. Annette was especially enthusiastic about the chocolate fudge squares that the White House kitchen had prepared for her to take to a dinner party, so the sweet became a frequent feature on Jeff and Annette's own special menus. Jeff was fond of cheese straws, which he liked prepared "Georgia-style," that is, made with a sharp cheddar in a crumbly dough. To differentiate the dish from the traditional cheese straws prepared from puff paste, the White House kitchen referred to Jeff's favorite crisp pastry as "cheese sticks."

Although the Carters' eldest son Jack never lived in the White House, he often brought his family to dinner. Jack fit in nicely, concurring with the Carters' culinary tastes and practicing the same friendly manners. On his frequent visits to the White House, Jack often stopped by the kitchen to say hello, demonstrating the Southern charm that characterized the Carter family and made it such a pleasure to serve them.

Makes 24

2 cups flour
2 teaspoons baking powder
½ teaspoon salt
¼ teaspoon cayenne pepper

½ pound sharp cheddar cheese, finely grated
1 stick (½ cup) butter

1. Preheat oven to 325°F.
2. In a large mixing bowl, sift together flour, baking powder, salt, and pepper.

3. Stir in grated cheese.

4. Cut in butter using a pastry cutter; mix by hand until dough is smooth.

5. On a lightly floured board, roll out dough to about ⅓-inch thickness.

6. Cut dough into two dozen 6 × ½-inch sticks, using a sharp knife.

7. Arrange sticks on an ungreased baking sheet; leave 1 inch space between sticks to allow for spreading.

8. Bake on middle shelf of preheated oven for 10 minutes, or until golden brown.

9. Cool on wire racks before serving. Serve with piping hot soup and/or a tossed green salad for a first course, or as an hors d'oeuvre or buffet item.

When they were first married, Jimmy Carter taught Rosalynn some of his favorite recipes. Mrs. Carter became an enthusiastic cook, and the young couple often prepared dishes together as a form of relaxation. While living in Atlanta in the Governor's Mansion, Mrs. Carter enrolled in a local cooking school to enhance her culinary skills. She also became adept at serving as a State Hostess, which eased the transition into her demanding role as the nation's First Lady.

At the White House, Mrs. Carter continued to serve simple menus with a Southern accent. She explained the reasoning behind her special style of hostessing:

> In the Governor's Mansion we thought we had to be sophisticated. But I found that people wanted to eat what we ate. . . . I don't think that lavish entertaining is what Southern hospitality is all about. To me, what it is, and always has been, is simply a genuinely warm welcome to anyone who drops in. People in the South really enjoy having company, even when it is unexpected. And, because we truly enjoy it, people always feel welcome.

Mrs. Carter enjoyed eating and serving many types of foods, and she made a number of special trips to the White House kitchen to share her menu ideas and family recipes. One of Mrs. Carter's favorite recipes was for a simple cheddar cheese mold. Served in a

ROSALYNN'S PLAINS CHEESE RING

When he noticed the chandeliers were quivering due to a weakening ceiling structure, President Truman convinced Congress to appropriate funds for a thorough White House renovation. The Trumans lived in nearby Blair House for most of the four years required for the interior of the White House to be fully reconstructed. At her afternoon teas in Blair House, First Lady Bess Truman often served a cheese ring, made with a mixture of American and cream cheese.

ring to be spread on crackers, the cheese appetizer was prepared for many of the Carters' family dinners and some of their official White House functions. One unusual ingredient in Mrs. Carter's "Plains Special" was the strawberry preserves served in the center of the ring. With its unique flavor combination, Rosalynn's special cheese ring was not only a family favorite, but a big hit with the Carters' many guests.

Serves 6 to 8

1 pound sharp cheddar cheese, finely grated
1 cup mayonnaise
1 cup chopped pecans
½ cup very finely chopped onions
6 twists freshly ground black pepper
A dash of cayenne pepper
One 12-ounce jar strawberry preserves
Whole-grain crackers or melba toast

1. In a mixing bowl, combine cheese with mayonnaise, chopped nuts, and onions. Mix in black pepper and cayenne, and blend thoroughly.

2. Press into a 3-cup ring mold. Refrigerate for at least 2 hours.

3. To serve, dip mold into a pan of hot water for 15 to 20 seconds before turning out onto a serving platter. Fill center with strawberry preserves, and serve at once with whole-grain crackers or melba toast.

THE CARTERS' FAVORITE
SOUPS AND SALADS

The Carters liked homemade soups, especially when served with sandwiches or warm homemade breads for simple but filling lunches. The soup-and-sandwich menu had long prevailed as standard midday fare for Jimmy and Rosalynn Carter. As busy young partners in the blossoming family peanut business, and later with growing political responsibilities, the Carters had learned to depend on these hot, fast, easy lunches.

With the demanding schedules they faced daily while living in the White House, the busy Carters continued to appreciate quick, hearty luncheon meals. Unless fresh-baked Corn Bread or Buttermilk Biscuits were available, the Carters liked to have their lunchtime soups served with simple sandwiches. Two of the family favorites included country ham with cheddar cheese, and grilled cheddar with bacon and tomato. Amy's favorite sandwich was cold meat loaf on white bread, which she often requested as part of her school lunch.

Amy's lunches were prepared each morning in the White House kitchen. We made sure to pack a nutritious meal that included fresh fruit and raw vegetable sticks, some type of sandwich, and frequently a small Thermos of hot soup. Amy purchased her milk along with the rest of her classmates at the public school she attended a few blocks away from the White House.

Amy carried her lunch to school in a paper bag, which certainly was in keeping with the Carters' strong belief that life in the White House should not be too different from their life in Plains. Amy brought her schoolmates home to the White House for after-school snacks and overnight slumber parties—just as she had while living in Plains. A treehouse was constructed for Amy in the midst of the gardens that border the South Lawn of the White House—a lot like the one she had in Plains. And the White House kitchen attempted to provide Amy and the rest of the Carters with the kinds of meals

CHICKEN NOODLE SOUP

President Eisenhower was an amateur chef, and he enjoyed thumbing through cookbooks and experimenting with recipes. "Ike" prided himself on his homemade soups, but his detailed recipe for a plain vegetable soup was more than two pages in length! He began with some practical instructions for preparing chicken broth, but ended with a rather unusual suggestion for garnishing the soup:

The best time to make ... soup is a day or so after you have had fried chicken and out of which you have saved the necks, ribs, backs, etc., uncooked.... As a final touch, in the springtime when the nasturtiums are green and tender you can take a few nasturtium stems, cut them up in small pieces, boil them separately ... and add them to your soup.

they had always enjoyed at home in Plains. As Mrs. Carter had explained, "Some things should remain constant."

Makes 2 quarts

2 tablespoons butter
1 cup julienned carrots
1 cup julienned celery
1 cup julienned fresh
　mushrooms
½ cup finely chopped scallions
2 garlic cloves, finely minced
Juice of 1 lemon
2 quarts hot chicken bouillon

¼ teaspoon freshly ground
　white pepper
4 ounces fine egg noodles
1 cup finely slivered cooked
　chicken meat
1 cup very finely julienned red
　bell pepper
2 tablespoons chopped fresh
　parsley

Amy Carter enjoyed visiting the kitchen at the White House, just as she had at home in Plains.

1. Melt butter in a 3-quart saucepan, and add carrot, celery, mushrooms, chopped scallions, garlic, and lemon juice. Cover, and simmer over medium heat for 5 minutes.

2. Pour in hot bouillon and bring to a boil. Cover, and simmer for 15 minutes.

3. Add white pepper and noodles. Set cover slightly ajar, and simmer for 5 minutes.

4. Add chicken slivers and red pepper strips. Simmer, partly covered, for 5 minutes more.

5. Just before serving, sprinkle with chopped parsley. Serve hot.

Soup is such a practical dish, inexpensive yet filling, tasty but healthful, quick and easy yet ultimately satisfying. In Switzerland, soup has long been regarded as an integral component of the daily cuisine, for the hard-working mountainfolk as well as the more comfortable classes. In America's Old South, soup was almost always available in the homes of rich and poor alike, kept hot in a big soup pot set atop the kitchen stove. An American favorite since colonial days, soup has evolved into a wide range of regional dishes.

Lentil and Franks Soup is a variation on a traditional New England specialty, franks and beans. Frankfurters (or "hot dogs") may be regarded as the quintessential American foodstuff—that is, inexpensive and accessible, easy to make, and readily eaten on the run. Balancing out this rather high-fat meat with low-fat lentils helps to create a nutritionally sound recipe. Although dried beans and peas have been long maligned as "poor man's meat," recent attention to the nutritional benefits of legumes has led to a gradual alteration of public opinion. Lentils are still not considered "chic," but they have developed a reputation for providing tasty, nutritious results in certain hearty recipes.

The Carters liked their soups to be tasty, nutritious, and hearty. They enjoyed thick vegetable soups made with dried peas or beans, lentils, even peanuts. Lentil and Franks Soup was one of their favorite luncheon selections, served with a sandwich or hot bread at many of the Carters' "working lunches."

Each Wednesday during her husband's administration, Mrs. Carter met with the President for a "working lunch" in the small pri-

LENTIL AND FRANKS SOUP

When invading British troops burned down the "President's Mansion" during the War of 1812, First Lady Dolley Madison was forced to flee—but not before she rescued the portrait of George Washington that hung in the East Room. President James Monroe was later involved in the final stages of the massive reconstruction of the newly named "White House." Monroe even commissioned an elaborate soup tureen from French silversmiths, which raised a storm of controversy as critics accused the President of wanton luxury inappropriate for a First Family's home. However, President Monroe succeeded in impressing visiting dignitaries from other countries, using gracious dining and fine cuisine to convince the world that Americans were truly cultured and dignified. An impressive thirteen-foot mirrored doré purchased by President Monroe remains on display in the State Dining Room of the White House, adorning the long table when it is not in use.

vate study adjacent to the Oval Office. This room opens out onto a secluded flagstone terrace, providing a lovely setting for dining during pleasant weather. President Carter also enjoyed working alone in the private study, and used both the room and terrace for each Monday's "working lunch" with Vice-President Mondale as well.

Mrs. Carter's favorite spot in the White House may have been the Truman Balcony, where the family rocking chairs were positioned for intimate sunset chats. Mrs. Carter redecorated the President's Bedroom as a comfortable study, complete with overstuffed chairs and a footstool in front of the fireplace. All of the Carter clan liked to relax in the Solarium, often in front of televised football games. The Carters were able to settle quite happily into life in the White House, which made this family a pleasure to cook for—from soup(s) to (pea)nuts.

Makes 2½ to 3 quarts

½ pound dried lentils	A dash of salt
2 tablespoons butter	⅛ teaspoon freshly ground
1 cup chopped onions	white pepper
1 cup chopped scallions, white	1 large Idaho baking potato,
parts only	peeled and finely diced
2 garlic cloves, finely minced	2½ quarts hot beef bouillon
½ cup finely diced carrots	4 frankfurters
1 cup diced celery	1 tablespoon chopped fresh
1 bay leaf	parsley
½ teaspoon dried thyme	

1. Cover lentils with cold water; let soak overnight. Drain well and discard any small stones.
2. In a 4-quart soup pot, melt butter; sauté onions, scallions, and garlic for 5 minutes. Do not brown.
3. Add diced carrots and celery, bay leaf, thyme, salt and pepper; mix well.
4. Cover, and simmer slowly for 10 minutes.
5. Add drained lentils, diced potato, and hot bouillon. Bring to a boil; set cover slightly ajar, and simmer briskly for 1½ hours. (To enhance flavor, add a pig's knuckle or ham bone.)
6. Slice franks into very thin rounds and add to soup pot; boil for 1 minute.
7. Just before serving, sprinkle with chopped parsley. Serve hot.

As a young man, Jimmy Carter fulfilled his boyhood dreams when he was admitted into the Naval Academy in Annapolis. He worked hard to become a respected naval officer, and he hoped to one day be Chief of Naval Operations. During his training in Annapolis, Jimmy Carter was exposed to the delicious dishes made with fresh Chesapeake crabs. He also fell for his sister's best friend, eighteen-year-old Eleanor Rosalynn Smith.

Midshipman Jimmy Carter was home on leave when he went on his first date with Rosalynn. Less than a year later, twenty-one-year-old Ensign Carter married Rosalynn in a small private ceremony held in their hometown of Plains, Georgia. Undecided on her own career, Rosalynn was grateful for the opportunity to travel with Jimmy, and found life as a Navy wife to be both exciting and rewarding. John ("Jack") Carter was born first, at the base in Portsmouth, Virginia. James E. Carter III, or "Chip," was born three years later in Hawaii. After an additional three years, the Carters' third son, Donnel Jeffrey, or "Jeff," was born in New London, Connecticut. Amy did not arrive until after Jimmy Carter had retired from the Navy and the young family had returned to Plains to help run the family peanut business.

As his wife, business partner, and best friend, Rosalynn served as Jimmy Carter's principal confidante from their Navy days right on through the White House years. President Carter acknowledged that they had long enjoyed "an absolutely unconstrained relationship, an ability to express our doubts and concerns to each other." An impressed mother-in-law, Miss Lillian, once explained, "Even if I, his mother, want Jimmy to do something, I ask Rosalynn first. She can do anything in the world with Jimmy. He listens to her." Rosalynn herself once summarized their successful marriage: "We have always done things as equals."

First Lady Rosalynn Carter revealed the fact that her husband had long shared in performing the household chores, including the food shopping and cooking. Jimmy Carter had also shared the recipes for his favorite dishes with his wife, who in turn furnished them to the White House kitchen. During their years in the White House, Mrs. Carter shared her husband's delight at the availability of his favored Chesapeake crabs. While the Carters were the nation's First Couple, the White House kitchen was pleased to serve them a mutual favorite, creamy Maryland Crab-Corn Chowder.

MARYLAND CRAB—CORN CHOWDER

Thomas Jefferson suppos-
edly served only the freshest
foods, at their seasonal
peaks. Like his fellow Vir-
ginian, George Washing-
ton, Jefferson was always
pleased when crabs were in
season, fresh from the
Maryland shores. America's
first gourmet President recorded his favorite recipes
for seasonal delicacies, and
included the following "Ob-
servations on Soup" in his
daughter's cookbook, The
Virginia Housewife: "When
the soup is done take it off.
Let it cool and skim off the
fat clear. Heat it again and
dish it up. When you make
white soups never put in the
cream until you take it off
the fire." In traveling to
Italy on diplomatic missions
before he was elected as
America's third President,
Thomas Jefferson observed
the Italian technique for
making genuine Parmesan
cheese while visiting
the city of Parma. He
later provided his own
cooks with Parmesan
cheese, and other food imports as yet unfamiliar to
most American palates.

Makes 2 quarts

6 *large live blue crabs*
2 *cups dry white wine*
3 *cups water*
1 *bay leaf*
1 *tablespoon salt*
2 *tablespoons butter*
2 *garlic cloves, finely minced*
2 *cups finely diced leeks, white*
  parts only
1 *quart chicken bouillon*
6 *ears fresh corn*
A *pinch of cayenne pepper*

1 *teaspoon Worcestershire*
  sauce
4 *drops of Tabasco sauce*
1 *tablespoon very finely diced*
  red bell pepper
1 *tablespoon very finely diced*
  green bell pepper
1 *cup heavy cream*
¼ *cup dry sherry*
1 *tablespoon chopped fresh*
  parsley
PARMESAN CROUTONS

1. Boil crabs in white wine and water seasoned with bay leaf and salt for 10 minutes. Remove crabs. Strain broth through cheese-cloth; reserve crabs and stock separately.

2. Melt butter in a 3-quart saucepan, add garlic and leeks and sauté over medium heat, covered, for 5 minutes.

3. Add crab stock and chicken bouillon, bring to a boil, and sim-mer, covered, for 10 minutes.

4. Remove corn from the cobs using a sharp knife, then scrape cobs with the back of the knife; add kernels and scrapings to the simmering soup. Set cover slightly ajar, and simmer for 10 minutes.

5. Add cayenne pepper, Worcestershire sauce, and Tabasco sauce.

6. Remove warm crabmeat from the shells. (Crabmeat separates from the shell more easily when crabs are still warm.) Flake into the simmering soup.

7. Add diced peppers, cream, and sherry. Bring chowder just to the boiling point over high heat; remove from heat.

8. Sprinkle with chopped parsley and serve at once, topped with PARMESAN CROUTONS.

PARMESAN CROUTONS

Makes 12

¼ loaf French bread
4 tablespoons melted butter

4 tablespoons grated Parmesan cheese

1. Slice bread into 12 rounds, each ⅛-inch thick. Arrange on a baking sheet.
2. Under a hot broiler, brown bread very lightly; turn once to brown both sides.
3. Use a pastry brush to coat top of each slice with melted butter; sprinkle with grated cheese.
4. Drizzle remaining butter over all.
5. Broil for 1 minute, or until golden brown. Use at once.

WALDORF SALAD

Whether dining alone or with family and friends, the Carters preferred simple dinners that included lots of vegetables and the freshest possible foodstuffs. They liked their vegetables served plain, raw or lightly steamed. The Carters also enjoyed eating salads, including the crunchy fruit-vegetable combination known as Waldorf Salad.

Commonly composed of diced apples and celery and chopped walnuts, all coated with a mayonnaise dressing, the original Waldorf Salad was reportedly created by the legendary Oscar of the Waldorf: In 1893, the famed maître d'hôtel devised a special salad to serve the 1,500 guests who attended the gala opening of the first Waldorf-Astoria Hotel in New York City. When Oscar Tschirky's cookbook, *The Cook Book by "Oscar of the Waldorf"* (1896), appeared a few years later, his recipe for Waldorf Salad did not contain walnuts: "Peel 2 raw apples, cut into small pieces about ½-inch square, cut some celery the same way, and mix with the apple. Add 'a good mayonnaise.'" Walnuts became a standard ingredient in the recipe by the 1930s, although some cooks substitute pecans and others add raisins or grapes. Waldorf Salad is now a staple menu item in America's hotels and fine restaurants.

President Carter was not partial to rich sauces, nor did he like most commercial condiments. But the President did like "a good mayonnaise," especially in salads and in homemade tartar sauce. Although Americans typically buy commercially produced mayonnaise, the French use several classic recipes to prepare mayonnaise dressings. Sauce Mahonaise was invented in 1756 by a desperate

Harry S. Truman was a down-to-earth, unpretentious person, even while living in the White House. He enjoyed plain, simple foods and was most fond of his wife's wholesome, all-American dishes, such as her homemade meat loaf and tuna casserole. President Truman was also a fan of puddings, especially chocolate, and he loved ice cream as well. Waldorf salad was one of his all-time favorites.

but creative French chef who, lacking both butter and cream, devised a new sauce using egg yolks and oil. These days, making a homemade mayonnaise might seem like a dispensable chore, but the results can prove to be well worth the modicum of time and effort required. A thick, freshly made mayonnaise can transform the traditional Waldorf Salad into a truly memorable dish.

Serves 6

1 cup thick HOMEMADE
   MAYONNAISE
½ teaspoon salt
⅛ teaspoon freshly ground
   white pepper
2 cups peeled, diced crisp
   apples

1 cup diced crisp celery
¾ cup coarsely chopped
   walnuts
1 head Boston lettuce, washed
   and well dried
Fresh parsley sprigs
24 walnut halves

1. In a 2-quart mixing bowl, combine HOMEMADE MAYONNAISE with salt and pepper.
2. Fold in diced apples.
3. Fold in diced celery and chopped walnuts. Refrigerate salad for 1 hour.
4. Arrange lettuce leaves on a serving platter. Mound salad in the center, and garnish with sprigs of parsley.
5. Decorate top of salad with walnut halves. Serve cold. This salad is best when served fresh; leftover salad should be kept under refrigeration.

HOMEMADE MAYONNAISE

Makes 1½ to 2 cups

1 tablespoon lemon juice
¾ teaspoon salt
⅛ teaspoon freshly ground
   white pepper
1 teaspoon Worcestershire
   sauce
1 tablespoon Dijon-style
   mustard

2 egg yolks
2 tablespoons cider or white
   wine vinegar
1 to 1½ cups olive oil, at room
   temperature.

1. In a blender, combine all ingredients except olive oil; blend at high speed for 10 seconds.

2. With blender running at low speed, gradually add oil; cover blender and blend at high speed for 10 seconds. (Increasing the quantity of oil thickens the mayonnaise but dilutes the seasoning.) Use at once, as refrigeration causes the mayonnaise to separate.

Southern farmers by heritage, the Carters lived a life-style that reflected this image. President Carter wanted to be recognized by the American public as a "common man," just another citizen hired to do a job. In serving as the First Family, the Carters chose to eliminate much of the pomp and circumstance typically associated with the presidency. Instead, they imbued the White House with their own brand of relaxed informality and down-home Southern charm.

President Carter elected to use a modest sedan in place of the presidential limousine. He gave his first televised "fireside chat" from the White House library dressed in a cardigan sweater and open-necked shirt. The Carters hosted many picnics out on the South Lawn, where guests followed the First Family's lead in dress, donning denims and casual clothes. When the President bounded up and down the stairs of the White House, most of the staff could identify his approach by the thud of his heavy work-boots. President Carter and his family were at home in the White House, as relaxed and as real as they were back in Plains.

Mrs. Carter wanted the First Family's menus to reflect their former farm life and simple style. Even when guests joined the Carters for family dinners, modest Southern-style fare was most often served. The Carters' family dinners usually included at least one fresh vegetable, plus some sort of vegetable salad. The Carters were especially fond of fresh carrots, served steamed or in salad combinations. One of their favorite recipes was for a simple Carrot-Raisin Salad, which became a very popular dish on the family dinner menus during their years in the White House.

CARROT-RAISIN SALAD

As America's twelfth President, Zachary Taylor held much appeal for the "common man" because of his unaffected manner and unpretentious tastes. President Taylor led such a relaxed, informal life that someone once said he looked "more like an old farmer going to market with eggs to sell than anything." President Taylor had simple tastes in food, and he was especially fond of dishes made with that Southern institution, hominy. After Taylor died in office, America did not elect another President from the deep South until over 125 years later, when Jimmy Carter took office.

Serves 6

½ cup seedless white raisins
1 cup water
½ cup mayonnaise
¼ teaspoon salt
⅛ teaspoon freshly ground white pepper
2 cups grated crisp carrots

1 cup drained crushed pineapple
1 head Boston lettuce, washed and well dried
Six 1-inch chunks fresh pineapple

1. In a small saucepan, combine raisins with water; bring to a boil. Remove from heat and drain; let cool.

2. In a 2-quart mixing bowl, combine mayonnaise with salt and pepper.

3. Fold in raisins, grated carrots, and crushed pineapple. Refrigerate salad for 1 hour.

4. Arrange lettuce leaves on a serving platter. Mound salad in the center, and garnish with pineapple chunks.

5. Refrigerate until serving time; serve cold. This salad is best when served fresh; leftover salad should be kept under refrigeration. If desired, prepare with a thick HOMEMADE MAYONNAISE (page 250).

CREAMY BLUE CHEESE DRESSING

Salads were traditionally served after a meal in order to help cleanse the palate. The 1887 edition of The White House Cook Book *provided a concise list of acceptable salad ingredients, followed by advice on preparing the "proper" dressing for a "good salad":*

Beetroot, onions, potatoes, cabbage, lettuce, celery, cucumbers, lentils, haricots, winter cress, peas, French beans, radish, cauliflower—all these may be used judiciously in salad, if properly sea-

The Carters' weekly dinner menus were revamped on occasion by the First Lady, who was always the best authority on her family's eating habits and food preferences. One fact that became quite clear early in the Carters' White House residency was that the entire family liked green salads, served with a homemade dressing on the side—especially cheese dressings made extra thick and creamy with the addition of sour cream.

Blue-veined cheeses like Roquefort and French Bleu are perhaps the most prized of all the fermented cheeses. In accordance with strict French laws, Roquefort cheese must be made entirely from the rich milk of ewes raised in the Roquefort region of France. The cheese is ripened in cool, damp caves for up to a full year. The less pungent blue cheeses are produced not only in France but also in a number of other countries, including the United States. (The French blue cheeses are exported with a telltale "bleu" label imprint to indicate origin.) Blue cheese is tangy semi-soft cheese made from either cow's or goat's milk.

An extra thick and creamy dressing made with rich blue cheese and a generous quantity of sour cream is certainly not a low-calorie topping for a bowl of salad greens. Even though the trim, active Carters did not need to count calories, they still limited their overall intake of rich foodstuffs. To assist them in their healthy eating habits, the White House kitchen served the rich salad dressing in judicious amounts. By creating a creamy, flavorful dressing, we found that a little bit could go a long way.

Makes 2 cups

1 cup sour cream
1/2 teaspoon Worcestershire
   sauce
1/4 teaspoon salt

6 twists freshly ground black
   pepper
2 tablespoons mayonnaise
3/4 cup crumbled blue cheese

soned. . . . All the art consists in introducing the oil by degrees, a few drops at a time. You can never make a good salad without taking plenty of time.

1. In a mixing bowl, combine sour cream with Worcestershire sauce, salt, and pepper; mix in mayonnaise.

2. Fold in blue cheese, and serve in a sauceboat. If desired, prepare with HOMEMADE MAYONNAISE (page 250). Serve dressing at room temperature; store in refrigerator in a covered jar.

CARTER FAMILY FAVORITE ENTRÉES

For their very first main meal as White House residents, the Carters enjoyed a special roast beef dinner. Mrs. Carter later urged the kitchen staff to serve the family less costly cuts of beef. And since they had been served steaks and roasts so frequently while out on the campaign trail, the new First Family often opted for chicken and fish as family dinner entrées, typically accompanied by a variety of fresh vegetables in season.

One of President Carter's favorite dishes was a chicken and vegetable stew. An old-fashioned Southern stew traditionally prepared by hunters, Brunswick Stew was originally made with squirrel meat. Various claims have been staked for the origin of the recipe. The residents of Brunswick County, Virginia, assert that a Dr. Creed Haskins of their state legislature requested the special squirrel stew for a political rally back in 1828. This story is challenged by the residents of both Brunswick County, North Carolina, and Brunswick, Georgia. Wherever the dish may have originated, the recipe eventually evolved into a chicken stew. Some cooks include

BRUNSWICK
STEW

Fresh dairy products, including butter and milk, have long been popular at the White House. President Andrew Johnson's daughter reportedly milked their Jersey cows each morning, providing enough milk to meet their White House needs. She also churned the household's butter supply. President Taft's cow, Pauline, was the last to graze on White House grass; later residents turned to local markets for their supplies of milk and butter. When lumps of butter have been removed from churned cream, the liquid that remains is called buttermilk. The 1887 edition of The White House Cook Book *encouraged consumption of this nutritious beverage, which was then regarded as a "waste product."*

other meats, such as rabbit or veal, or even a pig's head or ham hocks. The Carters preferred Brunswick Stew made with chicken and fresh vegetables, and served with homemade Buttermilk Biscuits.

Biscuits are small leavened rolls, long used in Southern homes in place of bread. In the Old South, "beaten biscuits" were especially popular. Fortunately, there was usually plenty of kitchen help available to beat the dough with a mallet for the required thirty minutes or more. Southern cooks advised on proper techniques for creating the crisp biscuits: Regularity in beating was desirable, but excessive beating "killed the dough."

Buttermilk Biscuits are softer than beaten biscuits, and should be fluffy and flaky when baked. The Carters regularly enjoyed the biscuits with family dinners, but did not confine the popular breadstuff to their own meals. At the White House, the Carters often offered freshly baked Buttermilk Biscuits to their guests, at breakfast buffets, picnics and parties, and on other occasions when Southern specialties were served to White House diners from all over the world.

Serves 6 to 8

2 tablespoons salt
1 teaspoon freshly ground
   black pepper
4 tablespoons flour
6 pounds stewing chicken, in
   parts
1 stick (½ cup) butter
1 cup diced onions
4 garlic cloves, finely minced
2 cups peeled, seeded, and
   diced very ripe tomatoes
2 cups fresh or frozen baby
   lima beans

2 cups fresh corn, scraped off
   the cob, or frozen corn
   kernels, thawed and drained
1 bay leaf
A pinch of cayenne pepper
1 tablespoon Worcestershire
   sauce
2 cups dry white wine
1 tablespoon chopped fresh
   parsley

1. Combine half the salt with the pepper and flour; dredge chicken pieces evenly in this mixture.

2. Melt butter in a large sauté pan, add chicken and brown on all sides over medium-high heat. Transfer to paper towels to drain.

3. In the same pan, sauté the onions and garlic for 1 to 2 minutes, or until golden brown.

4. Add tomatoes, lima beans, and corn. Season with the remaining tablespoon of salt.

5. Add chicken pieces, bay leaf, cayenne pepper, Worcestershire sauce, and wine. Cover, and simmer for 20 minutes, or until chicken is tender.

6. Use a slotted spoon to transfer chicken to a deep serving platter. Evenly distribute the vegetables and sauce over the chicken.

7. Sprinkle with chopped parsley. Serve hot, with steamed rice and freshly baked BUTTERMILK BISCUITS.

BUTTERMILK BISCUITS

Makes 18

3 cups sifted flour
1 teaspoon salt
3½ teaspoons baking powder

½ cup plus 2 tablespoons butter, at room temperature
1¼ cups buttermilk

1. Preheat oven to 425°F.
2. Sift flour, salt, and baking powder into a mixing bowl.
3. Use a pastry cutter to cut in butter until it is evenly distributed.
4. Gradually add 1 cup of the buttermilk, and knead lightly by hand to make a soft dough. (To ensure flaky biscuits, do not overmix or overhandle.)
5. Turn dough out onto a lightly floured board. Roll out to a thickness of ¾ inch.
6. Cut into rounds, using a 2-inch biscuit cutter.
7. Arrange rounds on an ungreased baking sheet, 1 inch apart. (For softer biscuits, set rounds closer together on the baking sheet before baking.) Brush tops with remaining ¼ cup of buttermilk.
8. Bake on middle shelf of preheated oven for 10 minutes, or until biscuits have risen and tops are lightly browned. Serve warm.

SOUTHERN-STYLE BARBECUED PORK

Faced with the selection of their third President, Americans began to enjoy campaign activities specially designed to attract their votes. Thomas Jefferson's political supporters were the first to plan parades and host big barbecues in order to honor their candidate and win votes. Parades and barbecues still remain a staple of modern campaign strategy.

During the final weeks of the 1976 presidential campaign, the women of the Democratic Party honored Mrs. Carter and her "running mate" Mrs. Mondale at a "Pig-pickin' Fundraiser for 500." The Southern-style barbecue included:

7 barbecued pigs
42 gallons of Brunswick Stew
8 gallons of watermelon rind pickles
8 gallons of mixed sweet pickles
40 pounds of Coleslaw
600 slabs of Corn Bread
900 pecan tassies
Lemonade for 500 thirsty diners

The Carters continued to enjoy Southern-style barbecues as White House residents. However, President Carter preferred serving spicy spareribs rather than barbecuing whole pigs, and the family often enjoyed barbecued meat in the dining room as well as outdoors.

During the colonial era, whole hogs were roasted on grills over smoldering coals, a culinary process that is still popular in the South. Modern Southern cooks chop or slice the roasted meat, season it with spices and hot pepper, and serve the barbecue with spicy sauces. Northern barbecues typically feature chicken and burgers instead, while barbecued spareribs are most common in the Southwest.

The key to success with barbecued ribs is proper preparation prior to cooking: The meat should be parboiled to reduce the fat content and augment the absorption of the sauce. A second secret for preparing President Carter's favorite barbecued ribs was the special spicy sauce, made with very hot crushed red pepper.

Serves 6

6 pounds lean spareribs   *3 tablespoons prepared mustard*
2 tablespoons salt   *3 cups HOT BARBECUE SAUCE*

1. Preheat oven to 350°F. Line a baking sheet with aluminum foil.
2. In a large saucepan, cover ribs with water. Add salt.
3. Cover pan, and bring to a boil. Let boil for 5 minutes.
4. Drain; transfer ribs to the lined baking sheet.

5. Use a pastry brush to coat ribs with prepared mustard on both sides.

6. Bake on lower shelf of preheated oven for 15 minutes; remove from oven.

7. Use the pastry brush to coat ribs generously with HOT BARBECUE SAUCE.

8. Return to lower shelf and continue baking for 1¼ hours, or until ribs are brown and tender; brush with barbecue sauce several more times during the baking period. If ribs stick to the baking sheet, add a few teaspoons of warm water. Serve hot, with fresh corn and sauerkraut, or with baked beans and HOME-STYLE COLE-SLAW (page 262).

HOT BARBECUE SAUCE

Makes 1 quart

3 tablespoons vegetable oil
1 cup diced onions
4 garlic cloves, finely minced
½ cup diced green bell pepper
½ cup diced celery
3 cups tomato juice
2 tablespoons tomato paste
½ cup cider vinegar
1 teaspoon crushed red pepper
2 tablespoons dry mustard

⅔ cup brown sugar
Tied cheesecloth "spice bag," containing rind of ½ lemon, 4 whole cloves, 24 whole black peppercorns, 1 bay leaf, a pinch of whole rosemary, and ¼ teaspoon each fresh thyme, oregano, and marjoram (or a pinch each dried)

1. Heat oil in a 3-quart saucepan, add onions and garlic and sauté for 2 minutes.

2. Add green pepper and celery; sauté for 2 minutes more.

3. Stir in tomato juice, tomato paste, vinegar, crushed red pepper, dry mustard, and brown sugar.

4. Bring to a boil, stirring constantly with a wooden spoon.

5. Add spice bag. Set cover slightly ajar, and simmer over low heat for 45 minutes, stirring often.

6. Remove spice bag. Process sauce in a blender until smooth and use at once, or keep refrigerated in a covered jar for up to 2 weeks.

SWEET-AND-SOUR PORK

When the Carters lived in the White House, they tried to set a national example by limiting their household expenses and trimming unnecessary costs. Although the State Department is responsible for all food expenditures for the official State Dinners, the First Family is like any American family in that they pay for their own meals and snacks. With their extended family and many house guests, the Carters required a generous food budget.

While the President cut the operating costs of the White House

—assisted by an efficiency expert—Mrs. Carter kept a firm grip on the family food budget. Fortunately, the White House kitchen was already an economy-minded operation, easily passing all efficiency checks and adjusting to any cost-cutting alterations. The kitchen staff was pleased that our department set such a fine example.

On Sunday nights, the entire White House kitchen staff was off-duty. To cut some expenses and give the staff a break, the Carters prepared their own supper that night, typically an informal meal consisting mainly of leftovers, usually sandwiches.

President Carter was fond of pork chops with corn bread stuffing. All of the Carters liked pork dishes spiced up with barbecue sauce or sweetened up with a side dish of piping Hot Fried Apples. They especially enjoyed a Chinese-style dish made with lean chunks of tenderloin in a sweet-and-sour sauce. Mrs. Carter often included the tangy dish on special menus for official buffets, and served any leftovers to her family for their informal Sunday night suppers. Like most Chinese food, Sweet-and-Sour Pork can taste even better the second time around!

Opposite page: Chef Haller was a favorite of the Carters, perhaps because he so enthusiastically re-created their Southern-style favorites in the White House kitchen.

On his farm in Virginia, Thomas Jefferson developed new breeds of pigs by crossing the local hogs with some strains from Calcutta. His neighbors were resentful when Jefferson dominated the local pig market with his superior stock, so they nicknamed him "the hog governor." As with many of his culinary innovations, Jefferson's incredible foresight was not recognized by most at the time.

Serves 6

2½ *pounds lean pork, in 1-inch* ⅓ *cup soy sauce*
   cubes 2 *quarts vegetable oil*
2 *teaspoons salt* 4 *cups* SWEET-AND-SOUR SAUCE
⅓ *cup cornstarch* 2 *cups fresh or canned*
⅓ *cup dry sherry*   *pineapple chunks*

1. In a mixing bowl, dredge pork cubes with salt and cornstarch.
2. Add sherry and soy sauce, and mix gently. Marinate for 1 hour.
3. In a French fryer or large cast-iron skillet, heat oil to 375°F.
4. Use a long-handled slotted spoon to transfer the marinated meat cubes to the hot oil. Fry for 3 to 4 minutes, or until brown and crisp.
5. Use the slotted spoon to remove cooked meat cubes; let drain on paper towels. Transfer to a 4-quart saucepan.
6. Cover pork with SWEET-AND-SOUR SAUCE and bring to a simmer, stirring constantly. (The cornstarch on the pork will cause the sauce to thicken.)
7. When sauce is bubbling, add pineapple chunks. Return to a simmer, stirring constantly.
8. Transfer to a serving dish and serve at once with steamed rice. (Kept hot in a chafing dish, this makes an excellent buffet item.)

SWEET-AND-SOUR SAUCE

Makes 1 quart

¼ cup vegetable oil
3 garlic cloves, crushed
1¼ cups sugar
¾ cup catsup
¾ cup pineapple juice

¼ cup soy sauce
1 cup cider vinegar
½ cup cornstarch
¾ cup water

1. Heat oil in a large skillet, add garlic and sauté for 3 minutes, or until golden brown.

2. Remove from heat. Remove garlic with a slotted spoon.

3. Add sugar, catsup, pineapple juice, soy sauce, and vinegar to the skillet; stir to blend, using a wooden spoon.

4. In a small bowl, combine cornstarch with water. Add to the skillet and blend well.

5. Transfer to the top of a double boiler; cover, and heat over hot water until sauce is thickened, stirring occasionally. Keep warm until use.

The kitchen staff enjoys a lunch break; on Sundays, the Carters gave us all the day off.

From their very first day as White House residents, the Carters made it quite clear that they preferred a simple American life-style. This fact was well received in the White House kitchen, where simple American foods have long been appreciated for their true elegance and fine taste. Plain chicken dishes turned out to be some of the Carters' favorite menu selections for family dinners. President Carter was especially fond of baked chicken breasts stuffed with cheddar cheese, and fried chicken made "Southern-style."

Fried chicken may just be the best known and best loved of all Southern dishes. However, Southern cooks do not agree on the best method for preparing this popular dish, nor on the best way to serve it. Everyone seems to agree on the desired results, however —that is, tender, juicy chicken meat encased in a crispy, savory crust. And eating fried chicken with the fingers appears to be accepted almost everywhere without argument.

The hundreds of recipes for Southern Fried Chicken vary on nearly every aspect of preparation, from initial batters to final cooking techniques. Some cooks dredge the chicken in flour, others shake the meat in paper bags containing flour or cornmeal or both. Some Southern cooks soak the chicken pieces in buttermilk before frying, while others bake the chicken encased in bread crumbs. Vegetable shortening is used for frying—unless corn oil, vegetable oil, or peanut oil is preferred. The frying pan—a well-seasoned cast-iron skillet is best—may or may not be covered during the cooking process, depending, of course, on the cook's point of view. Southern Fried Chicken is served hot with or without gravy, or cold on the following day.

To avoid controversy and confusion, Mrs. Carter came into the White House kitchen to show us exactly how the President preferred his Southern Fried Chicken. After her demonstration, we served Jimmy Carter's Southern fried chicken quite often, not only for the family's meals, but at a number of White House functions with a Southern flair.

The "best" accompaniments for Southern Fried Chicken are as numerous as the "best" recipes for preparing the dish. At the White House, President Carter's favored fried chicken was served with fresh cooked vegetables and a crisp salad, oftentimes a homemade coleslaw. No matter how it is prepared and served, Southern Fried Chicken is a simple, all-American dish that usually turns out to be finger-lickin' good.

JIMMY CARTER'S SOUTHERN FRIED CHICKEN

Even at the turn of the century, there was no single, universally accepted recipe for fried chicken. There was general agreement, however, on the acceptable manner for eating fried chicken. The 1887 edition of The White House Cook Book *provided the following guidelines as one of the "Small Points on Table Etiquette": "One may pick a bone at the table, but, as with corn, only one hand is allowed to touch it . . . one is, however, on no account to suck one's finger after it."*

Serves 6 to 8

2 quarts vegetable shortening
Three 2½ pound frying
  chickens
2 cups flour

2 tablespoons white cornmeal
2 tablespoons salt
2 teaspoons freshly ground
  white pepper

1. In a large, well-seasoned cast-iron skillet, heat shortening to 375°F.

2. Wash chickens and dry well, using a kitchen towel. Cut each into 8 serving pieces.

3. In a large mixing bowl, combine flour with cornmeal, salt, and pepper; dredge chicken and set on paper towels.

4. Fry chicken in hot oil, turning to brown evenly on all sides. (This will take from 10 to 12 minutes; white meat will cook faster than dark meat.) As each piece becomes golden brown and tender, transfer to paper towels to drain. Keep chicken hot until serving in a preheated 350°F oven: set well-drained pieces on an ovenproof serving platter on middle shelf of oven, with the door slightly ajar. For cold fried chicken, allow to cool, then wrap tightly and refrigerate overnight. Serve with fresh ears of corn, mashed potatoes with gravy, BUTTERMILK BISCUITS (page 255), and HOME-STYLE COLESLAW.

HOME-STYLE COLESLAW

Serves 6 to 8

1 medium-size head green
  cabbage (about 3 pounds)
1 cup shredded carrots
1 cup finely chopped onions
3 garlic cloves, pressed
1 cup cider vinegar
2 tablespoons celery seeds
1 tablespoon Worcestershire
  sauce

1 tablespoon Dijon-style
  mustard
1 tablespoon salt
¼ teaspoon freshly ground
  white pepper
1 tablespoon sugar
1½ to 2 cups mayonnaise
2 tablespoons chopped fresh
  parsley

1. Cut cabbage in quarters; remove core and outer leaves.

2. Use a very sharp knife to finely shred cabbage. Wash in cold water, drain well, and let dry on paper towels.

3. In a large mixing bowl, combine shredded cabbage and carrots; mix in chopped onions and pressed garlic.

4. In a small mixing bowl, combine vinegar with celery seeds, Worcestershire sauce, mustard, salt, pepper, and sugar. Pour over vegetables and mix well by hand.

5. Use a plate that fits into the mixing bowl to weigh down the vegetables and assist in the absorption of the marinade; let stand for 30 minutes.

6. Drain off excess marinade. Mix in mayonnaise a few tablespoonfuls at a time until vegetables are evenly coated.

7. Transfer to a serving bowl. Sprinkle with chopped parsley.

8. Refrigerate for several hours before serving. Serve very cold.

The state of Georgia is speckled with marshy and wooded areas that provide the resident gamesmen with ample opportunity for some excellent hunting. Wild duck and quail abound along the Kinchafoole Creek, one of Jimmy Carter's favorite spots for hunting game birds. It was not surprising that the list of the President's favorite foods included several dishes prepared from duck and quail.

The quail is a bird of passage, a native of hot countries that migrates with the change in seasons. For cooks who do not hunt their own game, dressed quail can be purchased from many meat markets and butcher shops. In America, quail are specially raised on farms for use by restaurants and home cooks. Quail can be roasted or grilled, and are often served with wild rice. One of President Carter's favorite dinners was braised quail with grits. All of the Carters were pleased when any leftover quail meat was served as an unusual but delicious hash.

Hash is a popular American dish, prepared in a variety of forms in a number of regional cuisines. In New England, corned beef hash is commonly served for a hearty breakfast or light supper meal. When the Carters moved "North" to Washington, they were willing to sample all sorts of dishes new to their Southern palates. In fact, before living in the White House they had never eaten corned beef! Upon discovering that they liked the dish, the Carters regularly included a New England-style corned beef dinner on the family's dinner menus. However, they still preferred their hash Southern-style, made with any of the fine-flavored meat left after a braised quail dinner.

QUAIL HASH

During the late 1800s, the presidential inaugurations were huge celebrations with impressive entertainment and enormous buffets, attended by crowds far too massive for the White House to accommodate. James Garfield's inaugural celebration was moved to the Smithsonian, where music was provided by John Philip Sousa and the U.S. Marine Band. President James Buchanan served saddles of venison and mutton in a building erected specifically for his inaugural celebration. The Old Pension Building was the site selected to celebrate the inauguration of President Benjamin Harrison. Quail was served as part of the massive buffet.

Serves 6

4 tablespoons butter	½ cup hot milk
2 tablespoons minced shallots	3 cups finely diced cooked
2 garlic cloves, pressed	quail meat
½ cup diced fresh mushrooms	1 tablespoon Worcestershire
½ cup diced celery	sauce
Juice of ½ lemon	6 twists freshly ground black
2 tablespoons flour	pepper
1 cup hot quail or chicken	1 tablespoon chopped fresh
stock	parsley

1. Melt butter in a 2-quart saucepan, add shallots and garlic and sauté for 2 minutes. Do not brown.

2. Add diced mushrooms and celery. Add lemon juice and simmer for 5 minutes, or until liquid has completely evaporated.

3. Stir in flour.

4. Add hot stock and hot milk, bring to a boil, and simmer for 2 to 3 minutes, stirring, until smooth.

5. Stir in diced quail meat. Add Worcestershire sauce and pepper.

6. Sprinkle with chopped parsley just before serving. (Keep warm until serving by setting saucepan in a pan of hot water; stir occasionally.) Serve topped with POACHED EGGS (page 149) or over toast. For hors d'oeuvres, serve in tartelettes or bouchées.

PRESIDENT CARTER'S FRIED FISH

After the Carters had been living in the White House for around two years, the President appeared in the Family Kitchen one day with a sheet of paper in hand. As he showed me the simple recipe he had written out, President Carter explained, "This is the way I like to have fish prepared, Chef." So that was the way we served fish to the President from that day on.

At the White House, swordfish was used to prepare the fried fish that appeared regularly on the Carter family dinner menus. For the Southern-style picnics held on the White House lawn, catfish was commonly substituted. In both situations, the fried fish was accompanied by the crisp balls of deep-fried cornmeal batter known as Hush Puppies. Southern cooks reportedly used to toss leftover scraps of fried cornmeal to their howling hounds in order to quiet the hungry dogs. Since the sated pups usually hushed up, the recipe for Hush Puppies was revamped for use in satisfying hungry guests.

Vice-President Mondale was another fan of a down-home fish fry. In fact, "Fritz" Mondale exhibited such a remarkably healthy appetite during his vice-presidency that his wife later admitted, "Not once in those four years did I worry about what we'd have for dinner. But I did worry about Fritz's weight." Vice-President Mondale was an amateur cook, so he often dropped into the White House kitchen to discuss recipes and chat about food. He was always very relaxed and friendly, a real regular guy. It was easy to understand why the Vice-President was able to establish such a fine working relationship with President Carter. They had a lot in common, including their down-to-earth attitudes and honest appreciation for good, simple food.

Calvin Coolidge was well known for his dry sense of humor. An avid fisherman, President Coolidge enjoyed fishing in the River Brule. When questioned by a reporter as to the number of fish in the river, the President estimated that there were some 45,000 trout, adding "I haven't caught them all yet, but I've intimidated them."

Serves 6

2 pounds fresh swordfish or
  catfish
2 tablespoons Worcestershire
  sauce
Juice of 1 lemon
1 tablespoon dry mustard

1 tablespoon salt
1 teaspoon freshly ground
  white pepper
2 quarts vegetable oil
2 tablespoons flour

1. Cut fish into French fry-size strips. Layer in a square pan or casserole dish.

2. In a small mixing bowl, combine Worcestershire sauce, lemon juice, mustard, salt, and pepper; pour over fish.

3. Cover pan tightly with plastic wrap. Let marinate for 2 to 3 hours.

4. In a large cast-iron skillet, heat oil to 375°F.

5. Spread flour in a shallow dish; dredge fish strips and transfer to the hot oil one at a time.

6. Fry for 5 minutes, or until golden and crisp; turn fish with a slotted spoon to brown evenly.

7. Drain on paper towels. Serve hot, with hot HUSH PUPPIES and catsup and tartar sauce, or SAUCE RÉMOULADE (page 213) and SAUCE TARTARE (page 266).

At President Carter's request, the White House's silver nut bowls were filled with peanuts during his administration.

HUSH PUPPIES   Makes 24

2 quarts vegetable oil
2 cups yellow cornmeal
1 tablespoon baking powder
1 teaspoon salt
¼ teaspoon freshly ground
    white pepper

2 eggs
½ cup cold milk
½ cup finely diced onion
2 garlic cloves, pressed

1. In a deep fryer or large cast-iron skillet, heat oil to 375°F.

2. In a large mixing bowl, combine cornmeal with baking powder, salt, and pepper.

3. In a smaller bowl, mix eggs with cold milk, diced onion, and pressed garlic. Add to large mixing bowl and stir until batter is well blended.

4. Carefully drop heaping tablespoonfuls of the batter into the hot oil.

5. Fry for 3 minutes, or until golden brown; turn to brown evenly, using a slotted spoon.

6. Drain on paper towels. Serve hot.

SAUCE TARTARE   Makes 1½ cups

1 tablespoon cider vinegar
Juice of ½ lemon
½ teaspoon salt
¼ teaspoon freshly ground
    white pepper
1 teaspoon Worcestershire
    sauce
1 tablespoon Dijon-style
    mustard

2 egg yolks
1 cup vegetable oil
2 tablespoons very finely
    minced onion
2 tablespoons very finely
    minced chives
2 hard-boiled egg yolks, very
    finely minced

1. In a blender, combine vinegar, lemon juice, salt, pepper, Worcestershire sauce, mustard, and raw egg yolks; blend at high speed for 10 seconds.

2. With blender running at low speed, gradually add oil; cover blender and blend at high speed for 10 seconds.

3. Stir in minced onions, chives, and cooked egg yolks. Use at once, as refrigeration causes the dressing to separate.

Bessie Lillian Carter raised her family in the small Georgia town of Plains. In 1966, at the age of sixty-seven, "Miss Lillian" joined the Peace Corps. She spent the next two years in a rural area of India, an experience she said had moved her deeply.

Miss Lillian symbolized the American dream that life can begin afresh at any age for those with the courage to adopt a new lifestyle. An independent, brave, forthright, and outspoken person, Miss Lillian was an excellent role model for a future President, to whom she offered the following sage advice: "If you are good, be *dynamically* good, don't be passively anything!" and, "Regardless of criticism, do what you think is right."

Jimmy Carter described his mother as "an extrovert, very dynamic, inquisitive in her attitude about life, compassionate toward others." He was the first American President to send his mother on a diplomatic mission when he appointed Miss Lillian to head the U.S. delegation attending the funeral of India's President Fakhruddin Ali Ahmed. Accompanied by her grandson Chip, Miss Lillian was warmly welcomed by the Indian people, who were openly grateful for the years of service she had given to their country.

Miss Lillian's Peace Corps duty was difficult and demanding, but one of her only complaints was a yearning for her favorite foods. In letters to her family, Miss Lillian expressed some of her cravings: "I'd give anything for a jar of peanut butter," she wrote once; and again, "I'd rather have a chunk of cheese than diamonds."

Miss Lillian enjoyed home-cooked Southern-style meals and, like the rest of the Carter clan, she loved cheddar cheese. On her frequent visits to the White House during her son's presidency, Miss Lillian was delighted with the Southern specialties and the various cheese dishes served for the First Family's meals. She often dropped by the White House kitchen to express her gratitude for the fine food and service, or simply to chat about everyday things. Miss Lillian even sent a gracious thank-you note from her home in Plains to bid a fond farewell.

One of Miss Lillian's favorite dishes was also popular with another gracious White House guest, Mrs. Ruth Carter Stapleton. As the President's sister and Rosalynn's childhood friend, Mrs. Stapleton was warmly welcomed on her frequent visits to the White House. Like her mother, she often stopped by the kitchen to say hello and chat with the staff. In was an honor to be able to prepare a beautiful cheese soufé for such beautiful Southern women as Miss Lillian and Ruth Carter Stapleton.

MISS LILLIAN'S CHEDDAR CHEESE SOUFFLÉ

Cheese appears to have been a popular gift for honoring America's early Presidents on a grand scale. In 1801, Thomas Jefferson received a 1,600-pound block of cheese, which had been transported from New England to Washington by sleigh; as late as 1803, the cheese was still being served to White House guests. President Andrew Jackson received a gift cheese weighing 1,400 pounds, which he decided to share at a public reception held at the White House in 1837. Set out on a stand in the main hallway, all of the cheese was devoured in some two hours by the crowd of hungry guests. It was reported that the aroma of aged cheese lingered in the White House for weeks afterward.

Plains, Ga -

To the Staff -

I want to thank you for all the wonderful treatment and care you gave me on my many visits to the White House -

To the Chef - butlers - kitchen help - a million thanks -

To Freddy who was always there to greet me - Thanks!

I'll probably never see you again, but I shall never forget you -

Please extend my thanks to everyone I know - and God bless you every one -

Love to you all -

Miss Lillian

[illegible] -
White House Residence
Washington
DC -

Please! Staff in Kitchen -

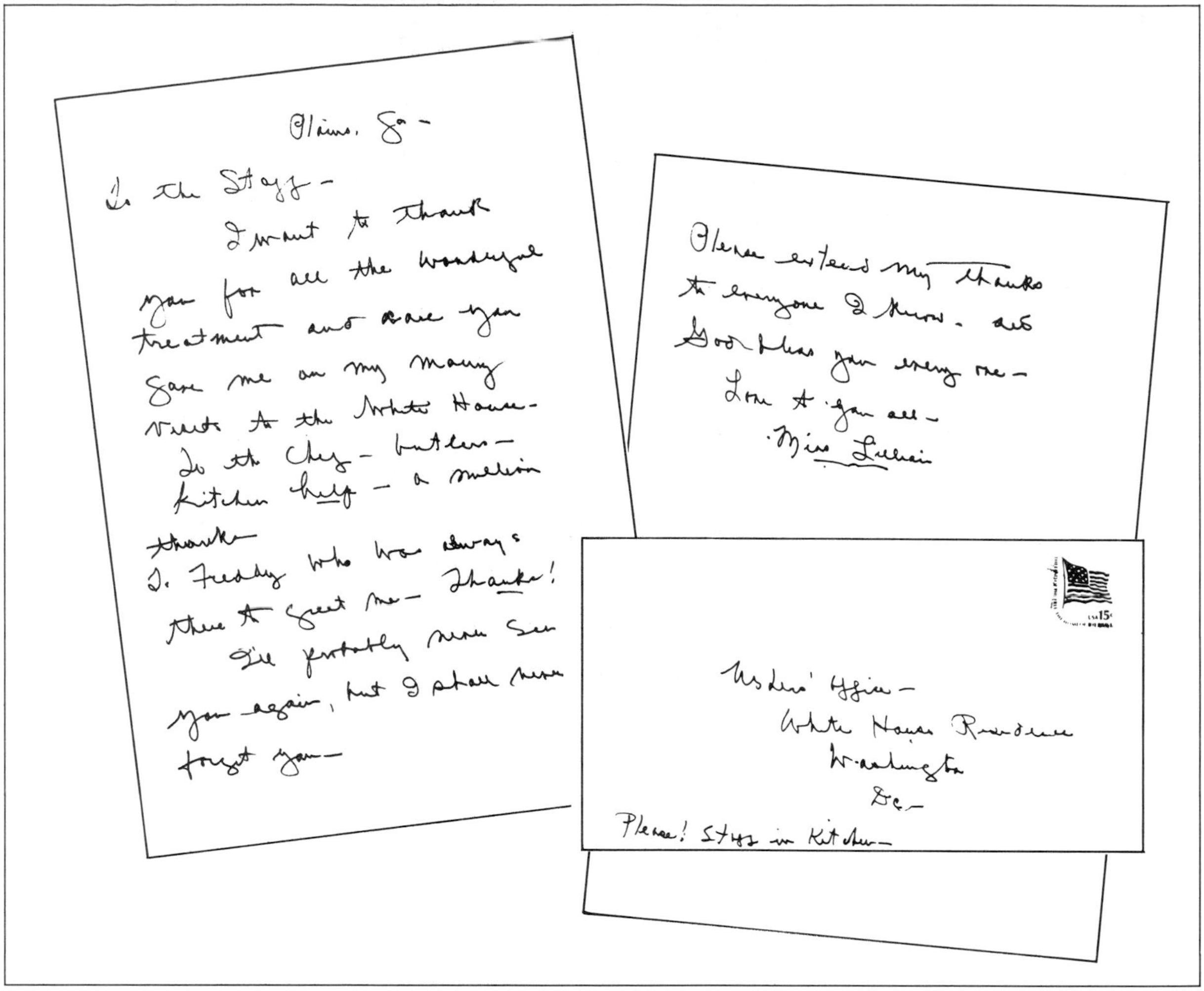

Serves 4

4 tablespoons butter
6 tablespoons flour
1 cup hot milk
1/4 teaspoon salt
1/8 teaspoon freshly ground white pepper
1/8 teaspoon nutmeg
4 egg yolks
6 egg whites, at room temperature
1/8 teaspoon cream of tartar
4 ounces sharp cheddar cheese, shredded

1. Preheat oven to 350°F. Use a pastry brush to generously coat the inside of a 1½-quart soufflé dish with soft butter; dust lightly with flour.

2. Melt butter in a 1-quart saucepan, add flour, and work into a roux. Cook for a minute or two, stirring constantly.

3. Add milk, salt, pepper, and nutmeg and bring to a boil, stirring vigorously. Cook over low heat for about 1 minute, or until thickened and smooth. Remove from heat.

4. Add egg yolks one at a time, stirring after each addition.

5. In a large, dry mixing bowl, slowly beat egg whites with cream of tartar; increase speed gradually, beating until egg whites are stiff.

6. Fold about one-quarter of the stiff whites into the egg yolk mixture.

7. Transfer egg yolk mixture to the mixing bowl, and fold in shredded cheese.

8. Blend gently until smooth and fluffy. Do not overmix.

9. Pour into the prepared mold to 1½ inches from the top. Smooth top lightly with a spatula.

10. Bake on lower shelf of preheated oven for 30 minutes, or until golden brown and puffed to about 2 inches above the rim. Serve immediately with a crisp green salad.

CARTER FAMILY FAVORITES ON-THE-SIDE

It is indeed unfortunate that a "mess of greens" remains a dish as yet unappreciated outside of the South. In the traditional Southern home, boiled greens were eaten on a daily basis. Collard greens, turnip greens, mustard greens, dandelion greens, kale, Swiss chard, and other greens were carefully cleaned, chopped into bite-size pieces, and cooked with some salt pork or bacon fat for flavor.

COLLARD GREENS WITH WHITE TURNIP

The 1887 edition of The White House Cook Book included instructions on boiling "greens":

About a peck of greens is enough for a mess for a family of six, such as dandelions, cowslips, burdock, chicory, and others. . . . Put greens into a large pot half full of boiling water, with a handful of salt, and boil steadily till stalks are tender—five to twenty minutes according to the maturity of the greens. Drain, chop them a little, season with salt, pepper, and butter. Vinegar may be added if liked.

After draining the cooked greens, the liquid was never discarded. Instead, the nutrient-rich "pot likker" was ladled over vegetables, used in soups, or eaten as broth to moisten crusty corn bread. A "mess of greens" and the accompanying "pot likker" are considered by some as the cornerstones of soul food.

Although "soul food" applies to the foods traditionally eaten by generations of American blacks, the actual term was adopted as recently as the 1960s during an era of marked growth in black ethnic pride. Soul food originated in the slave quarters of the Southern plantations, where no food was wasted, so that no one went hungry. With the advent of the Civil War, "poor man's food" became most Southerners' daily fare. A combination of necessity, availability, and culinary creativity, influenced by Afro-American and Southern cooking styles, led to a singular cuisine.

The Carters were very fond of certain soul food dishes, including fried chicken and fried catfish, hot biscuits, and boiled greens. Since the Carters preferred most vegetables raw or lightly cooked, they were especially enthusiastic about a recipe we created that combined the tender boiled greens with crisp cubes of white turnip. In the White House kitchen, soul food—like all food—was specially prepared to provide the First Family with the dishes they liked most, cooked in the manner that best suited their own personal tastes.

Serves 6

1½ pounds collards, stalks removed	1 cup diced onions
2 quarts water	2 garlic cloves, minced
1 tablespoon salt	1 ham hock
1 teaspoon sugar	2 cups peeled, diced white turnip
¼ teaspoon freshly ground white pepper	

1. Wash collard leaves thoroughly in cold water. Break into bite-size pieces.

2. In a 3-quart saucepan, place water and salt, sugar, and pepper. Add onions and garlic, and bring to a boil.

3. Add ham hock; cover, and simmer for 15 minutes.

4. Add collard leaves and continue to simmer, cover set slightly ajar, for 30 minutes.

5. Add diced turnip and simmer, cover slightly ajar, for 30 minutes more, or until liquid is almost completely reduced.
6. Spoon into a shallow serving dish; serve hot.

Succotash is an old-fashioned dish that dates back to America's colonial days and is still popular today in the deep South. The Carters were fond of the simple vegetable combination, with sausage links served on top in order to cater to the President's affinity for dishes made with pork. Plain succotash can serve as a tasty accompaniment to a variety of pork dishes. Topped with hot sausage links, it can be a perfect addition to a Southern-style buffet, picnic, or other informal dining occasion.

An Indian invention, succotash was served at the first Thanksgiving, held in 1621. Typically prepared from dried white beans and cooked dried corn, succotash—like many corn dishes—became a staple in the colonial diet. Creative Southern cooks elaborated on the original recipe, substituting fresh lima beans and young sweet corn. It is this particular vegetable combination that has won the allegiance of so many modern-day Southerners.

The name "succotash" was derived from the Narrangansett Indian word "misickquatash," which referred to a stew pot with an ear of corn, some dried beans, and a flavoring of bear grease. At the White House, a more modern version of this popular Southern dish was preferred. Succotash was often included on the menus for the Carters' many informal social functions, and was also enjoyed on a regular basis with the First Family's own Southern-style meals.

Serves 6

1 pound country sausage links
2 tablespoons butter
½ cup finely chopped onions
3 large ripe tomatoes, peeled and seeded
2 cups fresh or frozen baby lima beans
1½ cups fresh or frozen corn kernels

1 cup tomato juice
1½ teaspoons salt
¼ teaspoon freshly ground white pepper
1 tablespoon chopped fresh parsley

SUCCOTASH WITH SAUSAGE

Corn and beans flourished in the gardens of Thomas Jefferson's 10,000-acre Virginia estate. To ensure a rich and varied food supply for himself and his numerous house guests, Jefferson kept his woods stocked with wild game, the ponds and streams furnished with fish, and the fields filled with pigs, cattle, sheep, and goats. Jefferson's poultry runs were cluttered with chickens, peacocks, and fowl of all sorts, and his gardens and orchards bloomed with a wide array of produce. After his return from diplomatic duty in Europe, Thomas Jefferson continued to correspond with the American envoys who remained abroad, requesting additional agricultural enlightenment. For some 23 years, the superintendent of

a botanical garden in Paris responded, sending Jefferson packets of seeds so that he could cultivate new plants and share his results with his dinner guests and the rest of America.

1. In a large skillet, cook sausages over medium-high heat until they are cooked through and evenly browned, about 10 minutes. Drain off fat, cover, and keep warm. (To prevent sausages from bursting during cooking, prick holes in the skins with a sharp fork.)

2. In a separate skillet, melt butter; sauté onions over medum heat for 3 minutes, or until transparent. Do not brown.

3. Dice tomatoes and add to sautéed onions. Stir in lima beans, corn, tomato juice, salt, and pepper.

4. Cover and simmer for 25 minutes, stirring occasionally.

5. Transfer to a deep serving dish. Arrange sausage links across the top.

6. Sprinkle with chopped parsley, and serve at once, with batter-fried foods such as HUSH PUPPIES (page 266), PRESIDENT CARTER'S FRIED FISH (page 264), or JIMMY CARTER'S SOUTHERN FRIED CHICKEN (page 261).

JIMMY CARTER'S "EGGPLANT GOULASH"

Jimmy Carter liked to include some sort of fresh vegetable in his diet every day. However, when out on the campaign trail or traveling on a diplomatic mission, it was sometimes impossible to obtain fresh produce. The Carters were always glad to get back to Plains—and later to the Governor's Mansion in Atlanta—where the local markets could supplement whatever their own gardens did not supply. While living in the White House, President Carter and his family continued to enjoy a variety of fresh vegetables in season. The unusual market demands of the many embassies and consulates located in Washington has led to an impressive array of foodstuffs not always available elsewhere, including fresh Southern vegetables.

Butternut squash, zucchini, butter beans, vine-ripe tomatoes, and fresh corn were some of President Carter's favorite vegetables. He also liked greens such as collards and kale, and he even enjoyed a number of dishes made with okra, one of the least popular vegetables in America. But eggplant was undoubtedly Jimmy Carter's favorite vegetable. The President liked fresh eggplant straight out of the garden, thinly sliced and batter-fried, or baked in a soufflé or casserole.

Native to India, the eggplant was named by the colonists when the oddly shaped vegetable first arrived on American shores. Its mild flavor makes eggplant a versatile vegetable. Eggplant Parmagiana is a popular Italian-style dish featuring batter-fried eggplant layered with cheeses and baked in a rich tomato sauce. Eggplant Ticinese is a lighter casserole dish flavored with olive oil, garlic, fresh tomatoes, and oregano. The recipe has long been popular in Ticino, a Swiss canton that borders on Italy and for which the dish was named.

Jimmy Carter enjoyed experimenting with vegetable cookery and liked to try his favorites prepared in different ways. Although he referred to his very favorite eggplant casserole as "goulash," the staff in the White House kitchen actually prepared the dish according to the Italian-Swiss recipe for Eggplant Ticinese. This eggplant side dish appeared on the Carter family dinner menu quite often, partly because of its versatility, but mostly since the President liked it so much.

Thomas Jefferson is credited with introducing the eggplant to colonial America, but the new vegetable was not well accepted. By the turn of the century, however, more appealing recipes for the unfamiliar vegetable were available. The 1887 edition of The White House Cook Book provided guidelines for preparation:

Take fresh, purple eggplants of a middling size. Cut them in slices a quarter of an inch thick and soak them for half an hour in cold water with a teaspoonful of salt in it. . . . You must not remove them from the water until you are ready to cook them, as the air will turn them black.

Serves 6

¼ cup olive oil
1 cup finely chopped onions
4 garlic cloves, very finely minced
2 medium-size eggplants, peeled
4 ripe tomatoes, peeled and seeded, or one 14½-ounce can whole tomatoes with juice
2 teaspoons salt
6 twists freshly ground black pepper
1 teaspoon chopped fresh oregano, or ½ teaspoon dried
1 tablespoon chopped fresh parsley
½ cup dry bread crumbs
1 cup shredded mozzarella cheese

1. Preheat oven to 375°F. Butter inside of a 2-quart casserole dish.
2. Heat oil in a large nonstick sauté pan, add onions and garlic and sauté for 2 minutes, or until golden brown.
3. Cut eggplant into ½-inch cubes; add to pan, and sauté for 5 minutes, or until lightly browned.
4. Dice tomatoes and add to sauté pan; season with salt, pepper, and oregano, and simmer for 5 minutes.
5. In a small bowl, mix together chopped parsley, bread crumbs, and shredded cheese.
6. Transfer sautéed vegetables to the prepared casserole dish and sprinkle with the parsley-crumb-cheese mixture.
7. Bake on upper shelf of preheated oven for 20 minutes, or until golden brown. Serve hot as a side dish to accompany lamb, veal, chicken, or seafood.

FRENCH FRIED ONION RINGS

Onions were not well accepted by early Americans, and Benjamin Franklin succinctly expressed their sentiments: "Onions can make ev'n heirs and widows weep." The 1887 edition of The White House Cook Book *attempted to encourage reticent cooks to use the neglected vegetable:*

> *A little onion is not an injurious article of food, as many believe. A judicious use of plants of the onion family is quite as important a factor in successful cookery as salt and pepper . . . imparts a delicate appetizing aroma highly prized by epicures.*

During the Carter administration, the generally ignored Vidalia onion received much public attention. An ordinary yellow onion, the Vidalia develops an unusual sweetness when grown in the soils of a particular region of Georgia. The mild moist onion is also less pungent, causing somewhat less weeping than most other varieties.

As a favor to the President, one of the Carters' financial advisers from the Plains peanut business regularly brought along a bag of Vidalia onions on his trips to the White House. The Vidalias were perfect for making French-fried onion rings, one of the President's favorite dishes. Cooking onions in fat improves the flavor by enhancing their innate sweetness. Browning onions is undesirable, however, as the burning causes a bitter, acrid flavor to develop.

French-fried onion rings are currently very popular in America, where the crispy batter-fried vegetable typically accompanies hamburgers, fried fish, and other fast foods. Like most Americans, the Carters liked fast foods and fried foods, but since such foods are notoriously high in fat-calories, even the lithe Carter clan limited their intakes to moderate amounts. The Carters were unusually disciplined with both diet and exercise, so the White House kitchen was never worried about serving the First Family an occasional favorite high-calorie dish, including the batter-fried Vidalia onion rings.

Serves 6

1 quart vegetable oil
4 large sweet onions (Vidalia or Bermuda)
1 cup flour
1 cup heavy cream
2 eggs

1 teaspoon salt
⅛ teaspoon freshly ground white pepper
2 to 3 tablespoons dry bread crumbs

1. In a deep fryer or large cast-iron skillet, heat oil to 375°F.
2. Slice onions into ⅛-inch thick rings. Carefully separate out the larger rings; set aside smaller rings for use in other dishes.
3. Spread flour in a shallow bowl; dredge onion rings lightly.
4. In a shallow mixing bowl, combine cream with eggs, salt, and pepper, using a wire whisk. Dip in onion rings, coating well on each side.
5. Spread bread crumbs in a separate shallow bowl; coat onion rings on both sides.

6. Add batter-coated onion rings to the hot oil a few at a time; fry for 3 minutes, or until golden brown and crisp.

7. Drain on paper towels, and serve hot.

Precautions are advisable when peeling onions—unless they are sweet Vidalia onions from Georgia.

CHIP'S DEVILED EGGS

Eggs have long been recognized as a versatile food; they can be prepared in a variety of styles or added to recipes to enhance palatability and nutritional value. Professional chefs have long advocated creativity in egg cookery, and the 1887 edition of The White House Cook Book *provided home cooks with some encouragement in this regard: "There are so many ways of cooking and dressing eggs that it seems unnecessary for the ordinary family to use only those that are the most practical."*

In the twenty-plus years I have served as the Executive Chef at the White House, I have seen subtle changes in the home of the First Family. No family leaves the White House exactly as it was upon their arrival. Each family, in its own personal way, leaves a special impression on the White House that forever alters the character of the President's home.

The Carters were the first family from the deep South to occupy the White House since President Zachary Taylor (1849–1850). Quite a few of their Southern customs were new to the White House staff. Big family gatherings, for example, are held in the South on a regular basis. These affairs are typically informal, and plenty of home-style food is served. When the heat and humidity allow for outdoor entertaining, picnics and outdoor buffets are common. The Carters hosted many informal family-style parties out on the South Lawn. One of the standard menu items at these affairs was stuffed eggs.

Chip Carter was a real fan of stuffed eggs, especially served with a spicy "deviled" filling. Chip was a frequent visitor to the White House kitchen, where hard-cooked eggs were kept on hand for him to grab on the run. An energetic young man, Chip liked foods he could eat on the go since he was always busy, often traveling on business in his father's behalf. Chip was really a "chip off the old block" in his avid interest in political issues. He was a happy White House resident, working in the exciting world of politics and keeping energized with his favorite foods furnished by the White House kitchen.

Makes 12

6 hard-cooked eggs, chilled
½ cup soft cream cheese
½ teaspoon salt
¼ teaspoon freshly ground white pepper
2 tablespoons Dijon-style mustard

1 tablespoon Worcestershire sauce
Fresh parsley sprigs
Black olive slices

1. Remove shells from cold eggs; slice each in half lengthwise.
2. Carefully scoop out yolks and sieve into a small mixing bowl.
3. Arrange egg white halves on a tray, cavities up.
4. Add cream cheese, salt, pepper, mustard, and Worcestershire sauce to the mixing bowl; whip until smooth, using a wire whisk.

5. Transfer to a pastry tube fitted with a small (#4) tip and divide evenly among the cavities of the egg halves, filling each in a decorative manner.

6. Refrigerate until serving time. Garnish each egg with a tiny sprig of fresh parsley and several thin slices of black olive. Decorate serving platter with additional sprigs of fresh parsley, if desired.

The Carters enjoyed many of the humble foods of the Old South, including a variety of dishes made from corn. They preferred their corn dishes prepared with stone-ground white cornmeal instead of the degerminated yellow variety that is popular in the North. In the White House kitchen, the two types of cornmeal were often combined in order to create a soft, light product with a crunchy texture. Use of white cornmeal alone can result in dishes with too little body, while yellow cornmeal can yield products that are too dry. A combination of the two can provide the best of both worlds, such as the delicious Corn Bread that became a favorite of the Carters.

Since wheat was a luxury item until the development of the milling process, Corn Bread was the predominant bread in early American homes. Corn Bread is still baked regularly in the contemporary Southern kitchen and, with the Carters in residence, homemade Corn Bread became one of the staples of the White House kitchen. The First Family liked to serve hot, freshly baked Corn Bread at Southern-style breakfasts, with soup for simple luncheon meals, and to accompany a wide array of entrées for the family dinners.

Makes 9 squares

1 cup flour	1 tablespoon sugar
1/2 cup white cornmeal	1 egg
1/2 cup yellow cornmeal	1 cup warm milk
4 teaspoons baking powder	1 stick (1/2 cup) butter, melted
1/2 teaspoon salt	

1. Preheat oven to 425°F. Butter inside of an 8-inch square baking pan.

2. In a large mixing bowl, combine flour, yellow and white cornmeal, baking powder, salt, and sugar.

CARTERS' CORN BREAD

Early Americans often referred to their freshly ground cornmeal as "Indian meal," as in the following recipe included in the 1887 edition of The White House Cook Book:

Sift one quart of Indian meal into a pan; make a hole in the middle and pour in a pint of warm water, adding one teaspoonful of salt; with a spoon mix the meal and water gradually into a soft dough; stir it very briskly for a quarter of an hour or more, till it becomes light and spongy; then spread the dough smoothly and evenly on a straight, flat board (a piece of the head of a flour-barrel will serve for this purpose); place the board nearly upright before an open fire and put an iron against the back to support it; bake it well; when done, cut it in squares; send it hot to table, split and buttered.

3. In a smaller mixing bowl, beat egg with warm milk, using a wire whisk. Stir in melted butter.

4. Pour over dry ingredients and mix with the wire whisk until smooth. Let stand for 15 minutes. (It is important to let batter rest before baking so that the cornmeal absorbs the liquid and the resulting texture is smooth, never grainy.)

5. Scrape batter into the prepared pan. Bake on lower shelf of preheated oven for 20 minutes, or until top is golden and toothpick inserted near center comes out clean.

6. Let pan stand on a wire rack for 10 minutes before cutting into squares. Serve warm, with whipped butter, if desired.

CARTER FAMILY DOWN-HOME SWEETS

PEANUT BRITTLE

Peanuts were the Carters' family symbol long before they became White House residents. They enjoyed eating peanuts, plain or as an ingredient in a number of dishes, but no more than the typical American family. However, Jimmy Carter was the proud proponent of his family's peanut business, so he was pleased that his presidency advanced the reputation of the plain ol' peanut.

When Jimmy Carter was only 5 years old, he was already involved in the peanut business, selling small bags of boiled peanuts that he had picked fresh and prepared all by himself. Although he eventually left the family peanut business for a naval career, the death of his father provided young Jimmy with a new perspective on his own future. He returned to his roots and, with the assistance of his energetic young wife, gradually expanded the family business into a thriving commercial enterprise.

America is one of the world's foremost producers of peanuts. Georgia leads the country in peanut production. Therefore, in order to demonstrate his deep feelings of family, state, and national pride, Jimmy Carter requested a simple alteration in White House custom during his presidency: The silver nut bowls traditionally present on every table at the State Dinners, which had usually contained roasted mixed nuts, were to be kept filled with plain old peanuts during his administration.

President Carter liked to snack on peanuts, usually deep-fried and salted. His mother, Miss Lillian, had always prepared the nuts in this manner to have on hand for family and friends. The Carters also enjoyed several sweets made with peanuts, including Peanut Cookies and Peanut Brittle. Amy was especially fond of these two goodies, so the White House pastry chef prepared batches of both on a regular basis.

Although sugary sweets have long been recognized by concerned parents as non-nutritious foodstuffs best reserved for occasional treats, pastry chefs have devised many recipes to improve the reputation and health value of cookies and other desserts. The 1887 edition of The White House Cook Book *provided a recipe for a molasses cookie called* Our Little Ones, *which encouraged parental acceptance by citing them as "specially recommended as wholesome for children."*

Makes 2 pounds

1½ cups water
3 cups granulated sugar
1 cup white corn syrup
3 cups shelled raw peanuts

1 teaspoon salt
4 tablespoons butter
½ teaspoon baking soda

1. In a large saucepan, boil water with sugar and corn syrup for 5 minutes, or until the mixture reaches 200°F on a candy thermometer.

2. Add peanuts and salt; continue boiling until candy thermometer reads 295°F, stirring constantly with a wooden spoon. Nuts should be crackling hot, but syrup should not be browned.

3. Remove from heat, and stir in butter and baking soda.

4. Immediately pour out onto a well-buttered marble slab, or a large baking sheet set atop wire racks. Use a metal spatula to spread the mixture as thinly as possible. Work quickly!

5. Put on clean gloves to protect against burns and use the spatula to quickly loosen the mass and turn it over. Stretch quickly by hand until candy is transparent in appearance.

6. Let stand until cool. Use the metal spatula to lift the cooled candy and crack into bite-size pieces. Store candy in an airtight container.

PECAN DIAMONDS

The Georgia pecan is thin-shelled and delicious when toasted, lightly glazed, or baked in breads, pies, candies, and cookies. Pecans have long been appreciated by cooks all over the South for the unique rich flavor so appropriate in many traditional Southern desserts. Although the Carters reserved sweets for special occasions, desserts made with fresh Georgia pecans were some of their favorite treats.

A special type of rich pecan cookie was introduced to the White House by one of the pastry chefs who served during the Carter administration. The original recipe for Pecan Diamonds had been devised at the well-respected Culinary Institute of America, a training center for chefs located in Hyde Park, New York. The recipe is provided on the printed cards that accompany attractive gift packages of pecan diamonds, baked by students and supplied to fortunate recipients by administrators at the Institute.

During the Carters' White House years, many batches of the delicate pecan cookies were served at official teas and receptions. They proved to be a popular menu item at the concert receptions given on Sunday afternoons. The perfect little diamond pastries were offered to White House guests following Andrés Segovia's impressive guitar performance, and after the stellar presentation by Amy's favorite, ballet dancer Mikhail Baryshnikov.

Pecan Diamonds in smaller quantities were also included on the menu when the First Family entertained guests for dinner. Family and friends from the Carters' home state were especially appreciative of the rich cookies made with Georgia pecans. And guests from the rest of the country were introduced to this delightful dessert while enjoying the sweet flavor of Southern hospitality, White House-style.

Makes around 200 cookies

Crust

½ cup plus 2 tablespoons
    butter
9 tablespoons sugar
*6 tablespoons vegetable
    shortening*

1 egg
1 teaspoon vanilla extract
3 cups flour
1 teaspoon baking powder
½ teaspoon salt

1. In a large mixing bowl, cream butter with sugar and shortening. Blend in egg and vanilla.
2. In a smaller mixing bowl, sift together flour, baking powder,

and salt. Transfer to the larger bowl, and mix to form a smooth dough.

3. Wrap dough in plastic and refrigerate ovenight.

4. Preheat oven to 350°F.

5. Divide chilled dough into 3 equal pieces. Return 2 of the pieces to the refrigerator.

6. Set the piece of dough between 2 sheets of plastic wrap and transfer to a large board; use a rolling pin to roll out into a 5 × 12-inch rectangle about ⅛-inch thick.

7. Remove top sheet of plastic and turn dough over to line one end of a 12 × 16-inch ungreased baking sheet. Remove the other sheet of plastic.

8. Repeat with each of the remaining pieces of dough; arrange the pieces of rolled dough to evenly cover the baking sheet. (If dough breaks or crumbles while transferring to the baking sheet, press together gently to patch.)

9. Bake on middle shelf of preheated oven for 10 minutes, or until golden brown.

10. Let pan cool on a wire rack.

Pecan Filling

4 sticks (2 cups) butter
1⅛ cups honey
½ cup granulated sugar
2½ cups light brown sugar
8 cups chopped pecans
½ cup heavy cream

1. Make the filling: In a large saucepan, combine butter with honey and granulated and light brown sugars. Bring to a boil over medium heat; let boil for 3 minutes. Remove from heat and let stand until cool. Fold in chopped nuts and heavy cream.

2. Spread hot pecan filling onto the cooled crust. Bake on lower shelf of the hot oven for 35 minutes, or until bottom crust is completely cooked; filling will still be soft. Let cool completely on a wire rack.

3. Use a sharp knife to cut into 200 small diamonds: Slice diagonally across the sheet to make 15 lines, then repeat in the opposite direction to form diamonds, each measuring 1½ inches in diameter; discard incompletely formed diamonds from the perimeter.

4. Serve at once, or store in an airtight container.

PINEAPPLE UPSIDE-DOWN CAKE

In 1751, George Washington had his first taste of fresh pineapple during a trip to Barbados. The future first President of the United States announced that he preferred pineapple to any other fruit. Unfortunately, the perishable fruit neither traveled well nor grew well in the climate of Washington's homeland. Canned pineapple was not available to Americans either, until Dole established a Hawaiian pineapple company in 1921.

Pineapple Upside-down Cake is prepared so that the sweetened fruit is on the bottom during the baking process, and the finished cake is inverted before serving. The result is a rich cake saturated by the warm sweet syrup and spiked with the delicious flavor of pineapple. On the rare occasions when the Carters indulged in a "dessert by request," this sweet cake was a welcome treat.

Ever since Columbus discovered the bounty of the New World, pineapple has been one of the world's best loved tropical fruits. The natives of the West Indies used the plentiful fruit as a symbol of welcome, decorating the entrances to their huts with pineapples and pineapple tops. The Spanish carried on the tradition, and the American colonists carved pineapples onto their gates and door posts. Serving fresh pineapple or a delectable dish made with the popular fruit remains a hospitable way to welcome guests.

Fresh pineapple is not always available in today's markets, due to the perishability of the fruit. Fortunately for fans of Pineapple Upside-down Cake, the canned fruit makes a delicious substitute. The Carters served the cake warm, with a silver bowl of freshly whipped cream on the side, certainly a most delightful dessert for welcoming family and friends.

Serves 8

Two 8-ounce cans pineapple rings in heavy syrup
2 cups light brown sugar
1/3 cup melted butter
2 cups sifted flour
1 1/2 teaspoons baking powder
1/2 teaspoon baking soda
3/4 teaspoon salt
3/4 teaspoon cinnamon
1/2 teaspoon allspice
1/3 cup vegetable shortening
1 egg
7/8 cup buttermilk

1. Preheat oven to 350°F.
2. Drain pineapple; reserve 2 tablespoons of the syrup.
3. In a small mixing bowl, combine half the brown sugar with the melted butter and the reserved syrup.
4. Spread evenly over the bottom of a 9-inch cake pan. Arrange the 8 pineapple rings in a layer on top.
5. In a mixing bowl, sift together flour, baking powder, baking soda, salt, cinnamon, and allspice.
6. In a larger mixing bowl, cream shortening with the remaining cup of brown sugar. Add egg, and beat until light and fluffy.
7. Alternately mix in dry ingredients and buttermilk, adding a

little at a time and beating well after each addition. Continue beating until batter is smooth.

8. Spoon batter carefully over the pineapple rings. Scrape remaining batter into the pan using a plastic spatula.

9. Bake on middle shelf of preheated oven for 45 to 50 minutes, or until top is golden brown and firm to the touch.

10. Let pan cool on a wire rack for 5 minutes. Reverse onto a serving dish and remove pan; serve warm. Since the cake creates its own decorative top once it is turned over, additional garnish is unnecessary. If desired, freshly whipped cream can be served on the side.

GEORGIA PEACH COBBLER

Pies are popular desserts in the South, often prepared with a regional flair. Single-crusted open-face pies are favored, such as sweet potato or pecan pie. Deep-dish pies made with a variety of fresh fruits in season are also well liked. Fruit cobblers often adorn Southern dessert tables, prepared as deep-dish pies with a rich biscuit crust on top. The Carters' favorite pie was decidedly pecan, but they were also very fond of a fresh peach cobbler.

Although peaches enjoy a relatively brief season, usually peaking in July and August, the delicate fruit ranks second to the apple among America's leading fruit crops. Peaches are classified as firm-fleshed clingstone or soft-fleshed freestone. Clingstone peaches are best for pies and other baked goods. The most widely sold freestone peach is the Alberta, reportedly named after the wife of the Georgian who first grew this variety in 1870. Georgia is now a leading state in the production of America's commercial peach crop.

At the Carters' farm in Plains, peanuts were not the only crop that flourished. The Carters' gardens bloomed with fresh produce, their vines drooped with berries of various types, and an orchard housed fig trees and their prized pecan trees. The Carters put up their own fruits and vegetables, and prepared homemade preserves from wild berries and fresh peaches. And there was always plenty of fresh produce on hand at their Georgia home.

When the Carters moved to the White House, they found that plenty of fresh food was still available, including a wide variety of seasonal fruits. Since the Carters rarely requested a dessert following their family meals, the White House kitchen kept an ample

Historical accounts tend to emphasize the physiques of America's largest Presidents, all but ignoring the leaner leaders. Although the almost gaunt appearance of Abraham Lincoln is widely recognized, the diminutive size of James Madison is often overlooked. At 5 feet 4 inches and barely 100 pounds, Madison was America's slightest President. William Harrison was also thin, and suffered from a digestive disorder that severely restricted his diet. For those aspiring to an increase in weight, the 1887 edition of The White House Cook Book *offered the following "Health Suggestions":*

First, restore digestion, take plenty of sleep, drink all the water the stomach will bear in the morning on rising, take moderate exercise in the open air, eat oatmeal, cracked wheat, graham mush, baked sweet apples, roasted and broiled beef, cultivate jolly people, and bathe daily.

supply of fresh fruit on hand. Just-ripe bananas, crunchy apples, sweet pears, and grapes usually satisfied any after-dinner cravings. When peaches were in season, however, Mrs. Carter occasionally requested a "real" dessert for her family, the Southern deep-dish pie we called Georgia Peach Cobbler.

Serves 6 to 8

2 cups cake flour
¼ teaspoon salt
4 teaspoons baking powder
½ cup finely shredded sharp cheddar cheese
½ cup plus 1 tablespoon butter, at room temperature
½ cup buttermilk
8 medium-size very ripe peaches

½ cup water
¾ cup granulated sugar
¼ cup light brown sugar
Juice of 1 lemon
1 teaspoon vanilla extract
1 egg yolk, beaten with 1 tablespoon water

1. In a large mixing bowl, sift together flour, salt, and baking powder.
2. Stir in shredded cheese.
3. Cut in ½ cup butter until well distributed, using a pastry cutter.
4. Add buttermilk, and stir with a wooden spoon to form a soft dough. Do not overmix.
5. Transfer dough to the center of a large square of plastic wrap. Top with a sheet of plastic of equal size, and press by hand to form a square of 2-inch thickness.
6. Refrigerate dough for 30 minutes.
7. Preheat oven to 375°F. Butter inside of a shallow 1½-quart casserole dish.
8. Dip the peaches in boiling water for 2 to 3 seconds; transfer into ice water and peel immediately. Halve them and remove pits, then cut each half into thin, even slices.
9. In a 1-quart saucepan, combine the ½ cup water with granulated and light brown sugars, and bring to a boil.
10. Add lemon juice, and boil for 3 minutes.
11. Add sliced peaches, and simmer for 1 minute.
12. Remove from heat; stir in vanilla and the remaining tablespoon of butter.
13. Transfer to the prepared casserole dish, and let cool.

14. On a lightly floured board, roll out dough to ¼-inch thickness and the same dimensions as the casserole dish, using a rolling pin.

15. Carefully transfer to top of casserole dish to form a top crust; press edges to sides of dish. Use a pastry brush to coat crust lightly with beaten egg yolk.

16. Use a fork to prick holes in the crust in about a dozen places.

17. Bake on middle shelf of preheated oven for 45 minutes, or until crust is golden brown.

18. Let dish cool slightly on a wire rack. Serve warm.

BLACK CHERRY CHEESECAKE

The Carters were all devoted cheese fans. They especially liked sharp aged cheddar, either served with crackers for snacks or included in a wide variety of dishes. To fulfill the First Family's liberal cheese requirement, the White House kitchen invariably had a huge wheel of good cheddar on hand.

Other types of cheese were also well-received at the Carters' dining table. Gruyère in a soup or soufflé, blue cheese or Roquefort in a salad dressing, and mozzarella in casseroles were popular items on the family's dinner menus. The Carters even served cheese for dessert, as an accompaniment to a fresh fruit platter or, for a real rare indulgence, in a rich cheesecake.

Popular in various forms for hundreds of years, modern-day cheesecake appears in one of two main forms in the United States: Italian-style, with a rich ricotta cheese filling, or the more common New York-style, made smoother and even richer with the use of cream cheese. Cream, either sweet or sour, lightens a cheesecake and heightens the flavor. Cheesecakes can be served plain, or garnished with fresh fruit or fruited toppings. However it is made, though, cheesecake is a notoriously high-calorie dessert.

The Carters were lean and active, so they had no need to restrict calories. In fact, the physically draining weeks out on the campaign trail sometimes resulted in weight losses. As regular joggers, the President and his wife kept fit and expended additional calories. Cheese was a good way to add some needed calories to their daily diets. And cheesecake—as many a dieter can attest—was a sure means of supplementing their caloric intakes in a very delicious way.

Makes two 10-inch cakes

Sugar Dough Crust

4 cups flour   1 cup confectioners' sugar
2 sticks (1 cup) unsalted butter   1 extra-large egg

1. Sift flour into a large bowl.
2. Cut in butter, using a pastry cutter, until well distributed.
3. Use the back of a large spoon to form a well in the center and add sugar and egg. Blend thoroughly.
4. Turn out on lightly floured surface and work dough lightly with the palm of the hand until smooth.
5. Shape into a ball; flatten gently by hand to around 1½-inch thickness.
6. Wrap dough in plastic and refrigerate for 1 hour. (If refrigerated overnight or longer, let dough stand at room temperature for 30 minutes before proceeding.)
7. Preheat oven to 375°F.
8. With a sharp knife, cut dough in half. On a lightly floured board, roll out each piece of dough to form a large circle of ⅛-inch thickness.
9. Carefully transfer pastry to the bottom of two 10-inch spring-form pans; trim off excess.
10. Prebake crusts on lower shelf of preheated oven for 10 minutes, or until lightly browned. Let cool on wire racks.

Filling

5 pounds cream cheese, at   Grated rind of 1 lemon
   room temperature   Grated rind of ½ orange
3 cups sugar   1 teaspoon vanilla extract
12 eggs   1½ cups heavy cream

1. Preheat oven to 375°F.
2. In a large mixing bowl, beat cream cheese until very smooth.
3. Add sugar, and mix well.
4. Add eggs, 2 at a time, beating until smooth after each addition.
5. Add lemon and orange rind, and stir in vanilla.
6. Stir in heavy cream, mixing gently until smooth.
7. Divide batter evenly between the 2 prebaked crusts.
8. Set cakes on a large baking sheet or in a shallow pan with 2-inch sides. Add water to pan to make a shallow *bain marie*.

9. Bake on middle shelf of preheated oven for 55 minutes. Cakes will be golden brown.
10. Cool cakes completely on wire racks, and refrigerate overnight.

Black Cherry Topping

¾ cup sugar
¾ cup unsweetened orange juice
2 cups fresh black cherry halves, pits and stems removed

4 tablespoons cold water
Juice of 1 lemon
2 tablespoons cornstarch

1. In a 1-quart saucepan, dissolve sugar in orange juice. Bring to a boil, and let boil for 5 minutes.
2. Stir in cherries and boil for 8 minutes more, stirring occasionally with a wooden spoon.
3. In a small bowl, combine cold water with lemon juice and cornstarch, stirring until dissolved. Add to cherries, stirring gently until thickened.
4. Remove from heat and let cool.
5. Spread topping evenly onto surface of chilled cheesecakes. Serve at once. (Other fruit toppings or fresh fruit may be substituted if desired, or cheesecake can be served plain.)

AMY'S PEANUT BUTTER COOKIES

Amy was a frisky, freckled, strawberry blonde with an outgoing personality and an independent spirit. She loved to read, enjoyed playing alone or with friends, and was a good student. Amy was an active member of the Girl Scouts, and she practiced the piano and took violin lessons after school. While living in the White House, Amy attended a public school nearby, where she quickly made a host of friends. On many occasions, the ground floor of the White House reverberated with the pleasant sound of young girls' laughter as Amy and her friends rollerskated down the uncarpeted halls.

The Carters were strict with Amy because it would have been too easy for a child living in the White House to become spoiled. Amy was well behaved and undemanding, and her natural, friendly disposition made her a popular White House resident. Also popular with the press, Amy had her photograph on the cover of *Time* magazine, which described her as providing "an intangible aura of

Amy Carter became a popular figure with press and public alike during the Carter administration.

pleasure to the grit of day-to-day politics." Although the Carters were proud that Amy was so well liked by the American public, they eventually declared their daughter off-limits to the press in order to preserve some childhood normalcy.

Amy considered the White House "a great place to live." She also regarded herself as being "a real good cook," so she became a frequent visitor to the White House kitchen. Amy liked the fun of holidays and birthdays at the White House, and she enjoyed getting involved in the food preparation whenever possible. At Easter time, Amy loved readying the colored eggs for the annual Easter Egg Roll held out on the White House lawn. In her enthusiasm, however, Amy usually splattered the dye all over the kitchen—we even had to wash down the walls afterward!

At mealtimes, Amy always ate whatever was served. There was never a separate menu or special meal prepared for her. Her favorite foods included hamburgers and pizza, ice cream and cookies, the foods that most American children relish. Amy's parents made sure that her overall diet was healthful and well balanced, but Amy saw to it that she also enjoyed an occasional treat. There was always a fresh batch of homemade cookies available in the White House kitchen, stored in a special boot-shaped cookie jar. A handy supply of Amy's Peanut Butter Cookies was one way to ensure frequent visits from the most popular little girl in the White House.

Makes 60 cookies

1 stick (½ cup) soft butter
½ cup vegetable shortening
½ cup peanut butter
1 cup granulated sugar
1 cup light brown sugar

¼ teaspoon salt
2 eggs
1 teaspoon baking soda
¼ cup warm water
3 cups sifted flour

1. Preheat oven to 400°F.
2. In a large mixing bowl, cream together butter, shortening, and peanut butter.
3. Beat in the granulated and light brown sugars and salt.
4. Beat in eggs, one at a time.
5. In a small bowl, dissolve baking soda in warm water. Add to the large mixing bowl and stir well.
6. Stir in flour. Mix until dough is smooth.
7. Transfer dough to the center of a large sheet of plastic wrap;

During the annual Easter Egg Roll, the White House lawn is packed with happy children.

For many years, an annual Easter Egg Roll was held each Easter Monday on the grounds of the Capitol building. During the Hayes administration, however, Congress curtailed the custom because of complaints that the crowds of children were ruining the grass. President Hayes relocated the lively and well-loved event on the grounds of the White House, where two of his own children happily joined in the fun. The Easter egg tradition has continued ever since, held each spring on the South Lawn of the First Family's home.

top with another sheet of equal size. Press dough out by hand to form a square 2 inches thick.

8. Wrap up tightly and refrigerate for 1 hour, or until dough is firm enough to be workable.

9. Roll dough by hand into 1-inch balls. Arrange on ungreased cookie sheets, leaving 1 to 2 inches between cookies.

10. Gently press each ball flat with the tines of a fork; press each cookie again, crosswise, to flatten to ¼-inch thickness and to create the characteristic crisscross pattern. To prevent fork from sticking, occasionally dip in flour.

11. Bake in preheated oven for 15 minutes, or until golden brown.

12. Let stand for 10 minutes before transferring to wire racks to cool completely. Store in a tightly covered container.

SPECIAL EVENT RECIPES

SHRIMP GUMBO

By the time President Carter hosted the first State Dinner of his administration, I had already orchestrated over 200 such events. Yet the Carters' official events were definitely different. From the choice of beverage and the type of menu to the selection of entertainment and the composition of guest lists, the White House functions hosted by the Carters had a style all their own.

Upon his election as America's thirty-ninth President, Jimmy Carter had announced his intention to reduce the size and cost of political ceremonies. The trumpets and colorguards disappeared from state events, and pomp and circumstance was replaced with informal hospitality Southern-style. At the State Dinners, no hard liquor was available, but domestic wines and champagnes were served. The menus were printed in English, with little use of classic French terms, and an emphasis on Southern cuisine was evident. To reduce printing costs, the menus were attractively presented as part of the printed programs, which White House guests took home as unique mementoes of singular events.

The Carters' State Dinners usually began earlier than the traditional 8:00 P.M., and ended punctually at 11:00. Entertainers varied in experience and style from talented amateurs attending local universities to internationally acclaimed performers. A wide array of guests attended the gala events, including many of the Carters' loyal campaign workers, friends, and supporters. The First Lady once explained some of the reasons for the Carters' punctual State Dinners and eclectic guest lists: "We had State Dinners in Georgia and then Jimmy worked afterward. I expect he may [at the White House] . . . We just try to think of people we know in the country. At [one State Dinner], we had a couple from North Carolina who run a little store."

The menu for the Carters' first State Dinner in the White House included a Shrimp Gumbo, a thick soup made with okra. In the

South, a gumbo is a potpourri, anything that is put all together or occurs all at once. Spicy and served with a scoop of rice, gumbos are made with a wide variety of ingredients, including seafood, ham, and chicken, plus tomatoes, okra, peppers, and hot spices. At the White House, Shrimp Gumbo was mildly seasoned so that every guest could enjoy the Southern-style soup.

During her family's first State Dinner, Amy Carter sat at the head table, where she enjoyed her gumbo alongside the guest of honor, President Portillo of Mexico. The entertainment that followed, a piano performance by Rudolph Serkin, was selected especially for Mrs. Portillo, an accomplished pianist, who received a standing ovation when she played a few selections on his piano. The piano had actually been transported to the White House from Philadelphia for the performance. Serkin succinctly explained, "I usually bring my piano because I am not used to any other."

Since the Carters' first State Dinner at the White House was held on Valentine's Day, the menu and decor were specially designed to promote an atmosphere of warmth and friendship. The very next day, the White House kitchen received an equally warm and friendly note from the new First Lady, thanking the staff for helping to make the President's introductory State Dinner a success.

Makes 2½ quarts

6 tablespoons butter
1 cup finely diced onions
4 garlic cloves, finely minced
2 cups chopped leeks, white
    parts only
1 cup diced celery
2 quarts hot FISH STOCK
2 cups peeled, seeded, and
    diced fresh tomatoes
1 cup thinly sliced okra
1 bay leaf

2 tablespoons instant tapioca
1½ pounds small raw shrimp,
    peeled and deveined
1 teaspoon salt
A pinch of cayenne pepper
6 twists freshly ground black
    pepper
1 tablespoon chopped fresh
    chives
1 tablespoon chopped fresh
    parsley

1. Melt 4 tablespoons of the butter in a 4-quart soup pot, add onions and garlic and sauté over medium-high heat for 3 to 4 minutes, or until golden.

2. Add leeks and celery; sauté for 5 minutes, stirring often.

3. Add hot FISH STOCK, and bring to a boil.

4. Add tomatoes, okra, and bay leaf. Stir in tapioca, and return to a boil.

5. Cook gumbo over medium-high heat, stirring occasionally, for 30 minutes, or until thickened.

6. Melt the remaining 2 tablespoons butter in a nonstick sauté pan, add shrimp, and season with salt, and both kinds of pepper. Sauté over high heat for 3 minutes, stirring occasionally to cook evenly; stir in chopped chives and parsley.

7. Transfer shrimp to boiling gumbo; boil for 5 minutes more. Serve hot, with JEFF'S GEORGIA-STYLE CHEESE STICKS (page 240) for a first course, or with steamed rice and tossed salad for a light luncheon meal.

FISH STOCK

Makes 2 quarts

5 pounds fish bones (red snapper is excellent)
2½ quarts water
1 tablespoon salt
¼ cup cider or white wine vinegar
Juice of 1 lemon
1 leek (white part only), chopped

1 cup diced celery
1 large onion, peeled and coarsely diced
1 bay leaf
24 white peppercorns
Sprig of fresh parsley

1. Wash the fish bones and place them in a 4-quart stock pot. Add cold water to cover.

2. Add salt and vinegar and bring to a boil over medium-high heat.

3. Skim off the surface froth and add the remaining ingredients.

4. Let simmer over medium heat, partly covered, for 30 minutes.

5. Strain the stock through cheesecloth and discard the bones and vegetables. If not using immediately, let cool completely and store in a covered container in the refrigerator for up to 24 hours, or in the freezer for up to 2 weeks.

The whole purpose of this office and the social side of the White House is to provide a setting for the substantiative negotiations to be carried on.

—Emil Mosbacher, Jr.
Chief of Protocol, 1969–1972

WHITE HOUSE STUFFED MUSHROOMS

Of all the top-notch social functions that are held in Washington, the State Dinners hosted by the White House are undoubtedly the choicest. Preparation of appropriate menus for the meals to be served during a visit from a foreign head of state entails a great deal of careful planning and attention to detail. Given the vast importance of impressing and pleasing visiting dignitaries, it is obvious why "the social side of the White House" can impart a positive influence on world affairs. Thus we take our own role very seriously in the White House kitchen.

State Dinners are held at the White House an average of once per month. The majority of the official functions hosted by the First Family are less prestigious affairs, and therefore less stressful for the White House staff as well as for the President and his First Lady. During the Carter administration, the menus served at social functions ranged from formal sit-down dinners to down-home meals and festive buffets. One of the most popular menu items at these varied affairs was White House Stuffed Mushrooms.

Easy to prepare in advance, stuffed mushrooms can be served as a first course or side dish at a small formal dinner, or by the hundreds as an hors d'oeuvre for big parties and buffets. Nicely sized mushroom caps can be filled with a variety of stuffings—the recipe favored at the White House includes a pork sausage stuffing, sprinkled with a cheese topping—and can be refrigerated for a day or two prior to use. Stuffed mushrooms serve as a handy menu item since the desired number of pre-stuffed caps can quickly be heated when needed. This leaves time and space for cooking menu items that must be made just before serving.

Stuffed mushrooms are still popular at White House events, and were also served during the administrations that preceded the Carters. Thus it is indeed possible that "substantiative negotiations" have been made amid many a serving of the delectable dish.

Serves 6

16 medium-size fresh
   mushrooms
1 tablespoon butter
1 tablespoon minced shallots
2 garlic cloves, very finely
   minced
Juice of 2 lemons
1/2 teaspoon salt
1/2 pound pork sausage
1 egg

1/4 cup heavy cream
1 tablespoon chopped fresh
   parsley
1/2 cup bread crumbs
1/4 cup water
2 tablespoons grated Parmesan
   cheese
1/2 teaspoon sweet Hungarian
   paprika

1. Preheat oven to 400°F.

2. Wash mushrooms quickly in cold water; remove stems.

3. Dice mushroom stems very finely.

4. Melt butter in a small sauté pan, add shallots and garlic and sauté for 3 minutes. Do not brown.

5. Add diced mushroom stems, juice from 1 lemon, and half the salt. Simmer for 5 minutes, stirring constantly, until cooked through and well blended.

6. Add sausage; simmer for 10 minutes, or until all liquid has evaporated, stirring constantly.

7. Mix in egg, cream, parsley, and bread crumbs; blend well. Remove stuffing from heat.

8. In a small saucepan, combine water with the juice of the other lemon; add the remaining 1/4 teaspoon of salt.

9. Add mushroom caps, cover, and simmer over medium heat for 5 minutes; drain.

10. Arrange mushroom caps on a greased baking sheet, cavities up.

11. Divide stuffing evenly among mushroom caps, mounding on top of each cap.

12. Combine grated cheese with paprika, and sprinkle onto stuffed caps.

13. Bake on upper shelf of preheated oven for 6 minutes, or until tops are browned. Serve at once, as a side dish with broiled sirloin steak, lamb or pork chops, fish or seafood, or as an hors d'oeuvre or buffet item.

Maryland Crab Cakes are as popular along the Southeast coast line as Southern fried chicken is in the deep South. At the White House, the delicious crab patties have been served on numerous occasions, as both a buffet item at official functions and a family dinner dish. The Carters were especially fond of Maryland Crab Cakes, so the simple dish was often included on their menus, even for formal receptions and elaborate buffets. Mrs. Carter once served miniature crab cakes to a potentially critical crowd, some 200 food editors from the nation's most influential magazines and newspapers. We were all very pleased with the overwhelming success of the menu.

Following an all-day conference in the Executive Office Building, a late-afternoon reception was held for the food editors in the State Dining Room of the White House. The hors d'oeuvres and pastries were attractively arranged on three large tables, each offering an unusual array of colors, textures, and tastes. The White House kitchen staff created an extra special buffet for the food editors, since so many in the group had been so generous in the past when covering State Dinners and other special events.

One of the buffet tables was decorated in pinks and greens, with sculpted cantaloupes overflowing with green grapes and salmon hors d'oeuvres on cucumber rounds. On another table, golden puff pastries filled with Roquefort cheese were warmed in chafing dishes, along with the miniature Maryland Crab Cakes served with a spicy Mustard Sauce. The dessert table was garnished with edible handmade decorations, including delicate children's boots formed from dark chocolate and spun-sugar baskets filled with truffles and pastries. On each table, fresh summer flowers accentuated the colorful, appetizing, and delicious food displays.

As the reception buffet was openly admired by the hungry group, hostess Mrs. Carter rushed in to welcome the food editors to the White House. The First Lady apologized for her tardy arrival, explaining in her natural manner, "Jimmy and I had been fishing, and I had to fix my hair."

Mrs. Carter had arrived by helicopter from Camp David, the presidential retreat in the Maryland mountains. The President and Mrs. Carter loved to go fishing out at Camp David, often cooking up their catch for dinner. Before they left the White House, the Carters invited the entire staff to join them at Camp David for lunch and a tour of the grounds. I was impressed by the President's extensive knowledge of dendrology and agriculture as he described in detail the trees and wildlife that populated the area. Mrs. Carter

MARYLAND CRAB CAKES

proudly displayed their extensive collection of fly hooks, used with scientific expertise to lure the local fish from stream to table. At the unprecedented staff luncheon, the Carters served us a delicious Chinese-style seafood dish and generous portions of roast beef. It was a day that the White House staff will long remember.

Makes 12

1 pound lump crabmeat
4 tablespoons butter
1 tablespoon finely minced
   shallots
2 garlic cloves, pressed
Juice of 1 lemon
1 teaspoon dry mustard
¼ cup flour
1 cup hot milk
6 drops of Tabasco sauce
1 tablespoon Worcestershire
   sauce

2 egg yolks
1 tablespoon chopped fresh
   chives
1 tablespoon chopped fresh
   parsley
¼ cup bread crumbs
3 eggs
½ teaspoon salt
1 cup CLARIFIED BUTTER (page
   43)

1. In a small mixing bowl, carefully pick over crabmeat and remove bits of shell.

2. Melt butter in a 1-quart saucepan, add shallots and garlic and sauté for 2 minutes, or until golden. Do not brown.

3. Mix in lemon juice and dry mustard.

4. Use a wire whisk to stir in flour. Cook briefly over low heat, stirring constantly. Add hot milk, bring to a boil, and continue stirring over low heat until thickened.

5. Stir in Tabasco and Worcestershire sauce.

6. Remove from heat. Stir in egg yolks one at a time, and set sauce aside.

7. Transfer crabmeat to a large mixing bowl. Add chopped chives and parsley; add bread crumbs, mixing gently by hand.

8. Fold sauce into crab mixture.

9. Divide into 12 equal portions and form each into a small burger-shaped patty; flatten each slightly, using a metal spatula.

10. In a shallow bowl, beat eggs with salt.

11. Heat clarified butter in a large cast-iron skillet. (Frying in clarified butter helps to prevent burning and yields crispy, golden brown patties with extra flavor.)

12. Dip crabcakes in egg and fry in hot skillet over medium-high

heat; cook for 3 to 4 minutes on each side, or until golden brown and heated through.

13. Drain on paper towels. Arrange on an ovenproof serving platter.

14. Just before serving, reheat quickly under a hot broiler, turning to heat evenly. Broil for 2 to 3 minutes, or until crisply browned and bubbly; serve at once, with a mixed green salad or HOME-STYLE COLESLAW (page 262). A flavorful sauce can be served if desired, such as spicy MUSTARD SAUCE.

MUSTARD SAUCE

Makes 1½ to 2 cups

2 tablespoons cider vinegar or white wine vinegar
1 tablespoon lemon juice
1 tablespoon dry mustard
¾ teaspoon salt
⅛ teaspoon freshly ground white pepper
1 teaspoon Worcestershire sauce
1 tablespoon Dijon-style mustard
2 egg yolks
1 to 1½ cups olive oil, at room temperature

1. In a small mixing bowl, combine vinegar and lemon juice with dry mustard; mix with a wire whisk until mustard is dissolved.

2. Transfer to a blender and add salt, pepper, Worcestershire sauce, prepared mustard, and egg yolks; blend at high speed for 10 seconds.

3. With blender running at low speed, gradually add oil; cover blender and blend at high speed for 10 seconds. Use at once, as refrigeration causes the dressing to separate.

AVOCADO PEAR STUFFED WITH SEAFOOD

Most honored guests at the White House do not request special foods unless there is a religious or health reason. Cooperative efforts between the State Department, the White House, and the foreign embassies ensure that menus suitable to the visiting dignitaries can be carefully planned. For a returning guest of honor, state dinner menus are meticulously designed so that the meal does not duplicate dinners served on previous visits.

Possibly the most unusual State Dinner served during my twenty-plus years as the Executive Chef at the White House was prepared at the request of the guest of honor. When the Carters hosted a State Dinner in honor of Prime Minister Ohira of Japan, the White House kitchen was informed that the menu was to include roast suckling pig and grilled buffalo!

At that time, exotic meats had begun to emerge as a culinary trend. Thus the White House was able to purchase fresh buffalo meat without too much extra effort. Pieces of the buffalo meat were grilled, along with a whole suckling pig, out on the rooftop terrace that opens off the State Dining Room. Chicken was barbecued as well, which appealed to those guests with less adventurous appetites.

Although the kitchen staff was not exactly thrilled at the prospect of serving roast pig and grilled buffalo for a formal dinner, the remainder of the menu was more typical of such occasions. I was pleased to be able to serve one of my own favorite first courses, ripe avocado halves stuffed with fresh seafood. The avocado "pear" is a delightful fruit, with soft buttery flesh and a mild but rich flavor. Originally known as "alligator pears" because of their leathery skin and pear shape, avocadoes have recently become quite popular in the United States, with the increased interest in Mexican cuisine. Avocado tastes delicious spiced with chilies, garlic, pepper, and onions, as it is commonly served in the Mexican-style dip Guacamole. Ripe avocado is also very tasty served plain, sliced thin and sprinkled with lemon juice, salt, and pepper.

In spite of the eccentricity of the menu, the State Dinner featuring Prime Minister Ohira's special meat selections turned out to be an overwhelming success. Since the Prime Minister's daughter had informed the White House about her father's taste for contemporary American music, popular singer Bobby Short was scheduled to provide the evening's entertainment. Everyone who attended the State Dinner appeared to enjoy the music and the food provided by the White House on that fine spring evening, especially the guest of honor.

Serves 8

4 large ripe avocadoes
1½ cups thick HOMEMADE
    MAYONNAISE
½ cup diced cooked lobster
    meat
½ cup cooked tiny shrimp
½ cup cooked bay scallops
¼ cup finely diced celery
4 drops of Tabasco sauce
1 tablespoon Worcestershire
    sauce

1 tablespoon chopped fresh
    chives
4 hard-boiled eggs, finely
    chopped
1 tablespoon chopped fresh
    parsley
8 tiny black olives, pitted
8 fresh parsley sprigs

1. Peel avocadoes, cut each in half lengthwise, and remove pit.

2. Arrange avocado halves on a serving platter, cavities up.

3. In a 2-quart mixing bowl, combine 1 cup of the MAYONNAISE with lobster, shrimp, scallops, celery, Tabasco sauce, Worcestershire sauce, and chopped chives; mix to coat well.

4. Divide evenly among the avocado halves in smooth mounds.

5. Top the center of each mound with an additional tablespoon of MAYONNAISE.

6. In a small bowl, mix chopped eggs with chopped parsley. Arrange around the perimeter of each cavity.

7. Center a tiny olive and a sprig of parsley in the mayonanaise atop each avocado.

8. Refrigerate for at least 1 hour. Serve very cold, with JEFF'S GEORGIA-STYLE CHEESE STICKS (page 240), sesame sticks, or other fine crackers as a first course or light luncheon entrée.

SWISS GRUYÈRE SOUFFLÉ

Soufflés can be prepared with a variety of ingredients to suit any number of occasions. At the White House, a Swiss Gruyère soufflé proved to be one of the most popular dishes served at the special luncheons hosted by Mrs. Carter. In fact, soufflés of various types were included on many of the menus served during the Carters' White House years.

A feather-light Swiss Gruyère soufflé was featured on the menu of the private luncheon hosted by Mrs. Carter in 1977 to honor Empress Farah of Iran. At the time, the Shah of Iran was a frequent White House guest, once joking with the First Lady that he had attended more State Dinners there than she had! The delicate cheese soufflés were also served at Mrs. Carter's private luncheon for Mrs. Helmut Schmidt, the wife of the Chancellor of the Federal Republic of Germany and another frequent dinner guest at the

White House. On one of the Chancellor's many visits, the New York Jazz Repertory Company performed a moving tribute to Louis Armstrong. The menu served at this fine State Dinner featured an impressive spinach soufflé.

Zucchini soufflés were served in the spring of 1980 at one of Mrs. Carter's Senate Ladies' Luncheons. For these events, as with the First Lady's private luncheons for the wives of heads of state, the menus featured light, pretty foods, with emphasis on flavor and appearance but moderation in portion size. All of the ladies' luncheons served at the White House could be savored without undue worry about caloric excess. Since presentation is as important as taste for this type of event, the food was meticulously decorated and carefully coordinated.

At the 1980 Senate Ladies' Luncheon, the first course featured an unusual Italian delicacy, a tiny pasta turnover called *agnolotti*. In 1978, the first course served to the Senate ladies was mulligatawny soup, an East Indian dish made with apples and chicken and delicately flavored with curry. An original "Bouquet of Fresh Vegetables" was also introduced at this luncheon, a beautiful array of lightly steamed vegetables artfully arranged to highlight the contrasts in texture and color. The staff of the White House kitchen was very pleased that the hundreds of women attending Mrs. Carter's special luncheons were so openly delighted with the meals they were served, as the menus had been painstakingly prepared precisely to flatter their eyes and palates.

Opposite page: The menu for the State Dinner in honor of Prime Minister Ohira of Japan included roast suckling pig and—more typically—a beautiful, delicate dessert.

Serves 4

4 tablespoons butter	*4 egg yolks*
6 tablespoons flour	*6 egg whites, at room*
1 cup hot milk	*temperature*
½ teaspoon salt	*⅛ teaspoon cream of tartar*
⅛ teaspoon freshly ground	*4 ounces Gruyère cheese,*
white pepper	*shredded*
⅛ teaspoon nutmeg	

1. Preheat oven to 350°F. Use a pastry brush to generously coat inside of a 1½-quart soufflé dish with soft butter; dust lightly with flour.

2. Melt butter in a 1-quart saucepan, add flour, and work into a roux. Cook briefly over low heat, stirring constantly.

3. Add milk, salt, pepper, and nutmeg; stirring vigorously, bring to a boil, then simmer over low heat for about 1 minute, or until thickened and smooth. Remove from heat.

4. Add egg yolks one at a time, stirring well after each addition.

5. In a large, dry mixing bowl, slowly beat egg whites with cream of tartar; increase speed gradually, beating until egg whites are stiff.

6. Fold about one-quarter of the stiff whites into the egg yolk mixture.

7. Return egg yolk mixture to the mixing bowl, fold to combine with rest of whites, and fold in shredded cheese. Do not overmix.

8. Pour into the prepared dish to fill 1½ inches from the top. Smooth the top lightly with a spatula.

9. Bake on lower shelf of preheated oven for 30 minutes, or until golden brown and puffed to about 2 inches above the rim. Serve immediately, with a crisp green salad.

JAMBALAYA

President Carter was an enthusiastic advocate of big, fun outdoor parties with lively music and plenty of down-home food. One of the Carters' most memorable informal functions was the first all-jazz presidential concert ever given at the White House. Held out on the South Lawn, the jazz fest for 800 guests marked the twenty-fifth anniversary of the esteemed Newport Jazz Festival.

Some all-time jazz greats were featured on the day's program, such as Eubie Blake, Dexter Gordon, Sonny Rollins, McCoy Tyner, Herbie Hancock, Stan Getz, Lionel Hampton, Chick Corea, and George Benson. Even the President joined the music making, bravely pounding out "Salt Peanuts" on the piano with some help from Dizzy Gillespie.

The menu was short and simple, but perfect for a big outdoor party and appropriate for an authentic jazz festival: Jambalaya, salad, Pecan Pie, and cold beer and soft drinks.

Jambalaya is a Creole rice dish that features any number of combinations of main ingredients, including chicken, sausage, ham, pork, and seafood. Onions, tomatoes, and sweet peppers are usually added, and seasoning can include hot chili, and white, black, and cayenne pepper. The name "jambalaya" is believed to have derived from the French *jambon* or Spanish *jamon* (ham), the French *à la* ("in the style of"), which is used in Nova Scotia with almost everything, and the African *ya* (rice). The contributions of various nationalities, like the mixture of ingredients, is the trademark of Creole cookery.

The Jambalaya that was served at the Carters' jazz fest featured a mildly seasoned rice, flavored with generous chunks of tender chicken. To suit the varied tastes of a large crowd, the dish was only lightly peppered, with small bottles of Tabasco sauce available for those who wanted more "hots." A hundred pounds of onions were patiently chopped by members of the Jambalaya Festival Association from Gonzales, Louisiana, the self-proclaimed "Jambalaya Capital of the World." The ingredients were gently simmered in four huge cast-iron kettles set over oak fires on the White House lawn, where the experts from Louisiana helped the White House kitchen staff to carefully "turn" the jambalaya and prevent the rice from becoming mushy.

President Carter appeared to be enjoying the jazz festival as much as the rest of the crowd. He looked right at home in his denims, as he chatted with the musicians and guests scattered about the White House lawn. Amy made herself right at home as well, munching on Pecan Pie while taking in the view from up in her tree house.

Another fun festival hosted by the Carters was a down-east oyster bake held on the White House lawn. A New England catering company helped to prepare the seafood feast, which included fresh lobsters and clams in addition to the oysters. The Carters also held a huge picnic on the South Lawn to honor the black musicians who have contributed so much over the years to the music of America. One thousand guests feasted on roast beef and Louisiana rice, a peppery Southern dish that resembles a spicy rice pilaf, with a flavor not too different from the heartier Jambalaya.

Serves 6

Two 2½-pound chickens
2 teaspoons salt
6 twists freshly ground black
  pepper
4 tablespoons vegetable oil
2 cups finely diced onions
4 garlic cloves, finely minced
¼ pound pork sausage, diced
1 cup dry white wine

2 cups water
1½ cups uncooked long-grain
  rice
½ cup finely chopped scallions,
  white parts only
¼ teaspoon crushed red pepper
1 tablespoon chopped fresh
  parsley

1. Cut each chicken into 10 pieces: separate wings and legs, and cut each leg in half; cut the breast in quarters. Season with salt and black pepper.

2. Heat oil in a large sauté pan, add chicken pieces and brown evenly on both sides over medium-high heat. Drain on paper towels.

3. Add diced onions and garlic to the hot oil; sauté for 3 minutes, or until just beginning to brown.

4. Add diced sausage and sauté for 5 minutes, stirring constantly.

5. Add chicken pieces, wine, and water; bring to a boil.

6. Add rice, scallions, and red pepper. Cover, and simmer over medium heat for 25 minutes.

7. Remove from heat and let stand, covered, for 5 minutes.

8. Spoon into a serving dish, sprinkle with chopped parsley, and serve at once with a tossed green salad. Tabasco sauce can be served on the side for added "hots." (For pork jambalaya, substitute 2¾ pounds of lean pork cubes for the chicken pieces.)

The Carters enjoyed hosting large barbecues and picnics on the White House lawn.

When the Great Viceroy of China visited New York City in 1896, the chefs at the esteemed Waldorf Hotel spent many weeks planning an elaborate feast. To their utmost dismay, the Viceroy arrived with his own personal chefs who prepared all of his food for the entire sojourn. Fortunately for the White House kitchen staff, our own first feast for important visitors from the People's Republic of China was eaten appreciatively by all.

Vice Premier Deng Xiao-ping visited President Carter in 1979, with the first Chinese delegation to arrive on American soil since the Franklin D. Roosevelt administration. For the first time since 1949, the United States and China established formal diplomatic ties. In honor of the historic event, a special State Dinner was held at the White House.

Grand banquets are a Chinese tradition. To facilitate the "Peking Duck Diplomacy," the State Dinner held in honor of the Chinese Vice Premier included an unusually elaborate menu. The high-quality *plume de veau* ws a superb cut of roast loin of veal, served stuffed with a rich mixture of ground veal and cream flavored with sautéed shallots and dry sherry. The timbale of seafood was brimming with chunks of fresh lobster, scallops, and shrimp, served in a handmade pastry bowl. The pastry chef created 16 handmade chocolate boxes, which were filled with delicate dark and milk chocolate truffles. As a special favor to the White House, a Chinese-American calligrapher from the State Department prepared bilingual engraved menus for the 140 dinner guests.

The guests were all very impressed with the fine meal, including one former "regular" at White House State Dinners: Richard Nixon, in his first visit to the White House since his own presidency. President Nixon had been instrumental in resolving U.S. relations with the People's Republic of China during his own White House years.

Because of the time required for preparation and the cost of the ingredients used, the dishes served at this special State Dinner made quite an exceptional menu, even for the White House kitchen, where "only the best" has long been the motto. After Vice Premier Deng Xiao-ping left the White House and continued on his American tour, it seems that some sort of veal dish appeared on the menu at most every dinner he attended. Apparently, no one was quite sure just what to serve a delegation from the People's Republic of China, so most of their American hosts decided that it was wise to follow the fine example set by the White House. For-

CHINESE STIR-FRY VEGETABLES

tunately, the Chinese delegation appeared to be quite pleased with the "American Veal Diplomacy."

For one of their last special dinners as White House residents, the Carters enjoyed a Chinese dinner prepared by a visiting chef. At the suggestion of Press Secretary Jody Powell, President Carter invited the chef from a local restaurant specializing in Szechuan cuisine to prepare a meal at the White House. The Szechuan dinner menu was creatively designed, the food was attractively prepared, and everything tasted delicious, including a stir-fry vegetable dish made with Chinese mushrooms and crisp pea pods.

The Carters were very fond of stir-fry vegetable dishes. Various combinations were served at their family dinners, and at the frequent buffets held by President Carter as "working dinners" for select members of Congress. The lightly seasoned combination of julienned carrots, red pepper, mushrooms, bean sprouts, and snow peas so impressed Senator Heinz of Pennsylvania that he requested the recipe. This was quite a compliment, since the Senator was also chairman of the board of the highly respected Heinz corporation, where the recipes for many well-known products have been developed.

Chinese-style stir-fry vegetables served as a simple reminder of the most elaborate meal of the Carter administration, the State Dinner held to honor Vice Premier Deng Xiao-ping.

Serves 6

½ pound carrots, peeled	Juice of 1 lemon
1 red bell pepper, seeded	½ pound fresh snow peas
1 pound fresh bean sprouts	½ cup vegetable oil
½ pound small fresh mushrooms	1 tablespoon seasoned salt
	2 tablespoons soy sauce

1. Slice peeled carrots into julienne strips of around 2 inches in length.
2. Slice red pepper into fine strips of a similar length.
3. Wash bean sprouts in cold water and drain well.
4. Wash mushrooms quickly in cold water mixed with lemon juice; drain well. Cut into fine slices.
5. Cut tips from snow peas, and slice each in half lengthwise.
6. In a large sauté pan or Chinese wok, heat half the oil.
7. Fry carrot strips in hot oil over high heat for 1 minute, stirring constantly; add pepper strips, and fry for 1 minute more.

8. Add bean sprouts and sprinkle with half of the seasoned salt; stir-fry for 2 to 3 minutes, or until vegetables are steaming hot.

9. Use a slotted spoon to transfer the hot vegetables to the center of a serving platter.

10. Heat the remaining ¼ cup of oil in the sauté pan or wok.

11. Add sliced mushrooms and snow peas; sprinkle with the remaining seasoned salt. Stir-fry for 2 to 3 minutes, or until vegetables are steaming hot.

12. Use the slotted spoon to transfer to the serving platter; arrange the mushrooms and snow peas around the outer border of the centered vegetables.

13. Sprinkle with soy sauce, and serve at once, with steamed rice and broiled fish, chicken, or lean meats.

OLD-FASHIONED POUND CAKE

President Carter was of English descent, so his ancestors may have served their family and guests pound cake made the traditional way. Originally prepared with a pound each of butter, sugar, flour, and eggs, the extra-dense, extra-rich cake was popular in the Old World in the eighteenth century. During the 1830s, the colonists created their own New World version with an "Indian Pound Cake" made from the cornmeal that was so readily available at that time. By the turn of the century, the English-style pound cake had grown more popular in America, and the 1887 edition of *The White House Cook Book* provided a basic recipe for "Plain Pound Cake":

Beat to a cream one pound of butter with one pound of sugar; after mixing well with the beaten yolks of twelve eggs, add one grated nutmeg, one glass of wine, one glass of rose water. Then stir in one pound of sifted flour and the well-beaten whites of the eggs. Bake a nice light brown.

While serving as the White House hostess for President Thomas Jefferson, Dolley Madison often offered pound cake to visitors at tea time. Some 175 years later, pound cake was still being served to White House guests. The recipe favored by the Carters yields a plain, old-fashioned loaf cake, but the proportions for the basic ingredients are less uniform than originally required and the results are not quite as heavy and rich.

During their years in the White House, the Carters served pound cake a number of times, both for family meals when guests were in attendance and at special functions and parties. The Carters' Old-fashioned Pound Cake was usually served with fresh fruit in season, such as strawberries, raspberries, or blueberries. On certain occasions, fresh whipped cream was served as well. A properly prepared pound cake is delicious just plain, the perfect accompaniment to a hot cup of coffee or café au lait.

Old-fashioned pound cake proved to be a popular dessert on the Carters' picnic menus. The recipe can be easily adapted for serving to large-scale parties as well as family-size groups.

Makes 2 loaves

2 sticks (1 cup) butter	*Grated rind of 1 lemon*
1¼ cups sugar	*2 cups cake flour, sifted*
1 teaspoon vanilla extract	*5 eggs*

1. Preheat oven to 300°F. Grease two 9 × 5-inch loaf pans; dust lightly with flour.

2. In a large mixing bowl, cream butter with sugar. Mix in vanilla and lemon rind.

3. Gradually add flour, blending well.

4. Add eggs one at a time, beating well after each addition; continue mixing until batter is smooth.

5. Divide batter evenly between the prepared pans. Bake on lower shelf of preheated oven for 45 to 50 minutes, or until golden brown and firm to the touch. A toothpick inserted near the centers should come out clean.

6. Turn out cakes to cool on wire racks before slicing. Serve plain, toasted, or with fresh berries and whipped cream. Cake will remain fresh for weeks if wrapped airtight and refrigerated.

AMY'S PUMPKIN BIRTHDAY CAKE

Amy Carter's birthday fell twelve days before Halloween, so the Carters sometimes held a dual celebration. On her tenth birthday, Amy hosted a Halloween birthday party in the White House. Her friends arrived dressed in a colorful array of costumes, and the entire group headed for the China Room to carve jack-o'-lanterns from big orange pumpkins. Potato chips and dip were served, along with fruit punch ladled out of a festive bowl made from a hollowed pumpkin.

Amy and her party guests watched the original version of the scary old film *Frankenstein*, shown in the White House movie theater. Formerly used as a storeroom, the little theater is located on the ground floor of the East Wing. Major studios regularly supply the First Family with feature films, and will send special movies on request.

Appetites aroused by fun and fright, Amy's guests trooped up to the Solarium for hamburgers and soft drinks. A big orange birthday cake was served, a sponge cake shaped like a jack-o'-lantern with a carrot nose and a big grin. The cake was such a hit with the children that it was served at future dual celebrations held for Amy while she lived in the White House.

One year a surprise visitor joined Amy and her birthday guests. In honor of Mickey Mouse's special White House appearance, the pastry chef baked a terrific cake that looked just like the well-known Disneyland character. When Mickey arrived in the White House kitchen, I grabbed my camera to snap a few photos to take home to my own children. Unfortunately, the pictures did not come out very clearly because the uncomfortable Mr. Mouse asked me to please hurry: The heat of the kitchen was too much for him in his Disneyland garb, so Mickey Mouse was unable to stay and pose for very long. Amy's enthusiastic party guests made sure that her birthday cakes disappeared rapidly as well.

Makes 1 large cake

32 eggs, separated, at room temperature
4 cups confectioners' sugar
Grated rind of 4 lemons
¼ teaspoon salt
7½ cups cake flour
6 cups CUSTARD CREAM (page 113)
3 cups APRICOT GLAZE (page 114)

2 quarts warm CHOCOLATE FONDANT (page 114)
1¾ pounds marzipan
Orange and red food coloring
1 medium carrot, well-scrubbed, with top trimmed
1 medium spaghetti squash, cooked and cooled
4 cups SWEETENED WHIPPED CREAM (page 112)

1. Preheat oven to 325°F. Generously grease the inside of a 14-inch round cake pan with butter; dust lightly with flour. Generously grease the insides of two 9-inch ovenproof mixing bowls.

2. In a large mixing bowl, beat the egg yolks until fluffy. Add sugar and lemon rind; beat well.

Amy's birthdays were celebrated
with family, friends, fun,
and her favorite foods.
(COURTESY: JIMMY CARTER LIBRARY)

3. In a separate mixing bowl, beat egg whites with salt until stiff; fold into yolks. Gently fold in flour.

4. Divide the batter among the prepared pan and bowls; smooth the tops.

5. Set the pan on the lower shelf of the preheated oven; set the bowls in a shallow pan of boiling water and transfer to the middle shelf of the oven. Bake for 45 to 50 minutes, or until a cake tester or thin metal skewer inserted near the center comes out clean. The cakes should not brown.

6. Let pans cool on wire racks for 5 minutes; then turn the cakes out onto the racks and let cool completely. Cover with plastic wrap and refrigerate overnight.

7. Use a long, serrated knife to slice the flat cake into 2 layers. Spread the bottom layer with 3 cups of the CUSTARD CREAM; top gently with the other layer, being careful that the filling does not ooze out. Spread the top and sides of the filled cake with a light layer of APRICOT GLAZE, using about 2 cups. Pour on CHOCOLATE FONDANT and spread to cover entire cake evenly. This cake forms a base for the pumpkin.

8. Center a squat glass tumbler upside down on the frosted cake and press down to cut out a circle of cake; remove and insert the tumbler bottom-side up in the hole.

9. With a long, serrated knife slice each bowl-shaped cake into four even strips. Spread the cut surfaces with 2 cups of the CUSTARD

CREAM and reassemble into half-spheres. Spread the flat surfaces with the remaining CUSTARD CREAM and fit the two cakes together to form a sphere. Spread the entire cake sphere with a light layer of the remaining APRICOT GLAZE.

10. In a small mixing bowl, mix 1½ pounds of the marzipan with orange food coloring, 1 to 2 drops at a time, until it has reached a nice pumpkin color. On a board lightly dusted with confectioners' sugar, roll out the marzipan in a thin sheet, like a pie crust; lift it carefully and use it to completely cover the cake sphere. (You may have to roll out the marzipan in several pieces, smoothing the edges together with your fingers as you cover the cake.) Use the extra marzipan scraps to form a pumpkin "stem" at the top.

11. In a separate mixing bowl, mix the remaining marzipan with red food coloring, 1 to 2 drops at a time, until it is evenly colored. Form little eyes, ears, cheeks, and a mouth from the red marzipan and arrange to form a pumpkin face.

12. Insert the carrot to form a nose. Arrange strands of spaghetti squash on top to form hair.

13. *Carefully* transfer the pumpkin cake to the bottom cake, centering it on the upturned tumbler. Use a pastry bag fitted with a star tip to garnish the bottom cake with SWEETENED WHIPPED CREAM. Arrange birthday candles all around the bottom layer and light them just before serving. Serve with vanilla, chocolate, and pumpkin-flavored ice cream.

On Amy's birthday, a certain mouse was a welcome White House visitor.

MISS ALLIE'S HOLIDAY LANE CAKE

The Carter family traditionally gathered together in Plains over the Christmas holidays at the home of Rosalynn's mother, "Miss Allie." As America's First Family, the Carters continued to practice their holiday custom. Before leaving for Georgia, however, the Carters always hosted at least a dozen Christmas parties at the White House, in order to wish their staff and the nation a happy holiday season.

During their first Christmas season in the White House, the Carters hosted fifteen yuletide parties prior to their departure for Plains. There was a private party for the President's Secret Service, one for the White House guards, and another for the members of the press assigned to cover the First Family's activities. The President gratefully acknowledged the time and assistance donated by his volunteer staff with a seasonal fête in their honor, and he toasted the members of his Congress at a separate holiday party. Even ten-year-old Amy hosted a Christmas event, the annual party given for the children of the Diplomatic Corps. Some 430 children between the ages of 5 and 11 joined Amy for Christmas cookies and punch in the East Room, where the famous actress Helen Hayes held everyone spellbound with her rendition of "The Christmas Story."

On this particular Christmas, the White House Christmas tree was especially meaningful for the First Lady. The 20-foot fir had been decorated with 2,500 ornaments, including some that were painstakingly prepared by retarded children. In a project coordinated by the National Association for Retarded Citizens, the handmade Christmas tree ornaments were donated to the White House so that the nation's children could share in the holiday spirit of giving. Mrs. Carter was pleased that the press coverage helped to focus public attention on one of her major personal projects, improved mental health care for the nation's needy.

The Carters' family Christmas tree was traditionally decorated with homemade ornaments, strings of shell peanuts draped alongside strings of popped popcorn. Their customary Christmas dinner was served at Miss Allie's, who prepared as one of her holiday specialties a uniquely Southern concoction called Lane Cake. The four layers of plain cake are iced with a thin fondant containing a combination of chopped pecans, candied fruit, and coconut. The recipe first appeared in a cookbook published in 1898 by Mrs. Emma Rylander Lane of Clayton, Alabama.

Miss Allie was a lovely and exceedingly gracious person. Whenever she visited the Carters in the White House, she liked to drop by the kitchen. Miss Allie always seemed most interested in seeing the pastry chef in action, especially when he was decorating an intricate dessert or creating a delicate garnish from spun sugar. The kitchen staff was grateful for the chance to adopt Miss Allie's own dessert recipe, so that Southern Lane Cake could be served to the Carters' White House guests during the Christmas season.

The First Lady was grateful in turn to the kitchen staff during the hectic holidays, which she was kind enough to acknowledge, either in person or with handwritten notes. A "Yule Log" cake was served one year, a traditional Christmas dessert prepared by the White House chef with an authentic-looking "bark" of mocha frosting. For the Carters' Old-fashioned Christmas Party, the goodies were catered while the White House kitchen provided the snow! To create the fairyland atmosphere appropriate for the event, I summoned to the White House a Swiss associate who was an expert in the science of man-made snow. The artificial snow that covered the South Lawn was just perfect for the skating party, but seemed to last forever afterward. I had to listen to a lot of good-natured jokes around the White House about the "real Swiss snow" that refused to melt.

Makes one 9-inch 4-layer cake

3½ cups flour
3½ teaspoons baking powder
½ teaspoon salt
2 sticks butter, at room
temperature (1 cup)

2 cups sugar
1 cup milk
8 egg whites, at room
temperature
LANE FROSTING

1. Preheat oven to 375°F. Grease four 9-inch layer pans; line each with a round of greased wax paper.

2. Sift flour with baking powder and salt.

3. In a large mixing bowl, cream butter with sugar until light and fluffy.

4. Gradually add dry ingredients, alternating with milk; mix well after each addition, and mix batter until smooth.

5. In a clean, dry bowl, beat egg whites until stiff; fold into batter.

6. Divide batter evenly among the prepared pans. Bake on lower shelf of preheated oven for 20 minutes, or until golden brown and a toothpick inserted near the center comes out clean.

7. Let pans stand on wire racks for 5 minutes before turning cakes out onto the racks to cool completely.

8. Spread the top of each layer with a thin coating of *LANE FROST-ING,* and stack them.

9. Frost the entire cake with a thin coating of frosting.

10. Let stand for 30 minutes, until frosting hardens. Store at once in an airtight cake tin. If desired, cake may be decorated with a few whole candied cherries, whole pecans, and a sprinkling of shredded coconut.

The Carters celebrated Christmas with a variety of receptions, including an Old-Fashioned Christmas Party with skating performances by Peggy Fleming and others.

LANE FROSTING

Frosts one 9-inch 4-layer cake

8 egg yolks
1 cup sugar
2 sticks (1 cup) butter, at room temperature
2 tablespoons brandy
2 tablespoons water

½ cup finely chopped candied cherries
1 cup coarsely chopped raisins
1 cup chopped pecans
½ cup shredded coconut

1. In the top of a double boiler, combine egg yolks with sugar.

2. Cook over hot water for 6 to 7 minutes, stirring constantly with a wire whisk, until very smooth.

3. Gradually add butter, a tablespoonful at a time, stirring constantly after each addition until well absorbed.

4. Continue cooking for 3 to 4 minutes, stirring constantly with a wooden spoon, until thickened. Do not boil.

5. Transfer to a mixing bowl. Let cool slightly.

6. Stir in brandy and water.

7. Stir in chopped fruit and nuts and shredded coconut. Use at once, before the frosting hardens.

After a long winter of near-starvation, a big family feast was held in 1621 to celebrate the first harvest of Plymouth Colony. The Wampanoag Indians joined the colonists in giving thanks for the bounty of good food and the blessing of survival. Turkey was probably served at the now-traditional feast, along with an array of "current-day" favorites such as Corn Bread, Pumpkin Pie, and cranberry sauce.

Acres of cranberries grew wild in the acid subsoils of New England. The Indians used the wild berries to make medicines and dyes as well as food. The tart berries were served sweetened with maple sugar as a relish of sorts, which evolved into cranberry sauce. Most of the current cranberry harvest is still derived from the bogs of New England, with the majority now processed into commercial cranberry sauce.

The high acid content of cranberries makes the fruit unusually durable, which allows for freezing with minimal damage and year-round use in a variety of recipes. The Carters liked tart cranberries baked in lightly sweetened muffins, served in place of their routine Hot Biscuits or Corn Bread. While living in the White House, the Carters occasionally requested Cranberry Muffins for breakfast, and regularly included them in lieu of the traditional cranberry sauce for their annual Thanksgiving meal.

CARTERS' CRANBERRY MUFFINS

Makes 12

1 cup chopped fresh
  cranberries
¾ cup sugar
2 cups sifted flour
¾ teaspoon baking soda

¼ teaspoon salt
1 egg, beaten
¾ cup buttermilk
¼ cup melted butter

1. Preheat oven to 400°F. Grease twelve 2-inch muffin cups, and dust lightly with flour (or use paper muffin cup liners).
2. In a small mixing bowl, combine chopped cranberries with ½ cup of the sugar to coat well.
3. Into a large mixing bowl, sift together flour, baking soda, salt, and the remaining ¼ cup of sugar.
4. In a smaller bowl, combine the beaten egg with buttermilk and melted butter. Add to dry ingredients and stir; do not overmix. (Stir muffin batter as little as possible—just enough to moisten flour—as overmixing results in heavy, flat muffins.)
5. Fold in cranberries.
6. Spoon into prepared muffin tins, filling each two-thirds full.
7. Bake on lower shelf of preheated oven for 20 minutes, or until golden brown and a toothpick inserted in the center comes out clean.
8. Let cool on wire racks for 5 minutes before removing muffins from tins. Serve warm. Freeze extra muffins or keep in an airtight container; reheat in a 350°F oven for several minutes just before serving.

GEORGIA PECAN PIE

The Carters indulged in rich desserts only on special occasions. For large-scale celebrations, President Carter liked to serve traditional Southern favorites, especially desserts made with Georgia pecans. The White House kitchen staff became adept at turning out dozens of sweet pecan pies to be cooled and sliced, served plain or with fresh whipped cream at a variety of special events. The White House pastry chef also honed his skills in creating bite-size pecan desserts by the hundreds, such as the popular pecan tassies, Pecan Diamonds, and pecan pralines.

The pecan is a richly flavored nut that is often featured in Southern dishes. Pecans can be eaten plain out of hand, roasted, salted and spiced, or sweetened with a sugar glaze. The versatile nut can be introduced into a variety of recipes including quick breads and sweet rolls, stuffings and casseroles, ice creams and candies. The thin-shelled Georgia pecan is especially delectable when baked in a brown sugar syrup to make a Southern-style pie.

Pecan pie was served to some 800 guests on the South Lawn of the White House during President Carter's jambalaya jazz festival. The Southern-style pie was also enjoyed by 700 White House guests at the Carters' huge Halloween gala in 1978. At each event, the President and his family joined in the fun, donning appropriate garb and enjoying the food.

The simple menu from the jazz fest included Jambalaya and salad, both served in massive quantities in order to satisfy the crowd of hungry guests. Some 100 Pecan Pies were prepared for dessert. A slightly more elaborate menu was planned for the big Halloween bash, featuring pâté, roast beef with horseradish sauce, smoked turkey, baked ham, deep-fried mozzarella, crudités, cheese, crackers, rolls, bread, and pastries, including 50 pumpkin and 50 Pecan Pies. Hot and cold cider, sangria and wine, soft drinks and coffee were also served by the gallon. At both of these large-scale celebrations, White House guests got a sizable taste of true Southern hospitality, as well as the Carters' special dessert favorite, sweet Georgia Pecan Pie.

Serves 8

1 stick (½ cup) butter, at room temperature
1 cup firmly packed light brown sugar
3 eggs
½ cup light corn syrup

1½ cups broken pecans
1 teaspoon vanilla extract
½ teaspoon salt
One 9-inch PIE CRUST, prebaked (page 18)

1. Preheat oven to 375°F.
2. In a mixing bowl, cream butter with brown sugar until light and fluffy.
3. Beat in eggs, one at a time.
4. Stir in corn syrup and mix until smooth.
5. Stir in pecans, vanilla, and salt; blend well.
6. Pour into prebaked pie shell. Bake on lower shelf of preheated oven for 40 minutes, or until top is brown and firm to the touch.
7. Cool on a wire rack before slicing into wedges. Serve warm, with fresh whipped cream if desired. For an extra rich dessert, serve à la mode with vanilla ice cream.

HAZELNUT "GIANDUJA" MOUSSE

The science which feeds men is worth at least as much as the one which teaches how to kill them.

—Brillat-Savarin
French magistrate and gastronome

The road to peace in the Middle East took over 30 years, the treaty negotiations lasted more than 16 months, and the summit at Camp David required 13 intense days. When it was finally over, the time allotted for planning and preparing the celebration feast was a mere 8 days. To ready a fine meal for 1,340 guests, the largest sit-down dinner ever served in the history of the White House, the main obstacle was logistics. In the White House kitchen, we regarded the situation as a challenge.

On the Monday morning a week before the White House hosted the Peace Treaty Dinner, there was a short meeting in the East Wing to brief the White House staff on the upcoming event. The Carters had been planning the celebration for weeks, quietly assembling a guest list and discussing details. However, until the world leaders ascertained that the treaties would indeed be signed, the planning could not progress to actual preparation. Immediately upon receiving the go-ahead, the White House staff launched into action.

Fortunately for the staff, there already existed a comprehensive plan of action that had proven successful at an event of similar scale. When the White House hosted a huge outdoor celebration in 1973 to honor the Vietnam Prisoners of War, a sit-down dinner had been served to 1,300 guests. The White House kitchen staff felt a little more at ease this second time around.

By Monday, March 26, 1979, all of the preparations for the Peace Treaty Dinner had been successfully completed. The South Lawn of the White House was aglow with the bright yellow and orange of one huge and six smaller striped tents. One hundred thirty-four tables were housed inside, each topped by a starched white tablecloth, and glowing with a splash of fresh-cut flowers under the dim light of an old-style hurricane lamp. Adjacent to the dining area, strategically located mobile warmers and refrigerated trucks housed the food, while the wine and champagne chilled in two ice-filled aluminum canoes borrowed from the U.S. military.

The meal had been specially designed to delight the palates of the diners, while incorporating a preparation and serving schedule that was feasible for the chefs and waiters. The first course, a light

seafood mousse, and the dessert, a rich hazelnut-chocolate mousse, were both served cold, prepared in advance and held in the refrigerated vehicles. The food warmers worked exceedingly well in the below-freezing weather, retaining the warmth of 1,340 servings of strip sirloin and the accompanying green beans, carrots, and mushrooms ironically entitled "spring" vegetables. Some 280 waiters served the entire meal with militaristic precision, so that the hot food stayed appetizingly hot and the cold food retained both appearance and flavor. The dinner was a smashing success.

Guests at the Peace Treaty Dinner included President Carter's entire Cabinet, 39 Senators, 115 Representatives, and 5 Governors, as well as many prominent Americans of Jewish and Arab ancestry, members of the press, business and labor leaders, and a host of the Carters' friends and supporters. Guests were seated so that every table featured representatives of each of the three nations involved in the treaty. The entertainment included musical performers from each nation as well, with an Egyptian rock band, an Israeli duet, and America's own Leontyne Price. Even the menu was "tripartisan," with 110 kosher meals available for those who made the special request and juices for those who abstained from alcohol. A

President Carter's historic efforts helped pave the way for peace in the Mideast and brought good cheer to White House dining tables.

local kosher caterer supplied the dinners on this particular occasion, but when time permitted before certain other events, a rabbi came to the White House to kosher the kitchen and allow for the preparation of kosher meals.

Once the diners were seated and the toasts had been made, President Carter table-hopped as hosts usually do when the party is a success. President Sadat joined the rest of the crowd in thanking President Carter for his persistence, patience, and tenacious devotion to world peace: "As far as my historic experience is concerned, I think that he worked harder than our forefathers did in Egypt, building the pyramids."

After serving the largest sit-down dinner in the history of the White House, on incredibly short notice, the kitchen staff empathized with President Carter's devoted determination to overcoming obstacles. We also agreed that the hard work and concentrated effort certainly proved worthwhile, upon witnessing the glow of good cheer and the spirit of peaceful friendship that distinguished this historic event.

Serves 20

7 tablespoons sugar
1½ ounces sliced hazelnuts
2 packages (½ ounce)
   unflavored gelatin
½ cup water
5 ounces hazelnut chocolate
   ("Gianduja")

3 ounces semisweet chocolate
3 tablespoons Kirsch
1 whole egg
4 egg yolks
4½ cups very cold heavy cream

1. In a small saucepan, melt 3 tablespoons of the sugar over medium heat until light brown.

2. Add hazelnuts and sauté until golden brown; stir occasionally, using a wooden spoon.

3. Transfer to a well-greased pan and let "nougat" cool.

4. When nougat is cool, use a metal spatula to lift and break into very small pieces.

5. In the top of a double boiler, combine gelatin with water; melt over hot water.

6. In the top of another double boiler, combine the two chocolates; melt over hot water, keeping at 80 to 90°F.

7. Transfer melted chocolate to a large mixing bowl. Fold in melted gelatin; fold in Kirsch.

8. In a small mixing bowl, whip egg and egg yolks with the re-

maining 4 tablespoons of sugar until light and fluffy. Stir into the chocolate mixture.

9. Fold in nougat pieces.

10. Beat the cream in a chilled bowl until very stiff; fold in.

11. Transfer to two 1½-quart molds or soufflé dishes. Lightly smooth tops, using a spatula.

12. Refrigerate for 2 to 3 hours, or until firm.

13. To unmold mousses, dip dishes into hot water for 4 to 5 seconds. Turn out onto serving platters, and serve at once or keep refrigerated. Decorate with additional whipped cream, if desired, using pastry bag fitted with a small (#4) star tip.

> I promised you four years ago that I would never lie to you, so I can't stand here and say it doesn't hurt. I've wanted to serve as President because I love this country and because I love the people of this nation. . . . I am disappointed tonight, but I have not lost either love.
> —From President Carter's concession speech, 1980

When the Carter administration ended in January 1981, Jimmy Carter returned to Plains, where he has maintained an active voice in national issues and world politics. From a humble background as a family man and farmer, President Carter had brought his strong convictions regarding human rights and global peace all the way to the White House, where he had continued to practice and preach his philosophy of equality and good will.

Jimmy Carter was the first President to walk from the Capitol building to the White House following his inaugural ceremony. He grasped his wife's hand as they braved the winter cold to stride down the crowd-lined streets to their new official residence. Toward the end of the mile-plus walk, the Carters were joined by nine-year-old Amy and a contingent of family members. Their historic march served to symbolize the Carters' future four years as White House residents, that is, a close family with an independent spirit and a simple, unpretentious manner. When the new First Family arrived at the White House that day, they were welcomed and warmed with mugs of Hot Spiced Cider.

While living in the White House, the Carters continued to offer their own personal brand of Southern hospitality. The Carters did not serve hard liquor to White House guests, however, preferring to offer soft drinks and nonalcoholic beverages, with American wines at dinner. Amy was especially fond of lemonade, and Mrs. Carter was partial to the White House iced tea.

Amy had sold her own lemonade in Plains to the reporters covering her father's election. As a White House resident, Amy discontinued her marketing endeavors and enjoyed the lemonade available from the White House kitchen. Mrs. Carter's favored iced tea was made from an unusual recipe devised by one of the long-term maître d's at the White House. The "secret" ingredient in the maître d's special iced tea was lemonade, although for years his evasive response to requests for the recipe had always been, "The secret is in the brew."

After the 1981 inaugural ceremony, the Carters returned to the White House to bid a fond farewell to the household staff. We were genuinely sorry to see them go, and were amazed at how fast the four years had passed. As we shook hands for the last time with the departing President, Mrs. Carter reassured the staff: "You'll like the Reagans. They will be different from us, there's no doubt about that. But you'll like them."

The White House staff simply treated the Carters to the same fine hospitality that they so graciously provided to their own guests. When the Carters lived in the White House, we honored them with their own brand of humble service, and extended the good will of the nation's leader to his own loved ones in his own home.

HOT SPICED CIDER

Makes 2 quarts

2 quarts fresh apple cider
12 whole allspice berries

Two 2-inch strips lemon rind
2 cinnamon sticks

1. In a 3-quart saucepan, combine cider with spices.
2. Bring just to a boil.
3. Set cover slightly ajar, and simmer just under the boiling point for 20 minutes.
4. Strain. Serve hot.

AMY'S LEMONADE

Serves 1

Juice of 2 lemons
1 cup water

2 tablespoons THICK SUGAR
SYRUP

1. In a tall, frosted glass, combine all ingredients; stir with a long-handled teaspoon.
2. Add ice cubes, and serve at once.

THICK SUGAR SYRUP

1 cup water

1 cup sugar

1. In a small saucepan, combine water with sugar.
2. Slowly bring to a boil over medium-low heat.
3. Simmer for 10 minutes, stirring occasionally, until syrup is clear.
4. Remove from heat and let cool. (Keeps well under refrigeration.)

MAÎTRE D'S ICED TEA

Serves 1

8 ounces freshly brewed tea,
chilled
2 ounces freshly made AMY's
LEMONADE
1 thin slice lemon

1. Pour cold tea into a tall frosted glass filled with ice cubes.
2. Stir in lemonade with a long-handled teaspoon.
3. Garnish with lemon slice. Serve at once.

THE
REAGAN FAMILY

*From the Reagans'
Bread Board*

*Reagan Family Favorite
Soups and Salads*

The Reagans' Favorite Entrées

Reagan Family Favorite Desserts

Special Event Recipes

FROM THE REAGANS' BREAD BOARD

Two weeks after he was elected as the fortieth President of the United States, Ronald Reagan visited President Carter in the Oval Office. The outgoing President informed the President-elect about life in the White House, explaining that "the house runs itself." One of President Carter's aides noted that "nobody else could learn in four years what they do over there" to account for why the residence staff remained relatively constant. The Reagans concurred, and the White House kitchen staff carried on business as usual with the arrival of the new First Family.

We had planned to allow at least six months for adjusting to the new residents' tastes. After all, a Hollywood couple would certainly dine differently from a farm family from Plains, Georgia. Yet, many of the simple menus that the Carters had enjoyed appealed to the new First Family. And the Reagans were pleased with some of the favorites of the Fords, Nixons, and Johnsons as well. The White House kitchen staff was pleased to find the transition to the new administration so rapid and hassle-free.

As President Reagan has admitted, once he entered the political arena, he was hooked. And Mrs. Reagan has said that politics makes everything else the couple has done seem "dull as dishwater," even though both had been Hollywood film stars. The Reagans believe in celebrating the high office with pomp and circumstance, flash and flamboyance, and they demonstrated their love of excitement right from the start. Only the dazzle of their second inaugural celebration exceeded that of the first spectacular event.

On January 20, 1981, Ronald Reagan took the oath of office on the West Front of the Capitol, overlooking the city and its historic monuments. The new President wore a formal morning coat and striped gray pants. Mrs. Reagan donned a shimmering gown to join her husband in attending the eight balls held that evening in their honor. For partygoers and givers, the Reagan administration sig-

PRESIDENT REAGAN'S WHOLE WHEAT MUFFINS

When Thomas Jefferson was elected as the third President of the United States, he lived in a modest rooming house in Washington. After the swearing-in ceremony, the new President returned home for dinner only to find that his fellow boarders occupied all available seats around the dining table. Humbly observing the democratic principle of "first come, first serve," President Jefferson retired to his room without dinner.

The White House staff welcomes each new First Family to their new residence.

naled a rebirth of high style and fine taste. For all of America, the spirit and optimism of the new presidency was contagious.

During the 1985 inauguration, there was a constant stream of houseguests as the Reagan family celebrated with dozens of friends and thousands of fans. The White House kitchen kept busy preparing meals and snacks to fuel the family, as well as the more elaborate menus for the ceremonial receptions. The inaugural houseguests especially enjoyed the meals served in the Solarium, including a roast beef dinner with President Reagan's favorite Whole Wheat Muffins instead of Yorkshire Pudding.

Makes 18

1 cup whole wheat flour
1 cup all-purpose flour
4 teaspoons baking powder
½ teaspoon salt
¾ cup light brown sugar
¾ cup coarsely chopped
    walnuts

¾ cup seedless raisins
1 cup milk
2 eggs, beaten
⅔ cup melted vegetable
    shortening

1. Preheat oven to 425°F. Grease eighteen 2-inch muffin cups and dust lightly with flour (or use paper muffin cup liners).
2. Sift flour together with baking powder and salt.
3. In a large mixing bowl, combine dry ingredients with brown sugar, nuts, and raisins.
4. In a small mixing bowl, combine milk with beaten eggs. Mix in shortening and blend well.
5. Stir milk mixture into dry ingredients and combine until just moist. (Do not overmix, or you will have heavy, flat muffins.)
6. Divide batter evenly among the muffin cups, filling each a little more than half full.
7. Bake on lower shelf of preheated oven for 15 to 20 minutes, or until the muffins are evenly browned and a toothpick inserted in the center comes out clean.
8. Cool on wire racks for 5 minutes before removing muffins from tins.
9. Serve warm with whipped butter. Freeze extra muffins or keep in an airtight container; reheat for several minutes just before serving.

The only way to keep your health is to eat what you don't want, drink what you don't like, and do what you'd druther not.
—Mark Twain

HEALTHFUL BRAN MUFFINS

From their very first day as White House residents, Mrs. Reagan made clear her concern about the President's diet. She is careful to see that the First Family menus are well balanced and healthful, nutritious as well as delicious. Mrs. Reagan likes to serve light meals, designed around seasonal produce and artfully arranged to accentuate the natural beauty of fresh foods.

The Reagans typically eat breakfast together at 7:45 A.M., and their menu is as consistent as it is sensible. The nutrition-conscious First Lady is aware of the importance of including adequate amounts of fiber-rich foods in the diet, and of minimizing intake of fat and cholesterol. Therefore, the Reagans start the day with bran cereal, skim milk, fresh fruit, and decaffeinated coffee. Once a week, eggs are served—scrambled, poached, or soft-boiled for four minutes—a single egg for each of them. The President usually supplements his morning repast with whole wheat toast or a home-

First Families of earlier administrations may not have been exposed to the science of nutrition, but most were well aware of the importance of a well-balanced diet. The 1887 edition of The White House Cook Book *summarized the thinking of the day on "Regulation in Diet":*

> *The food we eat is a very important item, and one which it would be difficult to arrange any rule for which it would apply to all persons under different circumstances. . . . Avoid extremes in living too free or scanty; have a good nourishing diet and a sufficient quantity, and it should always be properly cooked. . . . It is very important that the food be taken with regularity at the accustomed time.*

Opposite page: Teamwork is key at every level of White House functioning.

made muffin. Mrs. Reagan is especially pleased when Healthful Bran Muffins appear on her husband's breakfast tray.

At 6 feet 1 inch in height and weighing a steady 185 pounds, President Reagan is in tip-top shape. His appetite is equally healthy, yet he stays trim with a daily exercise routine that includes morning calisthenics and a workout with the elaborate equipment in the Exercise Room on the second floor of the White House. Mrs. Reagan is naturally petite and so need not fret over calories, but she joins her husband in exercising regularly and following a healthful diet plan. Life in the White House is reflective of the current national fitness trend, but the Reagans also understand that concern for health need not be incompatible with eating enjoyment.

Makes 12

1 cup flour	¼ cup firmly packed light
1 cup unprocessed bran	brown sugar
1 tablespoon baking powder	⅔ cup milk
¼ teaspoon salt	1 egg, beaten
¼ cup vegetable shortening	¼ cup dark molasses

1. Preheat oven to 400°F. Grease twelve 2-inch muffin cups and dust lightly with flour (or use paper muffin cup liners).

2. In a small mixing bowl, stir together flour, bran, baking powder, and salt.

3. In a separate mixing bowl, beat shortening with brown sugar until light and fluffy. Blend in milk, egg, and molasses.

4. Stir in dry ingredients until just moist. (Do not overmix or you will have heavy, flat muffins.)

5. Divide batter evenly among the muffin tins, filling each about two-thirds full.

6. Bake on lower shelf of preheated oven for 12 to 15 minutes, or until tops are firm to the touch and a toothpick inserted in the center comes out clean.

7. Cool on a wire rack for 5 minutes before removing muffins from tins.

8. Serve warm with butter, honey or jam. Freeze extra muffins or keep in an airtight container; reheat in a 350°F oven for several minutes just before serving.

Monkey Bread is a heavy, sweet loaf that serves as a Reagan family tradition. The origin of the unusual name is uncertain—some believe the bread resembles a monkey puzzle tree, while others insist that the loaf looks like a pack of monkeys. Mrs. Reagan's explanation may actually be the best: she claims it is so named "because when you make it, you have to monkey around with it."

Reserved for special occasions and holidays, Monkey Bread is a definite deviation from the lighter fare preferred by the First Lady. When guests join the Reagans for dinner in the White House, though, the menu may be just a bit more elaborate, a little less sensible. In general, however, the meals served to the Reagans—

MRS. REAGAN'S MONKEY BREAD

The lovely young wife of President John Fitzgerald Kennedy informed the public, "I am, first, a wife and mother; second, the First Lady." Yet she set numerous precedents in hosting White House social events, and was actively involved in the menu planning for official occasions. Mrs. Kennedy also arranged for the White House to be established as a national museum, with its contents designated as part of a permanent collection. During the Kennedy administration, a fine arts committee was appointed to help refurbish the White House in a manner appropriate for a historical landmark. Mrs. Kennedy is remembered for a unique charm, grace, and style, which contributed to the "Camelot" atmosphere that characterized the Kennedys' brief tenure in the White House. Subsequent First Ladies have continued her work to enrich the social and historical significance of the White House.

with or without company—reflect Mrs. Reagan's keen attention to proper nutrition and attractive presentation in menu planning.

Mrs. Reagan is very conscious of style and beauty, and she is careful to ensure that the White House maintains the grace and dignity of a President's home. As soon as the Reagans moved into the White House, she energetically tackled the household task undertaken by so many of the First Ladies: maintaining the White House as a national museum while creating a comfortable atmosphere for both family and guests. Mrs. Reagan utilized as much of the White House furniture collection as possible in refurbishing the Family Quarters, supplemented with favorite pieces from the Reagans' California home. Needlepoint pillows and family photos create a homey environment for the President and his devoted wife.

When the Reagans host private dinner parties, their guests usually join them upstairs in the President's Dining Room. Before dinner, aperitifs may be served in the Yellow Oval Room. If the Reagans plan on dining alone, they relax together in the Family Quarters and forego formality in favor of simple trays served as they watch the network news. First Lady Nancy Reagan has been undeniably successful in establishing the Reagans' White House as both a dignified mansion that serves its honored guests with grace and style, as well as a comfortable home where the President can relax with family and friends.

Makes one 9-inch extra-high ring

1 package active dry yeast	*3½ cups flour*
1¼ cups warm milk (105°F to 115°F)	*¾ cup butter, at room temperature*
1 tablespoon sugar	*1 cup butter, melted*
1 teaspoon salt	*1 teaspoon water*
3 eggs	

1. Butter inside of a 9-inch tube pan and dust lightly with flour. To extend the height of the pan, use 2 collars of aluminum foil, each 4 inches high; secure one collar around the center ring, and use string to tie the other collar in place around the outside of the pan.

2. Dissolve yeast in ¼ cup of the warm milk.

3. In a large mixing bowl, combine the yeast mixture with sugar, salt, and 2 of the eggs. Blend well.

4. Add flour and the remaining warm milk; blend well.

5. Use a pastry cutter to cut in the unmelted butter until well distributed.

6. Mix with a dough hook or turn out and knead by hand for 5 minutes until dough is smooth and elastic.

7. Place dough in a well-greased bowl and cover with a damp cloth. Let rise in a warm place for 1¼ hours until double in bulk.

8. Punch down, knead again, and let rise for 35 minutes.

9. On a lightly floured board, roll out dough and shape into a log 2 inches thick.

10. Use a thin, sharp knife to slice dough into 24 even pieces; shape each into a Ping-Pong-size ball.

11. Roll the dough balls in the melted butter and layer evenly in the prepared pan. Let dough rise again in a warm place for 20 minutes.

12. Preheat oven to 375°F.

13. In a small bowl, beat the remaining egg with the water. Use a pastry brush to lightly moisten the top of the ring.

14. Bake on lower shelf of preheated oven for 25 minutes, or until bread rises above the foil collar and top turns golden brown.

15. Let pan cool on a wire rack for 10 minutes before removing foil collars.

16. Serve the warm loaf in a bread basket; it pulls apart easily to yield individual servings. Serve with butter and marmalade if desired.

The American public looked forward to a star-filled, exciting, and glamorous presidency when the Reagans moved into the White House in 1981. A widespread fascination with celebrities has long existed in this country; most everyone enjoys hearing stories about their favorite stars of film, television, sports, and society. The election of a President who had once been a well-known movie actor, television host, and Hollywood celebrity ensured plenty of fodder for the insatiable American appetite for star-studded anecdotes.

When the Reagans entertain friends at the White House, the guest list might include Frank Sinatra, Charlton Heston, or Audrey Hepburn. Private dinners are often followed by movie screenings in the White House theater. Sometimes the film is a new release provided by one of the major studios, other times an older film in

HOMEMADE PITA BREAD

Julia Grant, wife of President Ulysses S. Grant, was an avid socialite and enjoyed her role as White House hostess. Each Wednesday, First Lady Grant presided over a feast for 36 guests, encompassing some 20 to 29 courses at an estimated cost of $700 to $1,500 per meal. Mrs. Grant described her years in the White House as "quite the happiest period of my life. . . . When Congress and society get in session, Washington is a mecca for brains and beauty."

which the President or the First Lady had a role. The 1957 movie *Hellcats of the Navy* features both of them, and is always a hit. Popcorn is passed about the theater in large silver bowls.

Mrs. Reagan prefers to serve pretty, light, fashionable foods at most of their private dinner parties. The family dinner menus are not very different, except that wine (usually from California) is served only when guests are present. President Reagan has long been interested in wines and is proud to serve excellent selections from his home state. When the Reagans dine alone, they prefer to drink water with their meals, often sipping decaffeinated coffee with dessert.

When bread is included on the Reagan family dinner menus, it is most often in the form of wedges of pita. These round, flat loaves originated in the Middle East, but they have become popular in the United States, and are now served with a variety of ethnic cuisines. The First Lady likes homemade pita bread served with cold soup as a first course, or with the salad and one of their favorite cheeses such as goat, Brie, or Gruyère. Pita is also a popular menu item when the Reagans entertain, even at those White House dinners where the Hollywood stars seem to shine almost as brilliantly as the White House itself.

Makes six 10-inch round loaves

1½ cakes compressed yeast
1½ cups warm water (105°F to 115°F)
1 teaspoon salt

1 teaspoon sugar
3 tablespoons vegetable shortening
4 cups sifted flour

1. Dissolve yeast in ½ cup of the warm water.

2. In a large mixing bowl, combine yeast mixture with salt, sugar, and shortening. Blend thoroughly.

3. Stir in flour one cup at a time, alternating with the remaining warm water.

4. Mix with a dough hook or turn out and knead by hand until dough is smooth and elastic.

5. Place dough in a well-greased bowl and cover with a damp cloth. Let rise in a warm place for 1 hour, or until double in bulk.

6. Preheat oven to 500°F. Preheat baker's stones or quarry tiles on floor of oven.

7. Knead dough briefly in the bowl and turn out onto a lightly floured board.

8. Divide dough into 6 even pieces and shape each into a smooth ball.

9. Roll each dough ball out to form an 8-inch round about ⅛-inch thick.

10. Transfer rounds onto baker's stones or quarry tiles. Bake in the hot oven for 8 to 10 minutes, or until bread is brown and puffed up like a balloon.

11. Let the rounds cool on wire racks (they will deflate). Store in refrigerator or freezer, stacked and tightly wrapped in plastic. Stuff with sandwich fillings such as cheese and country-style ham, or slice in wedges to serve with soup or salad.

REAGAN FAMILY FAVORITE SOUPS AND SALADS

PRESIDENT REAGAN'S HAMBURGER SOUP

Everyone wonders what the President of the United States eats. Residing in the White House, the nation's leader has access to whatever foods he wishes, prepared on demand by a skilled staff. So most people expect that the President "dines like a king" every day. This is certainly not the case with Ronald Reagan.

Raised in a small town in Illinois, "Dutch" Reagan attended Eureka College, where he was a three-letter man in football and captain of the swim team. He landed a job as a sports announcer at a radio station in Iowa, and soon became one of the best-known sportscasters in the Midwest. Accompanying the Chicago Cubs to spring training in California, "Dutch" took a screen test at Warner Brothers. Jack Warner immediately said, "Okay, sign him," and Ronald Reagan had a seven-year contract at the age of twenty-six. Immensely likeable both on and off the screen, Ronald Reagan (he dropped his nickname when he left radio) acted in some fifty-five movies. Yet he maintained his small-town humbleness and unpretentious manner throughout his Hollywood years. And he retained an appetite for simple, home-style meals.

Thomas Jefferson is remembered as a discerning gourmet and a connoisseur of wines, attributes unusual in his day. He was also a farmer and a man of simple tastes, as he once explained: "I would rather be shut up in a modest cottage dining on simple bacon and letting the world roll by as it liked, than to occupy the most splendid post."

Even in the White House, Ronald Reagan prefers the plain foods of his early days, and Mrs. Reagan makes sure that her husband is served his favorites on a frequent basis. These include such homey dishes as Macaroni and Cheese, Meat Loaf, and Hamburger Soup. Whether he dines on the more elaborate fare popular with the First Lady or his own simple favorites, President Reagan is easy to please. His dinner plate always returns to the kitchen clean as a whistle!

The President usually has lunch in the Oval Office, and he prefers a light meal such as soup, bread, and a fruit dessert. He likes minestrone with a wedge of fresh Italian bread, lentil soup with sliced frankfurters, navy bean or black bean soup, and Scotch broth made with barley. His favorite soup, however, is a home-style hamburger soup made with beef broth, lean ground beef, fresh tomatoes, and hominy. Served with a slice of toasted French bread and perhaps a medley of fresh fruit for dessert, such a simple meal is just as good as "dining like a king" for President Reagan.

Makes 4 quarts

¼ cup butter
2 pounds lean ground beef
2 cups diced onion
4 garlic cloves, finely diced
1½ cups diced carrots
2 cups diced celery
1 cup diced green bell pepper
3 quarts hot beef broth
4 large ripe tomatoes, peeled and chopped (or one 14½-ounce can stewed tomatoes)

½ teaspoon freshly ground black pepper
2 bay leaves
One 15-ounce can hominy
2 tablespoons chopped fresh parsley

1. Melt butter in a heavy skillet, add meat and brown quickly over high heat.

2. Add diced vegetables, cover, and simmer over medium heat for 10 minutes, stirring occasionally.

3. Add hot broth, tomatoes, pepper, and bay leaves. Cover, and simmer over medium heat for 35 minutes, stirring occasionally.

4. Stir in hominy. Set cover slightly ajar, and simmer over medium-high heat for 10 minutes.

5. Remove bay leaves and add chopped parsley. Serve at once, with thick slices of toasted French bread. Soup freezes well, and can be kept refrigerated for several days in a covered container.

(REPRINTED WITH SPECIAL PERMISSION OF KING FEATURES SYNDICATE, INC.)

I had two role models when I was growing up: Jane Wyman, who chose to be a motion-picture star; and Nancy Reagan, who chose to be a professional homemaker. They both made their choices. So when I got to be nineteen years old, I knew that I could be anything in the world I wanted to be, as long as I was willing to work at it, and I could make the choice of what I wanted to be because those women had done it.

—Maureen Reagan

The Reagans' eldest child is the daughter of Ronald Reagan and his first wife, actress Jane Wyman. Maureen is a regular guest at the White House, usually accompanied by her husband, Dennis Revell. Although she does not always agree with her parents' politics—Maureen is known as the "house feminist"—they enjoy each other's company and are mutually supportive. Maureen was active in her father's overwhelmingly successful reelection campaign, and was subsequently named co-chairperson for the Republican Party.

Maureen's sense of adventure has led her to sample a wide array of careers; she has been an actress, a television and radio show hostess, a U.S.O. volunteer with a tour of Vietnam, and the president of a firm that boosts U.S. exports. She met Dennis through the Young Republican Club, and they were married in Beverly Hills during her father's first year in the Oval Office. Since Dennis is 6 feet 7 inches tall, the couple sleeps in the Lincoln Bedroom on

MAUREEN'S VEAL AND VEGETABLE SOUP

President Taft so enjoyed turtle soup that he brought a special cook to the White House specifically to prepare this one dish. One may wonder whether our stoutest President—Taft weighed in at 332 pounds on his inaugural day—adhered to the "Small Points on Etiquette" spelled out in the 1887 edition of The White House Cook Book:

Soup is always served for the first course, and it should be eaten with dessert spoons and taken from the sides, not the tips of them, without any sound of the lips and not sucked into the mouth audibly from the end of the spoon . . . Never ask to be helped to soup a second time. The hostess may ask you to take a second plate, but you will politely decline. Fish chowder, which is served in soup plates, is said to be an exception which proves this rule, and when eating of that it is correct to take a second plateful, if desired.

President Kennedy, a Bostonian and an athlete, favored hearty New England fish chowder, sometimes requesting it several days in a row. He would have been totally in agreement with the "exception that proves this rule."

their frequent visits to the White House—Abraham Lincoln's bed is seven feet long.

Maureen is a very professional and extremely busy person, yet she always takes time for friendly chats with the White House staff. She also finds time to be considerate of others, calling the kitchen or dropping by to inform the staff of her meal plans. Sometimes she leaves a note to let us know what she would like for breakfast. Other times, she notifies us that she will be out late, telling the kitchen staff not to bother to stay. She is grateful on such occasions for the pot of homemade soup left for her to enjoy when her day's work finally draws to a close.

Because of their hectic social schedules, Maureen and Dennis do not always join the Reagans for meals when visiting the White House. When they are able to dine at the family dinner table, though, both are very easy to please. Dennis is lean and active, and he has a hearty appetite. Maureen likes to eat lightly, but she has become an admitted fan of the special vegetable soup I concocted when she paid her parents an unexpected visit. I used only the ingredients I had on hand, and voilà! Now when Maureen is out working hard to support her father and his party, a pot of her favorite Veal and Vegetable Soup may be simmering on the stove at the White House, awaiting her return.

Makes 3 quarts

2 tablespoons butter
1 cup diced onions
1 cup diced leeks, white part only
4 garlic cloves, finely chopped
1 cup halved and thinly sliced carrots
2 cups finely diced lean veal

¼ teaspoon freshly ground white pepper
2 quarts hot chicken stock
1 bay leaf
1 cup heavy cream
1 tablespoon chopped fresh parsley

1. Melt butter in a 4-quart saucepan, and add onions, leeks, garlic, and carrots. Cover, and simmer over medium heat for 10 minutes.

2. Add diced veal and sprinkle with pepper; sauté for 3 minutes, stirring constantly.

3. Add hot stock and bay leaf. Cover and simmer over medium heat for 30 minutes, stirring occasionally.

4. Stir in heavy cream and chopped parsley; bring just to the boiling point over high heat.

5. Remove from heat and serve at once with CHEESE TOAST triangles or wedges of HOMEMADE PITA BREAD (page 333).

CHEESE TOAST

Makes 4 triangles

2 slices white or whole wheat
  bread
2 ounces cheddar cheese,
  grated

A pinch of paprika

1. Toast bread lightly.
2. Remove crusts and discard.
3. Set toast on a foil-lined baking sheet.
4. Sprinkle toast evenly with grated cheese and paprika. Cover each slice with wax paper and press gently by hand to flatten; discard wax paper.
5. Broil on upper oven shelf for 3 minutes, turning pan around once to brown evenly. Tops should be golden brown and bubbling.
6. Let cool for 1 minute before slicing in half diagonally. Serve warm triangles at once.

RIVERSIDE SALAD

The Reagans' eldest son was adopted as a baby by Ronald and his first wife, Jane Wyman. Michael Reagan is a successful businessman who lives in California with his wife, Colleen, and their two young children. Now a devoted parent and family man, Michael exhibited the typical Reagan sense of adventure, acting and racing speedboats for a time before he settled down.

When his father was reelected in 1984, Michael brought his family to the White House to participate in the inaugural celebration. Like his father, Michael is a football fan, so he hosted a little celebration of his own at the White House: On the day before the inauguration, nine guests joined Michael in the Family Theater for a Superbowl Party. "We're number one!" is a chant that can be heard from time to time, even in the White House!

When President Reagan and his wife travel to California to visit Michael or other family members and friends, they often stay at the luxurious Century Plaza Hotel in Beverly Hills, which is fre-

The healthfulness of vegetables has long been recognized by Americans. The virtues of a vegetable diet have also long been exaggerated, just as they are today in some popular fad diet books. The 1887 edition of The White House Cook Book *provided sensible guidelines on including fresh vegetables in the diet, but overstated the case a bit: "Watercress will neutralize chalk in the blood, which limy matter is the great cause of aging and stiffening of the fibers. Those who would feel young and look young, therefore, should eat watercress."*

quented by the rich and famous, from Dolly Parton and Frank Sinatra to King Juan Carlos of Spain. The dining room caters to the weight- and health-conscious, serving the light dishes that are currently so popular. Once President Reagan ordered a chicken salad plate for lunch in the hotel dining room. The other patrons followed suit, and the hotel kitchen was suddenly inundated with orders for chicken salad! The salad plate, which was made with sliced kiwi and garnished with fresh vegetables, was subsequently added to the restaurant menu.

At the White House, the Reagans like a variety of California-style salad plates prepared from native vegetables and/or fruits such as avocadoes, oranges, and grapefruit. One of Mrs. Reagan's favorites is Riverside Salad, its crisply tart chicory accentuated by tangy grapefruit and a light dressing that makes it as refreshing and healthful as the California surf.

Serves 6 to 8

½ head chicory
2 bunches fresh watercress
½ teaspoon salt
¼ teaspoon freshly ground
  black pepper

LIGHT OIL AND VINEGAR
  DRESSING
2 medium-size grapefruits,
  peeled and sectioned

1. Discard outer leaves from the chicory. Shred leaves into fine strips, and wash carefully in cold water.
2. Cut off and discard the bottom two-thirds of the stems from each bunch of watercress. Wash leaves carefully in cold water.
3. Dry greens in a towel and transfer to a large salad bowl.
4. Sprinkle with salt and pepper. Add dressing and toss lightly.
5. Divide salad evenly among individual serving plates. Garnish each with 2 to 3 grapefruit sections, and serve at once.

LIGHT OIL AND VINEGAR DRESSING

Makes 1 scant cup

1 tablespoon Dijon-style
  mustard
1 teaspoon salt
¼ teaspoon freshly ground
  black pepper
Juice of ½ lemon

¼ cup red wine vinegar
½ cup olive oil
2 teaspoons chopped fresh
  parsley
1 tablespoon chopped fresh
  chives

1. In a small mixing bowl, combine mustard with salt, pepper, lemon juice, and vinegar; stir with a wire whisk until well dissolved.

2. Gradually add oil, stirring constantly until thickened.

3. Stir in chopped parsley and chives. Serve at once, or store in the refrigerator in a covered jar; let warm to room temperature before use.

Following in their parents' footsteps, the two youngest offspring of Ronald and Nancy Reagan have both chosen careers on stage and screen, right smack in the public eye. Ron Jr. left Yale to study ballet, but resigned from the famed Joffrey Ballet troupe for a career in print and television journalism. Patti adopted Nancy Reagan's maiden name to make it on her own as Hollywood actress Patti Davis. She, too, has recently turned her talents to writing, authoring a best-selling novel. Both are married and living in California.

Ron Jr. was a more frequent guest at the White House when he lived in New York City. Mrs. Reagan was always concerned about her active son's diet and made sure the kitchen had plenty of healthy snacks on hand. When Ron Jr. was in town with his ballet troupe, for example, the refrigerator was stocked with lean meats, various cheeses, and fresh produce. The White House kitchen also kept a selection of imported beer on hand, a refreshing liquid much appreciated by athletes and dancers.

All of the Reagans appreciate fine food and drink, but all have benefited from Mrs. Reagan's concern for good nutrition. They are very fond of delicate salads prepared with a wide variety of ingredients. Some family favorites include watercress and alfalfa sprouts salad, Caesar Salad, Spinach Salad, and antipasto. Mrs. Reagan also enjoys unusual salad ingredients such as peppery arugala, crispy mâche, the red chicory known as radicchio, and delicate Belgian endive.

Long popular in Europe, and developing a following in the United States, Belgian endive is green chicory that is cultivated under specially controlled conditions. Grown almost exclusively in Belgium, it must be harvested by hand from the sandy soil where it flourishes. It is both grown and stored in total darkness, as exposure to light will turn the creamy white leaves green and cause loss

BELGIAN ENDIVE SALAD

A number of America's Presidents have been reelected, but only one brushed aside the then-unwritten law against three terms of office and successfully ran for a fourth. Franklin D. Roosevelt was amused by the quip Chief Justice Charles Evans Hughes made at a White House dinner prior to his third inauguration: "Mr. President, after I have read the oath and you have repeated it, how would it do for me to lean forward and whisper, 'Don't you think this is getting a little monotonous for both of us?'"

of flavor. Belgian endive is an excellent salad green, and the smooth, crisp leaves provide a delicious contrast to strips of lean meats and Swiss cheeses. The Reagans are especially fond of a Belgian Endive Salad made with julienned ham and crisp red pepper.

Serves 6 to 8

6 Belgian endive hearts
¼ pound lean smoked ham
½ red bell pepper, seeded
½ cup LIGHT OIL AND VINEGAR
   DRESSING (page 340)

6 to 8 large leaves Boston
   lettuce, washed and well
   dried
1 tablespoon chopped fresh
   parsley

1. Slice endive hearts in half lengthwise; carefully remove the bitter core and discard.
2. Slice endive into fine julienne, wash in cold water, and dry well in a towel.
3. Slice ham into fine julienne.
4. Slice red pepper into fine julienne.
5. In a large salad bowl, combine endive, ham, and red pepper strips. Add dressing, and toss lightly.
6. Arrange Boston lettuce leaves on individual serving plates.
7. Divide endive salad evenly among the leaf-lined plates; sprinkle with chopped parsley, and serve at once.

THE REAGANS' FAVORITE ENTRÉES

PRESIDENT
REAGAN'S SUNDAY
NIGHT ROAST BEEF
HASH

The White House has magnificent quarters and we're very well treated there, but you are a kind of a bird in a gilded cage, and they don't open the door very often to let the bird out.

—President Reagan

President Reagan is remarkably fit for a man of his years, in spite of the degree of stress his public position entails. He copes with the constant barrage of national and international problems by allowing himself to "take time out" on a regular basis. As Governor of California in a time of political unrest, Ronald Reagan arrived home each evening at around 6:00 P.M. to have a relaxing dinner with his family. Never a workaholic, he learned to preside as "chairman of the board," providing direction and leaving execution to his staff. When he was Governor, Ronald Reagan was known to advise his aides as he left the office for the day, "Hey, you guys, get out! Go home to your wives!"

In combination with a healthful diet and regular exercise, President Reagan's ability to handle stress has contributed to his youthful vigor. He takes regular breaks from the pressures of the Oval Office and heads for the tranquility of Camp David. Mrs. Reagan also enjoys the peaceful environment of the Maryland camp, where she and her husband are able to take brisk walks, eat hearty meals, and watch movies after dinner.

When they return, relaxed and refreshed, after a weekend at Camp David, the Reagans like to have a light dinner. Sunday night

For "an excellent breakfast dish," the 1887 edition of The White House Cook Book *provides the following recipe for "Beef Hash":*

Chop cold roast beef, or pieces of beefsteak; fry half an onion in a piece of butter; when the onion is brown, add the chopped beef; season with a little salt and pepper; moisten with the beef gravy, if you have any, if not, with sufficient water and a little butter; cook long enough to be hot, but no longer, as much cooking toughens the meat. Some prefer to let a crust form on the bottom and turn the hash brown side uppermost.

All the beautiful rooms at the White House are scenes of important decision making.

If you can't stand the heat, let somebody else take it.

©1985 HERBLOCK

(COPYRIGHT © 1985 BY HERBLOCK IN THE WASHINGTON POST)

fare typically consists of a simple main dish, fresh vegetables, salad, and fruit.

The Reagans are fond of hash made with chicken, but the President's favorite is an old-fashioned roast beef hash. Sometimes they enjoy a hearty dinner of roast beef with Yorkshire Pudding. They are also fans of a California favorite, steak with chili. Mrs. Reagan likes her meat cooked medium-well, while the President prefers his well-done. Both agree that the best roast beef hash is cooked crisp, yet juicy and flavorful, a delicious way to end a pleasant weekend.

Serves 6

2 tablespoons butter
1 cup finely diced onions
3 garlic cloves, finely minced
1 cup finely diced celery
½ cup finely diced green bell pepper
4 cups finely diced cooked roast beef
1 large cooked potato, peeled and finely diced (leftover cooked potatoes are fine)

1 cup stewed tomatoes
¼ teaspoon freshly ground black pepper
¼ teaspoon dried thyme
2 tablespoons chopped fresh parsley

1. Melt butter in a large nonstick sauté pan, add onions and sauté for 3 minutes. Add garlic and sauté for 2 minutes more.

2. Add diced celery, green pepper, and roast beef; sauté for 5 minutes, stirring constantly.

3. Stir in diced potato and tomatoes, and season with pepper, thyme, and parsley.

4. Simmer over medium heat for 10 minutes, until hash is golden brown and holds together well. Remove from heat.

5. Set a large nonstick sauté pan over medium-high heat. Scoop generous spoonfuls of hash into the pan and cook the patties for 5 minutes, or until nicely browned; flip to brown other side for 5 minutes more. The patties should be heated through and crisp but not dry.

6. Serve at once, topping each patty with a fresh POACHED EGG (page 149) or a fried egg, if desired. Hash tastes best if prepared a day in advance and refrigerated, then made into patties and fried just before serving. Serve with a hot green vegetable and a crisp green salad.

This ranch really casts a spell. . . . You turn in the gate—it's just a road for a few ranches that are up here—and once you're inside, there's no sense of traffic or the outside world at all. . . ."

—Ronald Reagan, on Rancho del Ciero

During his second term as Governor of California, Ronald Reagan purchased a 688-acre ranch located in the Santa Ynez Mountains east of Santa Barbara. Built in 1872, the adobe house has a stone hearth and a rustic atmosphere. At their home away from the White House, the Reagans enjoy riding horses, tending to the cattle, and working in the gardens and orchards. President Reagan likes to clear the brush and chop wood, which they use to heat their "ranch in the sky." All of the outdoor exercise can really work up an appetite. Although she does not aspire to be a fancy cook, Mrs. Reagan will occasionally "rustle up some eggs" when the couple are out at the ranch.

Dinner menus at Rancho del Ciero are similar to the hearty meals served at Camp David. Some of their vacation favorites are also prepared for family meals at the White House. Although the Reagans prefer chicken, veal, and fish to beef, several of their best-liked dishes do feature lean beef. Beef and Kidney Pie is one, whether served in the rustic dining room of a century-old adobe ranch, or at the fine dining tables of the White House.

BEEF AND KIDNEY PIE

The 1887 edition of The White House Cook Book *included a variety of recipes for the meat pies traditional in the Old World, adapted to the foodstuffs available to the early American settlers. Beefsteak pie, chicken pie, and pigeon pie were more appealing but perhaps less intriguing than the pie made with "Snow Birds":*

One dozen thoroughly cleaned birds; stuff each with an oyster, put them into a yellow dish, and add two ounces of boiled salt pork and three raw potatoes cut into slices. Add a pint of oyster liquor, an ounce of butter, salt, and pepper. Cover the dish with a crust and bake in a moderate oven.

Serves 6 to 8

1 tablespoon salt
¼ teaspoon freshly ground
   black pepper
2 tablespoons flour
2 pounds round of beef, thinly
   sliced
¼ cup vegetable oil
2 fresh veal kidneys, trimmed
   of all fat and coarsely diced,
   then sprinkled lightly with
   salt

2 tablespoons butter
2 tablespoons finely minced
   shallots
2 garlic cloves, finely minced
3 cups dry red wine (preferably
   Burgundy)
Prebaked PUFF PASTE, OR POT
   PIE CRUST (page 353)
1 egg, beaten with 1 tablespoon
   water

1. Preheat oven to 375°F.
2. In a shallow bowl, combine salt, pepper, and flour. Dredge beef slices in this mixture.

3. In a heavy skillet, heat 2 tablespoons of the oil; add beef and brown for 5 minutes, stirring constantly.

4. Transfer beef slices to a colander to allow fat to drain.

5. Heat the remaining oil in the skillet; add kidneys and sauté for 3 minutes, or until browned. Transfer to the colander and let drain.

6. Melt the butter in the skillet, add shallots and garlic, and sauté until golden.

7. Return the beef and kidneys to the skillet. Add wine, cover, and simmer over low heat for 45 minutes, or until meat is tender.

8. Make prebaked cover to fit a 2-quart casserole dish with PUFF PASTE, or prepare POT PIE CRUST. Transfer the meat mixture to the dish. Top with the prebaked PUFF PASTE and cover with foil; or place POT PIE CRUST over meat mixture, and press edges to the sides of the dish to seal. Prick in several places with a fork, and brush lightly with the egg-water mixture.

9. If a prebaked PUFF PASTE cover is used, bake until heated through. Bake on upper shelf of preheated oven for 20 minutes, or until crust is golden brown. Let cool slightly on a wire rack before cutting pastry into squares. Serve with BELGIAN ENDIVE SALAD (page 341) or other crisp greens.

PUFF PASTE

To top 1 pot pie

4 sticks (2 cups) butter, at room
   temperature
Ice water

4 cups sifted flour
½ teaspoon salt

1. Knead butter until smooth, moistening it with a little ice water, and squeezing out any pockets of water that form. Shape into a rectangular cake and wrap tightly in plastic; refrigerate until ready to use.

2. In a large mixing bowl, combine flour with salt. Gradually add 1½ cups ice water, mixing well to form a firm dough.

3. Chill dough in the refrigerator for 30 minutes.

4. On a lightly floured board, roll out dough to form a square 1½ inches thick.

5. Set the butter cake in the center of the dough; fold up the dough to encase the butter in a "package." Chill for 15 minutes.

6. On the lightly floured board, roll out dough to form a rectangle that is 3 times as long as it is wide; fold one third of the rectangle

toward the center, then fold the other third over the top, to form 3 layers. This process is a "turn."

7. Make another turn. Chill for 20 minutes.

8. Make 2 more turns; chill for 20 minutes more.

9. Make another 2 turns; then wrap the dough tightly in plastic and refrigerate overnight. (Dough will keep for 1 week in the refrigerator, or as long as 3 weeks in the freezer.)

10. Preheat oven to 400°F. Grease a baking sheet.

11. On a lightly floured board, roll out dough to ⅛ inch thick.

12. Cut dough to fit pot pie dish, allowing a little overlap, and transfer to the prepared sheet. Prick with a fork 10 to 12 times, or use a small sharp knife to cut an attractive design into the crust.

13. Bake on lower shelf of preheated oven for 10 minutes.

14. Reduce heat to 350°F and bake for 10 minutes more, or until crust is dry and lightly browned.

"In Hollywood, you were never over twenty-five. At least I progressed beyond twenty-five."

—Nancy Reagan

Ronald Reagan is the oldest President in the history of the United States, elected at age 69 and reelected at 73. He was born during the Taft administration, when there were only 46 states. His lifetime has spanned 2 world wars, the Great Depression, and 14 American presidencies, including his own. Asked how he has maintained his youthful appearance, the President explains, "I keep riding younger and younger horses."

In 1981, four of the Reagans' closest friends co-hosted a birthday celebration for the President at the White House. One hundred guests attended the surprise party to wish the President a happy, healthy seventieth birthday. The cake—an impressive array of vanilla sponge layers—was presented on individual spun sugar stands, so that every table had its own birthday cake. The top layer, for the President's table, was garnished with a beautiful white spun-sugar horse.

The menu for the President's big birthday bash included Lobster en Bellevue with Sauce Rémoulade and stuffed veal with a wine sauce. When President Reagan celebrated his seventy-fifth birthday in 1986, the party was smaller in size but the menu was equally

OSSO BUCCO

William Henry Harrison was the oldest President in history when he was inaugurated in 1841 at the age of 68. After only one month in office, however, President Harrison succumbed to pneumonia from a cold he had contracted during the inaugural ceremony. He was the first U.S. President to die during his term of office.

Mrs. Reagan joins family and supporters in helping the President to celebrate an annual event.

impressive—a lean loin of veal stuffed with a flavorful combination of pork, veal, shallots, garlic, buttery bread crumbs, and fresh parsley, and an unusual dessert of coconut-covered balls of cake stacked in a spun-sugar "corral," each initialed with the President's monogram. A chocolate sauce provided a deliciously rich complement to the coconut, the President's favorite dessert flavor.

In 1982, the President's birthday dinner menu featured yet another veal dish, Osso Bucco, or "bone with a hole." This Northern Italian dish is a favorite of the Reagans and is served for both family dinners and special meals. Other veal dishes favored by the Reagans include veal scallopine in Marsala, Veal Piccata, and Veal Parmigiana, each of which can make any meal a celebration.

Serves 6

6 slices center-cut veal shank
(each 1½ inches thick) and
shank bone
½ cup flour
1 tablespoon salt
1 teaspoon freshly ground
white pepper
2 tablespoons olive oil
2 tablespoons finely minced
shallots
2 garlic cloves, finely minced
1 cup diced carrots

1 cup diced celery or celery
root
2 cups dry white wine
1 cup tomato juice
2 teaspoons chopped fresh
oregano, or 1 teaspoon dried
2 medium-size ripe tomatoes,
peeled and coarsely diced
Gremolata: 2 finely minced
garlic cloves, 2 tablespoons
chopped fresh parsley, and
grated rind of 1 lemon

1. In a shallow bowl, dredge veal slices with flour, salt, and pepper.

2. Heat oil in a heavy skillet, add veal slices and brown over medium heat, cooking for about 5 minutes on each side. Transfer to paper towels to drain.

3. Add the minced shallots and garlic to the hot oil; sauté for 2 minutes.

4. Add diced carrots and celery or celery root; sauté for 3 minutes more.

5. Add wine and tomato juice and bring to a boil.

6. Add the oregano and the shank bone; return to a boil.

7. Cover and simmer over medium heat for 20 minutes. Turn bones over and simmer for 20 minutes more, or until meat is tender and falls away from the bone.

8. Transfer the shank bone to a deep serving platter and surround with the rest of the veal.

9. Add diced tomatoes to the sauce and bring to a boil.

10. Spoon sauce over the meat, sprinkle with the *Gremolata*, and serve at once with steamed rice or noodles.

There is no official job description for the First Lady, and special training is not provided. Each First Lady creates her own niche, as advocate for the President, hostess for the White House, and role model for the nation. The causes she chooses to champion automatically attract much press and public attention, so the support of the First Lady is always a great advantage.

PAELLA À LA VALENCIANA

The First Lady receives thousands of letters each month, with requests for aid or advice. The phones at the White House ring some 6,000 times a day, with many of the callers in search of the ear and heart of the First Lady. She must entertain foreign and domestic dignitaries, wives of heads of state and the U.S. Congress, members of women's groups and Girl Scout troops with equal grace and diplomacy. She also sees to it that the White House provides a warm home for the First Family, as well as a fitting environment for political business and entertainment. The First Lady must grow into her position quickly, learning to meet public accolades and criticisms with both humility and good humor. While her efforts are rarely unappreciated, the demanding job of being America's First Lady is decidedly unsalaried.

Mrs. Reagan is comfortable in the White House, and she has impressed the press and the public with her devotion to her husband and her active involvement in national issues. She has taken

The First Lady frequently stops by the kitchen to confer with Chef Haller on menu plans for special occasions.

a major role in managing the presidential household, from helping to organize official functions to working with the kitchen staff to plan family menus and special meals. She often comes into the White House kitchen to participate in the final presentation of a fancy platter or celebratory dessert. And she is always considerate of the kitchen staff, leaving friendly notes to inform us of any changes in menus or meal times.

If a specific dish strikes Mrs. Reagan's fancy, she will compliment the kitchen and request that the recipe be kept on file for future use at family or special meals. She is a sophisticated diner with an artist's eye for visual appeal. Mrs. Reagan is pleased when the kitchen comes up with a new dish for her to try, so we are able to practice culinary artistry and employ our creative skills in working with her. Since Mrs. Reagan prefers light foods, including entrées made with chicken or fish, she especially enjoys Paella à la Valenciana, a pretty dish of Spanish origin that combines the two in an unusually seasoned rice base.

Eleanor Roosevelt served the longest term as America's First Lady, and she was both a controversial and an admired figure. She spent much time and energy in championing her causes. White House entertaining was conducted in a casual, open-house atmosphere. At a private luncheon for King George VI and Queen Elizabeth, the Roosevelts served hot dogs and baked beans. The First Lady said, "I shall be myself"—and she was.

Serves 6

One 3½-pound chicken
1 tablespoon salt
½ teaspoon freshly ground
   white pepper
¼ cup olive oil
1 cup diced onions
4 garlic cloves, finely minced
2 cups diced red and green bell
   peppers
½ pound sliced chorizo (spicy
   red Spanish sausage)
2 cups long-grain rice

1 teaspoon saffron
1 tablespoon tomato paste
2 cups dry white wine
3 cups hot chicken stock
1 cup fresh green peas
1 pound large fresh shrimp,
   peeled and deveined
½ pound small fresh scallops
12 fresh mussels, thoroughly
   scrubbed
2 tablespoons chopped fresh
   parsley

1. Cut the chicken into 10 pieces: Cut off the wings, remove the back and reserve for stock, separate the legs and thighs, and quarter the breast.

2. Mix together salt and pepper; season chicken pieces lightly and reserve the extra seasoning.

3. In a large sauté pan or paella pan (a large heavy skillet with 2 handles), heat olive oil, brown chicken on all sides, and let drain on paper towels.

4. Add the onions, garlic, and peppers to the hot oil; sauté for 3 minutes.

5. Stir in sliced sausage and sauté for 3 to 4 minutes to brown on all sides.

6. Stir in rice, saffron, and tomato paste. Add the chicken.

7. Pour in wine and 2 cups of the hot stock. Bring to a boil over medium-high heat, stirring constantly.

8. Cover, and simmer over medium heat for 10 minutes.

9. Remove cover; sprinkle in the peas.

10. Sprinkle the shrimp and scallops with the reserved seasoning, and arrange over the rice along with the mussels.

11. Cover, and simmer over medium heat for 10 minutes more.

12. Add the remaining cup of hot chicken stock. Cover, and let stand for 10 minutes on top of the stove.

13. Sprinkle with parsley and serve at once, right from the pan. Accompany with crisp greens such as a watercress and mushroom salad. If desired, fresh lobster and clams can be included in the paella, in addition to or in place of the other seafood.

CHICKEN POT PIE

Although the expression "a chicken in every pot" has been attributed to President Hoover, his campaign speech actually included a different line: "The slogan of progress is changing from the full dinner pail to the full garage." It was Henry IV who, in the late sixteenth century, expressed a wish that "there would not be a peasant so poor in all my realm who would not have a chicken in his pot every Sunday."

Mrs. Reagan volunteers her time to various projects, focusing her energies on several areas of concern. When Ronald Reagan was Governor of California, Mrs. Reagan became involved in the Foster Grandparents Program. The overwhelming success of the project convinced her to continue the work as First Lady, sponsoring senior citizens all over the United States who tutor children with physical or mental handicaps and provide guidance to troubled teens classified as juvenile delinquents. Mrs. Reagan is also active in other social programs that help young people, including the Special Olympics, Girl Scouts of America, and Public Education of Handicapped Children. Perhaps her biggest project, however, is Mrs. Reagan's fight against drug abuse.

At a time when drug and alcohol abuse have become major problems in America, the attention to the issue emanating from the White House is proving to be highly effective. Mrs. Reagan has also appeared in public service spots on both television and radio to help increase awareness about substance abuse. On her sixty-third birthday, one of the numerous anti-drug abuse programs for which Mrs. Reagan serves sent a huge bouquet to the White House, sixty-three red carnations accompanied by a giraffe statuette and a card that read, "On behalf of every parent and grandparent in America, the National Federation of Parents for Drug-Free Youth thanks you for sticking your neck out on this issue."

Mrs. Reagan has talked to the Pope about the international ramifications of drug abuse. She has hosted an international conference on drug abuse for wives of heads of state from seventeen other countries. She hosted a television documentary, "The Chemical People," and made the issue a national priority. "Nobody wanted me to do it, the drug issue," she admits. "I guess they thought it was kind of a downer. It's not a cheery subject. But I think I've brought it to a level of awareness that wasn't there before. I hope people are more aware of how bad the drug problem is, and how widespread and dangerous it is."

The First Lady deserves a great deal of credit for her strong commitment to an "uncheery" subject of national and global concern. Her staff is extremely proud of Mrs. Reagan's efforts, so we do all that we can to support her in such worthy endeavors. Whenever the First Lady holds a luncheon meeting or a dinner to honor her program participants, the White House works hard to provide her with a setting that reflects her own shining example. At a luncheon hosted for "The Chemical People," this delicate Chicken Pot Pie was almost as deserving of applause as the documentary itself and those who help champion the First Lady's cause.

Serves 6

One 4-pound roasting chicken
1 medium-size onion, quartered
2 garlic cloves, crushed
2 medium-size carrots, peeled
    and chopped
2 stalks celery, chopped
Tied cheesecloth "spice bag,"
    containing 24 black
    peppercorns, 1 bay leaf,
    2 cloves, ¼ teaspoon each
    dried marjoram, thyme, and
    rosemary
2 teaspoons salt
Juice of 1 lemon
2 cups dry white wine
2 to 3 cups cold water

1 cup 1- × ⅛-inch carrot sticks,
    cooked tender-crisp
1 cup 1 × ⅛-inch celery sticks,
    cooked tender-crisp
½ cup pearl onions, boiled and
    drained
1 cup fresh button mushrooms,
    boiled and drained
½ cup shelled fresh green peas
3 cups CHICKEN VELOUTÉ SAUCE
1 tablespoon chopped fresh
    parsley

POT PIE CRUST
1 small egg, beaten with
    1 tablespoon cold water

1. Cut the chicken into 6 pieces: Cut off the wings, remove the back and set aside for stock, cut off the legs and thighs and slice the breast in half.

2. In a large soup pot, combine onion and garlic with carrots and celery. Add the spice bag and arrange chicken pieces on top.

3. Sprinkle with salt and lemon juice. Pour in wine, and add enough cold water to cover.

4. Cut a circle of wax paper the size of the soup pot and set atop the chicken. Top with a heatproof plate of the same size to weigh down the ingredients.

5. Bring to a boil over medium-high heat; reduce to medium-low and simmer for 5 minutes.

6. Remove from heat and let stand for 10 minutes.

7. Preheat oven to 350°F. Butter inside of a 2-quart casserole dish.

8. Remove and bone the cooked chicken; slice it into bite-size pieces.

9. Arrange half of the chicken pieces in the casserole dish. Cover with a vegetable layer consisting of half of the carrot and celery sticks, half of the pearl onions and button mushrooms, and half of the peas.

10. Layer the remaining chicken on top of the vegetable layer.

11. Cover with half of the CHICKEN VELOUTÉ SAUCE.

12. Cover with a layer of the remaining vegetables and pour the rest of the CHICKEN VELOUTÉ SAUCE over all.

13. Sprinkle with chopped parsley and top with the POT PIE CRUST.

14. Press the edges of the pie crust to the sides of the casserole dish to seal well and flute them. Prick the top 10 to 12 times with a fork to allow steam to escape.

15. Brush crust lightly with the egg-water mixture.

16. Bake on upper shelf of preheated oven for 20 minutes; brush again with more eggwash and bake for 20 minutes more, or until crust is golden brown and pot pie is steaming hot throughout. Serve at once, with BELGIAN ENDIVE SALAD (page 341) or other crisp greens.

CHICKEN VELOUTÉ SAUCE

Makes 3 cups

3 tablespoons butter
3 tablespoons flour
3 cups hot chicken stock
1/2 cup heavy cream
1 tablespoon Worcestershire
   sauce

1/4 teaspoon salt
1/4 teaspoon freshly ground
   white pepper
1/8 teaspoon nutmeg

1. In a 2-quart saucepan, melt butter; add flour and work into a roux.

2. Cook for 1 minute over medium heat, stirring constantly with a wire whisk.

3. Stir in hot stock and bring to a boil, stirring constantly.

4. Simmer over medium heat for 10 minutes, stirring often.

5. Add heavy cream and bring to a boil, stirring constantly.

6. Remove sauce from heat and stir in Worcestershire sauce, salt, pepper, and nutmeg. Keep warm until use.

POT PIE CRUST

Makes 1 pie crust

3 cups flour
1 teaspoon salt
½ teaspoon baking powder
1¼ cups vegetable shortening

1 egg
2 teaspoons white wine vinegar
5 to 6 tablespoons cold water

1. Sift flour with salt and baking powder into a mixing bowl.

2. Use a pastry cutter to cut in shortening until well distributed.

3. Beat egg with vinegar and 5 tablespoons of the water; add to mixing bowl and blend quickly by hand until dough is smooth. Add more water if needed; handle dough as little as possible.

4. Form by hand into a smooth ball. Wrap tightly in plastic and refrigerate for 2 hours to ease handling.

5. On a lightly floured board, roll out dough to fit the casserole dish, allowing an extra inch or two for fluting edges.

HOMEMADE PIZZA PIE

What are the odds of your being invited to dinner at the White House? About the same as Tom Selleck appearing at your Tupperware party in search of a melon keeper.
— Erma Bombeck, humorist and syndicated columnist

Contrary to widespread public opinion, dinner at the White House is not altogether different from dinner in the typical American household. Of course, when the Reagans entertain honored guests or celebrate special events, the menu is designed to suit the occasion. Yet the Reagans also enjoy casual family meals. A favorite that is regularly included on weekend menus is Homemade Pizza Pie.

Many of the nation's leaders have preferred all-American fare to the fancier foods served at White House dinners. President Grant was reportedly a man of simple tastes, but became a victim of the times when he was forced to endure lengthy dinners in accordance with his wife's wishes and the social customs of the day. Theodore Roosevelt became upset when the press labeled him a "gourmet," since he preferred that the public regard him as a man of simple tastes. President Cleveland also preferred plain foods to finer fare, once complaining prior to a White House social event, "I must go to dinner. I wish it was to eat a pickled herring, Swiss cheese, and a chop at Louis's instead of the French stuff I shall find."

Pizza is eaten in an estimated 96 percent of America's households, with the average individual enjoying a slice or two some 30 times a year. One of the most popular fast foods in America today, pizza was created in Naples sometime during the sixteenth century. According to legend, a Neopolitan pizza maker *(pizzaioli)* was the first to add mozzarella cheese to the flat tomato-topped pie when he created a dish to honor the visit of Queen Margherita in 1889. Neopolitan immigrants who settled along the Eastern seaboard adapted "pizza Margherita" to ingredients available in the New World, and by the time the first pizzeria opened in New York City in 1905, the pie had evolved into the form now popular all over the United States.

The key to a traditional pizza is a brick oven, which bakes the pie until the crust is crispy on the outside, firm yet soft in the middle, and the cheese browns and bubbles without turning tough. In the home kitchen, the best results are achieved with use of a baker's stone or quarry tiles. Popular variations on the standard "pizza Margherita" include thick-crusted Sicilian-style, deep-dish "Chicago style," and pizza "alla marinara," with garlic, tomatoes,

In the White House kitchen, "Happy Days" include visits from favorite celebrities.

and olive oil but, as in the early days, sans cheese.

The Reagans like their pizza topped with an array of fresh ingredients, including onions and garlic, sliced mushrooms, red and green peppers, black olives and spicy pepperoni. The President and his wife often join many of their fellow Americans in enjoying a good homemade pizza on Saturday night, and they concur with most pizza fans in requesting "no anchovies, please!"

Makes two 13-inch pies

Dough

1 cake compressed yeast
1⅓ cups warm water
2 tablespoons vegetable oil

1 teaspoon salt
1 teaspoon sugar
4 cups sifted flour

1. In a large bowl, dissolve yeast in ½ cup of the warm water.
2. Stir in oil, salt, and sugar.
3. Gradually add flour, alternating with the remaining warm water, to make a stiff dough.
4. Knead dough by hand on a lightly floured surface for 10 minutes, until smooth and elastic.
5. Place in a greased bowl and cover with a damp towel. Let rise in a warm place for 1½ hours, or until doubled in bulk.

Tomato Sauce

2 cups homemade tomato
  sauce, or a good home-style
  commercial sauce
Two 14-ounce cans whole plum
  tomatoes
1 teaspoon sugar

1 teaspoon dried oregano
½ teaspoon dried thyme
½ teaspoon freshly ground
  black pepper
1 tablespoon chopped fresh
  parsley

1. In a large saucepan, slowly heat tomato sauce.
2. Drain plum tomatoes and chop fine; add to sauce.
3. Stir in remaining ingredients.
4. Let simmer over medium-low heat for 5 to 10 minutes, or until thickened. Keep warm.

Vegetable Topping

2 tablespoons olive oil
2 cups thinly sliced onions
4 garlic cloves, finely chopped
1 cup thinly sliced red and
  green bell peppers

2 cups thinly sliced fresh
  mushrooms

1. In a large sauté pan, heat oil, add onions, and sauté for 3 minutes. Do not brown.

2. Add remaining vegetables and sauté for 5 minutes more. Let cool.

Final Garnish and Assembly

1 cup sliced black olives
8 ounces sliced pepperoni

4 cups coarsely shredded
mozzarella cheese

1. Preheat oven to 475°F. Lightly oil two 13-inch pizza pans.

2. Punch down dough and divide into 2 equal portions.

3. On a lightly floured board, roll out each piece to a 10- to 12-inch round; stretch by hand to the desired dimensions and transfer to the prepared pans.

4. Pinch up edges of dough to form a thick outer crust. Prick inner area with fork 10 to 12 times.

5. Spoon on the warm tomato sauce and spread evenly to within 1½ inches of the thick perimeter.

6. Arrange vegetable topping evenly over the sauce, to within 2 inches of the edge.

7. Sprinkle the center of one pie with sliced olives; arrange the sliced pepperoni evenly in the center of the other pizza.

8. Sprinkle shredded cheese evenly over the vegetables and sauce.

9. Bake on middle shelf of preheated oven for 25 minutes, or until crust is brown and cheese is golden and bubbling. (If available, baker's stones can be preheated on the oven floor and pizzas can be baked directly on the hot tiles.)

10. Use a pizza wheel or knife to slice each pie into 6 wedges. Serve at once with a crisp green salad and ice cold beer or soft drinks.

PRESIDENT REAGAN'S MACARONI AND CHEESE

It's something that you don't forget. I thought, maybe, it would fade a little, but it doesn't. Every time he leaves the house, particularly to go on a trip, I think my heart stops till he gets back. I really didn't worry before. You know that that's a possibility and so on, but you never think it's going to happen to you, and when it does, it's a shock that stays with you.

—Nancy Reagan

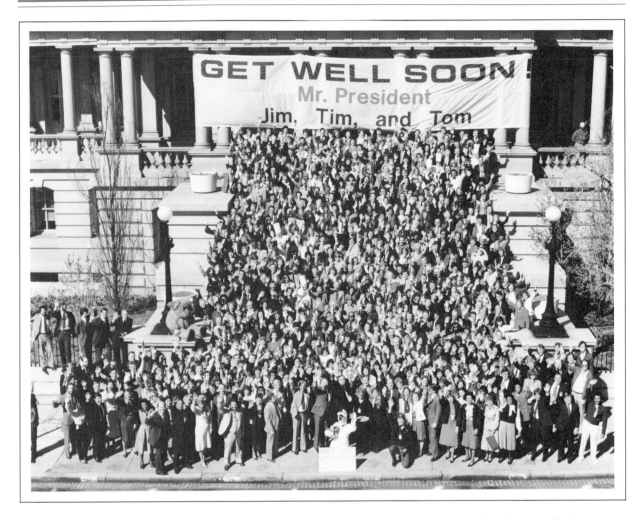

GET WELL SOON!
Mr. President
Jim, Tim, and Tom

On March 10, 1981, after only two months in office, President Reagan was wounded in an assassination attempt. As he emerged from the Washington Hilton hotel where he had given a speech to union leaders, a twenty-five-year-old man fired a .22 revolver, hitting the President in the left side and seriously wounding three others, including press secretary James Brady. After two hours of surgery to remove the bullet, President Reagan made a remarkably fast recovery and returned to the White House in less than two weeks. His good humor during the ordeal elevated the President in the eyes of the public to a national hero.

At the Academy Awards ceremony that year, Johnny Carson ad-

The White House staff welcomes the President home from the hospital.

In 1787, Thomas Jefferson traveled to Italy in search of a gadget to husk rice and a machine to make macaroni. When he was unsuccessful in obtaining the pasta maker, Jefferson appealed to a friend who was on his way to Naples. The emissary returned with a machine for making spaghetti and warned Jefferson, "I procured at Naples according to your request, the mould for making macaroni. . . . It is of smaller diameter than is used in the manufacture of macaroni, but of the diameter that has been sent to gentlemen in other countries."

mitted to the audience, "I was tempted to call the President and ask if he had any more of those one-liners I could use." Despite the bullet lodged near his lungs, President Reagan walked into the emergency room of George Washington University Hospital and joked with the doctors, "Please assure me that you're all Republicans." When his worried wife arrived at his bedside, the President calmed her fears with a jaunty "Honey, I forgot to duck." A few months later, President Reagan was asked by reporters if there was anything he would have done differently during the first six months of his presidency. He quickly responded, "I wouldn't have gone to the Hilton hotel."

The White House staff attempted to provide support for the First Lady during that stressful time by providing Mrs. Reagan with the sustenance she needed in order to preserve her strength and continue coping with the situation bravely. The White House kitchen was also happy to provide the President with some of his favorite foods during his recovery at the nearby hospital. At his request, we sent over some of his all-time favorites, including Macaroni and Cheese. The dish was prepared in the manner the President prefers, the noodles well cooked and covered with a very light cheese sauce spiked with mustard.

Serves 4 as an entrée, or 6 to 8 as a side dish

½ pound macaroni	*1 teaspoon salt*
1 tablespoon butter	*1 teaspoon dry mustard*
1 egg, beaten	*½ teaspoon Worcestershire*
3 cups grated sharp cheddar	*sauce*
cheese	*A pinch of paprika*
1 cup warm milk	

1. Preheat oven to 350°F. Butter a 2-quart casserole dish.
2. Add macaroni to 2 quarts of boiling salted water and cook for 10 minutes.
3. Drain well in a colander. Transfer to a mixing bowl.
4. Stir in butter and beaten egg. Add 2½ cups of the grated cheese.
5. In a small bowl, combine milk with salt, mustard, and Worcestershire sauce.
6. Spoon macaroni and cheese into the prepared casserole. Pour milk mixture over and sprinkle top with the remaining cheese.

7. Sprinkle with paprika. Bake on middle shelf of preheated oven for 35 to 40 minutes, or until macaroni is firm to the touch and the top is crusty and browned.

8. Serve at once, either as a light entrée accompanied by a hot green vegetable and a crisp salad, or as a side dish with Hamburgers or Meat Loaf.

SWORDFISH STEAK WITH LEMON BUTTER

I've always said that without her, Dad wouldn't be President of the United States. She gives him inner strength that he really needs, and that keeps him going every day, knowing that at the end of the day, he has her to go home to.

—Michael Reagan

They are absolutely a team. You do not get one without the other, ever.

—Maureen Reagan

The President and the First Lady serve as America's primary marital role models, a couple united by love and commitment to each other as well as to a common goal. President Reagan and his wife have been working together in a strong partnership since the early days of their marriage. From Hollywood careers to parenting and politics, the Reagans have led a shared life with obvious success. In spite of the many obstacles to be overcome along the way, the First Couple has remained a mutually supportive and undeniably loving team.

President Reagan relies on his wife's solid judgment, and he values her opinion. Mrs. Reagan is devoted to her husband and is protective of his well-being. Each is very grateful to the friends and supporters who help to make the "other half" happy. In the White House kitchen, we please the President by catering to the tastes of the First Lady, and we satisfy Mrs. Reagan by serving foods that help to keep President Reagan fit and healthy. Fortunately, a great many dishes fit this double bill.

Fish is a healthful food, light and nutritious yet versatile and readily garnished for an attractive presentation. President Reagan is especially fond of broiled swordfish napped with lemon butter. Mrs. Reagan is fond of a number of fish dishes, including salmon mousse, grilled halibut steak, broiled trout with kiwi fruit, and

Popovers are an American-ized version of the English favorite known as Yorkshire Pudding. Created by the settlers who founded Portland, Oregon, the light and crusty pastry was known as "Portland popover pudding" in 1886. The 1887 edition of The White House Cook Book *did not include a recipe for the airy delicacies, but did provide advice on use of lemon butter in "Meats and Their Accompaniments": "Lemon juice makes a very graceful addition to nearly all the insipid members of the fish kingdom. Slices of lemon cut into very small dice and stirred into drawn butter and allowed to come to the boiling point . . . is a fine accompaniment."*

swordfish Véronique. To preserve the delicate texture, it is essential to avoid overcooking fish and to serve it at once, with an appropriate sauce or wedges of fresh lemon. Popovers, the hollow puffed bread made with an egg batter similar to that for Yorkshire Pudding, make a nice, light accompaniment to fish dishes. The batter rises and falls over the sides of the pan during baking; hence the name. A well-seasoned cast-iron popover pan, designed to yield only 11 airy popovers, yields the best results, but standard muffin tins can be used as well.

Serves 6

*Six 8-ounce fresh swordfish
    steaks*
1 teaspoon salt
*¼ teaspoon freshly ground
    white pepper*
2 tablespoons vegetable oil
2 teaspoons sweet paprika

1 stick (½ cup) butter, melted
Juice of 1 lemon
*1 tablespoon chopped fresh
    parsley*
6 lemon wedges
Fresh parsley sprigs

1. Preheat oven to 425°F.
2. Remove skin from swordfish and discard. Season steaks with salt and pepper.

3. In a small bowl, combine oil with paprika. Use a pastry brush to coat the steaks on both sides.

4. Transfer the fish to a casserole dish. Bake on upper shelf of preheated oven for 10 to 15 minutes, or until firm to the touch and lightly browned.

5. In a small mixing bowl, combine melted butter with lemon juice and chopped parsley.

6. Place baked swordfish steaks on a serving platter and spoon on lemon butter. Garnish platter with lemon wedges and fresh parsley sprigs. Serve at once, with hot POPOVERS and a crisp green salad.

Opposite page: The Reagans can serve as a universal role model of a strong marriage and a good working relationship.

POPOVERS

Makes 11 popovers

1 cup milk, at room
   temperature
2 eggs, at room temperature
1/4 teaspoon salt
A pinch of freshly ground
   white pepper

A pinch of nutmeg
1 cup sifted flour
1/4 cup warm water
1 tablespoon bacon drippings
   or vegetable shortening
Whipped butter

1. Preheat oven to 400°F.

2. In a mixing bowl, combine milk with eggs, salt, pepper, and nutmeg, using a wire whisk.

3. Add flour and whisk well. Add water and whisk until batter is well blended.

4. Grease insides of a popover iron liberally with bacon drippings or shortening; preheat in the hot oven for 5 minutes.

5. Divide batter evenly among the 11 popover cups, filling each no more than three-quarters full.

6. Bake on middle oven shelf for 15 minutes.

7. Turn oven down to 375°F and continue baking 10 to 15 minutes more, or until popovers are puffed up, golden brown, and crisp on the outside. (If they are removed prematurely from the oven, popovers will fall.) Serve at once, with crocks of whipped butter.

REAGAN FAMILY
FAVORITE DESSERTS

**APPLE BROWN
BETTY**

I can't talk for anybody else. I can talk for me—what makes me happy, what makes my husband happy, what makes our marriage happy. For me, my husband and my family come first. And that makes me happy. I assume it makes them happy.

—Nancy Reagan

How do you explain it? We're happy. I don't know how to answer it. From a man's standpoint, I could say what I think Clark Gable once said to someone—"There's nothing more important than approaching your own doorstep and knowing that someone on the other side of the door is listening for the sound of your footsteps."

—Ronald Reagan

As a young actress, Nancy Reagan dated film stars Clark Gable and Robert Stack, and a host of other attractive men. But the only man she ever met who lived up to her criteria for a lifelong partner was Ronald Reagan. Looking back, Mrs. Reagan has admitted, "I think I knew from the moment I opened the door on our first date that this was the man for me."

At that time, Ronald Reagan was a successful movie actor whose name had been romantically linked with Doris Day, Ann Sothern, and a number of Hollywood's other beautiful young stars. A friendly, unpretentious young man, Ronald Reagan was popular both on and off the set. But in Nancy he found a woman who truly believed in him and was willing to support him with all her heart —a real friend and confidante. Ronald Reagan soon realized that life with Nancy was "a wonderful world of warmth and contentment."

The Reagans were wed on March 4, 1952, in a small private ceremony with their close friends the Bill Holdens as witnesses. More than thirty-five years later, the Reagans are still happily married. As daughter Maureen has testified, "They have the ultimate relationship. They are each other's best friends. We all want to have that kind of relationship."

Mrs. Reagan clearly enjoys her role as the President's wife. She is protective of her "best friend," and keeps a close eye on her husband's health and happiness. Mrs. Reagan understands the President's love of sweets, for example, but she is careful to ensure that his diet is well balanced and that the "treats" are, for the most part, nutritious and healthful.

Unlike the other four First Families for whom I have served as Executive Chef, the Reagans do not restrict sweets to special occasions but enjoy some sort of light dessert after most every meal. Fruit desserts are especially popular, including a wide array of apple dishes, such as compotes, mousses, custards, tarts, and apple meringue pie. The President is fond of honey-baked apples, and Mrs. Reagan's favorite is an old-fashioned Apple Brown Betty. The layered fruit-and-sweet crumb dessert is served warm, with Lemon Sauce or a scoop of vanilla ice cream.

Serves 6 to 8

4 cups dry bread cubes, lightly toasted
6 tablespoons butter, melted
4 medium-size tart green apples, peeled and cored
1 teaspoon cinnamon
½ cup plus 1 tablespoon light brown sugar
Juice and grated rind of 1 lemon
⅔ cup hot water

1. Preheat oven to 375°F.
2. Mix bread cubes with melted butter. Spread one-third of the mixture in the bottom of an 8-inch-square casserole dish.
3. Coarsely dice the peeled apples. Dredge with cinnamon.
4. Spread half of the diced apples on top of the bread layer in the casserole dish. Top with ¼ cup of the brown sugar, then cover with another layer of bread cubes.
5. Spread the remaining diced apples on top of the second bread layer; sprinkle with another ¼ cup of the brown sugar. Sprinkle with the lemon juice and rind.
6. Top with an even layer of the remaining bread cubes. Spoon on the hot water and sprinkle the top with the remaining tablespoon of brown sugar.
7. Bake on lower shelf of preheated oven for 35 to 40 minutes, or until top is golden brown and crusty.

America has carried on a long love affair with sweets. The majority of Americans rate ice cream as their favorite dessert since childhood. George Washington is still remembered for his passion for the frozen sweet; he kept "two pewter ice cream pots" at his Mount Vernon estate, and returned from a business trip to Philadelphia with "a Cream Machine for Making Ice." Thomas Jefferson was also an admitted ice cream fan, and his hostess Dolley Madison introduced the frozen cream to the White House. At President Madison's second inauguration in 1812, a special ice cream, which had been prepared with fresh cream from the Madisons' own dairy and fresh strawberries from Dolley's own garden, was served.

8. Let stand on wire rack for 2 to 3 minutes before cutting into squares. Serve warm with ice cream or LEMON SAUCE on top.

LEMON SAUCE

Makes 1 cup

½ cup sugar
1 tablespoon cornstarch
A pinch of salt
A pinch of nutmeg

1 cup boiling water
1 tablespoon butter
2 tablespoons lemon juice

1. In a small saucepan, combine sugar with cornstarch, salt, and nutmeg.
2. Gradually add the water, stirring with a wire whisk to blend thoroughly.
3. Bring to a boil, and simmer over low heat for 2 minutes, stirring constantly, until sauce is thick and clear.
4. Add butter and lemon juice. Stir until well mixed.
5. Keep warm until serving time.

PRUNE WHIP

Ronald Reagan has always been an optimistic, happy person, and he has certainly led an interesting and exciting life. He appears to be a man who can attain success in any number of arenas. The radio voice of young "Dutch" Reagan attracted quite a following for his simulated sportscasts, and his personable stage presence transformed Ronald Reagan into a popular screen star. As the president of the Screen Actors Guild, Ronald Reagan was highly respected by his peers. As the President of the United States, he has earned the admiration of the world.

In an ever-changing environment, one aspect of Ronald Reagan's life has remained constant for over thirty-five years—his wife adores him. And history has illustrated time and again that a man can overcome great obstacles and achieve grand success when backed by the love of a good woman. The Reagans represent the ultimate in modern-day marriage, an equal partnership between a man and a woman who love and support each other through all that life may offer.

The staff at the White House joins the world in respecting America's leader and admiring his strong marriage, and we are always

pleased to assist the First Lady in maintaining her husband's youthful vigor and love of life. To keep the President's physique trim, yet satisfy his penchant for sweets, the family menus include light, nutritious desserts. During the summer months, the Reagans' dessert menu includes a wide variety of fresh fruits prepared as icy sorbets, cold mousses, or en gelée. In the winter, the Reagans enjoy warm fruit soufflés and compotes. At any time of the year, the menu may include an airy fruit whip. Purées made from dates or prunes make delicious whips, naturally sweet from the high sugar contents of these nutritious dried fruits.

Serves 8 to 10

1 pound 5 ounces pitted prunes
1 cup sugar
8 egg whites, at room temperature

1 teaspoon lemon juice
¼ teaspoon salt
½ cup chopped pecans

1. In a 2-quart saucepan, cover prunes with cold water.
2. Add ⅔ cup of the sugar; bring to a boil over medium-high heat.
3. Cover, and simmer over medium heat for 45 minutes, or until prunes are very tender.
4. Drain off any excess juice. Use a wire whisk or food processor to whip the prunes into a smooth purée.
5. Transfer to a mixing bowl and let stand for 1 hour.
6. Preheat oven to 350°F. Rinse a 7-cup ring mold in cold water.
7. In a clean bowl, beat egg whites until just stiff. Gradually add lemon juice, salt, and the remaining ⅓ cup of the sugar, beating constantly until very stiff; fold into prune purée.
8. Fold in chopped nuts.
9. Spoon into mold to fill up to ½-inch from the top. Smooth the surface.
10. Set mold in a shallow pan of water. Bake on lower shelf of preheated oven for 30 minutes, or until firm to the touch.
11. Let stand in water bath for 10 minutes.
12. Loosen the mold by running the blade of a thin knife carefully around the inside rim. Turn out onto a round serving platter.
13. Serve at once, warm or at room temperature. Fill center with COINTREAU FRUIT and serve with a chilled sauceboat of COINTREAU SAUCE if desired, or garnish with freshly whipped cream and finely sliced prunes.

Thomas Jefferson enjoyed entertaining guests for dinner, sometimes serving as many as a dozen desserts at what he called his "sinful feasts." His dessert table included sweets popular at that time, such as blancmange, meringues, and macaroons. Martha Jefferson Randolph included some of her father's favorite recipes in her 1824 cookbook, The Virginia Housewife, *among them a sweet fruit purée known as Gooseberry Fool:*

Pick the stems and blossoms from two quarts of green gooseberries. Put them in a stewpan with their weight in loaf sugar and a very little water; when sufficiently stewed, pass the pulp through a sieve, and when cold, add rich boiled custard till it is like thick cream. Put it in a glass bowl and lay the brothed cream on the top.

COINTREAU FRUIT

Fills one 7-cup ring mold

1 *medium-size apple*　　　6 *dried apricot halves*
1 *ripe pear*　　　6 *dried pear halves*
1 *medium-size banana, ripe but*　　　1 *tablespoon sugar*
　not brown　　　2 *tablespoons Cointreau*
6 *dried figs*　　　¼ *cup chopped walnuts*

1. Core apple and cut into thin, even slices.
2. Core pear and cut into thin, even slices.
3. Slice banana into ⅛-inch rounds.
4. In a small mixing bowl, combine sliced fruit with dried fruit.
5. Sprinkle with sugar and Cointreau. Stir to combine.
6. Spoon into center of ring mold and sprinkle with chopped nuts.

COINTREAU SAUCE

Makes 3 cups

7 *egg yolks*　　　2 *cups hot milk*
⅔ *cup sugar*　　　½ *teaspoon vanilla extract*
1 *cup cold milk*　　　3 *tablespoons Cointreau*

1. In the top of a double boiler, combine egg yolks with sugar and cold milk; mix thoroughly, using a wire whisk.
2. Slowly add hot milk, stirring constantly with the whisk.
3. Set over a pan of hot water and cook over medium heat, stirring constantly with a wooden spoon, for 6 to 7 minutes, until thickened and able to coat the spoon. Remove from heat.
4. Set the pan in a bowl of ice water to cool; stir constantly with the wooden spoon.
5. When the sauce is cold, stir in vanilla and Cointreau. Refrigerate until serving time.

OLD-FASHIONED FLOATING ISLANDS

We can hardly start a meeting or make a decision without passing around the jar of jelly beans. . . . You can tell a lot about a fella's character by whether he picks out all of one color or just grabs a handful.

　　　　　　　—Ronald Reagan

When the Reagans moved into the White House, jelly beans were immediately elevated to the esteemed position of America's First

Candy. Oblivious to the concern of dentists and nutritionists, the President continued his lifelong habit of snacking at will on the sticky little candies. At the 1980 inauguration, an estimated 40 million jelly beans were consumed at the various celebrations around the city. President Reagan still keeps a crystal jar filled with jelly beans on the table during his Cabinet meetings, sharing his favorite snack with his closest advisers.

In spite of his sweet tooth, Ronald Reagan follows a sensible diet and has retained the athletic physique of his youth. His energy and optimism defy the years and the stresses of his job. His healthful life-style and positive attitude reflect both traditional wisdom and the advice of today's medical experts. Ronald Reagan represents an American dream, that is, a long and healthy life filled with exciting experiences and happy memories.

One of the President's favorite desserts is Old-fashioned Floating Islands, meringue puffs afloat in a vanilla custard. Like jelly beans, this sweet is sugar-rich but light and refreshing. The Reagans sometimes serve it with a colorful fruit topping, such as Raspberry Sauce with sliced kiwi, or Crème Anglaise and fresh red berries. The classic dish makes a pretty presentation, so is sometimes served at special dinners as well as at the Reagans' family meals.

Serves 10

10 egg whites, at room temperature	4¼ cups milk
¼ teaspoon cream of tartar	1 cup granulated sugar
A pinch of salt	10 egg yolks
1 cup plus 1 tablespoon confectioners' sugar	1 teaspoon vanilla extract

1. In a clean bowl, beat egg whites with cream of tartar and salt until soft peaks form.

2. Gradually increasing the mixing speed, add 1 cup of the confectioners' sugar, a few tablespoonfuls at a time, beating until stiff.

3. Continue beating until meringue is very stiff and glossy but not dry.

4. In a large sauté pan, combine 4 cups of the milk with the granulated sugar. Slowly warm over medium heat until hot but not boiling, stirring occasionally.

5. Spoon out meringue by heaping tablespoonfuls and use a second spoon to ease the "islands" into the warm milk. Poach the

In 1771, Benjamin Franklin mentioned in a letter that he had eaten "custard with floating masses of whipped cream or white of eggs." Thomas Jefferson called the French dessert "snow eggs," and Mrs. John Adams served Floating Islands at the very first White House reception in 1801, when the "President's Palace" was formally opened to the public. The 1887 edition of The White House Cook Book included a recipe for the dish:

Beat the yolks of five eggs and the whites of two very light, sweeten with five tablespoons of sugar and flavor to taste; stir them into a quart of scalded milk and cook it until it thickens. When cool pour it into a glass dish. Now whip the whites of three remaining eggs to a stiff froth, adding three tablespoonfuls of sugar and a little flavoring. Pour this froth over a shallow dish of boiling water; the steam passing through it cooks it; when sufficiently cooked, take a tablespoon and drop spoonfuls of this over the top of the custard, far enough apart so that the "little white islands" will not touch each other. By dropping a teaspoonful of bright jelly on the top or center of each island, is produced a pleasing effect; also by filling wine glasses and arranging them around a standard adds much to the appearance of the table.

meringues for 1 minute, or until they puff up; turn them with a slotted spoon and poach for 1 minute more.

6. Use the slotted spoon to transfer the poached meringue mounds to a baking sheet. Refrigerate the meringues and keep the milk warm.

7. In a mixing bowl, blend egg yolks with the remaining ¼ cup milk. Stir this mixture into the warm milk.

8. Transfer the milk mixture to the top of a double boiler. Cook over simmering water, stirring constantly, until the mixture coats a wooden spoon. (Do not overcook, or the yolk will scramble.)

9. Stir in vanilla; set pan in a bowl of ice to cool, stirring often with the wooden spoon.

10. Pour the cold custard into a large glass serving bowl.

11. Remove the meringues from the refrigerator and dust lightly with the remaining confectioners' sugar. Quickly glaze under a hot broiler for 2 to 3 seconds, just enough to lightly brown.

12. Use a metal spatula to carefully set the meringues on top of the custard.

13. Cover tightly and refrigerate for several hours or overnight. Serve very cold, topped with CRÈME ANGLAISE AU KIRSCH, (page 109) or RASPBERRY SAUCE (page 29), and fresh fruit such as strawberries, kiwi or raspberries, if desired.

PLUM PUDDING

A number of America's Presidents are remembered for their stage presence and ability to charm the public. A few have been true humorists. Abraham Lincoln was once praised in the Saturday Review for his keen wit: "One advantage the Americans have is the possession of a President who is

For President Reagan, politics and theater have long been linked; in both he has captivated audiences for years with his personable style and a voice that projects earnestness and excitement, warmth and honesty. The President speaks a language that the everyday person is able to understand, and he delivers his messages laced with anecdotes and humor. President Reagan has proven even more popular as a politician than he was as a Hollywood celebrity, and equally as entertaining.

Although he is extremely busy and always on a tight schedule, the President takes the time to be friendly to his hard-working staff. He will crack a joke or smile that winning smile, waving hello as he hurries to or from the Oval Office. His likeable nature is irresistible, as is his overwhelming sense of optimism. He gives the White House an agreeable and upbeat air, with a hint of positive expectation.

Holidays are especially pleasant times in the Reagans' White House. Both the President and his wife are fond of tradition, so all sorts of special activities and decorations enliven the various holi-day seasons. Christmas is the Reagans' favorite time of year, when family and friends join them to help celebrate the future and give thanks for the past.

From the very first year of their administration, the Reagans have chosen to celebrate Christmas at home in the White House. As Mrs. Reagan once explained, "Christmas is my favorite season, and the White House seems like a perfect place to be." Volunteers assist the First Lady in decorating the rooms on the State Floor with hundreds of bright poinsettias, candles and wreaths, tiny white lights, and special little ornaments. More than a dozen Christmas

not only the First Magistrate, but the Chief Joker of the Land." Calvin Coolidge was also able to deliver quick one-liners, although he rarely smiled or laughed himself: "I think the American people want a solemn ass as a President. And I think I'll go along with them." Two of his more memorable quips were made during formal dinners at the White House. When a fellow diner attempted to coax the President into a discussion by stating, "I have made a bet that I could get more than two words out of you," Coolidge answered coolly, "You lose." And when another chatty dinner guest remarked, "You go to so many dinners. They must bore you a great deal," President Coolidge responded, without even looking up from his dinner plate, "Well, a man has to eat somewhere."

THE WHITE HOUSE

a Mother Goose

Christmas 1986

trees are set up in and out of the White House, with the "official" Christmas tree situated in the Blue Room. In 1986, the 18-foot Noble fir was garnished with around 750 wooden "cookies" carved by the White House carpentry staff, plus gold foil snowflakes, velvet and lace balls, hand-blown glass ornaments, and thousands of miniature white lights. Each year the Reagans top the tree with a different decoration; in 1986 this ornament was donated by a nonprofit organization that employs the physically and mentally handicapped. Even the traditional gingerbread house, prepared each year by the White House assistant chef, has included a special Reagan touch requested by the First Lady: Every Christmas since 1981, the old-world creation made from gingerbread dough has featured the usual marzipan figurines of Hansel, Gretel, and the Witch artfully arranged on a sugar "snow"-covered path lined with—what else?—jelly beans.

The Reagans enjoy a fun-filled Christmas day every year in the company of family and their closest friends. Someone dresses up as Santa Claus and everyone gets a chance to sit on his or her knee and make a Christmas request. Christmas music and lots of laughter help to create the warm family atmosphere that the Reagans enjoy so much. The White House kitchen provides a traditional Christmas dinner, and Old-fashioned Plum Pudding is a regular menu feature.

Serves 12

1 cup ground beef suet
1 box (2½ cups) seedless raisins
1½ boxes (3 cups) currants
½ box (four ounces) chopped candied lemon rind
½ box (4 ounces) chopped candied orange rind
½ cup flour
1 tablespoon freshly grated nutmeg
2 teaspoons allspice

1 teaspoon cinnamon
⅓ cup light brown sugar
1 teaspoon butter
2 tart green apples, peeled and diced
3 eggs
1 cup bread crumbs
¼ cup brandy
¼ cup rum
3 cups warm BRANDY SAUCE

1. In a large mixing bowl, combine suet with raisins, currants, and candied fruit rind. Dredge with flour.
2. Stir in grated nutmeg, allspice, cinnamon, and sugar.

3. In a small nonstick pan, melt butter, add diced apples and sauté for 5 minutes, or until tender.

4. Blend cooked apples with the dried fruit mixture. Add eggs and bread crumbs; blend together until well mixed.

5. Add brandy and rum. Blend well.

6. Generously grease the inside of a 2-quart plum pudding mold; sprinkle lightly with granulated sugar. (An airtight earthenware crock can be substituted, but the top must be sealed with a wax paper layer and a foil cover to prevent leakage.)

7. Pour pudding into the prepared mold to fill up to the top. Smooth out top.

8. Cover mold and set inside a 3-quart soup pot. Add 2 quarts of water, and bring to a boil over medium-high heat.

9. Cover the pot and reduce heat to low. Simmer for 4 hours; as water evaporates, add a little hot water to maintain steam.

10. Remove from heat and uncover the soup pot. Let stand for 1 hour; do not uncover the mold.

11. Turn out onto a serving platter and serve at once, with a sauceboat of warm or flaming BRANDY SAUCE.

BRANDY SAUCE

Makes 3 cups

7 egg yolks
⅔ cup sugar
1 cup cold milk

2 cups hot milk
½ teaspoon vanilla extract
3 tablespoons brandy

1. In the top of a double boiler, combine egg yolks with sugar and cold milk; mix thoroughly using a wire whisk.

2. Slowly add hot milk, stirring constantly with the whisk.

3. Set over a pan of hot water and cook over medium heat, stirring constantly with a wooden spoon, for 6 to 7 minutes, until thickened and able to coat the spoon. Remove from heat.

4. Stir in vanilla and brandy. Keep warm until serving time; sauce may be flamed upon serving if desired.

SPECIAL EVENT RECIPES

MRS. REAGAN'S COLD CURRY SOUP

There has been a gradual evolution in the cuisine served at the White House, notable even during the two decades I have been the Executive Chef. From the Johnsons' family-style meals to the Nixons' French fare, to the Fords' all-American and the Carters' Southern favorites, the food that has graced the First Families' dining tables has changed from administration to administration, and I foresee an excellent future for White House cuisine.

Mrs. Reagan prefers light and sophisticated food, with equal emphasis on appearance and taste. Like her family menus, Mrs. Reagan's special event meals include lots of fresh fruits and vegetables, healthful foods rich in flavor without heavy sauces. Her special ladies' luncheons, in particular, are carefully designed to appeal to the eye as well as the palate. The annual Senate Ladies' Luncheon is hosted in the spring, when the warm Washington weather usually inspires Mrs. Reagan to include a cold soup on the menu.

Chilled soups are prepared with fruits or vegetables in a light broth, to be enjoyed as a refreshing and nonfilling first course. Served in glass bowls with French or Pita Bread, cold soups are as pretty as they are palatable. They are also pleasing to the kitchen staff since they can be prepared in advance and served on a hot day without added heat in the kitchen. Standard fare in the world's repertoire of cuisines, cold soups vary from the ancient beet broth, borscht, to the French-sounding American invention, vichyssoise. Mrs. Reagan's favorite is a Cold Curry Soup.

Curry is a general term applied to many dishes in Indian cuisine, but commercial curry powder is actually a blend of several spices, including coriander, cumin, and red peppers, that Indians do not utilize in their standard fare. Along the coastal areas of India, certain dishes are flavored with curry leaf, an herb distinguished by its strong fragrance. When curry leaves are dried, much of the flavor is lost and the characteristic aroma diminishes. Thus most commercial curry powders do not contain dried curry leaves, although the mild flavor of their combined ingredients contributes a delicate yet distinctive taste and aroma to a variety of dishes, including hot or cold soups.

Curry powder enlivens mulligatawny soup, a hot chicken and apple concoction favored by Mrs. Reagan that has been popular with preceding First Ladies as well. Every First Family I have served has enjoyed cold cucumber soup, and the light, creamy dish appears quite often on Mrs. Reagan's family and special event menus. She also likes cold jellied madrilene, avocado soup, and black bean soup served with lemon slices. Her number-one chilled favorite combines the unique flavor of curry with an unusual ingredient, chutney.

Makes 2 quarts

4 tablespoons butter
1 cup chopped onions
4 garlic cloves, chopped
½ cup chopped celery
½ cup chopped carrots
4 tablespoons curry powder
4 tablespoons flour

6 cups hot chicken stock
2 tablespoons chutney
  (preferably Major Grey's)
¾ cup heavy cream
¾ cup milk
1 cup peeled, finely diced tart
  green apples

1. In a 3-quart saucepan, melt butter over medium heat, add onions and sauté for 3 minutes. Do not brown.

2. Add garlic, celery, and carrots; sauté for 3 minutes more.

3. Stir in curry powder and flour. Slowly pour in hot stock, stirring constantly with a wooden spoon.

4. Bring soup to a boil, stirring constantly. Add chopped chutney.

5. Reduce heat. Set cover slightly ajar and let soup simmer over medium heat for 30 minutes, stirring occasionally.

6. Remove from heat and let cool.

7. Transfer soup to a blender or food processor; purée for 2 minutes, until very smooth.

8. Transfer soup to a clean saucepan and bring to a boil over medium-high heat.

9. Stir in cream and milk. Thin to desired consistency with additional milk, if necessary.

10. Transfer soup to a tureen. Refrigerate for at least 4 hours, until very cold.

11. Just before serving, add diced apples. Serve with sesame seed

twists, JEFF'S GEORGIA-STYLE CHEESE STICKS (page 240), or other fine crackers.

GAZPACHO

Our supper was of the simplest kind; all the serving men and maids of the hostelry had gone to the dance, and we had to be content with a mere Gazpacho . . . It is the favorite dish of the Andalusians, and the prettiest women do not shrink from swallowing bowlfuls of this hell-broth of an evening. Gazpacho is considered highly refreshing, an opinion which strikes me as rather rash, but, strange as it may seem, the first time one tastes it, one ends by getting used to it and even liking it.

—Theophile Gautier, French poet and novelist,
on his trip to Spain in 1840

Gazpacho is an Andalusian dish that has become increasingly popular as a result of the current trend toward lighter, healthier eating. There are actually two forms of the cold soup: one a white creamy version made with grapes and almonds, the other the better-known spicy vegetable broth with chopped cucumber, tomato, and green peppers. Bread should accompany a good Gazpacho, preferably as croutons placed on top, or set in the bottom of the soup plates before the soup is served. Gazpacho can be presented in frosty plates with an ice cube for additional chill, and a relish tray filled with toppings—diced vegetables and the croutons—can be served on the side.

Mrs. Reagan has included Gazpacho on the menu for important special events, such as the luncheon held in honor of The United States delegation to the U.N. for the Decade for Women Conference. And the Reagans often enjoy the chilled soup in more informal settings, including their California ranch. During a rigorous day of horseback riding and outdoor chores, the Reagans welcome an energizing midday meal that features the refreshing Spanish soup. The following recipe for Gazpacho comes from the Reagans' housekeeper at Rancho del Ciero, adapted for use by the White House kitchen staff.

Makes 1½ quarts

4 large ripe tomatoes, peeled
1 cup peeled, chopped
  cucumber
1 cup chopped green bell
  pepper
1 garlic clove
1 cup clear beef stock or
  consommé
2 tablespoons chopped fresh
  chives
2 tablespoons chopped fresh
  parsley
2 tablespoons chopped fresh
  basil, or 1 teaspoon dried

2 tablespoons chopped fresh
  tarragon, or 1 teaspoon dried
1 tablespoon Worcestershire
  sauce
6 drops of Tabasco sauce
⅛ teaspoon freshly ground
  black pepper
1 cup peeled, finely diced ripe
  tomato
½ cup peeled, seeded, and
  finely diced cucumber
½ cup finely diced green
  pepper
1 cup fresh CROUTONS

1. In a blender, combine whole tomatoes, chopped cucumber and green pepper, and garlic clove with the beef stock. Purée until smooth.

2. Add chives, parsley, basil, tarragon, Worcestershire sauce, Tabasco sauce, and pepper. Blend until thoroughly mixed.

3. Refrigerate soup or set bowl in a pan of ice for 2 hours.

4. Pour soup into individual serving bowls. Top each with a sprinkling of the finely diced tomato, cucumber, and green pepper. Sprinkle with CROUTONS and serve at once.

CROUTONS

Makes 1 cup

4 slices white bread
1 cup olive oil

1 garlic clove

1. Trim crusts from bread and discard; cut into ¼-inch dice.

2. Heat oil in a small sauté pan, add garlic and sauté until brown.

3. Remove garlic and discard.

4. Add diced bread to hot oil and sauté quickly, until golden brown on all sides.

5. Remove croutons with a slotted spoon and drain on paper towels before use.

GUACAMOLE

The Reagans do not dine outdoors very often, but they have hosted a number of informal events on the South Lawn. Their big barbecues and staff picnics have been memorable events with lively entertainment and delicious menus. The Reagans' Jazz Picnic held in the summer of 1986, for example, featured performances by the famed Preservation Hall Jazz Band and the cast of the Broadway smash *Hot Mikado*. The 800 guests feasted on hot dogs and burgers, baked beans and cold beer. When a Congressional reception for 500 was held on the South Lawn in the fall of 1981, the California-style barbecue featured juicy charcoal-grilled steaks and California beans, a West coast specialty made with chili and brown beans. The 1985 Congressional barbecue included country music by Mickey Gilley and a Tex-Mex feast that ranged from frijoles and fajita to flan.

At such outdoor fests, the popular dip known as Guacamole often accompanies the informal fare. Prepared from fresh avocadoes, Guacamole is lightly seasoned with lemon, lime, and the distinctive flavor of cilantro (coriander leaves, also known as Chinese parsley). It can be served as a salad or garnish as well as a dip, and may include chopped tomatoes and sweet peppers, hot spices and jalapeño peppers, depending on the chef's preferences and the diners' desires. For White House special events, Guacamole is prepared in a mildly spiced form in order to accommodate the tastes of a wide audience. The President and Mrs. Reagan also prefer the mild version when Guacamole is included on the family menus, usually to accompany tacos as a salad or garnish.

When Jacques Cousteau was invited to the White House in 1981, lunch was served outdoors on the Pool Patio, a lovely garden spot outside the Oval Office. The President was especially enthusiastic about entertaining the famed underwater explorer, as adventurers and athletes are some of his favorite guests. When the *Stars & Stripes* recaptured the Americas Cup from the Australians in 1987, skipper Dennis Conner and his crew came to the White House at the President's request. Although the large press reception did not feature any spicy refreshments, the tanned skipper caught my attention with a humble request for a glass of water. I was honored to oblige the dehydrated sailor, and obtained an autograph in return. Before the crew departed for New York and a ticker tape parade held in their honor, the President congratulated them and praised their skipper as "a regular American guy, a smart guy who worked his way up from the bottom and deserves the credit for what he's done." One might consider such praise from President Reagan a case of the proverbial pot calling the kettle black!

Serves 8 to 10

6 ripe California avocadoes
1 cup finely chopped white
   onions
1 tablespoon finely chopped
   cilantro
Juice of 2 limes
Juice of 1 lemon
4 tablespoons olive oil

¼ teaspoon or more Tabasco
   sauce
2 large ripe tomatoes, peeled
   and diced
1 bunch scallions, finely
   chopped, white part only
Additional fresh cilantro sprigs
   for garnish

1. Peel avocadoes and slice each in half. Remove the pits and set them aside.

2. Mash the avocado flesh in a large mixing bowl, then whip until smooth, using a wire whisk.

3. Fold in chopped onions and cilantro, lime and lemon juice, and olive oil.

4. Season to taste with Tabasco sauce.

5. Transfer to a glass serving bowl. Top with avocado pits to prevent discoloration; cover and refrigerate until serving time.

6. Just before serving, remove pits. Sprinkle dip with diced tomato and chopped scallions, garnish with additional cilantro leaves, and serve with warm tortilla chips.

SPINACH SALAD

Mrs. Reagan is very much involved in the planning for State Dinners and other official functions hosted by the White House. She enjoys the responsibilities that accompany the supervision of large parties, and is exceptionally skilled at coordinating gala affairs to the satisfaction of both guests and staff. For each of the State Dinners and for many other important White House meals and buffets, Mrs. Reagan appreciates the chance to preview the menu.

Once she has ensured that the menu is suited to the season, the eye, and the guest of honor, Mrs. Reagan likes to give it her personal touch. Mrs. Reagan usually reviews the menu early on in the planning of the event, to allow time for a "dry run" whenever she deems it appropriate.

In such cases, the White House kitchen will prepare a scaled-down version of the special meal from soup to dessert, including the proposed sauces and garnishes, for the First Lady and several guests. For some occasions, Mrs. Reagan will suggest a preview of a single course or just the dessert. The First Lady carefully evaluates the food for presentation and balance as well as taste, then comes to the kitchen to share her insights and offer her suggestions. When we succeed in pleasing the First Lady's eyes and palate, we know that the satisfaction of her future dinner guests is guaranteed.

At the White House, we allow the seasons to guide us in menu planning, making every dish from the freshest ingredients. Another important feature of a well-designed dinner is simplicity—a dish should always delight diners without overwhelming them visually or overstimulating their taste buds. Mrs. Reagan is fond of fresh, simple salads that can be varied to suit the season, the event, and the guests. Spinach salads, served on glass plates at elegant formal dinners or in wooden bowls on casual occasions when a rustic look is desired, are popular with the First Lady.

When the President of Portugal was honored in 1983 at a State Dinner, a simple spinach salad was served along with a fine French cheese. Later that same year, a spinach and water chestnut salad adorned the menu of a State Dinner for the King and Queen of Nepal. And in 1985, a private dinner held to honor Thailand's Queen Sirikit included a spinach salad made with mandarin oranges and tossed with Poppy Seed Dressing. A fresh, simple Spinach Salad is a welcome addition to most menus, from the First Family's carefully planned special event meals to the daily dinners served in any family's home.

Serves 6

6 slices bacon
1 pound small-leaf spinach
1 teaspoon Dijon-style mustard
2 teaspoons Worcestershire
    sauce
1/4 cup red wine vinegar
1/2 teaspoon salt

1/8 teaspoon freshly ground
    black pepper
2 hard-boiled eggs, finely
    chopped
1 tablespoon finely chopped
    fresh parsley

1. In a heavy skillet, fry the bacon until crisp. Drain well on paper towels; keep fat warm in the pan.

2. Remove spinach stems and wash leaves thoroughly under cold water; drain well and dry in a towel.

3. In a large salad bowl, combine mustard with Worcestershire sauce and vinegar; whip with a wire whisk until well blended.

4. Add the spinach leaves. Sprinkle with salt and pepper, and toss lightly.

5. Pour on the warm bacon fat and toss again.

6. In a small bowl, combine chopped eggs with parsley. Sprinkle over salad.

7. Crumble cooked bacon and sprinkle over salad. Serve at once with broiled fish or seafood, or with broiled meats such as filet mignon or lean lamb chops.

A dinner party invitation, once accepted, is a sacred obligation. If you die before the dinner takes place, your executor must attend.

—Advice to New York socialites in 1890s

Ah, you'd be nuts to come.
—President Eisenhower to a declining dinner guest

The Reagans' State Dinners and state visits are formal and ceremonial, with each step carefully choreographed. The arrival of an

ANGEL HAIR PASTA WITH SEAFOOD

In the White House kitchen, we make our own pasta.

honored guest on the South Lawn is attended by national anthems, a gun salute, and troops in review. Receiving lines are conducted for official visitors, and meals are served with decorum. The post-dinner entertainment is concluded at precisely 10:55 P.M., the dancing always ends by 11:30 P.M. An exacting schedule ensures that the Reagans' special events are conducted smoothly and efficiently, each function proceeding from start to finish without a hitch. During his two terms in office, President Reagan has hosted an average of one State Dinner per month with numerous official functions every week. Assisted by the perfecting ministrations of the First Lady, each event has proven flawless.

For their first special function, the Reagans hosted a State Luncheon in honor of Prime Minister Edward Seaga of Jamaica, with a menu that began with fresh artichoke hearts stuffed with king crab. The Reagans' premier State Dinner was held a month later, in honor of Prime Minister Margaret Thatcher, and the menu included another delectable seafood dish, Suprème of Pompano in Champagne. Another of Mrs. Reagan's favorite formal first courses also features fresh seafood, in combination with another Reagan passion: homemade pasta. Delicate angel hair pasta laced with fresh scallops, shrimp, and lobster in a light cream and Romano cheese sauce was the first course for the Reagans' State Dinner in 1986 in honor of Prime Minister Brian Mulroney of Canada.

Pasta has grown tremendously in popularity in the United States during the past few years. Up until 1914, America imported pasta from Naples and limited its purchases almost exclusively to spaghetti and macaroni. Today's pasta fans enjoy homemade noodles in a wide variety of shapes and sizes. In the White House kitchen, homemade pasta is prepared in a pleasing array of colors and forms. Puréed tomato or spinach is mixed into the pasta dough in order to create pretty red or green ravioli, canneloni, and lasagna noodles. Sauces for the Reagans' pastas also vary in appearance and flavor, from the traditional tomato topping to a light primavera or a rich Romano Cheese Sauce.

Angel hair pasta, or *capelli d'angelo*, are very fine strands of pasta, thinner even than thin spaghetti. In the White House kitchen, we prepare the noodles by hand, half spinach-green and the other half wheat-white. Due to the recent "pastarization" of America, the unusual noodles can now be purchased ready-made in supermarkets and specialty shops.

Serves 6 as an entrée, or 12 as a first course or side dish

Two 2-pound fresh lobsters
3 tablespoons olive oil
½ cup warm brandy
1 bay leaf
24 black peppercorns
¼ cup cider vinegar
2 cups dry white wine
1 tablespoon salt
1 pound tiny fresh scallops
2 dozen medium-size fresh
  shrimp, butterflied (peeled
  and split lengthwise down
  the backs)

2 tablespoons butter
¼ cup vegetable oil
¾ pound green angel hair pasta
¾ pound white angel hair
  pasta
¾ cup grated Romano cheese
ROMANO CHEESE SAUCE

1. Remove stomachs and crack claws of each lobster. Heat olive oil in a large heavy pot, add whole lobsters, and pour in warm brandy.

2. Carefully flame brandy, using a long match; let flames die out.

3. Add bay leaf, peppercorns, vinegar, wine, and salt. Cover and simmer over medium heat for 10 minutes.

4. Remove from heat and let stand for 10 minutes.

5. Drain broth into a small saucepan; keep warm for use in the ROMANO CHEESE SAUCE.

6. Chill lobsters in refrigerator (to make it easier to remove the meat from the shells). Preheat oven to 350°F.

7. Remove lobster meat from shells and cut into 1-inch pieces; reserve shells for use in preparing the ROMANO CHEESE SAUCE.

8. Boil scallops in 2 cups of salted water for 2 minutes; drain.

9. Sauté butterflied shrimp in the butter for 3 minutes; cover, and let stand for 5 minutes.

10. In a large pot, add vegetable oil to 5 quarts of salted water; bring to a boil over high heat. Add pasta and cook over high heat for 3 minutes.

11. Drain pasta in a colander; rinse with cold water, and drain well.

12. Arrange pasta in 12 mounds on a large oven-proof platter. Sprinkle each mound with a tablespoon of grated cheese.

13. Arrange lobster, scallops, and shrimp evenly around the pasta mounds.

14. Transfer platter to preheated oven for 5 minutes to thoroughly heat; remove from the oven.

15. Pour 2 cups of ROMANO CHEESE SAUCE over all to cover. Serve at once, with additional sauce on the side. Serve with a crisp green salad for a light entrée, or as an unusual side dish to accompany veal.

ROMANO CHEESE SAUCE

Makes 4 cups

1 stick (½ cup) butter
2 tablespoons finely minced shallots
2 garlic cloves, finely minced
2 tablespoons tomato paste
2 tablespoons flour
3 cups warm lobster broth
A pinch of cayenne pepper

Shells from the 2 boiled lobsters, chopped or broken into small pieces
1 cup heavy cream
2 leeks, chopped, white part only
2 tablespoons grated Romano cheese

1. Melt butter in a 2-quart saucepan, add shallots and garlic and sauté until golden.
2. Stir in tomato paste using a wooden spoon. Stir in flour.
3. Add warm lobster broth, stirring constantly with a wire whisk. Add cayenne pepper and lobster shells to the sauce.
4. Bring to a boil, reduce heat to medium and simmer for 10 minutes, stirring constantly, until sauce is smooth and velvety.
5. Add cream and simmer for 10 minutes more; thin with a little milk if sauce seems too thick.
6. In a small saucepan of boiling water, blanch leeks for 2 minutes; drain.
7. Strain sauce and stir in leeks.
8. Stir in grated cheese. Cover and keep warm until use.

SMOKED TROUT AND WATERCRESS MOUSSE

The discovery of a new dish does more for human happiness than the discovery of a new star.

—Brillat-Savarin

Mrs. Reagan is always enthusiastic about innovations in the White House kitchen, welcoming unusual flavor combinations and use of exotic ingredients. Since both she and her husband are fond of seafood mousses, we have created a number of delicious variations

on that theme, which have been well received at the Reagans' State Dinners.

At the State Dinner held in 1984 in honor of President Jayewardene of Sri Lanka, the first course consisted of a delicate pink salmon and cucumber mousse served with an exquisite red caviar sauce. The menu was carefully designed around the preferences and dietary restrictions of the honored guest and his official party. The State Department had issued a detailed list of menu specifications, including the prohibition of pork products, shellfish, and anything colored blue! (Blue was the official color of the opposition-separatist party.)

When Prime Minister Rajiv Gandhi was the honored guest at a State Dinner held in 1985, the White House kitchen served a light crab and cucumber mousse with a piquant Creamy Horseradish Sauce. The menu also included an unusual French import known as grape cheese—a creamy cheese with a mild, buttery flavor that comes encased in a rind coated with the skins and seeds of the black grapes used by local wineries.

A salmon mousse ushered in the meal served to honor the 1986 visit of Mohammed Khan Junejo, the Prime Minister of Pakistan. The delicate first course included lightly smoked trout, herbed toast rounds, and a flavorful tarragon sauce. The guest list included George Peppard, star of the popular television show "The A Team." Asked if he thought President Reagan was a fan of the show, Mr. Peppard responded that he had no idea, nor did he plan to ask, but Maureen Reagan later reported that her father was indeed an occasional viewer.

Prior to the annual Governors' Dinner held in February 1987, Mrs. Reagan requested a try-out of the proposed meal. She was extremely pleased with every item on the menu, from the light Trout Mousse with a Creamy Horseradish Sauce to the coconut cream with Raspberry Sauce. Despite the stormy weather on the evening of the dinner itself, Mrs. Reagan warmed the governors and their wives with her usual fine hospitality, and the President cheered the guests with a timely joke: In Roman times, a group of frightened Christians were herded into the public arena to face their demise from savage lions, but were surprised to see the beasts quickly lie down; when the Emperor asked why the lions were not attacking their victims, he discovered that the animals had been warned that "there would be speeches after the meal." At the White House, such information does not appear to dampen the appetites of the Reagans' special dinner guests.

Serves 10

1¼ pounds smoked trout
2 packages (½ ounce)
  unflavored gelatin
¼ cup dry sherry
2 tablespoons butter
1 tablespoon flour
1 cup hot milk
¼ teaspoon salt
¼ teaspoon freshly ground
  white pepper

1 tablespoon Worcestershire
  sauce
1 cup finely chopped
  watercress leaves
2 cups heavy cream
10 cherry tomatoes
10 black olives
10 small lemon wedges
Fresh parsley sprigs

1. Grind the trout through a meat grinder, then mince very finely in a food processor, and transfer to a large mixing bowl.

2. In the top of a double boiler set over hot water, dissolve the gelatin in the sherry.

3. In a small saucepan, melt butter over medium heat, stir in flour, and cook for 1 minute. Add hot milk, stirring constantly; bring to a boil, and continue cooking until cream sauce thickens. Season with salt, pepper, and Worcestershire sauce.

4. Pour cream sauce over minced trout. Stir in chopped watercress and mix gently; fold in gelatin mixture.

5. In a cold, clean bowl, whip cream until stiff. Fold into trout mixture.

6. Pour into a 1½-quart mold, filling to ½ inch from the top. Smooth the surface.

7. Refrigerate for at least 6 hours or until mousse is set.

8. Dip mold in hot water for a few seconds, then turn out onto a serving platter.

9. Decorate top with cherry tomatoes and black olives; garnish platter with alternating lemon wedges and parsley sprigs. Serve at once with a bowl of CREAMY HORSERADISH SAUCE and crisp crackers such as sesame seed sticks.

CREAMY HORSERADISH SAUCE

Makes 2 cups

1 cup sour cream
½ cup mayonnaise
½ cup freshly grated
  horseradish (or well-drained
  commercial horseradish)

A pinch of salt
1 teaspoon Worcestershire
  sauce

1. In a small mixing bowl, combine sour cream with mayonnaise.
2. Fold in horseradish. Season with salt and Worcestershire sauce.
3. Spoon into a glass bowl. Refrigerate until serving time.

To commemorate the one hundredth birthday of the Statue of Liberty, a huge celebration was held over the July Fourth weekend of 1986. Millions of spectators lined the New York harbor to watch the majestic 18-mile procession of the Tall Ships, the largest such parade in modern history, which featured 22 full-rigged tall ships as well as some 250 sailing vessels from 30 different nations. President Reagan unveiled the newly refurbished Statue of Liberty, whose reconstruction had taken three years. An incredible fireworks display concluded the celebration, specially choreographed to illuminate the famous statue that has welcomed millions of arrivals to America. Liberty Enlightening the World, better known as the Statue of Liberty, was the scene of an exciting and memorable centennial event.

A historic ceremony was held at Governor's Island that weekend with President Reagan, President Mitterrand of France, and some 3,000 dignitaries, diplomats, journalists, and honored guests. Two identical luncheons followed, one hosted by Mrs. Reagan and the other served simultaneously in a separate location to the two presidents.

Given free reign in creating the menu for the occasion, we devised an impressive display, which featured a crab mousse with intricate garnishings and a beautiful dessert of red, white, and blue sorbet topped with chocolate replicas of the Statue of Liberty. The meal generated a round of applause from the diners.

Since the food was to be prepared in the White House kitchen, transporting it from Washington to New York posed a problem. The best solution was for the staff to fly with the food platters to Governor's Island on the morning of the luncheon. A military helicopter transported us with our fragile foodstuffs, carefully packed to survive the bumpy ride. It turned out to be a fretful few hours, as the copter vibrated like a laundry room full of unbalanced washing machines. I was concerned that the delicate mousse platters would quiver into disarray, while White House pastry chef Roland Mesnier secured his chocolate sculptures in an ice chest, which he held

CHESAPEAKE BAY CRAB MOUSSE

protectively in his lap. Fortunately, the food arrived intact, and with minor adjustments all was ready to serve. Our efforts were well rewarded by the return trip to Washington, when the helicopter ride afforded us a perfect vantage point from which to view the historic ships in the harbor on a glorious and memorable holiday.

COLD BEET SOUP
WITH CAVIAR
GRUYÈRE CHEESE TWISTS
CRAB MOUSSE AMERICAN—
HORSERADISH SAUCE
BABY CARROTS AND
ARTICHOKES VINAIGRETTE
LADY LIBERTY SORBET:
RED CURRANT,
COCONUT, BLUEBERRY
PETITS FOURS SEC
LA GRANDE DAME 1979

Chef Haller's special Chesapeake Crab Mousse was decorated in fine detail to celebrate the hundredth birthday of the Statue of Liberty.

Serves 10

1½ pounds cooked lump crabmeat (fresh from East Coast waters, if available)

2 packages (½ ounce) unflavored gelatin

½ cup dry vermouth

¼ cup finely chopped scallions

¼ cup finely diced red bell pepper

¼ cup finely diced celery

Juice of 1 lemon

1 tablespoon chopped fresh parsley

1 tablespoon chopped fresh tarragon, or ¼ teaspoon dried

1 teaspoon salt

¼ teaspoon freshly ground white pepper

A pinch of cayenne pepper

1 cup mayonnaise

1 cup heavy cream

10 thin slices of black truffle or black olive

10 pimiento rounds

Fresh dill sprigs

1. Purée one pound of the crabmeat and break the other half pound into small pieces; reserve 10 pieces for garnish.

2. In the top of a double boiler set over hot water, dissolve gelatin in vermouth.

3. In a large mixing bowl, combine crab purée with chopped scallions, diced pepper and celery, lemon juice, parsley, and tarragon. Season with salt, white pepper, and cayenne pepper.

4. Stir in mayonnaise and melted gelatin. Fold in crab pieces.

5. In a cold, clean bowl, whip cream until stiff. Fold into crab mixture.

6. Pour into a 1½-quart ring mold, filling to ½ inch from the top. Smooth the surface.

7. Refrigerate for 4 to 6 hours, or until mousse is set.

8. Immerse mold briefly in hot water, then turn out onto a serving platter.

9. Decorate top with the reserved crab pieces, truffle or olive slices, and pimiento rounds; garnish platter with fresh dill sprigs. Serve at once, with AURORA SAUCE and JEFF'S GEORGIA-STYLE CHEESE STICKS (page 240).

AURORA SAUCE

Makes 2 cups

1 cup mayonnaise

½ cup chili sauce

½ cup sour cream

2 teaspoons Worcestershire sauce

¼ teaspoon Tabasco sauce

1 tablespoon chopped fresh parsley

1. In a small mixing bowl, combine all ingredients. Mix well.
2. Transfer to a sauceboat. Chill until serving time.

LOBSTER MOUSSELINE

When Prince Charles visited the White House in the spring of 1981, President Reagan toasted his upcoming marriage at a private dinner for 32. The President offered a sage observation: "The step you are about to take is really a very serious step, but your sense of humor will carry you through." Returning to the White House 4½ years later, Prince Charles retained his good humor as he shared his beloved wife with throngs of American fans.

Princess Diana has become a British national monument, a symbol of old-fashioned royalty with modern-day flair and universal appeal. She is living proof that a princess can be regal without being stuffy, and her style is at once traditional and contemporary. It is obvious to her many admirers that the Prince adores her, and her glamour, grace, and natural beauty have mesmerized most of the rest of the world.

As part of a 19-day tour to Australia and America, Prince Charles and Princess Di spent 3 busy days in Washington. The world's most closely watched couple arrived in the nation's capital amid a storm of frenzied publicity, and maintained their charm despite the onslaught of reporters and masses of excited admirers. Before departing for polo matches and a charity ball in Palm Beach, the royal couple attended to royal business in Washington, including a viewing of the National Gallery exhibit "Treasure Houses of Britain," and an endorsement of a department store's "Best of Britain" merchandising campaign. The climax of their brief stay in the capital was a grand White House dinner.

Many weeks in advance, Mrs. Reagan collaborated with Buckingham Palace in preparing a guest list for some 80 fortunate individuals. The private dinner was held in the spacious State Dining Room, where Mikhail Baryshnikov sat next to Princess Diana, while her husband was seated between Beverly Sills and the First Lady. Other well-known personalities who attended the elegant affair included some of Princess Di's American idols such as Neil Diamond, John Travolta, and Clint Eastwood. The star-studded guest register also listed fashion notables Estée Lauder and Gloria Vanderbilt, Olympic athletes Dorothy Hamill and Steve Lundquist, architect I. M. Pei and heart-throb Tom Selleck.

The menu served at the private dinner for the royal couple was carefully designed to suit the noble tastes of the Prince and Princess, and to appeal to the varied palates of their table mates. Since the Prince favors fish and fowl, the meal featured fennel-flavored lobster mousse as the first course and lightly glazed chicken for the entrée. Everyone appeared to enjoy the lovely dinner, the crowning glory of an exhilarating visit from a majestic and well-loved couple.

Serves 10

Two 2-pound fresh lobsters
4 tablespoons olive oil
½ cup finely minced shallots
2 garlic cloves, finely minced
1 cup chopped leeks, white part
  only
1 tablespoon salt
⅛ teaspoon black pepper
2 teaspoons fennel seed
½ cup warm brandy
1 cup home-made or
  commercial tomato sauce

1 tablespoon sweet paprika
¼ teaspoon cayenne pepper
1 cup heavy cream, hot
2 packages (½ ounce)
  unflavored gelatin
4 tablespoons dry sherry
2 cups heavy cream
10 thin slices of black truffle or
  black olive
10 thin strips of red bell pepper
10 fresh parsley sprigs
10 thin slices of lemon

1. Remove stomach and crack claws of each lobster.

2. In a large sauté pan, heat oil over medium-high heat, add whole lobsters and sauté until shells turn red.

3. Add shallots, garlic, leeks, salt, pepper, and fennel seed; sauté for 7 to 8 minutes.

4. Pour in warm brandy and flame carefully, using a long match; let flames die out.

5. Cover and simmer over medium heat for 5 minutes.

6. Stir in TOMATO SAUCE, paprika, cayenne pepper, and hot cream.

7. Cover, and simmer 5 minutes more.

8. Transfer lobsters to a casserole dish and refrigerate (to make removal of meat from the shells easier).

9. Reduce the lobster broth over medium-high heat to about 1 cup. Remove from heat and pour into a food processor.

10. Remove lobster meat from the shells; chop fine and add to food processor.

11. Purée lobster meat with broth for 3 minutes until very smooth.

12. In the top of a double boiler, dissolve gelatin in sherry. Add to the lobster purée, and blend for 10 seconds.

13. Transfer mixture to a large mixing bowl. In a clean, cold bowl, whip the cream until stiff and fold in.

14. Pour into a 1½-quart ring mold, filling to ½ inch from the top. Smooth the surface.

15. Refrigerate several hours or overnight.

16. Immerse mold briefly in hot water, then turn out onto a serving platter.

17. Decorate top with alternating truffle or olive slices and red pepper strips.

18. Garnish platter with alternating fresh parsley sprigs and lemon slices. Serve at once with chilled CREAMY HORSERADISH SAUCE (page 386) and JEFF'S GEORGIA-STYLE CHEESE STICKS (page 240) or slices of herbed French bread.

MRS. REAGAN'S VEAL PICCATA

Veal has been valued since biblical times for its tenderness and flavor. Italians have long savored delicacies that feature the best cuts of veal, and by the time of the Renaissance the lean meat was also popular in France, Germany, and elsewhere in Europe. Many Old World recipes for veal have been adapted by modern-day cooks to suit the current taste for light meat dishes with little fat and lots of flavor.

In Italian cookery, *piccata* means larded. In larding, slivers of fat are inserted into very lean cuts of meat with a special larding needle in order to prevent toughening and provide juicy flavor. Veal Piccata was originally prepared by larding scaloppine, thin pieces of the choicest cut from the top round. The modern method of preparation involves coating thin slices of veal in flour and sealing in the natural juices by browning quickly in fat before braising in veal broth and white wine. Veal Piccata is both flavorful and lean, the perfect dish for health-conscious connoisseurs. It is one of Mrs. Reagan's favorite entrées, simple enough to serve at family dinners, yet elegant enough to grace the fine tables set before the First Family's special guests. When the Reagans hosted a State Dinner to honor the Grand Duke and Duchess of Luxembourg, the 125 guests were able to share the First Lady's enthusiasm for Veal Piccata.

Veal is a rather fragile meat and is best when aged for no more than a few days and cooked until well-done but still juicy. Braised dishes such as Osso Bucco accentuate the delightful flavor of the meat while preventing it from drying out, and the Reagans like that dish almost as much as their favorite Veal Piccata. They are quite fond of Veal Marsala and stuffed veal loin as well. Mrs. Reagan prefers to serve the light veal dishes with homemade pasta or a flavorful "two-toned" rice dish made with both wild and white rice.

At the elegant State Dinner held to honor the royal couple from Luxembourg, the Veal Piccata was accompanied by a savory Saffron Rice. The delicate endive and watercress salad was served with two rich French cheeses: Reblochon, a soft, buttery cheese produced in the mountains from fresh alpine milk; and St. Paulin, a mild cow's milk cheese that is slightly pressed and full of flavor. The salad and cheese course served to cleanse the dinner guests' palates prior to the grand finale, a dozen airy soufflés flavored with fine hazelnut liqueur and accompanied by a light almond sauce. The entire dinner was light enough for modern appetites, yet luxurious enough to set before two regal rulers, an approving First Lady, the President, and their distinguished dinner guests.

Serves 6

12 very thin slices (1½ to 2 ounces each) veal tenderloin, well trimmed
½ cup flour
1 tablespoon salt
½ teaspoon freshly ground white pepper
2 eggs, beaten
1 tablespoon Worcestershire sauce

1 tablespoon chopped fresh parsley
¼ cup grated Romano cheese
¾ cup CLARIFIED BUTTER (page 43)
6 thin slices lemon
A pinch of paprika
A pinch of finely chopped fresh parsley

1. Set veal slices between sheets of aluminum foil and use a wooden mallet to flatten to ⅛-inch thickness.

2. In a shallow bowl, combine flour with salt and pepper.

3. In a separate shallow bowl, combine beaten eggs with Worcestershire sauce, chopped parsley, and grated cheese.

4. Dredge each veal slice in the flour mixture, then dip in egg mixture to coat both sides.

5. In a cast-iron skillet, heat clarified butter, add veal slices and sauté for 3 minutes on each side, or until evenly browned.

6. Transfer slices to paper towels to drain before arranging on a serving platter.

7. Sprinkle each lemon slice with a little paprika and a little pars-

ley, to color one half red and the other half green; garnish each slice of veal with a colorful lemon slice. Serve hot with rice, pasta, or TOMATO CONCASSÉ.

TOMATO CONCASSÉ

Serves 6

1 tablespoon olive oil
1 tablespoon finely minced
    shallots
1 garlic clove, finely minced
3 medium-size ripe tomatoes,
    peeled and coarsely diced

½ teaspoon salt
¼ teaspoon freshly ground
    white pepper
1 tablespoon chopped fresh
    parsley

1. In a sauté pan, heat oil over medium-high heat, add shallots and garlic and sauté for 1 minute.
2. Add diced tomatoes; sprinkle with salt and pepper.
3. Simmer over medium heat, stirring gently with a wooden spoon, for 3 minutes. Do not brown.
4. Serve at once, sprinkled with chopped parsley.

SALTIMBOCCA OF VEAL

In ancient Rome, veal was preferred to beef; Italian recipes combined veal with a variety of ingredients, including tuna fish, tomatoes, melted cheese, and Marsala. Italians still prize their veal dishes, and cooks the world over now embrace veal recipes as their own.

Since veal is a lean, delicate meat, care must be taken to prevent it from turning dry during the cooking process; sauces and stuffings are often employed to maintain tenderness and enhance taste. One delicious method calls for fastening paper-thin slices of tasty prosciutto ham to flattened slices of lean veal with toothpicks. The fattier ham provides juices for its leaner counterpart during sautéing; when the toothpicks are removed, the meats remain intact, and the "saltimbocca" practically melts in the mouth.

The Reagans favor veal over beef for their own family dinners, and special veal dishes are often prepared for their State Dinners and other official functions. Saltimbocca was served at a luncheon hosted by President Reagan in 1981 to honor President Portillo of Mexico, and again in 1983 at the State Luncheon for Dr. Osvaldo

Hurtado Larrea, then President of Ecuador. At the State Dinner held in 1986 to honor President Febres-Cordero of Ecuador, delicate medallions of veal flavored with a light Marsala wine sauce were accompanied by another Italian delight, Gnocchi Romano.

Gnocchi are little dumplings made from potatoes, cereal grains, or wheat flour. Probably Italian in origin, the name was derived from the city of Genoa, but gnocchi have been incorporated into a variety of international cuisines. Potato gnocchi made with the strong-flavored Sbrinz cheese is a popular dish in Switzerland, as is Gnocchi alla Ticinese, prepared with a milder Swiss cheese and baked until crisp. Gnocchi are typically shaped into tiny balls the size of walnuts, then boiled in water or heated in a tomato or cheese sauce. Gnocchi Gorgonzola are potato dumplings made with the blue-veined cheese named for an Italian city. Gnocchi Romano, which is favored by the Reagans, combines whole wheat dumplings with the hard Italian cheese named after another Italian city. It makes a delectable melt-in-the-mouth side dish to serve with family meals or to highlight special occasion dinners.

Serves 6

12 thin slices (1½ to 2 ounces each) veal tenderloin, well trimmed
12 leaves fresh sage
12 thin slices (½ ounce each) prosciutto ham
½ cup flour
1 tablespoon salt
¼ teaspoon freshly ground white pepper
¼ cup CLARIFIED BUTTER (page 43)
6 thin slices lemon
1 tablespoon finely chopped fresh parsley
6 fresh parsley sprigs

1. Set veal slices between sheets of aluminum foil and use a wooden mallet to flatten each to ⅛-inch thickness.

2. Cover each slice with a sage leaf, then top with a slice of ham, folded to the size of the veal slice. Secure with a toothpick.

3. In a shallow bowl, combine flour with salt and pepper. Dredge each veal package on both sides.

4. In a cast-iron skillet, heat CLARIFIED BUTTER over medium heat, add veal packages with the ham side facing down, and sauté for 3 minutes, or until brown.

5. Use a metal spatula to carefully turn veal packages over; sauté for 3 minutes more.

6. Transfer to an ovenproof serving platter. Gently pull out the toothpicks but leave each package intact.

Opposite page: Favorite foods have their special place with all of us —even Mr. President.

7. Dip the lemon slices in chopped parsley to coat half of each; set one atop each veal package. Garnish platter with fresh parsley sprigs and serve at once with RICE PILAF (page 16), or some kind of gnocchi, such as GNOCCHI ROMANO.

GNOCCHI ROMANO

SPECIAL EVENT RECIPE

Serves 6 as an entrée, or 10 as a side dish

4 *tablespoons butter*
½ cup finely chopped onions
2 *cloves garlic, finely minced*
3 *cups hot chicken stock*
*¼ teaspoon freshly ground
    white pepper*
9 *tablespoons uncooked cream
    of wheat cereal*

3 *egg yolks*
1 *cup milk*
*1½ cups finely grated Romano
    cheese*
2 *tablespoons chopped fresh
    Italian parsley*

1. Grease a baking sheet with 1-inch sides with vegetable oil.
2. In a 3-quart saucepan, melt 2 tablespoons butter over medium-high heat, add onions and garlic, and sauté until golden. Do not brown.
3. Add hot stock and bring to a boil; season with white pepper.
4. Stir in cream of wheat and continue cooking over medium-high heat, stirring constantly with a wire whisk, until thickened.
5. Reduce heat to low and continue stirring with a wooden spoon.
6. In a small bowl, blend egg yolks with milk. Stir into the cereal mixture.
7. Add ¾ cup of the grated cheese and continue stirring until cheese is melted. Remove from heat.
8. Spread evenly in the prepared pan using a plastic spatula. Let cool for 1 hour, or until firm.
9. Preheat oven to 375°F. Butter inside of a 2-quart casserole dish.
10. Use a 2-inch biscuit cutter to cut out rounds of gnocchi.
11. Layer gnocchi in the buttered casserole dish, arranging so that each round is half-covered by the next.
12. Sprinkle with the remaining grated cheese and the chopped parsley. Melt remaining 2 tablespons butter and drizzle over all.
13. Bake on upper shelf of preheated oven for 20 to 25 minutes, or until golden brown. Serve at once.

According to the traditions of classical French cuisine, Duckling à l'Orange should be prepared with the rinds of the bitter fruit known as Seville oranges, which are not commonly found in American markets. The tartness of the Seville is the perfect complement to the richness of duck or goose; the rinds of other types of oranges can be substituted to create the right balance of sweet and sour, tart and rich.

Since Mrs. Reagan is not especially fond of duck, Duckling à

DUCKLING À L'ORANGE

l'Orange is usually reserved for luncheons and dinners hosted by the President in her absence.

When the Soviet Minister of Foreign Affairs met with President Reagan at the White House in the fall of 1985, the luncheon menu featured young duck flavored with fresh basil and orange. In 1983, the Countess of Snowdon was honored by the Reagans with a State Dinner. The entrée was a variation on Duckling à l'Orange, prepared with tender chicken breasts and served with wild rice. The First Lady pronounced it a delightful alternative to the traditional version given here.

Serves 6

2 medium-size oranges
One 4½-pound fresh or frozen
  duck
3 tablespoons salt
½ teaspoon freshly ground
  white pepper
½ teaspoon ground rosemary
1 medium-size carrot, coarsely
  chopped
1 medium-size onion, coarsely
  chopped
2 garlic cloves, crushed
24 black peppercorns

1 bay leaf
7 fresh parsley sprigs
Fresh thyme sprig
Fresh rosemary sprig
2 cups dry white wine
3 cups hot chicken stock
1 cup unsweetened orange
  juice
½ cup red currant jelly
2 tablespoons cornstarch
¼ cup Cointreau
2 tablespoons water

1. Preheat oven to 375°F.
2. Peel oranges, separate into sections, and set aside. Blanch zest in boiling water for 2 minutes; drain and set aside.
3. Remove wings from duck and discard.
4. Mix together salt, white pepper, and ground rosemary; season duck with this mixture.
5. In a large nonstick skillet, brown duck on all sides.
6. Transfer duck to a large roasting pan, one leg-side facing up.
7. Roast duck for 30 minutes on lower shelf of preheated oven.
8. Drain off fat and turn duck so that other leg faces up.
9. Surround duck with chopped carrot and onion. Add garlic, peppercorns, bay leaf, and 1 sprig each of parsley, thyme, and rosemary.
10. Return to the hot oven and roast for 30 minutes more; stir vegetables occasionally, using a long-handled fork.

11. Turn duck breast side up. Reduce heat to 325°F.

12. Roast duck for 15 to 20 minutes, or until tender; if vegetables get too brown, remove and keep warm.

13. Transfer the roast duck to an ovenproof platter and keep warm.

14. Drain fat from the roasting pan and set pan over medium-high heat; stir in wine, hot stock, orange juice, and currant jelly.

15. Simmer until sauce is reduced by one-third, stirring constantly. Strain through cheesecloth and return to heat.

16. In a small bowl, combine cornstarch with Cointreau and water; add to simmering sauce, stirring with a wire whisk.

17. Add orange zest and bring sauce to a boil; simmer for 3 minutes, stirring constantly. Remove from heat.

18. Carve duck into 8 serving pieces: Separate legs and thighs, then quarter breast.

19. Arrange duck pieces on the ovenproof platter and garnish with orange sections. Keep warm until serving time.

20. Just before serving, glaze sliced duck with about ½ cup of the orange sauce. Garnish with the remaining parsley sprigs and serve at once, with a sauceboat containing the remaining orange sauce.

Do you ever have times when you think of other Heads of State and you think, oh, they must be so brilliant, so marvelous, and so extra special? And then you realize that you're a Head of State, and you think, I'm just an ordinary person.
—Prime Minister Margaret Thatcher
to President Ronald Reagan

COCONUT CUSTARD

Coconut Custard has been a favorite of each of the five First Families I have served. Rich with eggs and milk, and sweetened with fresh coconut milk and flakes of coconut meat, this custard is a special favorite of President Reagan, since his number-one flavor is coconut. He is very fond of coconut ice cream, coconut sorbet, and coconut cake, as well.

The coconut is a large pod that grows on the coconut palm tree. The sweet white meat comes encased in a hard brown shell, and remains moist in a syrupy "milk." Most coconuts are processed for consumer use: The meat is dried, shredded, and flaked, and often sweetened as well; the rich milk is canned for use in drinks and desserts. Since coconut is naturally high in fat, the oil can be separated from the nuts for commercial use. Many processed foods contain coconut oil, which provides flavor and has a lengthier shelf life than many other vegetable oils. Most of the coconut eaten in America is imported from the Philippines and other Pacific island countries.

When newly elected President Corazon Aquino of the Philippines first visited the White House in the fall of 1986, she really took the United States by storm, impressing all, from Capitol Hill to the White House, with her charming manner, amazing intelligence, strong goals, and passionate commitment to country. The Reagans were proud to be able to please the visiting President of the Philippines with a warm welcome from the American public and a lovely luncheon in the privacy of the nation's First Home, which concluded with a luscious Coconut Custard garnished with slices of fresh pineapple.

Serves 8

1½ cups sugar   2 cups half-and-half, warm
6 eggs, beaten   1 medium-size coconut
Grated rind of 1 lemon

1. Preheat oven to 350°F. Butter inside of a 1½-quart casserole dish.
2. In a mixing bowl, combine sugar with beaten eggs, lemon rind, and warm half-and-half. Blend well.
3. Pour custard into the prepared casserole dish.
4. Crack open coconut. Grate the meat coarsely and sprinkle over the custard. (Coconut milk can be reserved for use in other recipes.)
5. Set casserole in a shallow pan of water. Bake on lower shelf of preheated oven for 40 minutes, or until golden brown and firm to the touch. Serve warm or cold, with fresh pineapple chunks and freshly whipped cream, if desired.

FRESH PINEAPPLE
SORBET

What is patriotism but the love of the good things we ate in our childhood?"

—Lin Yutang, Chinese author and philologist

Ice cream is undeniably America's favorite sweet, but the current trend toward low-fat fare has led to a dramatic increase in the popularity of lighter desserts, such as fresh fruit sorbets. The Reagans are extremely fond of light sorbets, which they enjoy at family meals and serve to guests on special occasions. A simple fruit sorbet can be transformed into a spectacular dessert with the proper garnish and the special attention of a pastry chef.

When the Reagans hosted a State Dinner in January 1984 for Premier Zhao Ziyang of the People's Republic of China, the guest of honor was joined by some 125 guests, including Burt Reynolds and Dinah Shore, newscaster Connie Chung, E. G. Marshall, and Gregory Peck. Washington Redskins quarterback Joe Theismann sat at the First Lady's table, where Foreign Minister Wu Xuegian was seen examining his impressive Super Bowl ring. Dessert was a pomegranate-flavored sorbet presented in a spun-sugar bowl that was decorated with a beautiful bird painstakingly crafted out of sugar. When the Reagans again met with the Chinese Premier on their visit to China the following spring, an exquisite dinner was held at the majestic Great Wall Hotel in Beijing; the dessert was a light, sweet Ice Praline, a variation on sorbet.

A sorbet is prepared from liquefied fruit, sugar, and juice or water, with plenty of flavorful pulp. Sherbet is usually made with milk, resulting in a creamier product that is still lighter than ice cream. Ices do not contain milk, but are typically richer in sugar than the fruity sorbets. The Reagans enjoy a wide array of sorbets, including kiwi, mango, cranshaw, cranberry, black currant, blueberry, and raspberry. The President is especially fond of grapefruit, cantaloupe, and pineapple sorbets—unusually refreshing flavors that can be attractively garnished with fresh fruit to suit most any dining occasion.

Makes 1¼ quarts

1½ cups plus 1 tablespoon
  sugar
1 cup water

3 cups pineapple purée (made
  from fresh, ripe fruit)

1. In a saucepan, combine sugar with water. Bring to a boil over medium-high heat.
2. Remove from heat and let cool.
3. Place pineapple purée in a large bowl and gradually blend in

sugar syrup. Add only as much syrup as needed for taste; pineapple can be naturally very sweet, and excess sugar will produce a granular sorbet.

4. Freeze in an ice cream freezer according to the manufacturer's directions. Garnish with fresh pineapple chunks if desired. Sorbet tastes best on the day it is made, and should be prepared from only the ripest fruit.

Variations

For cantaloupe sorbet, substitute 4 cups cantaloupe purée and the juice of 2 lemons for the pineapple purée and water. Blend all ingredients thoroughly and freeze as directed. Garnish with fresh melon balls, if desired. For

grapefruit sorbet, blend 1¾ cups sugar with 4 cups unsweetened grapefruit juice and the juice of 1 lemon. Freeze as directed and garnish with fresh mint leaves if desired.

FRESH PEACH MOUSSE CARDINAL

On October 8, 1981, a solemn reception was held in the Blue Room for 23 honored guests, including 3 former U.S. Presidents and President Reagan. The historic event was the sole gathering of 4 American Presidents in the White House. Unfortunately, the circumstances were ceremonial rather than celebratory in nature. Former Presidents Nixon, Ford, and Carter were en route to represent President Reagan and the American people at the funeral of assassinated Egyptian President Anwar Sadat. Only 2 months earlier, President Sadat and his lovely wife, Jihan, had been the guests of honor at a State Dinner hosted by the Reagans. The White House kitchen had served a special dessert, Fresh Peach Mousse Cardinal.

This colorful dessert is prepared with very ripe, very juicy peaches and freshly whipped cream. It gets its "cardinal" color from a topping of fresh strawberry purée.

Recently, I re-created the dessert before some 200 culinary students as part of the "Distinguished Visiting Chef" program at Johnson and Wales College in Providence, Rhode Island. As I was showing the students how we make a meal suitable for serving to the President and his honored guests, I was interrupted by the arrival of a telegram from President Reagan, who was in Tokyo participating in an economic summit:

Chef Henry Haller has made my day many a day. His service to the White House goes far beyond his dazzling mastery of the culinary arts.

Many different people come to visit us at the White House: Diplomats, artists, and heads of state from almost every country under the sun. Chef Haller always finds a way to please every palate. It's not an easy job, but he does it brilliantly. I know he will have much to say based on his unique experience.

Mrs. Reagan and I think the world of him. We're sure you will, too. To all of you we send our warm regards.

—Ronald Reagan

It was a historic if solemn occasion when four American Presidents gathered together in the White House.

The President's laudatory message definitely made *my* day, along with the students' standing ovation in honor of a beautiful Fresh Peach Mousse Cardinal.

Serves 10

2 pounds ripe peaches
Juice of 2 lemons
1¼ cups granulated sugar
2 packages (½ ounce)
  unflavored gelatin
¼ cup peach brandy, warm

2 cups heavy cream
One 10-ounce package frozen
  strawberries
2 tablespoons confectioners'
  sugar
2 cups whipped cream

1. In a large saucepan, cover peaches with water and bring to a boil.
2. Add lemon juice. Cover and simmer over medium heat for 5 to 10 minutes, until peaches are tender; a sharp fork should pierce them easily.
3. Remove from heat and let cool.
4. Peel peaches and cut each in half; remove pits and discard.
5. Purée peaches in a blender. Transfer 2 cups of purée to a 3-quart mixing bowl.
6. Mix in granulated sugar until well blended.
7. In the top of a double boiler set over hot water, dissolve gelatin in the warm brandy. Stir into peach purée and let cool.
8. In a cold mixing bowl, whip heavy cream until stiff peaks form. Fold into peach purée.
9. Transfer peach mixture to a 1½-quart mold, filling to ½ inch from the top. Smooth the surface.
10. Refrigerate for 3 to 4 hours or overnight, until mousse is set.
11. In a blender, combine strawberries with confectioners' sugar; purée until very smooth. Refrigerate sauce until serving time.
12. Just before serving, dip mold briefly in hot water, then turn mousse out onto a serving platter. Top with the chilled fruit sauce and garnish with whipped cream. (Use a pastry bag fitted with a small star tip to create a decorative effect with the whipped cream, if desired.) Serve at once, with ALMOND TUILES.

ALMOND TUILES

Makes 60

½ cup sugar
1½ cups coarsely chopped
  almonds
1 egg

1 egg white
¼ cup flour
½ teaspoon almond extract

1. Preheat oven to 325°F. Generously grease a baking sheet.
2. In a small mixing bowl, combine sugar with chopped almonds.
3. Use a plastic spatula to stir in egg; then stir in egg white.
4. Stir in flour; add almond extract and stir until batter is smooth.
5. Spoon out 6 teaspoonfuls of the batter onto the prepared sheet, leaving plenty of space between the spoonfuls to allow for spreading. Flatten each mound of batter to 1/16-inch thickness by tapping gently and repeatedly with the back of a fork.
6. Bake in preheated oven for 5 minutes, or until lightly browned.
7. Use a thin, flexible spatula to quickly remove hot cookies from the baking sheet to a rolling pin, smooth sides facing down; let set for 3 to 4 minutes.
8. Remove tuiles to wire racks to cool completely. Store in an airtight cookie tin.

WHITE HOUSE CHRISTMAS GOODIES

Together, let us make a new beginning. . . . I ask you to trust that American spirit which knows no ethnic, religious, social, political, regional, or economic boundaries; the spirit that burned with zeal in the hearts of millions of immigrants from every corner of the earth who came here in search of freedom. The time is now, my fellow Americans, to recapture our destiny, to take it into our own hands.
—President Reagan's acceptance speech, July 1980

Christmas season at the White House is a warm and happy time of year, distinguished by the traditional festivities and lots of parties. In addition to their own private Christmas dinner, the Reagans host a large number of guests at the annual holiday receptions and other White House Christmas functions, beginning in early December.

For the White House kitchen staff, the Christmas season is an exceptionally busy time of year, as we prepare foodstuffs for the numerous buffets, teas, and various White House gatherings. Prior to most every party, generous quantities of eggnog, the traditional Christmas punch, are prepared and chilled. Rich and sweet but not overpowering, it is always well received by the Reagans' many guests.

Nog is an old English term for ale. The traditional eggnogs of other countries may contain beer or even wine, and some taste quite different from the holiday beverage popular in America, which is typically laced with rum and other spirits. The eggnog prepared in the White House includes rum, bourbon, and brandy; a nonalcoholic version can be prepared by substituting rum and brandy extracts for the three liquors. Eggnog tastes best when served very cold.

To accompany the creamy beverage, a variety of Christmas cookies are served at the Reagans' holiday parties. One of the favorites is the spicy gingersnap cookie, baked in the familiar form of gingerbread men in homes all over the world. The ginger and molasses dough is "a snap" to prepare, but decorating the little cookie men by the thousands can be quite a task. The delight of White House guests of all ages always makes the effort worthwhile.

Gingerbread is prepared each Christmas in the White House kitchen in order to build the traditional gingerbread house. Assistant Chef Hans Raffert created the first in 1969, when he joined the White House staff. The gingerbread house has been baked every year since, with slight variations to suit the times and the administrations. The White House gingerbread house stands some 3 feet tall and can take a week to build and decorate, but a simple gingerbread is easy to bake and can be beautifully presented with a sprinkling of confectioners' sugar or a garnish of freshly whipped cream.

Other holiday treats of all shapes and sizes are also baked in the White House kitchen to serve at the many Christmas celebrations. In 1986, a favorite of many visitors was a crunchy Almond Crescent, rich with butter and ground nuts. President Reagan gave his guests bright wool scarves, the red and green stripes embroidered with white lettering boasting "White House" and "Christmas 1986." With his contagious optimism, President Reagan is looking forward to happy holidays to come, both in the White House and in the years that follow. I join the Reagans and the rest of America in a national climate of hope and anticipation.

HOLIDAY EGGNOG

Serves 16

6 eggs, separated
1¾ cups sugar
½ cup rum
1 cup brandy
1 cup bourbon

1 tablespoon vanilla extract
3 cups heavy cream
3½ to 4 cups milk
1 tablespoon freshly ground
   nutmeg

1. In a large mixing bowl, beat egg yolks with 1¼ cups of the sugar until light and frothy.

2. Stir in rum, brandy, bourbon, and vanilla.

3. Chill for 2 to 3 hours.

4. Stir in cream. Gradually stir in milk to attain the desired consistency.

5. In a large clean bowl, beat egg whites just until stiff. Gradually add remaining sugar, beating until very stiff and glossy but not dry.

6. Fold stiff egg whites into the eggnog. Chill until serving time; sprinkle generously with nutmeg and serve at once.

GINGERBREAD MEN

Makes 24 to 36

¾ cup vegetable shortening
1½ cups sugar
2 eggs
¾ cup molasses
4 teaspoons baking soda
4 teaspoons hot water

4 cups flour
2 teaspoons ground ginger
1 teaspoon cinnamon
1 teaspoon ground cloves
Raisins

1. In a large mixing bowl, cream shortening with sugar until light and fluffy.

2. Add eggs one at a time, beating well after each addition.

3. Stir in molasses and blend batter thoroughly.

4. Dissolve baking soda in hot water. Stir into batter.

5. Sift together flour, ginger, cinnamon, and cloves. Stir into batter and blend thoroughly to form a smooth dough.

6. Refrigerate dough for 1 hour to ease handling.

7. Preheat oven to 350°F. Grease 2 to 3 baking sheets and dust lightly with flour.

8. On a lightly floured surface, roll out dough to ¼-inch thickness.

9. Use cookie cutters to cut out gingerbread men from the dough. Arrange on baking sheets. Use raisins to make eyes, mouths, and buttons.

10. Bake in preheated oven for 10 to 15 minutes, or until cookies are browned and crisp.

11. Set cookie sheets on wire racks and let stand for 5 minutes.

12. Carefully remove cookies from baking sheets using a metal spatula, and let cool completely on the wire racks. Pipe an outline

of WHITE FONDANT (page 119) around the gingerbread men, if desired. Store in an airtight container.

GINGERBREAD

Makes 16 squares

1 cup granulated sugar
1 cup vegetable shortening
3 eggs, at room temperature
1 cup dark molasses
1 cup milk, at room
    temperature
3 cups flour

1 teaspoon baking soda
2 teaspoons baking powder
1 tablespoon ground ginger
1 teaspoon cinnamon
1 teaspoon ground cloves
Confectioners' sugar

1. Preheat oven to 350°F. Grease an 8-inch square baking pan and dust lightly with flour.

2. In a large mixing bowl, cream sugar with shortening until light and fluffy.

3. Add eggs one at a time, beating well after each addition.

4. Stir in molasses and milk; blend batter thoroughly.

5. Sift together flour, baking soda, baking powder, ginger, cinnamon, and cloves. Stir into batter and blend well.

6. Pour into prepared pan. Bake on lower shelf of preheated oven for 35 minutes, or until evenly browned and firm to the touch.

7. Let pan cool on wire rack before dusting gingerbread with confectioners' sugar and cutting into squares. Serve warm or cold, with a bowl of freshly whipped cream, if desired.

ALMOND CRESCENTS

Makes 36

2 sticks (1 cup) unsalted butter,
    softened
2/3 cup granulated sugar
2 cups flour

1 1/4 cups ground almonds
1 teaspoon vanilla extract
1/2 teaspoon salt
3/4 cup confectioners' sugar

1. In a large mixing bowl, cream butter with granulated sugar until light and fluffy.

2. Sift in flour one-half cup at a time, mixing well after each addition.

3. Stir in nuts, vanilla, and salt; blend thoroughly into the dough.

4. Press dough into a square. Cover tightly with plastic wrap and refrigerate for 1 hour.

5. Preheat oven to 350°F. Grease 2 baking sheets and dust lightly with flour.

6. Shape dough into little balls each around 1¼ inches in diameter; roll each between the palms to form a ¼-inch-thick cylinder with slightly tapered ends.

7. Arrange cookies on prepared sheets and shape each into a crescent.

8. Bake on middle shelf of preheated oven for 15 to 20 minutes, or until light gold in color.

9. Let pan cool on wire racks for 5 minutes before removing cookies. Dust with confectioners' sugar, and let cool completely before serving. Store in an airtight container.

SWISS CHRISTMAS COOKIES

Americans have adored cookies ever since Dutch immigrants introduced *koekjes,* or "little cakes," to their early settlements. Now Americans purchase over $2 billion worth of cookies every year, and countless batches are prepared "from scratch" in many American homes.

Before the early settlers brought their recipes to the New World, Christmas cookies were customary only in Europe. Despite their different names and varied shapes, today's Christmas cookies are surprisingly similar the world over. Some have become year-round favorites.

Like many of the world's peoples, the Swiss celebrate Christmas with some traditional foods, such as a sweet braided egg bread and a variety of holiday cookies. However, since the Swiss have no traditional Christmas dinner, each family adopts its own special menu to serve as a holiday ritual. Some Swiss tables feature duck each year, others goose or, less often, America's traditional turkey. Almost all Swiss homes boast Christmas trees, brightly lit and attractively decorated, many adorned with foil-wrapped chocolate ornaments in the form of colorful clowns, Santas, and other holiday figures. Local pastry shops go all out at Christmastime, offering a host of beautiful goodies to serve to family and friends throughout the holiday season.

The Christmases of my own youth were filled with joy and family celebration. My mother, Rosa, prepared our big traditional dinner

on Christmas Day while the rest of the family went skiing in the fresh mountain air. We would return ravenous to find the holiday tree sparkling with decorations and the table set with enticing foodstuffs. I can still remember the delicious blood oranges from Spain, the fresh nuts, and the steaming cups of after-dinner café

Kirsch topped with freshly whipped cream. Some years we would have meringues for dessert, flavored with Kirsch and spread with rich whipped cream. And every year we enjoyed Rosa's home-baked Christmas cookies.

It is difficult to say absolutely which of the many wonderful Swiss Christmas cookies are best, but my own three favorites are *Leckerli, Maïlenderli,* and *Linzer* cookies. Leckerli were developed by dissatisfied pastry chefs of the fifteenth century who wished to improve upon their basic gingerbread recipes. These honey cakes are flavored with candied fruit peel and Kirsch, shaped in a special mold, and brushed with a light white glaze. Baseler Leckerli are made with coarsely ground almonds, while Berner Leckerli contain ground filberts as well. Maïlenderli are rich butter cookies that can be cut into all sorts of holiday shapes and designs. The dough may be flavored with Kirsch and/or fresh almonds, depending on individual tastes. Linzer Cookies are thin butter cookie sandwiches, each filled with a teaspoon of raspberry jam. All three of these cookies can be baked in giant batches and kept fresh in airtight containers for a week or longer. But I must warn you that they hardly ever last this long!

BERNER LECKERLI

Makes 30

1 cup coarsely ground almonds	1 tablespoon honey
1 cup coarsely ground filberts	5 egg whites
2 cups sugar	1/2 cup WHITE FONDANT (page
1/2 cup flour	119)
2 teaspoons cinnamon	1 teaspoon Kirsch
1/2 cup finely chopped candied orange peel	Colored sugar crystals

1. In a large mixing bowl, combine ground nuts with sugar, flour, and cinnamon. Stir in candied peel and honey; mix thoroughly.
2. In a clean, dry bowl, beat egg whites until stiff. Fold into nut mixture.
3. Gently press dough into a square; cover tightly with plastic wrap and refrigerate for 6 hours or more.
4. Preheat oven to 350°F. Grease 2 baking sheets.
5. On a lightly floured board, roll out dough to 1/2-inch thickness.
6. Using a lightly floured Leckerli mold, cut out cookies. Arrange

on the prepared sheets, leaving 1½-inch spaces in between to allow for spreading.

7. Bake in preheated oven for 5 to 6 minutes, or until golden brown.

8. Let cookies cool for 5 minutes before frosting.

9. Mix WHITE FONDANT with Kirsch, and brush lightly onto warm cookies. Sprinkle with colored sugar crystals.

10. Cool completely on wire racks before storing in an airtight container.

MAÏLENDERLI

Makes 60

½ cup soft butter
¾ cup sugar
Grated rind of 1 lemon
1 tablespoon Kirsch

¼ teaspoon salt
3 eggs
2½ to 2¾ cups flour
1 tablespoon water

1. In a large mixing bowl, cream butter with sugar until light and fluffy.

2. Beat in lemon rind, Kirsch, and salt.

3. Beat in two of the eggs, one at a time, blending well after each addition.

4. Stir in flour gradually, adding just enough to make dough that is workable and no longer sticky.

5. Knead gently until smooth; do not overhandle dough.

6. Press dough into a square; cover tightly with plastic wrap and refrigerate for 4 hours or more.

7. Preheat oven to 350°F. Grease several baking sheets; dust lightly with flour.

8. On a lightly floured board, roll out dough to ¼-inch thickness.

9. Using small cookie cutters, cut out dough to form stars, hearts, crescents, and/or other desired shapes. Arrange on the prepared sheets, leaving 1 inch in between to allow for spreading.

10. Beat together remaining egg and the tablespoon of water; use a pastry brush to coat cookies lightly with this egg wash.

11. Bake in preheated oven for 15 minutes, or until golden.

12. Cool cookies completely on wire racks before storing in an airtight container.

Makes 60 to 72

LINZER COOKIES

1 cup unsalted butter
¾ cup granulated sugar
1 egg
3 cups sifted flour
½ teaspoon salt

2 cups finely grated hazelnuts
2 egg whites, lightly beaten
1 to 1½ cups raspberry jam
2 to 3 tablespoons
 confectioners' sugar

1. In a large mixing bowl, cream butter with granulated sugar until light and fluffy.

2. Beat in egg.

3. Sift together flour and salt. Resift into the creamed mixture.

4. Add grated nuts. Mix until dough is smooth.

5. Press dough into a square; cover tightly with plastic wrap and refrigerate for 2 hours.

6. Preheat oven to 375°F. Grease 4 to 5 baking sheets.

7. On a lightly floured board, roll out dough very thinly to less than ⅛-inch thickness.

8. Use a round cookie cutter with scalloped edges to cut out 1¾-inch rounds from half of the dough; use a ½-inch insert in the cookie cutter to cut remaining dough into 1¾-inch scalloped rounds with ½-inch center "windows."

9. Arrange rounds on prepared sheets and brush tops with egg whites, using a pastry brush.

10. Bake in preheated oven for 10 to 12 minutes, or until lightly browned.

11. Let cool on wire racks for 5 minutes.

12. Spread each of the full rounds with a scant teaspoon of jam; use a thin metal spatula to spread in a thin, even layer.

13. Top each with a "windowed" cookie; press gently so that the jam puffs up through the "window." Let cool completely.

14. Sprinkle lightly with confectioners' sugar before serving; store in an airtight container.

NUTRITION NOTES

Nutrition has long played an important role in influencing the diets of America's foremost leaders as well as determining the health of the rest of the nation's populace. It was not until relatively recently, however, that the science of nutrition began to be practically applied. For centuries, diet had been determined solely by food availability and individual preferences. Sometimes grandmother's age-old health advice was also taken into account in diet planning. Rigorous scientific studies conducted during the latter half of the twentieth century have confirmed some and contradicted many other of the ancient diet doctrines, so that modern-day diners can now base their food choices on sound nutrition knowledge. With the last five First Families, varying degrees of nutrition awareness and actual application in daily diet have been observed. To a certain extent, America's recent Presidents have indeed been what they ate.

Nutrients are the essential chemical substances we obtain from foods that are required for:

- growth, upkeep, and repair of body tissues
- regulation of body processes
- energy for the body

No single food contains the fifty-plus nutrients required by the body in the amounts adequate for proper growth and health. Theoretically, however, all of the essential nutrients can be obtained from a combination of foods. A well-balanced diet contains the proper array of nutrients, and since foods vary in the kinds and amounts of nutrients they provide, it is important to include a variety of foods in the diet each day.

Nutrients are separated according to their chemical compositions into six categories: protein, carbohydrate, fat, vitamins, minerals, and water. Nutrition scientists have incorporated the bodily needs of individuals and the nutritive values of foods into what they call the Basic Food Groups. These five groups separate foods in accordance with the similarities of their individual nutrient contents. Each group includes a variety of different foods with comparable nutrient compositions. Most people can ensure an adequate intake of the needed nutrients by including in the diet the recommended number of daily servings of various foods from four of the Basic Food Groups: the Fruit and Vegetable Group, the Grain Group, the Milk and Cheese Group, and the Meat and Alternates Group. The so-called Others Group includes those foods for which the overall nutrient content is outweighed by the caloric content. These foods typically contain appreciable amounts of fat, sugar, and/or alcohol. The body does not require a specific number of servings from the Others Group. Unfortunately, these foods tend to be the most tempting and may overshadow a balanced diet, contributing an unbalanced portion of the daily caloric intake, unless discipline and moderation are employed. The chart on the next page illustrates the suggested daily servings from the Basic Food Groups that comprise a well-balanced diet. Note that nutrition supplements are usually unnecessary for the normal, healthy individual who has a well-balanced diet containing a wide variety of foods.

In 1980, the U.S. Department of Agriculture and the Department of Health, Education and Welfare (now Health and Human Services) released a landmark report entitled *Nutrition and Your Health—Dietary Guidelines for Americans*. This report has been revised several times during the ensuing years with input from both the interested public and expert scientific advisory committees. The gist of the original guidelines remains the same, however, and includes the following sensible suggestions:

- Eat a variety of foods
- Maintain a reasonable body weight
- Avoid too much fat, saturated fat, and cholesterol

Basic Food Group	Number servings per day	Serving size	Food sources
Fruit and Vegetable	4	½ cup juice	Citrus fruit or juice daily
		1 cup raw or ½ cup cooked	Dark green leafy vegetable or bright yellow fruit/vegetable 3–4 times per week Starchy vegetables are included in Grain Group
Grain	4	1 slice ½–¾ cup ½ cup ⅓–½ cup	Bread—whole-grain or enriched Cereal—cooked, dry, flours, grains Pasta—macaroni, noodles, spaghetti Starchy vegetables—corn, lima beans, peas, potato, pumpkin, winter squash
Milk and Cheese	3 (4 for teens)	1 cup 1½ ounces 1 cup	Milk—buttermilk, skim, whole Cheese (calcium contents are higher in harder varieties) Yogurt
Meat and Alternates	2	2 ounces cooked 2 1½ ounces 1 cup 4 tablespoons 1 cup	Meat, poultry, fish Eggs Cheese Cottage cheese Peanut butter, nuts Dried beans or peas
Others	–		Fats—butter, margarine, oils, salad dressings, shortening, cream Sweets—candy, cake, cookies, donuts, gum, jams, jellies, pastries, pies, soft drinks, sugars, syrups Alcoholic beverages—beer, wine, spirits

- Eat foods with adequate starch and fiber
- Avoid too much sugar
- Avoid too much sodium
- If you drink alcohol, do so in moderation

In practical terms, this means modification of the typical all-American diet in the following ways:

- Increase consumption of fruits, vegetables, and whole grains
- Reduce consumption of meat, and substitute high-protein low-fat alternatives such as poultry and fish
- Reduce intake of high-fat foods (whole milk, cream, butter, fried foods, fatty meats), and partially substitute unsaturated fats (vegetable oils, salad dressings, margarine) for saturated fats ("hydrogenated" or solid fats, coconut and palm oil, butter)

- Reduce consumption of sugar and foods high in sugar content (soft drinks, pastries, presweetened cereals, candy, desserts, sweets)
- Reduce consumption of salt and foods high in salt content (pickles, chips, crackers, condiments, soups)
- Moderate intake of alcoholic beverages to 1–2 drinks a day (i.e., wine, beer, or spirits)

The key to following a *well-balanced* diet is to learn to make wise food choices. Try to plan daily intakes to include adequate amounts of a wide variety of foods selected from the Basic Food Groups, with an emphasis on the nutrient-rich choices and discretion with the less nutritious selections (i.e., the Others Group). And try to keep the Dietary Guidelines in mind when making daily dietary decisions in order to adhere to a healthful eating plan. There is really no need to sacrifice dining pleasure so long as one eats moderately. In this manner, we can all be what we eat: moderate and well balanced, healthy and wise—nutritionally speaking, that is.

During the past few decades, the public interest in self-help health has grown markedly, which has led to a more nutrition-conscious society with a predominance of diet-conscious diners. It is possible to trace America's recent nutrition evolution by examining the general dietary patterns followed by the last five First Families. From the Johnson era through the reign of the Reagans, the dining table at the White House has served to exemplify the overall trends of the rest of the nation with regard to eating habits and dieting behaviors as well as the most contemporary American cuisine.

During the 1950s, food and dining often functioned as the central focus of family life. The typical family followed a diet based on all-American fare, which included national staples and regional specialty favorites. Nutrition and waist watching took back row seats to food palatability and individual tastes. Large meals were as traditional as the sweet desserts served afterward. For most Americans, eating was an enjoyable event unmarred as yet by health concerns and weight-watching woes. It took an American President's serious heart attack to awaken the national consciousness regarding the important influence of individual life-style on physical health. President Eisenhower's subsequent allegiance to a life of moderation, including regular exercise, stress reduction, and attention to dietary habits, set the pace for future decades of fitness awareness.

Lyndon B. Johnson suffered a heart attack around the same time as President Eisenhower. By the time the Johnson family moved into the White House, their menus were reflective of the new health attitude of America. All-American fare was featured along with certain Texan favorites, but moderation in meal size was stressed and desserts were frequently prepared in low-calorie versions. Dining pleasure was accompanied by attention to nutrition in preparing meals at the White House, while the "health food" movement began to crop up elsewhere in the United States. The Nixons were even more weight conscious than their predecessors, often dining on light salad plates and requesting cottage cheese platters prior to and following their frequent rich special event meals. Salad bars began to spring up in restaurants across America around this time, and cottage cheese became a staple in the kitchen of perennial dieters. For many Americans, continual dieting replaced normal dining and food denial became

as popular as food indulgence had been in the past.

By the time the Fords arrived at the White House, however, self-starving Americans were hungry for a new diet plan. The Fords ate heartily and exercised enthusiastically so that restrictive dieting was not necessary in maintainaing their healthful physiques. Americans picked up the exercise ball and ran with it. The Carters were daily joggers, and adhered to a lean diet as well. During the late seventies, vegetarian diets and spartan eating plans became more popular throughout the country. Environmental concerns, food waste, and the safety of the American food supply developed into burning issues for many Americans. However, around the time the Carters exited the White House, self-denial and limitations on liberal life-style patterns had lost popularity with the fickle American public.

The Ronald Reagans represent Americans of the 1980s. They lead a disciplined life-style but are able to combine moderate living patterns with eating enjoyment. The Reagans' diet is neither spartan nor intemperate. Instead, they limit themselves to a single serving of imported and fanciful fare, and forego "seconds" with the home-style foods they enjoy with equal enthusiasm. They do indulge in daily desserts, but usually opt for the more nutritious choices such as light sorbets and naturally sweet fruit dishes. Various low-fat milk products, light margarines and low-oil salad dressings, and whole-grain breads and bran cereals serve as some of the Reagans' kitchen staples, which have made healthful eating the norm in today's White House dining room. As this country's oldest President, Ronald Reagan illustrates the new American eating style: eat moderately and sensibly but enjoyably. If we must be what we eat, we might just as well enjoy it—and for as long as possible!

In a society where fast food is sometimes synonymous with dining out and cooking can mean five minutes in the microwave, health-conscious individuals may feel frustrated in attempts to eat wisely without exhaustive effort. For the vast majority of Americans who are not fortunate enough to employ a professional chef to prepare delicious and nutritious daily meals, the required menu planning, shopping, and cooking can pose some real obstacles to healthful eating. Dining out wisely can prove especially challenging for the nutrition conscious. Fortunately, there are practical steps that all of us can make in order to provide ourselves and our families with a moderate, well-balanced, healthful yet enjoyable diet. The following "Tip Sheets" may be able to assist health-and-nutrition-conscious individuals in making wise food choices in the modern home, the supermarket, and when dining out, all settings noted these days for hustle, bustle, and a confusing barrage of diet misinformation.

TIP SHEET: KITCHEN SMARTS

Set some time aside each week to plan out menus for the next seven days:

- Keep the Basic Food Groups and the Dietary Guidelines in mind to plan meals that are moderate, well-balanced, and healthful.
- Include low-fat sources of protein for every meal (e.g., lean meats and poultry; fish and seafood; eggs and dried beans and peas; low-fat milk, cheese, and yogurt).
- Include fiber-rich sources of carbohydrate for every meal (e.g., whole-grain breads and cereals; pastas and rice; fresh fruits and vegetables).
- Design menus that achieve a balance between hot and cold, crispy and creamy, spicy and mild, plain and colorful.
- Utilize cookbooks and recipes to assist in developing menus that emphasize variety and avoid redundancy.

Keep light, nutritious snack foods on hand:
- Cut up an array of raw vegetables into finger foods to keep on ice.
- Spice up low-fat yogurt and/or cottage cheese with herbs and seasonings to use as "dips" for the raw vegetables.
- Slice baked potatoes or sweet potatoes into thin rounds and oven-brown into crisp, nutritious "chips."
- Mix together a variety of whole-grain cereals, nuts and dried fruits, and store in an airtight container or as individual servings in small plastic bags.
- Buy low-fat cheeses and whole-grain crackers, plus plenty of fruit juices and club soda or sparkling water.

Prepare and store foods properly to retain nutrients and reduce waste:

- Wash produce quickly and avoid lengthy soaking to reduce loss of water-soluble nutrients.
- Peel fruits and vegetables only when necessary to retain fiber and nutrients stored in and near the skin.

- Reserve bones, vegetable trimmings, potato peelings, etc., for use in homemade stocks.
- Use plastic wrap and airtight containers to keep foods fresh and seal out the nutrient-robbing air.
- Prepare salads just prior to serving and keep extras fresh in a crisper or Ziplock bag.
- Keep uncooked meats, poultry, and fish in the coldest section of the refrigerator and use as soon as possible, or freeze and then thaw out in the refrigerator a day or two before cooking.
- Store herbs and spices in a cool, dark place to retain potency.

Employ low-fat cooking techniques for nutritious dishes without excess fat calories:

- Boil foods in as little liquid as possible and reserve the nutrient-rich broth for use in stocks.
- Vegetables should be steamed to reduce the leaching losses of water-soluble nutrients.
- Nonstick sauté pans reduce the need for added fats.
- Nonstick sprays can ease clean-up without adding fat calories to the meal.
- Poach foods in low-fat broths.
- Stir-fry foods in small amounts of peanut or vegetable oil.
- Broiling and grilling can serve as low-fat cooking procedures by using racks that allow the excess fat to drip out.
- Try to cook foods as quickly as possible to seal in nutrients and flavor.

Use cast-iron cookware to increase the intake of iron (an essential mineral often inadequate in the average American diet):
- Cook iron-rich foods (e.g., meat sauces, stews, legumes, liver) in cast-iron pots and pans so that the mineral will leach into the food.
- Add foods rich in vitamin C (e.g., tomato sauce, lemon juice, green peppers) to items cooked in cast-iron in order to enhance absorption of the mineral.

Cook at home as often as possible for the best nutrition and the most diet control at the lowest cost:

- Bake large batches of whole-grain breads and extra servings of nutrient-rich meals when time allows, then freeze for later use.
- Bake your own homemade sweets (e.g., peanut butter cookies, banana bread, carrot cake) instead of purchasing the less nutritious commercial treats.

- Reduce use of "convenience foods" to a practical minimum, and prepare your own low-fat soups, sauces, dressings, etc., whenever possible.
- See Tip Sheet: Recipe Readjustments (page 420) for additional hints on improving nutrition in the home kitchen.

TIP SHEET: SUPERMARKET SAVVY

Prepare a detailed shopping list to accommodate each week's menu plan:

- Adhere to your list to avoid falling prey to impulse purchases and strategic supermarket persuasions.
- Purchase foods in the required amounts to avoid leftovers and reduce food waste.
- Purchase fresh foods in season whenever available, and substitute frozen only when necessary; sometimes canned foods (e.g., pineapple chunks) are preferable in cooking certain dishes, and may prove to be the sole alternative in some circumstances.
- Keep an eye out for sales and coupons in newspapers and magazines for discounts on the foods included in your shopping list.
- Shop at consumer-oriented supermarkets whenever possible. (Some stores provide helpful nutrition and diet information at point of purchase and for take-home guidance.)

Read food labels carefully:

- Examine the ingredient list to note the contents of fat, salt, sugar, etc. (The predominant ingredient is listed first with each item given in order of amount present in the product.)
- Check exact serving size for practicality (e.g., some diet soft drinks list *two* servings per 12-ounce can).
- Check nutrition labeling for estimated calories per serving, and note fat (in grams).
- Foods labeled as low-calorie must contain no more than 40 calories per serving, and reduced-calorie items must offer one-third fewer calories than their non-diet counterparts.
- Some nutrition labeling lists sodium content (in milligrams), cholesterol content (in milligrams), and sugar content (as percent of total carbohydrate).
- For whole-grain products, check to see that "100 percent whole" grains or flours appear first on the ingredient list; fiber content (in grams) per serving is sometimes given.

- Be wary, as labels can be highly misleading (e.g., certain brands of vegetable oil may be labeled "no cholesterol" but *no* vegetable product contains cholesterol, and anything can be labeled "light" or "natural" since these terms have no legal definition).
- Check the "freshness date" on baked goods and the "sell date" on milk products and other perishable items to avoid purchasing readily spoiled foods.

Consider your own life-style and personal priorities before making food purchases:

- Is convenience more important to you than cost?
- Is convenience more important to you than caloric content and nutritional value?
- Is it worth the added cost to purchase special diet products (e.g., low-calorie, low-fat, low-sodium, low-cholesterol)?
- Can you allot some extra time and effort to prepare more dishes at home in order to cut food costs while improving nutrition?
- See Tip Sheet: Recipe Readjustments (page 420) for additional hints on wise food selection.

TIP SHEET: DISCRIMINATING DINING

Frequent restaurants offering varied menus for wide (and wise) food selection:

- Cafeterias allow diners to make their own food choices without taking chances on menu items sight unseen.
- Italian menus include high-carbohydrate pasta dishes that serve as low-fat yet filling meals.
- Chinese, Japanese, Korean, and Thai restaurants offer steamed vegetables and rice plus plenty of other low-fat fare.
- Indian cuisine and vegetarian restaurants can offer diners high-fiber legumes and whole-grain dishes.
- Steak and seafood restaurants can provide lean sources of high-quality protein if menu selections are made carefully to avoid well-marbled cuts, batter-fried fish, and dishes in drawn butter.
- Salad bars are available in many restaurants (including some of the fast-food chains) for a light vegetable meal or a bulky low-calorie side dish.
- More and more restaurants are catering to their health-conscious patrons by offering "light" menu choices, and most establishments will attempt to meet special menu requests.

Choose carefully from restaurant menus to select the most individually satisfying yet nutritious dishes:

- Light appetizers such as fruit cups or consommé can temper a hearty appetite, while several selections in combination with salad can even replace an entrée.
- Keep portion sizes small or share an entrée with other diners, and note that the "doggie bag" is a completely acceptable means for avoiding overindulgence in favor of enjoying leftovers later.
- Order foods prepared without added butter or sauces, and request dressings on the side to control serving size.
- Limit butter on bread, sour cream on potatoes, and other added fats to the absolute minimum required for flavor.
- Use discretion at the salad bar to keep the high-fat toppings (e.g., potato or egg salad, bacon bits, creamy dressings, and oils) to a minimum.
- Desserts need not prove devastating as there are some light choices (e.g., fresh fruit in season, sorbets, angel food cake) and the richer selections can be shared by several diners.

Be moderate and choose carefully when dining at work, on the road, at parties, and on special occasions:

- Skip coffee-break doughnuts and vending machine sweets in favor of nutritious snacks such as low-fat yogurt, fresh fruit, and homemade muffins.
- Pack your own nutritious "brown bag" in order to control your luncheon menu in the workplace.
- Many commercial airlines cater to diet-conscious travelers, so special meals (e.g., low-fat, vegetarian, fruit, or seafood plates) can be reserved simply by calling a day in advance.
- To supplement the typical traveler's fare, bring along your own breakfast foods and nutritious snacks (e.g., individual boxes of bran cereal and powdered nonfat milk, fresh and dried fruit, whole-grain crackers, and peanut butter).
- More and more hotels entice patrons with health clubs and jogging trails, special diet menus, and gourmet lean cuisine.
- Before attending a dinner party or other food-focused affair, have a light snack such as a cup of broth or a piece of fruit in order to avoid arriving in a ravenous daze.
- Whenever those inevitable overindulgences do occur—away from home, on vacations, at social events, and on special occasions—avoid self-destructive guilt-driven deprivation dieting afterward in favor of a light menu for a few days, accompanied by a mild increase in the length and/or intensity of your exercise routine.

In order to adhere to a healthful diet plan, certain adjustments may need to be instituted in re-creating recipes, especially dishes described in earlier cookbooks and those that grandmother used to make. The recipes included in this book have been reproduced to represent the genuine dishes prepared for the last five First Families and their guests, so have not been adjusted to accommodate contemporary nutrition concerns. The following Tip Sheet may assist those home cooks who wish to alter some of the preceding recipes in order to suit individual dietary needs. Be aware that the final results will be different from the original dishes as created by Chef Haller in the White House kitchen.

TIP SHEET: RECIPE READJUSTMENTS

Reduce the overall fat content of recipes by substituting low-fat ingredients for the richer elements:

- Buy lean meats, trim the fat before cooking, and integrate small servings of meat as only one aspect of a meal rather than the focal point of the menu.
- Remove skin from poultry before cooking and opt for the leaner "white meat" over the fattier dark cuts.
- Use low-fat milk in place of whole milk, and replace cream or half-and-half with evaporated skim milk.
- Try some of the new low-fat cheeses, and use neufchâtel in place of cream cheese.
- Replace sour cream and mayonnaise with plain low-fat yogurt.
- Prepare reduced-fat "cream" sauces using low-fat milk (but expect a thinner consistency).
- Use nonstick pans and sprays for low-fat cooking, and "sauté" in broth and/or wine instead of butter and oil.
- Replace butter with soft margarine for less *saturated* fat (although the total fat content will be the same).
- Substitute olive or vegetable oils for shortening and butter to reduce *saturated* fat (but the total fat content will be the same).
- Watch out for some of the surprising sources of fat such as avocadoes, olives, nuts and seeds, and even coconut.

- See Tip Sheet: A Few Reliable References for the Kitchen (page 422) and experiment by using special cookbooks with low-fat recipes in order to devise dishes to suit your own particular needs and individual tastes.

Reduce the overall cholesterol, sodium, and/or sugar content of recipes by using the appropriate substitutions:

- To keep egg intake moderate, replace some of the high-cholesterol yolks with plain egg white.
- Reduce serving sizes for red meats and substitute low-fat animal foods whenever possible.
- Flavor foods with herbs and spices with a minimum of added salt.
- Moderate the use of high-sodium flavorings such as soy sauce, meat marinades, and commercial bouillons and stocks.
- For those on restrictive low-sodium diets, use of unsalted butter can contribute to a reduced sodium intake.
- In many dessert recipes, the sugar content can be reduced by one-third without destroying palatability.
- Naturally sweet fruits and juices can be used to flavor desserts.
- See Tip Sheet: A Few Reliable References for the Kitchen (page 422) and experiment by using special cookbooks with low-cholesterol, low-sodium, low-sugar recipes in order to devise dishes that will suit your own particular dietary needs and still satisfy your individual tastes.

Increase the overall nutritional value of recipes by using vitamin-, mineral-, and fiber-rich ingredients:

- Incorporate whole-grain flours into recipes for breads and rolls, quick breads and muffins, pancakes and waffles, and cookies and crackers.
- Try brown rice and wild rice, barley and buckwheat, millet and bulgur, whole wheat or vegetable pastas, plus a variety of legumes including navy beans, black beans, chick-peas, and lentils.
- Use wheat germ, unprocessed bran, cornmeal, and rolled oats to increase the nutrient value and fiber content of baked goods.
- Vary salad greens with romaine and Bibb lettuce, escarole and chicory, spinach and kale, bok choy and savoy cabbage, watercress and Belgian endive; add texture and color with bean sprouts and water chestnuts, cauliflower and broccoli florets, apple wedges or orange sections, seedless raisins or grapes, shredded or grated low-fat cheese, and homemade whole wheat croutons.
- Use powdered nonfat milk to thicken sauces, enrich batters, and bind casseroles as well as to increase the nutritional value of the dish.
- Add nutrients as well as decoration by using a sprinkling of chopped dried fruits or slivered nuts, fresh lemon or orange slices, sprigs of fresh parsley or watercress.
- See Tip Sheet: A Few Reliable References for the Kitchen (page 422) and experiment with light, healthful recipes to suit your own particular needs and individual tastes.

Creative health-conscious cooks may want to consider the following concepts in experimenting with the recipes included in this cookbook and from other resources:

- The culinary trend of the times is toward light, healthful menus that feature fresh foods and homemade dishes that appeal to both the eye and palate while contributing essential nutrients to the diet.
- To cook nutritious dishes, no ingredients have to be forbidden but all must be consumed in moderate amounts.
- Oftentimes, the simpler the recipe, the more healthful the dish.
- Certain recipes should never be revised, but most can be readjusted to suit your individual needs and tastes.
- In readjusting recipes, you should be prepared to experiment and you must be willing to practice, practice, practice.

As nutrition concerns have become increasingly important to the general public, the all-American diet has shifted toward an emphasis on the more healthful food choices. Yet, with the growing number of food items from which to choose and the unending expansion of today's fast-food society, it has become increasingly difficult for many individuals to keep pace and eat wisely. The only solution to the discriminating dieter's dilemma is to try to maintain an open mind while attempting to stay abreast of the contemporary and ever-changing nutrition scene. The following Tip Sheet is an abbreviated list of available resources that offer sound nutrition information and/or healthful recipes.

A FEW RELIABLE REFERENCES
FOR THE KITCHEN

American Dietetic Association Foundation. *Dietians' Food Favorites*. Chicago: The American Dietetic Association, 1986. (Delicious and nutritious recipes with nutritional values per serving.)

American Heart Association. *American Heart Association Cookbook*, 4th ed. New York: David McKay, 1984. (Low-fat, low-cholesterol, low-sodium recipes.)

Aronson, Virginia. *Thirty Days to Better Nutrition*. Englewood Cliffs, N.J.: Prentice-Hall, 1987. (Step-by-step guide to eating healthfully.)

Better Homes and Gardens. *The Dieter's Cook Book*. Des Moines, Iowa: Meredith Corporation, 1983. (Delicious low-calorie recipes with caloric values per serving.)

Brody, Jane. *Jane Brody's Good Food Book*. New York: W. W. Norton, 1985. (Informative guide with recipes for a high-carbohydrate diet.)

Burros, Marion. *You've Got It Made*. New York: William Morrow and Co., 1984 (Quick and easy recipes that conform to the Dietary Guidelines.)

Connor, Sonja, and William Connor. *The New American Diet*. New York: Simon and Schuster, 1986. (A gradual approach to dietary improvement.)

Dietary Guidelines for Americans, 1986. Superintendent of Documents, U.S. Government Printing Office, Washington, D.C. (Brief brochure outlining the updated guidelines.)

Hamilton, Eva, and Eleanor Whitney. *Nutrition—Concepts and Controversies*, 3rd ed. St. Paul, Minn.: West Publishing Co., 1985. (Comprehensive text written in the layperson's language.)

Jacobson, Michael, and Sarah Fritscher. *The Fast-Food Guide*. New York: Workman Publishing Co., 1986. (Nutrient values and ingredient information from some popular fast-food chains.)

Stare, Frederick J., and Virginia Aronson. *Rx: Executive Diet*. Norwell, Mass.: The Christopher Publishing House, 1986. (Easy-to-read guide with menu plans and coordinated daily index cards designed for the working person.)

Underwood, Greer. *Gourmet Light*. Chester, Conn.: The Globe Pequot Press, 1985. (Delicious recipes with reduced calories, fat, sodium, and sugar.)

U.S. Department of Agriculture. *Eating for Better Health—Food and Nutrition Service Program Aid No. 1290*. Superintendent of Documents, U.S. Government Printing Office, Washington, D.C. (Informative brochure with easy recipes that meet the Dietary Guidelines.)

———. *Nutritive Value of American Foods in Common Units—Agriculture Handbook No. 456*. Superintendent of Documents, U.S. Government Printing Office, Washington, D.C. (Comprehensive tables with caloric and nutrient values for some 2,500 food portions.)

KITCHEN NOTES

Even though cooking at home in your own kitchen is quite different from preparing a meal in the White House, proper culinary practices should always be employed. The equipment available in the home cook's kitchen may not be equivalent to the advanced gadgetry found in the professional chef's kitchen, but respectable recipe results are still possible. With a general understanding of basic cooking techniques and utilization of the appropriate culinary tools, even a novice cook can re-create recipes, just like a professional chef. All that is required is a creative imagination, a flexible attitude, and the patience required to practice, practice, practice.

Listed below are some very basic kitchen terms and brief descriptions of kitchen procedures and equipment to assist home cooks in their culinary endeavors.

Cutting up a chicken: First cut off the wings, then the leg sections and separate into drumstick and thigh. Slice through the ribs to separate the back from the breast and cut the breast into four equal portions; reserve the back section for use in stocks. TIP: bone breasts at home since boneless are more expensive; reserve the bones for use in stocks.

Deveining shrimp: Peel off the end of the tail and the thin skin of each shrimp. For cooked shrimp, peel back to expose the dark vein and rinse under cold water to remove. For raw shrimp, use a small, sharp knife to make a shallow slit down the back; use the tip of the knife to scrape out the thin black line that lies just underneath.

Carving a duck: Remove the leg sections and separate into drumstick and thigh. Slice the breast from the carcass in four even portions; slice into additional portions, if desired.

Filleting fish: Since this can be a complicated procedure, it is easiest to purchase fish in fillets. If you do fillet your own, reserve heads and spines for use in stocks. Slice fish into even portions for baking, grilling, poaching, or frying. TIP: Fattier fish can be baked or grilled without excessive drying, but leaner fish should be poached in liquid or cooked in fat.

Flaming foods safely: An artful show, flaming a dish can also enhance flavor but must be conducted carefully.

1. Bring the liqueur, dish to be flamed, a long kitchen match, and a chafing dish or small burner to the dining table.

2. Set up in a clear spot. Dim the lights.

3. Warm the liqueur in a small pan or a ladle held over the flame; do not boil.

4. Light the long match and hold it to the liqueur to ignite.

5. Quickly pour the flaming liqueur over the dish. Let flames die out. Serve at once.

TIP: For cold dishes such as ice cream, pour on the hot liqueur and flame at once.

Selecting a flour: Bread flour has more gluten for extra elasticity, whereas cake flour is softer for a crumblier texture, and pastry flour is finely milled with a low gluten content for delicate pastries. All-purpose flour is a blend of hard and soft flours, suitable for use in most recipes calling for flour. TIP: For a more delicate texture, substitute ⅞ cup rice flour for 1 cup all-purpose; for a heartier result, replace each cup with 1⅛ cups whole-grain flour.

Measuring out flour: Sift before measuring; stir whole-grain flour instead of sifting. When a range is called for in a recipe (e.g., 1½ to 2 cups), add the smaller amount first, then gradually add more—up to or exceeding the remainder—until the desired consistency is attained.

Fluting a pie crust: Roll out chilled pastry dough until 1 inch larger in circumference than the pie pan and ⅛ inch thick; fold in half to ease transfer into the pan, then arrange evenly. Pinch edges between the thumb and forefinger and twist slightly. For a two-crust pie, turn the edges of the top crust under the bottom crust to seal in the juices; for a one-crust pie, flute edges to stand up and pour in the filling after pie is set on the oven rack. TIP: To roll out an even-size crust, use a pastry cloth marked with concentric circles.

Frosting a cake and slicing it into serving portions: Transfer cooled cake to a serving platter and frost the sides first, using a thin metal spatula; frost the top last, spreading evenly or swirling in a decorative design. Use a cake cutter to slice into portions, dipping in hot water between slices to clean. Although serving sizes may vary depending on purpose (i.e., dessert or snack) and appetite, the approximate number of portions from common cake sizes can be estimated.

- 8-inch round layer = 8 servings
- 8-inch square layer = 6 servings
- 9-inch round layer = 8 to 10 servings
- 9-inch square layer = 6 to 8 servings
- 13 × 9 × 2-inch layer = twenty-four 2-inch squares *or* twelve 3-inch squares
- 9- or 10-inch spring form pan = 10 to 12 servings

Using fresh garlic: Always peel before use. Loosen the skin by laying 2 to 3 cloves close together on a cutting board; whack firmly, using the flat side of a kitchen knife. TIP: Sauté onions before adding garlic to the sauté pan in order to prevent garlic from browning too rapidly.

Preparing unflavored gelatin: In the top of a double boiler, mix powdered gelatin with a liquid such as water or brandy; set over a pan of hot water until gelatin is fully dissolved.

Kneading dough: After worked by hand for a time, dough will become elastic and leave the sides of the bowl; this indicates that it is ready for kneading. Transfer to a lightly floured surface and use firm, even hand motions to develop the gluten and form a smooth, elastic dough: First, fold dough toward you, press with the heel of your hand, and give it a slight turn; then fold and press again; repeat rhythmically. Whenever a second kneading is required, it can be completed right in the greased bowl. Always let dough rise in a warm (75°F to 85°F), sheltered spot away from drafts, and bake in the center of a preheated oven to allow air to circulate. TIP: To flour a board, use 1 tablespoon of flour for each cup included in the recipe.

Trimming lean meats: Use a sharp knife to remove visible (white) fat and gristle from lean cuts of meat before cooking. Prior to serving, trim off any remaining fat that may have become visible upon heating.

On poultry, most of the fat is in or just under the skin, which makes fat removal easy.

Cleaning fresh mushrooms: Rinse quickly under cold water. To whiten, rinse again in a solution containing 1 tablespoon flour per quart of cold water.

Selecting cooking oils: Olive oil tastes best in salad dressings; peanut oil is good for stir-frying; vegetable or corn oil can be used in deep-fat frying and to replace fat in most recipes. TIP: Sauté in a mixture of butter and oil if you want to both provide a rich flavor (from the butter) and allow rapid browning (because of the higher smoking point of the oil).

Using a pastry bag: Fill the bag no more than two-thirds full, leaving room at the top so that squeezing does not cause leakage. Use parchment paper to construct a homemade pastry bag: Cut out a triangle, roll it into a cone shape, then snip off the tip to the desired width. Commercial tips include plain tubes for lettering, star tubes to form shells and ridged edges, and crescent moons for leaves and scrolls, each in a range of diameters for piping everything from dainty flowers to thick piped potatoes.

Grating citrus peel: Wash fruit first, then rub against a grater to remove only the outermost portion of the rind; reserve juice and/or fruit for other uses.

Scalding milk: In the top of a double boiler, heat milk over hot water just until tiny bubbles appear around the edges. Do not allow the milk to boil.

Using herbs and spices: Fresh herbs are most flavorful; chop very fine to extract the full flavors. Freshen dried herbs by soaking in a little lemon juice prior to use. Freshly ground peppercorns are most flavorful. White pepper is the mildest, red pepper the hottest. To prepare a "spice bag," measure out the various seasonings into the center of a small square of cheesecloth; tie into a bundle using fine string. TIP: To avoid a bitter flavor, add spice bag only during the final hour of cooking.

Setting oven temperatures: Preheating will take no longer than 15 minutes. Warm foods at 225°F. To broil, set the pan so as to directly expose the food to the heat source; turn pan around once so that browning is even. TIP: Oven temperatures vary, so get to know your own oven in order to estimate cooking times and temperatures most accurately.

Using a candy thermometer: Always be sure to immerse the bulb completely in the hot liquid without letting it touch the sides or bottom of the pan.

- soft ball = 234°–240°F
- firm ball = 244°–248°F
- hard ball = 265°F
- soft crack = 270°–290°F

- hard crack = 300°–310°F
- brittles = 310°F

Recognizing French culinary terms: Since many common cooking terms also have classic French titles, it can be helpful to utilize a culinary dictionary such as *Larousse Gastronomique.* Such guides can prove especially helpful to the novice pastry cook.

Unmolding a ring or other set mold: First, dip the pan up to the rim in hot water for 5 to 6 seconds; then run a long thin spatula around the inside edges, tilting slightly to loosen the mold. Cover with a serving platter, invert, and shake gently to loosen before removing the pan.

Cooking with wines: Only cook with wines that you would also drink at the table because, although the alcohol evaporates upon cooking, the wine imparts special flavors to the final product. If desired, stock can be substituted for wine in savory sauces, and fruit juice can be used to replace the wine in most sweet sauces.

Using yeast: Active dry yeast is less perishable than compressed yeast cakes but requires more heat and moisture for activation. Very hot liquids will kill the yeast organisms; use of lukewarm (105°F for dry, 95°F for cake yeast) water is suggested.

REFERENCES

THE JOHNSON FAMILY

Aikman, Lonnelle. *The Living White House*. Washington, D.C.: National Geographic Society, 1966.

Barber, James David. *The Presidential Character —Predicting Performance in the White House*, Englewood Cliffs, N.J.: Prentice-Hall, 1972.

Bishop, Jim. *A Day in the Life of President Johnson*. New York: Random House, 1967.

Carpenter, Liz. *Ruffles and Flourishes*. New York: Doubleday, 1969.

Harwood, Richard, and Haynes Johnson. *Lyndon*. New York: Praeger, 1973.

Johnson, Lady Bird. *A White House Diary*. New York: Holt, Rinehart and Winston, 1970.

Johnson, Richard Tanner. *Managing the White House*. New York: Harper & Row, 1974.

Montgomery, Ruth. *Mrs. LBJ*. New York: Holt, Rinehart and Winston, 1964.

Mooney, Booth. *Lyndon—An Irreverent Chronicle*. New York: Thomas Y. Crowell, 1976.

Reedy, George. *Lyndon B. Johnson—A Memoir*. New York: Andrews and McMeel, 1982.

Smith, Marie. *Entertaining in the White House*. Washington, D.C.: Acropolis Books, 1967.

———. *White House Brides*. Washington, D.C.: Acropolis Books, 1966.

Taylor, Tim. *The Book of Presidents*. New York: Arno Press, 1972.

West, J. B. *Upstairs at the White House*. New York: Coward, McCann, and Geoghegan, 1973.

THE NIXON FAMILY

David, Lester. *The Lonely Lady of San Clemente*. New York: Thomas Y. Crowell, 1978.

Nixon, Richard. *The Memoirs of Richard Nixon*. New York: Grosset & Dunlap, 1978.

THE FORD FAMILY

Ford, Betty. *The Times of My Life*. New York: Harper & Row, 1978.

Ford, Gerald. *A Time to Heal*. New York: Harper & Row, 1979.

Hersey, John. *The President—A Minute-by-Minute Account of a Week in the Life of Gerald Ford*. New York: Alfred A. Knopf, 1975.

terHorst, Jerry. *Gerald Ford and the Future of the Presidency*. New York: Joseph Okpakee, 1974.

Vestal, Bud. *Jerry Ford Up Close—An Investigative Bibliography*. New York: Coward, McCann, and Geoghegan, 1974.

THE CARTER FAMILY

Barnhart, Clarence (ed.). "William Tell." In *New Century Cyclopedia of Names*. New York: Appleton-Century-Crofts, 1954.

Carter, Hugh. *Cousin Beedie and Cousin Hot*. Englewood Cliffs, N.J.: Prentice-Hall, 1978.

Carter, Lillian. *Away from Home—Letters to My Family*. New York: Simon and Schuster, 1977.

Carter, Rosalynn. *First Lady from Plains*. Boston: Houghton-Mifflin, 1984.

Dyer, Ceil. *The Carter Family Favorites Cookbook*. New York: Delacorte Press, 1977.

Hewitt, Jean. *The New York Times Southern Heritage Cookbook*. New York: G. P. Putnam's Sons, 1976.

Mondale, Joan. *The Mondale Family Cookbook*. Washington, D.C.: Mondale for President Committee, Inc., 1984.

Norton, Howard. *Rosalynn, A Portrait*. Plainfield, N.J.: Logos International, 1977.

Talmadge, Betty. *How to Cook a Pig and Other Back-to-the-Farm Recipes*. New York: Simon and Schuster, 1973.

Walter, Eugene. *American Cooking—Southern-Style*. New York: Time-Life Books, 1976.

Wooten, James. *Dasher—The Roots and Rising of Jimmy Carter*. New York: Summit Books, 1978.

THE REAGAN FAMILY

Butel, Jane. *Women's Day Book of New Mexican Cooking*. New York: Pocket Books, 1984.

Cannon, Lou. *Reagan*. New York: G. P. Putnam's Sons, 1982.

Clancy, John. *John Clancy's Christmas Cookbook*. New York: Hearst Books, 1982.

Fadiman, Clifton (ed.). *The Little Brown Book of Anecdotes*. Boston: Little, Brown, 1985.

Hazan, Marcella. *Marcella's Italian Kitchen*. New York: Alfred A. Knopf, 1986.

———. *More Classic Italian Cooking*. New York: Alfred A. Knopf, 1978.

Langseth-Christensen, Lillian. *Cold Foods*. New York: Doubleday and Co., 1974.

Leamer, Lawrence. *Make Believe—The Story of Nancy and Ronnie Reagan*. New York: Harper and Row, 1983.

Reagan, Nancy. *Nancy*. New York: William Morrow, 1980.

Reagan, Ronald. *Where's the Rest of Me?* New York: Karz Publishers, 1965.

Sheraton, Mimi. *Visions of Sugarplums*. New York: Harper and Row, 1981.

Wallace, Chris. *First Lady—A Portrait of Nancy Reagan*. New York: St. Martin's Press, 1986.

GENERAL REFERENCES

Beck, Bruce. *Produce*. New York: Friendly Press, 1984.

Boller, Paul. *Presidential Anecdotes*. Oxford University Press, 1981.

———. *Presidential Campaigns*. Oxford University Press, 1984.

Claiborne, Craig. *The New York Times Food Encyclopedia*. New York: Times Books, 1985.

DeGregorio, William. *The Complete Book of U.S. Presidents*. New York: Dembner Books, 1984.

Field, Michael, and Frances Field. *A Quintet of Cuisines*. New York: Time-Life, 1970.

Grigson, Jane, ed. *The World Atlas of Food*. New York: Simon and Schuster, 1974.

Hazelton, Nika. *The Swiss Cookbook*. New York: Atheneum, 1967.

Jones, Evan. *American Food—The Gastronomic Story*. New York: E. P. Dutton, 1974.

Kane, Joseph. *Facts about the Presidents*. New York: H. W. Wilson, 1981.

Kellerman, Barbara. *All The Presidents' Kin*. New York: The Free Press, 1981.

London, Anne. *The American International Encyclopedia Cookbook*. New York: Thomas Y. Crowell Co., 1972.

Mariani, John. *The Dictionary of American Food and Drink*. New York: Ticknor and Fields, 1983.

Martin, Ruth. *International Dictionary of Food and Cooking*. New York: Hastings House, 1974.

Marx, Rudolph. *The Health of the Presidents*. New York: G. P. Putnam's Sons, 1960.

Montagné, Prosper. *Larousse Gastronomique*. New York: Crown Books, 1961.

Nestlé. *Culinary Art and Traditions of Switzerland*. Private ed. Vevey, Switzerland: Nestlé Products, Ltd, 1985.

Oxford American Dictionary. New York: Oxford University Press, 1980.

Parents' Magazine Enterprises. *The First Ladies' Cook Book*. New York: Parents' Magazine Press, 1969.

Perl, Lila. *Foods and Festivals of the Danube Lands*. New York: World Publishing Company, 1969.

Pitch, Anthony. *Exclusively Presidential Trivia*. Washington, D.C.: Mino Publications, 1985.

Reader's Digest. *Eat Better, Live Better*. Pleasantville, N.Y.: Reader's Digest, 1982.

Trager, James. *The Food Book*. New York: Avon Books, 1970.

Ziemann, Hugo, and Mrs. F. L. Gillette. *The White House Cook Book*. New York: Saalfield Publishing Co., 1887.

INDEX

(Major recipe categories and ingredients are indicated in boldface.)

ABOUT THE AUTHORS

HENRY HALLER has served as the Executive Chef of the White House for over twenty years. Summoned to the White House in 1966 by Lady Bird Johnson, Chef Haller has supervised the kitchen operation there during the last five administrations. After completing comprehensive culinary training in his home country of Switzerland, Chef Haller moved to Quebec in 1948 and took a position in the kitchen of the Ritz-Carlton Hotel.

After a dozen years of preparing fine meals in a number of New York's most exclusive hotels, including the Astor, the Hampshire House, and the Sheraton-East, Chef Haller accepted the challenging post as the head of the kitchen of the most important household in America. Yet Chef Haller has been able to devote the time required to raise a family of four in Potomac, Maryland, with his Brooklyn-born wife, Carole. He is a member of the Vatel Club, La Société Culinaire Amicale, Les Amis d' Escoffier, and the American Culinary Federation. In 1985, Chef Haller was named "Outstanding Chef of the Year" by the Culinary Institute of America. In 1986, he received the "Antonin Carême Award" from the American Culinary Federation, and in 1987, the federation selected him as "Outstanding Chef in America."

An honorary member of Le Cercle des Chefs de Cuisine of Zurich and Berne and the Order of the Golden Toque, Chef Haller is currently president of Les Chefs des Chefs d'Etat (The Chefs of Heads of State).

VIRGINIA ARONSON is a registered dietitian and has published nine books on nutrition, including several textbooks and *Thirty Days to Better Nutrition*. She is a regular contributor to popular health and fitness publications. An avid runner, Ms. Aronson has been able to stay a step ahead of the potential caloric consequences of sharing Chef Haller's no-longer-secret recipes.